Poets on the Peaks

POETS ON

Gary Snyder

Philip Whalen &

Jack Kerouac

in the North Cascades

Text and Photographs by John Suiter

THE PEAKS

COUNTERPOINT WASHINGTON, D.C.

Library of Congress Cataloging-in-Publication Data
Suiter, John, 1948–
Poets on the peaks : Gary Snyder, Philip Whalen & Jack Kerouac in the North Cascades / text and
photographs by John Suiter.
p. cm.
ISBN 1-58243-148-5 (alk. paper)
1. Beat generation—Biography. 2. Snyder, Gary, 1930–   .—Homes and haunts—Cascade Range.
3. Whalen, Philip, 1923—Homes and haunts—Cascade Range. 4. Kerouac, Jack, 1922–1969—
Homes and haunts—Cascade Range. 5. Authors, American—Homes and haunts—Northwest,
Pacific. 6. Authors, American—Homes and haunts—Cascade Range. 7. Authors, American—
20th century—Biography. 8. Northwest, Pacific—Biography. 9. Cascade Range—Biography.
I. Title.
PS228.B6 S78 2002
811'.5409—dc21   2001047248

Frontispiece photograph: Dawn at Sourdough Mountain Lookout, September 1998.

Jacket and text design by David Bullen

Printed in Canada

COUNTERPOINT
P.O. Box 65793
Washington, D.C. 20035-5793

Counterpoint is a member of the Perseus Books Group

10 9 8 7 6 5 4 3 2 1

This book is for Hozomeen

Contents

As the light increased I discovered around me an ocean of mist,

which by chance reached up exactly to the base of the tower,

and shut out every vestige of the earth, while I was left floating

on this fragment of the wreck of a world, on my carved plank, in cloudland . . .

All around beneath me was spread for a hundred miles on every side,

as far as the eye could reach, an undulating country of clouds,

answering in the varied swell of its surface to the terrestrial world it veiled.

It was such a country as we might see in dreams,

with all the delights of paradise.

Thoreau on Mount Greylock,
A Week on the Concord and Merrimack Rivers

The miners' lives were bold and ingenious, but we need not limit our narrative simply to the anecdotes of a half century of mineral exploitation — as lively as they were. We're here today to make deeper connections to the earth.

Gary Snyder, *A Place in Space*

After the Gold Rush

Granite Creek, 1952

GARY SNYDER was heading for Japan. For the time being he was only in the woods at the foot of Crater Mountain, but he was on the way.

Late in June 1952, Snyder had arrived at the District headquarters of the U.S. Forest Service at Marblemount, Washington, the last town on the Skagit before the big country upriver. The Marblemount ranger compound was a snug oval of brown-painted, low-roofed, CCC-built bunkhouses, with a cookhouse and tool sheds, an office and fire school classroom, and some older cottages arranged around a cluster of shady oak trees. Next to the compound were a long stable and corral and some open pasture for the Forest Service pack mules and saddle horses. Rising up abruptly behind the compound was a fir-timbered no-name hill with a steep trail leading to a place called Cow Heaven. To the east and north were solid mountains.

Each June the sleepy Ranger Station came alive as the few year-round Forest Service men who ran the place were joined by an influx of college kids, schoolteachers, "seasonal men," and Native Americans from around the region, all drawn to the woods by Forest Service jobs. Most would be working trail crews in the forest, clearing windfalls, shoring footbridges on existing trails, or opening new trails for "timber cruisers" staking out the woods for future sales. Of the forty or more men on the compound, less than a dozen would be going into the mountains to be fire lookouts.

In those days, trails in the North Cascades were built and maintained not for recreationists but for the businesses of mining, logging, and fire fighting. More often than not, trails terminated at ugly backwoods stamp mills and placer operations, or forest "units" slated for cutting. Some trails led to spectacularly scenic fire lookouts, but those lookouts existed only because wildfire had been deemed bad business, and total suppression the official paradigm.

In addition to the trail crew hands and lookouts, there were men training to be fire guards and smoke chasers, and there were also packers, wranglers, and back-country carpenters. Occasionally there might be a female fire lookout—perhaps part of a husband-wife team—but by and large, Marblemount in those days was an all-male milieu. It had not always been so. In fact, before the Forest Service existed, lookouting was considered women's work. The first fire watcher in the country, according to lookout historian Ray Kresek, was a woman named Mabel Gray, a timber camp cook from Idaho who spotted smokes on the North Fork of the Clearwater River in 1902. With the creation of the Forest Service in 1905, lookouting became paid work, and men took over. Forest Service Chief Gifford Pinchot even issued a directive to discourage publicity on women lookouts, after a series of articles about Hallie Daggett, a lookout in Siskiyou County, California, (she was the daughter of the Lieutenant Governor) swamped the service with female applicants.

During World War II, with so many men overseas, the Forest Service had been glad to have women as fire watchers again. One of them, a Seattle high school teacher named Martha Hardy, published an account of her 1943 season on Tatoosh Lookout in the Goat Rocks wilderness south of Mount Ranier. *Tatoosh* had briefly been a best-seller in 1947, popularizing the notion that a woman could handle the rigors of a remote, solo mountaintop summer just as well as a man—and write about it, too. In 1951, the year before Gary Snyder went on lookout at Crater Mountain, a woman, Bonnie St. Aubin, had "manned" Crater—along with her husband Earle. But despite these exceptions, the postwar Forest Service had by 1952 reverted to being a man's outfit.

Some of the men were from families that had come into the Skagit before Washington was even a state; others were transient outdoor types from coastal towns, who couldn't stay put when the weather got good. Nearly everyone on the compound had done a little logging at some point. Some had helped build Ross Dam and boasted that they "knew every stone in it." Others had worked on the railroad that ran up to Diablo. A few of the older guys had even done some mining on Thunder Creek and Ruby Creek before the war, or packed for the miners. Altogether there were a lot of manual skills and woodsmanship gathered together at the mountain-ringed compound.

Although he had just turned twenty-two that May, Snyder's own logging skills were fairly impressive. On his family's dairy farm on the outskirts of Seattle, his education had begun early. By the time he was ten, his father had already put him on a crosscut saw, schooled him in the ritual of setting the handles and how to clean the blade. From thirteen to fifteen, Gary had worked his way through YMCA summer camp at Mount Saint Helens, doing part-time trail crew and carpentry work. At nineteen he'd taken his first job in the Forest Service, hand logging on trails on the Gifford Pinchot Forest (then called the Columbia National Forest) out of Spirit Lake. At twenty-one he'd been a timber scaler for the Indian-owned lumber company at Warm Springs reservation in eastern Oregon.

Back in February when he had applied for his fire watch, Gary requested, with some hubris, the "highest, most remote, and most difficult-of-access lookout" in the district. The Assistant Ranger at Marblemount, Blackie Burns, had obliged, assigning him immediately to the L.O. on 8,129-foot Crater Mountain, fifteen miles from the nearest roadhead, two thousand feet higher than any of his other lookouts, the last of the 8,000-foot fire watches in the whole state. "Boy," said Blackie when he met Gary that first week of fire school, "you have no idea what you've gotten yourself into."

By the end of June, the summit of Crater Mountain was still snowed in. Gary was sent to Granite Creek Guard Station to do trail crew work for a couple of weeks, until the trail melted enough for him to get through to the lookout. The guard station was situated at the base of Crater Mountain, in the shady valley where Granite and Canyon creeks flowed together to form Ruby Creek, one of the main tributaries of the Upper Skagit.

Granite Creek Guard Station was deep in the back country behind Ross Dam, twenty-five miles from Marblemount. From the Forest Service compound in Marblemount there was paved road only to Newhalem; after that, a rough gravel road wound through the Skagit Gorge to Diablo. After Diablo there was no road at all; a funicular lift took Snyder to the lake above Diablo Dam, and from there a tugboat ferried him for a half an hour to the foot of Ross Dam. There, a "sky hook" crane hoisted him up the 650-foot face of the dam on a wooden platform — quite a ride, but at the top of the dam it was still another day on foot through the woods of Ruby Mountain and up Ruby Creek to the guard station.

When Gary arrived at Granite Creek Guard Station in early July, two other men were already there — Harold Vail and Jim Baxter. Harold was a nineteen-year-old fellow from Marblemount, working for the Forest Service during his summers off from college. Harold's family had "followed the shingles" to Marblemount, he said — meaning that the Vails had moved up the Skagit working in each new shake mill that opened as logging had expanded up the river. The year before, Harold had done a fire watch on Hidden Lake Lookout — the "Hidden Lake Hilton," as it was ironically known — and had also been up to Crater to help pack down a husband-and-wife lookout team at the end of the season. Harold knew the Ruby Creek country quite well. He had been coming to it ever since Ross Lake had been opened to public fishing and several times had stayed at the guard station, with a high school friend whose father was a Forest Service ranger.

The other guard — Jim Baxter — was a seasonal man, thin and wiry, about forty years old at the time. Baxter loved the woods, and had a lot of back-country skills. Not quite a hobo, there was something of the fruit tramp about Baxter. He was temperamentally unsuited to holding down a straight job in the towns, or even in the woods for very long. At Granite Creek he tended to disappear for a two- or three-day solo camping trip from time to time, leaving Harold to run the place. Harold had no use for him, but Gary liked Baxter right away. Baxter spent his summers working trail for the Forest Service, picked apples and pulled hops in the fall, and holed up in cheap hotels in Bellingham or Ferndale during the rainy West Washington winters.

For three weeks, Gary worked out of Granite Creek while waiting for the lookout trail to melt out. Meanwhile, he helped inventory the guard station, ordered supplies, repaired breaks in the telephone wires strung through the woods, cleaned and sharpened the various tools, split firewood for the cabin's wood stoves. With Baxter or Harold he also worked up and down the creeks — to Ruby Landing to haul

Gary Snyder at Crater Mountain Lookout, August 1952.

"*. . . so I wrote the Ranger in Marblemount in February, listed my qualifications, which were trail crew and fire fighting work in various national forests, and experience with logging and carpentry and all that kind of thing, outdoor work, and mountaineering, and then I added: 'So I would like your highest, most remote, and most difficult-of-access lookout.'*"

Apparently it was a big joke in the Ranger Station that somebody had volunteered for that lookout. They said, "He's the guy!" and "We've got somebody who actually wants it!" Gary Snyder

hay for the horses, to Four Mile Cabin to clean up after a bear raid, to Slate Creek to shore up a washed-out footbridge on the trail.

One day while Gary and Harold were working in Slate Creek, a fire started back near Marblemount, on B&W Hill, a 5,000-foot mountain three miles northeast of town. The B&W Fire, as it came to be known, raced up the mountain all one day. Shubert Hunter, the lookout on Sourdough Mountain, had a good view down the Skagit and saw a huge column of smoke churning up the valley. By late afternoon black flakes of soot were wafting down through the trees twenty-five miles east of the burn in the Slate Creek drainage behind Mount Ballard. "You could reach out your hand in Slate Creek and catch ashes from that fire in Marblemount," recalled Harold Vail. He and Gary — out of radio contact and unable to see out of the Slate valley — did double time back to the guard station to get on the phone and find out where the smoke was coming from. By the time they got back the fire was under control, but not before two men died battling it. That July, news of it reached even to San Francisco, where Gary's roommate Philip Whalen heard the report. "The radio told of a great fire near Marblemount," wrote Whalen. "Are you singed?"

At that time, Snyder and Whalen had been friends for three and a half years, going back to their undergraduate days at Reed College in Portland, Oregon. At Reed they had been housemates, and, although Whalen was seven years older than Snyder (Philip was a World War II veteran going to Reed on the GI bill), they had graduated together in the class of 1951. Always simpatico, they had kept in touch after graduation and reunited in San Francisco's North Beach in the spring of 1952. Their apartment was on the second floor of a gray stucco building at Montgomery and Green streets, high on the south slope of Telegraph Hill — "like living on the bow of a ship," said Gary, with San Fran's famous fogs breaking around the hill and the lights of Coit Tower blinking like a ship's stack in the mist. The rent was $35 a month. Gary had found the place on his arrival in late March, shortly after dropping out of grad school at Indiana University. Within days of moving in he had landed an easy rent-paying job, at a Kodak film processing lab on the waterfront. A few weeks later, Philip Whalen joined him, coming up from L.A., where he had been hanging out, unemployed, with friends from Reed.

For Snyder, settling in San Francisco was a homecoming of sorts. He had been born in the city, at the old Stanford University Hospital in the Fillmore, in 1930, when his parents, Lois and Harold Snyder, had come down from Depression-wracked Seattle looking for work. There was none, and a few months after Gary's birth, the struggling couple and their new baby returned to Washington. Gary spent his boyhood on the family's hardscrabble farm outside Seattle and his teen years in Portland, living with his mother and sister after his parents' divorce. He went to Reed College on scholarship from 1947 to 1951, and by the time of his graduation, was, like so many other Reedies, "itching to get away from Portland, Oregon."

"West Coast of those days, San Francisco was the only city," Snyder would later write, "and of San Francisco, North Beach. Why? Maybe no place else in urban America where a district has such a feel of on-foot: narrow streets, high blank walls and stairstep steeps of alleys and white-wood houses cheap to rent; laundry flapping in the foggy wind from flat topped roofs. Morocco; or ancient terraced fertile crescent pueblos."

At Indiana University Snyder had been in the graduate linguistics and anthropology program, but that was all over now. He had done well at IU; in fact, he'd been offered an assistantship by the chair of the anthropology department. At Reed he'd been a brilliant and efficient scholar: his 200-page senior thesis, an interdisciplinary study of the Haida Indian version of the Swan Maiden myth — a world wide cycle of folk stories — became "the most copied Reed thesis of all time." Had he continued on at Indiana there is little doubt an illustrious academic career awaited him. But it was clear even after one semester of grad school that university life would never content or contain the young Snyder. He would always love the texts and the myths, of course; but he was finding he had another voice for them, one too poetic — and potent — for academe. At the beginning of February, Gary left Indiana and returned west, first for a brief visit with old Reed friends in Portland, then down to the Bay Area, arriving at his father's house in Oakland a few days after the spring equinox.

The apartment house where Snyder and Whalen lived in 1952 and 1953 was built right into the shoulder of Telegraph Hill, at the foot of the Montgomery Street steps — on foggy nights a setting straight out of Dashiell Hammett. Gary, however, thought of the locale in terms of terrain: "on the Montgomery Street drainage — at the top of a long scree slope just below a cliff." Certainly the streets of upper Telegraph Hill were some of the steepest in town, with enough gain to keep a hiker's legs and lungs in mountain shape all winter. From above the Montgomery steps, at the crest of Union Street, Gary could look down to the palm-lined Embarcadero and the stone-arched façades of the waterfront piers slanting out toward the flats of Treasure Island. To the east lay the hump of Yerba Buena Island, with the steel of the Bay Bridge bending to it, and Oakland and Berkeley on the far shore, the gray stone spike of the Campanile at UC Berkeley, small but distinct against the dark green of the background hills. For a full three-sixty, Gary could always climb a few more blocks to Coit Tower, take the elevator to the top, and peer out the arched windows at one of the most dramatic urban-natural panoramas on the continent, east to Mount Diablo, north to Point Richmond, west to the fresh green breast of Mount Tamalpais (with a fire watch tower — Gardner Lookout — on its East Peak, if one knew to look), south to San Bruno Mountain. Only Seattle rivaled it.

Even before leaving Indiana, Snyder had applied to the Forest Service for his summer lookout. He had been wanting to get into the North Cascades for some time. As a boy growing up on the outskirts of Seattle he had lived with the "unearthly glowing floating snowy summits" of Mount Baker and Glacier Peak watching him from the northern edges of his world, but by the time he was old enough to climb them his parents had divorced and he had moved down to Portland with his mother. All his early snowpeak climbing had been in the southern Cascades. He hadn't seen those ethereal beckoners of his boyhood again until 1947, when from the top of Rainier he'd looked up the range beyond Snoqualmie Pass to the big country to the north.

So in the winter of 1952, from Indiana he had applied to Marblemount, headquarters for the Skagit District of the Mount Baker Forest, which, from his maps, had several promising back-country lookouts. Soon after settling in at Montgomery Street, Gary received the forwarded Forest Service letter saying that he had been accepted and assigned for the season to Crater Mountain Lookout, in the North Cascades Primitive Area.

On his green quad map of the forest, spread out on the floor of his Montgomery Street flat in early April, Crater Mountain had looked very good. The L.O. was marked with a small triangle at 8,129 feet. The interval lines defining the bald summit ridge were very, very close together on the map, and there were blue and white patches showing glacier ice on the north slopes. He could visualize the whole

Ross Dam Trail, Ross Lake National Recreation Area, July 1997. ➤

scene: a craggy, precipitous, barren, wind-swept place, with lots of good rock. The dotted line of the lookout trail scaled out to seven and a half miles, wriggling down through the green of dense forest to a small square indicating a guard station at the foot of the mountain.

AT GRANITE CREEK, Gary was in the heart of what had once been the Skagit mining country. In 1879, Jack Rowley, a prospector from Seattle, set off the first Skagit gold rush with a highly publicized strike on Canyon Creek, just a few miles upstream from the later site of the guard station. To the newspapers, Rowley claimed that he had been led to his lucky diggings by a God-like "Hidden Hand" that had appeared to him in a dream and pointed him precisely to where the gold lay. The *Bellingham Bay Mail* pounced on the story. John Sutter, one of Rowley's cohorts, also mentioned finding some "rubies"—actually garnets embedded in schist—at the mouth of the stream, and so named it Ruby Creek. The headlines screamed: "Ruby Creek has gold from one end to the other!" And the rush was on.

Throughout the 1880s miners invaded the Ruby Creek area, many of them packing down from British Columbia on an old Indian trail along the east bank of the Skagit, others blasting their way upriver through the precipitous gorge above Newhalem, where they constructed an insane route of rope ladders and flimsy plank bridges called the Goat Trail. Carcasses of fallen mules and miners alike could be seen fairly often floating down the Skagit, but not often enough to drown the optimism of the oncoming goldrushers. At one point there were two thousand men working six hundred claims from the mouth of Ruby Creek far up into the watershed. An encampment of tents sprang up at the mouth of Ruby Creek, then a bunkhouse and blacksmith's and eventually—sure sign of civilization—a whorehouse. Ruby City, it was called. The pass where Jack Rowley had first dreamed his dream was named Hidden Hand Pass, the creek that flowed through it Hidden Hand Creek, and the big 9,000-foot mountain that loomed over it all—"Nokomokeen" to the region's Native Americans—became Jack Mountain.

In subsequent decades there were various booms and busts as promising new deposits were struck and then played out. Gold fever lingered on the Upper Skagit for a long time, both at Ruby Creek and downriver at Thunder Creek as well. As late as 1934 a lucky miner showed up in the town of Concrete with $30,000 worth of gold from diggings on Ruby. On Thunder Creek, the Azurite mine had sixty-five full-time men tunneling for ore right up until World War Two, when the government closed down all the Skagit mines to divert manpower into the army. Clearly there was gold to be had, but without a road to the claims there was no way to get heavy mining equipment in, or to get the rock back out in large enough quantities to pay.

Meanwhile, it was discovered that the real riches of the Skagit were in hydroelectric power. It was Skagit water power that provided the juice for the rise of Seattle as the premier metropolis of the Northwest—"Makes trolley buses run/Through the streets of dim Seattle far away," as Philip Whalen would later muse from a lookout high above Ross Dam. Seattle City Light had built Gorge Dam on the Skagit in 1919 and Diablo Dam in 1929 and after the Second World War was moving toward completion of its third and biggest, Ross Dam, situated less than a mile downriver of Ruby Creek. The power company had begun buying old mining claims and dismantling Ruby City even before the war, in anticipation of possible challenges to its plan to flood the creek once the dam was finished. Then, low postwar prices for gold further discouraged any major resumption of mining in the Upper Skagit. Finally, the filling of the reservoir behind Ross Dam delivered the symbolic coup de grâce to the gold rush era in 1949 when the Skagit waters began backing over the ruins of the miners' old settlement on lower Ruby.

By the time Gary Snyder arrived at the Granite Creek Guard Station in July '52, the gold rush days seemed like ancient history, even though it had been less than twenty years since the last serious mining. That summer, the Skagit had risen to nearly its full elevation behind Ross Dam, and what was left of Ruby City lay submerged and forgotten, deep in the cold green waters of Ruby Arm. Further upstream, the old mine cabins that had once dotted the banks of Ruby and Canyon creeks were nearly all gone—broken by bears, swept away by avalanche and wildfire, quietly swallowed in vine maple and berry thickets.

Originally, the Granite Creek Guard Station had itself been a miners' cabin, built back in 1902 by three shipwrights who had come up to the gold rush from the Seattle shipyards on the advice of a waterfront fortune teller. The men built a solid little cedar log cabin on the banks of Granite Creek, fitting it expertly with double dove-tailed corner joints, which would hold for a hundred years. They themselves were gone in two.

In the early 1920s the cabin was taken over by one Frank Beebe, who had first come to Washington from Ohio in 1895 at the age of twenty. On the train west, Young Beebe had fallen in with some prospec-

655-foot Ross Dam, in the Skagit gorge between Sourdough and Ruby mountains. "At the foot of Ross Dam they stocked a big barge with food and gear, then they put all of the mules and horses in the barge and eight or ten bales of hay for the horses and pack stock, and all of the personnel that were going in there, including two lookouts. . . . Then the tug pushed the barge up to the foot of Ross Dam, and there was a sky cable above and a cable line came down and they hooked on to the lines on the barge and lifted the barge all the way over Ross Dam with the horses and hay and everything on it, and us — I just couldn't believe it, that they were having us ride that up — and swung us across, and lowered us down into Ross Lake." Gary Snyder

tors on their way to the "Glory Hole" on Ruby Creek. Feeling lucky, he went along with them and spent a hopeful season panning the streams, but in the end came in to Bellingham, where he took a job in a shingle mill. Later, Beebe made his living on fishing boats in Alaska. But the Skagit had gotten into his blood, and in his middle age, he began making trips back to Ruby Creek, no longer seeking gold, but trapping for ermine, marten, and mink. Sometimes Beebe camped at the shipwrights' old abandoned cabin on Granite Creek; around 1920 he decided to claim it and moved the whole thing, log by log and shake by shake, down to the shady flat in the fork of Granite and Canyon creeks.

At the confluence of the creeks, the cabin was in a much more strategic position in the valley, and became a way station of sorts for travelers crossing back and forth between the Skagit Valley and the passes of the Cascade Crest. Over the next few years Beebe added a shake-walled kitchen and a sleeping room onto the rear of the original cabin. In 1928 he went to work for the Forest Service, and his place became the guard station. When Frank Beebe eventually retired and moved back to Bellingham, the Forest Service purchased the cabin from him and maintained it until the late 1950s.

The Granite Creek Guard Station, although it was one of the most remote outposts on the forest, was at the same time one of the most comfortable, having once been a family home. In the early 1930s, Frank Beebe's wife and daughter had joined him at the cabin and left behind many domestic touches. Just inside the front door of the guard station was a small living room, with a table and chairs, a pot-bellied wood stove, and a battered old couch to sprawl out on. At night Gary, Harold and Baxter sat around playing cards, writing letters, telling jokes and reading Damon Runyon stories. After Baxter and Harold turned in, Gary lay reading the T'ang dynasty poet Po Chü-i by kerosene lantern with the roar of swollen Canyon Creek outside mixing with the buzz of a billion insects in the moonlit woods. "It is only the sound of running water," wrote Po, "But I never grow tired of listening to it." Gary copied the lines in his journal. It was like the old poet was in the room with him.

On his arrival at the guard station, Gary had written in his journal, "I am not writing poetry at the time, it doesn't bother me much, perhaps something will develop." Snyder later dropped these lines from the published version of his lookout journals in *Earth House Hold*, but the casual entry is telling, as it apparently typifies the organic, non-coercive, relaxed approach toward his own creativity that he fostered from the beginning of his life as a poet.

In the early summer of 1952, Gary had good reason to feel confidence in his muse. Just before leaving San Francisco to come to the Cascades, he had finished "A Berry Feast," one of the poems for which he would be best known throughout the late '50s and '60s. Indeed, from its unabashed opening image of berry-studded scat in a "neat pile on the fragrant trail" to the mischievous "Fuck you!" of its Coyote hero, "A Berry Feast" would become a favorite of early ecology radicals, as well as the signature work of what was later wryly called "The Bearshit-on-the-Trail School of Poetry."

Working from notes taken at Oregon's Warm Springs Indian Reservation in late August of 1951 during the annual berry feast, Gary had built his poem throughout that fall and into the winter of 1952 while at Indiana University, completing it at Montgomery Street in the spring. It was the longest and by far the most ambitious poem Snyder had attempted to that date — his first try at the ethnopoetic merging of Native American, Asian, and personal myth for which he would become famous — a remarkable achievement for a twenty-one-year-old. Only a year before its writing, while still at Reed, Gary had modestly and realistically assessed his poetic talent at the time in a letter to his father, saying, "I have been turning out poems of minor importance but careful craftsmanship all fall, and am really feeling some control over the medium, and see the potentialities of complete expression." With "A Berry Feast," that potential had been realized.

Gary dedicated "A Berry Feast" to Homer and Joyce Matson, friends and fellow Reed College anthropology students with whom he lived at Warm Springs in the summer of 1951. Gary had first come to the Warm Springs rez with Homer, during their Christmas break from Reed in 1949. It had been very cold then, and they camped in Gary's mountaineering tent down by the Deschutes River, with Gary overseeing all the cooking and heating for four days while Homer conducted research for his graduation thesis. Gary, then in his third year at Reed, had collected "a fine folktale and a fragment of a flood legend" from an old Tsimshian man. This was Gary's first folklore project, as well as his introduction to the Tsimshian mythology that would inform his own senior thesis on Haida myth.

In the summer of 1951, after graduation, Gary had gone to Warm Springs and lived with the Matsons and their newborn baby in a small cabin on Schoolie Flats. While Homer Matson went about his ethnographic fieldwork among the local Wishram and Wasco people, and Joyce raised their baby, Gary worked as a timber scaler for the reservation's lumber company — that is, he kept a board-foot tally of the daily cut as the logs came into the yard. By the time of the late August berry feast, Gary had made several friends in the native logging operation and was in a perfect position to take in the festivities — no longer as an anthropology student but as an accepted fellow worker and neighbor.

The Warm Springs berry feast was a traditional "first-fruits" festival — that is, a ritual gathering, offering, and eating of the season's first berries, after which all the people were free to partake of the various wild berries growing in the area. The entire festival lasted nearly two weeks, with songs, story-telling, deer hunts, and dances, leading up to the first-fruits rite on the final weekend, when native women gatherers ceremonially brought in the first ripened huckleberries to the great public feast. Indi-ans came from all over the reservation and the surrounding areas — Wasco and Wishram and Puyallup and "Yakima horsemen, hair black as crows/shovel-shaped incisors, epicanthic fold." There was wild gambling as well, and horse races — and Gary had caught the whole thing.

On one of his days off at the guard station, Snyder hiked into Rowley Chasm on Canyon Creek to see if he could locate any of the mine shacks from the first gold rush and perhaps find some usable antique tools "or an old brass safety razor with teeth." He hiked all day until he finally discovered some tilting ruins in the hemlock gloom, but behind the heaped tailings and broken door frame there was only a tangle of rusty picks and gears no older than the Depression. Gary didn't turn up any artifacts, but he did come away with grist for a new poem, which he called "History Must Have a Start."

Tools of our time, nothing for an
Archeologist, unless washboards are rare —
The whole works packed in on muleback
In pieces, and never enough gold to pay.

In the 1950s, and well into the 1980s, Upper Skagit history "started" with stories of Jack Rowley and the miners of seventy-five years before. Few people then paid any attention to native elders who told about the old ways and uses of the remote valleys and mountainsides by their recent ancestors. Even less was known about the prehistoric people of the Skagit. Indeed, their existence was not even sus-pected. It was generally thought that the Cascades had acted as a natural barrier between coast and interior cultures, not a vast stage for a prehistoric human drama of its own. It had been assumed that Skagit natives had made little use of the Cascadian interior, except to cross over for purposes of trade.

That view largely went unchallenged until the 1970s. The first archeological survey of the Upper Skagit was not undertaken until 1971, and no evidence of ancient human activity was found until 1975. As late as 1986 there were only fifteen known archeological sites behind Ross Dam. By the year 2000 there were more than 150.

In fact—as is now known—the place where the Granite Creek Guard Station sat at the juncture of the creeks had been an important node in the watershed long before the miners. Not for hundreds but for thousands of years, native people had used Granite and Canyon creeks as conduits between the Skagit and the mountain passes to the east.

Even Snyder, with his anthropology degree (his Bachelor's from Reed was in anthropology and literature) and intense interest in Native Americans, was unaware of the deep layers of human culture buried in the valley of Ruby Creek where he worked and hiked that month. Long before the miners panned Ruby Creek for gold, Skagit Indians had fished there and ancient hunters had roasted elk and deer under rock shelters along its banks.

At Granite Creek, Snyder found himself in a situation very much like what he would encounter twenty years in the future when he established a homestead in the Sierra Nevada amid the wasted gravels and hackneyed lore of California Forty-Niners. It was a typically Western situation whereby the hundred-year-old feats and hijinks of the miners were accepted as ancestral and for a long time blotted out any previous cultural recall. Snyder had no problem giving the miners their historic due. He knew that in another time he would have no doubt been among them in camp—"you bastards/my fathers . . . Your itch/in my boots too." He acknowledged and admired their grit and would have been pleased to have retrieved some still-usable tool from Jack Rowley's day. Still, the irony of his title, "History Must Have a Start," expresses the young Snyder's hunch that our true spiritual ancestry lay buried at some deeper, yet-undiscovered cultural level.

When the Warm Springs berry feast had ended in late August of 1951, Gary had quit his scaler's job with the reservation lumber company and gone on a week-long solo camping trip to the Olympic Peninsula. From the Olympics, he then hitched down and spent a few days at his father's home in Berkeley before heading east to take up his graduate studies at Indiana University. In San Francisco, on the eve of his departure for the Midwest, he connected up with Philip Whalen, who had come down to

Remains of Granite Creek Guard Station in August 1998.

Granite Creek Guard Station, August 1952. Guard stations were part of the Forest Service's extensive fire suppression network, remote outposts where firefighting tools, food, and supplies were cached. In the event of a burn, guard stations also served as bases for smoke chasers. One or two seasonal "forest guards" or "fire guards" were usually stationed there as well. It was the guards' job to build and maintain area trails, put out small fires in the vicinity, and in general lend support to packers and lookouts.

San Francisco after graduating Reed in June. They met for dinner at the old Buon Gusto restaurant on the corner of Columbus and Broadway. Philip liked the city a great deal but hadn't been able to gain a foothold during his first summer; now broke, he was heading south to L.A., to stay rent-free with a friend from his army days, and hoping to accumulate a stake for an eventual return to the Bay Area.

Gary too would have preferred to remain in San Francisco, and was leaving for Indiana with some reluctance. Still, Indiana University, with its excellent folklore and linguistics programs, made good sense from a Native American anthropological point of view—it was a natural segue from his work with David H. French at Reed and the themes he had explored in his thesis on the Swan Maiden. Also, fellow Reed grad Dell Hymes was already there, and just up the road from Bloomington, another of Gary's very good friends, Lew Welch, had settled in Chicago. So, when Indiana offered him a small scholarship in the spring of 1951, Gary had accepted.

Always in the back of his mind, however, was another plan: to stay out of school for a year, live in San Francisco, work to pay back his loans from Reed, and take Chinese-language classes part-time in UC Berkeley's renowned Far Eastern languages department. Philip had wanted to tap into the same program, but like Gary, he could not afford the tuition for out-of-state residents. After dinner, the two friends took a wistful walk down through Chinatown to Union Square, to a metaphysical bookshop that stocked hard-to-find Oriental titles. Among the books Gary bought that night was *Essays in Zen Buddhism: First Series,* by D. T. Suzuki. It proved to be a momentous purchase.

Gary already knew something about Zen in the summer of 1951, but not much. In those days there were few books on the subject in English, and those were not that easy to come by. Most of what he'd gleaned about Zen had come tangentially from his professors at Reed—David H. French and Lloyd Reynolds—and from friends like Bob Richter and Charley Leong. French and Reynolds introduced Snyder to Zen academically—French from an anthropological, and Reynolds from a literary-artistic perspective. Charles Leong was a Chinese-American war veteran, twenty years older than Snyder, going to Reed on the GI Bill. Leong coached both Gary and Philip Whalen in many things Oriental, from Chinese language and calligraphy to the proper way to handle chopsticks. Robert Richter was a fellow Reed student, who sat next to Gary in Contemporary European Literature in the fall of 1949—"the first person I ever talked to who had actually made contact—living contact—with Zen," according to Snyder. (Richter had met the Zen Master Nyogen Senzaki in the spring of 1949.)

All these were preparatory influences. Suzuki was the first writer in the young Snyder's experience to speak of Zen with real authority and practicality, and his effect would turn out to be nothing less than life-changing. A few days after his dinner with Whalen, Gary set out from Oakland on the 2,300-mile hitch to Bloomington, Indiana, making his way first up to Sacramento on Highway 99, then heading east on the old two-lane Route 40 through Donner Pass and beyond into Nevada. In Nevada, the highway ran northeast between the Trinity and Humboldt ranges up to Winnemucca, then turned east, to follow the banks of the Humboldt River through seemingly endless echelons of spectacular mountains all the way across the state. This, Snyder well knew, had been the route of the California Trail that a hundred years before had brought the emigrant wagons from Fort Hall in Wyoming down to Stephens Pass. Later, the rails of the Central Pacific had been driven along the same course, at some points right in the Forty-Niners' wagon ruts. The original steel still ran out of sight into the heat shimmers of the river plain. For more than a hundred years, Euro-Americans had trapped and whipped and hammered their way along this route, moving with the west-flowing Humboldt across the ancestral territory of the Paiutes and Shoshoni. On the edge of each town, tilting tombstones marked the graves of the ones who hadn't kept up.

Somewhere on the outskirts of one of those dusty little eye-blink towns between Winnemucca and Elko — Golconda, perhaps, or Battle Mountain or Dunphy — Gary let his rucksack down and sat by the road shoulder to await the next eastbound car. Exactly a century before, in the late summer of 1851, ten thousand people a month had pressed on past the spot where he was now stationed, all going in the opposite direction on their way to the gold rush. The last anxious parties would have been coming through at exactly the same time of the season, praying that they could beat the early autumn snows through the Sierra passes. Eastward motion in that place felt retrograde, almost unnatural. The sun, the river, the land itself seemed to tend subtly toward California, as though still listing in the backwash of the great groaning human passage of a century before.

Cars were few, east or west, and to pass the time, Gary fished up his new Suzuki book from his pack and began to read. What impressed him most that September afternoon by the side of the road were Suzuki's accounts of the great T'ang Dynasty Chinese masters, their struggles and satoris — Rinzai and Obaku smacking and clobbering each other like a couple of vaudevillians; Baso tweaking Hyakujo's nose; but also the ultimate dignity of the student Koho, newly enlightened, stopping the stick of his master in mid-swing, saying, "You cannot give me a blow today!" There was humor and drama and mystery, even majesty, in Suzuki's stories.

Many of Suzuki's examples underscored the importance of self-knowledge and direct experience versus book learning. In fact, several of his accounts were of former scholars who had only reached satori after abandoning intellectual careers and taking to the hills or the highway — Kyogen, the tenth-century Chinese scholar trading his genteel study for a homeless shanty, finally enlightened by the hollow sound of a bit of scree striking a bamboo shoot; Tokusan, hitting the road after setting fire to a life's work of learned commentaries on the Diamond Sutra, saying, "However deep your knowledge of abstruse philosophy, it is like a piece of hair placed in the vastness of space . . ."

In that clear-aired Nevada landscape dominated by the distant 9,000-foot peaks of the Shoshone Range to the south and the Tuscaroras on the north, Suzuki's Zen was profoundly magnified. "It catapulted me into an even larger space," Gary would remember several years later. "And though I didn't know it at the moment, that was the end of my career as an anthropologist."

Zen, insisted Suzuki, was "a matter of character and not of the intellect." Gary, despite his own scholarliness, had felt this to be true for some time. Earlier that summer, hitching down from Portland to Warm Springs, he had read Thomas Merton's *The Seven Storey Mountain* — also by the roadside — where Merton had stressed the same thing. But Suzuki's message was even more to the point. "In Zen there must be *satori*," wrote Suzuki, "there must be a general mental upheaval which destroys the old accumulations of intellectuality and lays down the foundation for a new faith."

In a road-shoulder revelation — "a practical epiphany," in Snyder's phrase — suddenly it hit him: Route 40 was equally empty both East and West. He was free to go either way. He should be heading in exactly the opposite direction, back to California, and from there, to Japan for practical Zen training.

Of course, he had already committed to the semester at Indiana, and when his next eastbound ride appeared, Gary continued on into Utah and Wyoming. It took him four days to reach southern Indiana, reading Suzuki's essays all the way across — "Enlightenment and Ignorance," "History of Zen Buddhism from Bodhidharma to Hui-Neng," "On Satori," "Practical Methods of Zen Instruction," and "The Ten Cow-Herding Pictures." By the time he arrived in Bloomington, he was saturated with Suzuki's Zen and vowed inwardly that his Hoosier time would be short. His resolve had even taken auspicious form in the apartment he landed on his first day in town: a second-floor flat above a Chinese cafe called "The Orient."

ANOTHER D. T. SUZUKI title that Gary had picked up that 1951 night in San Francisco with his friend Whalen was the *Manual of Zen Buddhism,* one of the first authoritative collections of Chinese and Japanese Zen classics in English, containing many of the traditional sutras, koans, and sermons by the most famous Zen masters. Suzuki's *Manual* also had key excerpts from the main scriptures of the Buddhist canon—the Heart Sutra, the Diamond Sutra, the Lankavatara and Surangama sutras, and the Sutra of Hui-Neng. In those days, it was never far from the top of Gary's backpack, always near at hand.

While at Granite Creek Guard Station Gary read the Sutra of Hui-Neng—the Platform Sutra—for the first time, beginning a lifelong relationship with its teaching. The ramshackle old prospectors' cabin, with its cedar log walls and fresh-split cord wood piled outside was the perfect place to absorb Hui-Neng, the unschooled woodcutter who became one of the greatest Zen masters of T'ang Dynasty China.

Like many of Snyder's early heroes, Hui-Neng was an underdog and an outsider who set the established order on its ear with the force of his originality and spiritual independence. In addition to being poor and uneducated, Hui-Neng was also from one of Southern China's despised ethnic minorities. His spiritual awakening is said to have come about spontaneously, without any formal training or the customary scriptural studies. "Like Blake, Hui-Neng never went to school and did not need to go," commented the Zen scholar R. H. Blyth—another recent Snyder discovery. "Even if he had gone, like Thoreau he would have suffered no ill effects."

The story goes that while piling firewood in the market at Kwangchow, Hui-Neng was suddenly enlightened upon hearing a random phrase from the Diamond Sutra chanted by a passing monk. According to tradition, the line that so pierced Hui-Neng was: "Awaken the mind without fixing it anywhere." This wood-stacking satori of Hui-Neng's is one of the greatest moments in Zen history, comparable, says Blyth, to the sudden awakening of St. Paul on the road to Damascus.

Hui-Neng spent many years in the mountains, hiding out from jealous monks out to kill him after his secret confirmation as the Sixth Patriarch. For ten years, he lived incognito among hunters and trappers in the mountains of Southern China. It was a Zen adventure story that could have taken place in the American West.

"Hui-Neng's Platform Sutra is in a way the first clear philosophical statement of Zen thought. It's almost *the* founding text of Zen in China," Snyder says today, reflecting back on that first reading. "It is so early and so strong, and what it does is it takes Mahayana Buddhist philosophy and gives it a wonderful Zen turn. And that was like a foundation for me also, in reading that, reading it several times over. Everybody that does Zen has a close relationship with that text. So it was a very good thing for me to be reading at that time—better than I even knew."

Hui-Neng's "Discourse on Prajna," which Snyder was reading at Granite Creek, stresses the superiority of self-reliance and spontaneous intuition over scriptural authority. "Seeing into one's own nature"—the most profound phrase ever coined in the development of Zen, according to D. T. Suzuki —summed up Hui-Neng's pragmatic, visionary (the emphasis on seeing), and egalitarian philosophy. "People know thereby that their own Nature is originally endowed with Prajna-wisdom and that all things are to be viewed in the light of this wisdom of theirs, and they need not depend upon letters."

For Gary, it was a further corroboration that he was on the right spiritual track with his decision to break with academia. In his journal, following his entry on Hui-Neng, Snyder noted:

> *one does not need universities and libraries*
> *one need be alive to what is about*

Aeschylus had no doubt visited such scenery as this.
Thoreau, "Ktaadn," *The Maine Woods*

Youngsteiger

Crater Mountain, 1952

I T W A S T I M E for Gary to pack to his lookout. The creeks were down, the trails had melted out, he was ready to go. He had been in the Skagit for nearly a month and had yet to get into any high country. On the afternoon of July 19th, Andy Wilcox arrived at Granite Creek to take him up. Andy the Packer, or "One-Eyed" Wilcox, as he was also known, was a ringer for every Hollywood mule skinner from Gabby Hayes to Slim Pickens — a squinting, profanely hilarious character who could work a chew of Copenhagen snoose on one side of his mouth while the other cheek was full of berries and never get them crossed. "That Andy Wilcox could throw a diamond-hitch quicker than anybody in the Skagit," remembers Shubert Hunter, the lookout on Sourdough that year. "His whole world was those mules." Packer Wilcox showed at the guard station late in the day, slouching in on his mount and leading a string of three mules bearing Gary's lookout supplies, including a sack of brown rice and a gallon tin of soy sauce. "Shit Snyder, you gettin just like a damned *Chinaman*," he snorted. The "Chinaman" tag — always a loaded nickname in the Northwest woods (and especially so in that Korean stalemate summer) — stuck with some of the Forest Service guys. Gary wore it like a badge for the next two years.

Tommy Buller, a Forest Service man who first met Gary at Marblemount that summer, remembers Snyder's rice, and that "he wouldn't set in a chair like you or me, he would set cross-legged. He was really working on being able to be a monk. From here he was supposed to go into a monastery, and he told us it was going to be a tough show, and he was training himself. Everything he did pointed in that direction. . . . He knew that he was going to have to live on rice and he might as well make up his mind to do it. And me, I'm about eighteen years old and I see all this, and I said, 'Is that boy in this world or some other world?'"

At first light the next morning they set out — Gary, Harold Vail and Jim Baxter leading on foot with Andy Wilcox behind them bringing up the mules. They followed the misty trail above Canyon Creek until the sound of its rush was lost to the wind in the overhead firs. Crater Mountain Trail was a steep, switchbacking Forest Service trail built for pack stock. It went up the densely wooded south flank of Crater Mountain, now and then bending sharply around the huge girth of some old-growth conifer, but mostly the stands they trudged through were less than a century old, predominantly Douglas fir, ponderosa, and lodgepole pine, with some silver fir mixed in as they moved higher up. During the gold rush days, fires from the mining camps along Ruby Creek had routinely swept the lower flanks of Crater; the 1952 forest was a complex mix of tough old survivors of those turn-of-the-century burns and younger trees that had grown up in the aftermath. The stands were dense and allowed no vistas until almost 6,000 feet. Snyder recalls the mountain being socked in by clouds on the day of his packing up, with no views anyway, even above timberline.

After a couple of hours on the trail they came to Crater Lake — a shallow green tarn rimmed by a mile-long amphitheater of steep talus slides and metamorphic crags piling up to Crater's cloud-hidden summit. From the lake, the trail wriggled up the southwest shoulder of the mountain through the last of the wind-bitten alpine fir and at 7,000 feet opened on the final patch of level ground, with another 1,000 feet of elevation and a mile more to the top.

At 7,500 feet the terrain became too difficult for the mules. The pack trail devolved into a narrow foot path hewn into the southwest wall of the mountain, and ended abruptly at the bottom of a steep-pitched gully of boulders and scree. Gary and Harold went ahead to where a protruding flange of basalt served as a sort of natural platform for off-loading the mules and stacking supplies. On this stone plat-form was a weather-beaten wooden pallet with turn buckles for securing a load and an attached cable line going out of sight over the higher rocks. Gary had been told about this: everything had to be loaded off the pack stock here and hand-hoisted to the next level.

Andy brought up the mules one at a time, each one stepping surefootedly along with its heavy panniers bulging out over the edge of the narrow, steep-walled path and Andy leading it closely by the bridle. In the fog, it was hard to tell how much of a drop there actually was, but it felt like an immense void, and when a bit of scree would slide off under the shoe of one of the mules, the pebbles could be heard clattering down the rocks for a sickeningly long way. Accidents did happen: just two weeks before, while packing to Hidden Lake L.O., Harold Vail's younger brother Roger had lost a fully loaded mule — one of "Andy's mules" — over the side of the lookout trail. Now, Gary and Harold unpacked each new mule smoothly and quietly while Andy steadied it, then expertly and cussingly brought the animal about and led it back. There was barely enough room for the mule to turn around, but the operation went off without mishap.

Wilcox and Baxter returned with the mules to the guard station. Harold stayed behind to help Gary open up the lookout. Snyder remembers standing at the foot of the gully, with six weeks of supplies piled on the ledge beside them and the winch cable going up the rocks and disappearing into cold white fog. They buckled a load of heavy radio batteries and kerosene cans on the pallet and went on up the gully. There were eye-bolts drilled in the rocks with fixed ropes to haul themselves up. The gully went up about 300 feet and came to an exposed ledge with old yellow paint blazes showing the way up the rocks. At the top they found the tripod and windlass for hoisting up the load, and began cranking. It was like trawling in a huge fish; it took forever until the pallet appeared out of the mist, jerking forward on the cable eight inches at a time. It was amazing to think that the L.O. had been constructed this way, that all the shiplap siding, roof shakes, window glass, kegs of nails and all the tools to build it had come up the gully on this same hoist.

They were at 8,000 feet now, on a broad, treeless, seemingly barren platform sloping toward the summit ridge, a dreamscape of whipping fog and bizarre rock apparitions. When a gap blew open in the clouds, they got their first glimpse of the lookout perched on the gnarly hump of the summit, looking small and hapless and barely real in the mist, nothing but a box, still closed up from the winter with its wooden storm shutters battened down over the windows.

Harold Vail stayed with Gary the first night to help him get the lookout opened up. Together they unbolted the heavy wooden "weather door" and raised out the drop shutters from the rows of windows all around the lookout. Inside they got the kerosene stove going and brought in a basin full of snow—there were still drifts piled outside the north and west walls—to melt for drinking and cooking water, and they got the two-way radio going and checked in with the fire office back in Marblemount.

During the night the weather grew worse, and in the morning when Harold headed back down to the guard station there were four or five inches of new wet snow on the summit and inverted icicles sticking up on the guy wires of the lookout. Forty-six years later Harold Vail still recalled: "When I was up there in the middle of July it was cold enough to freeze and with the fog to make the moisture there were icicles on those guy wires out maybe six inches and they angled upwards 'cause the wind was coming up the cliff and blowing the icicles uphill."

Inside the lookout ice formed on the north and west walls. "My fingers are too numb to write," Snyder scratched in his journal when he was finally alone. "And this is mid-July. . . . One has to go to bed fully clothed." His first days in the lookout were harsh, and at first nothing seemed to go right. The weather remained wretched, lashing Crater Mountain summit with three days of wind, hail, sleet, and snow. The storm shutters kept slamming down in the wind and had to be propped back up; the two-way radio—his only contact with the world below—kept breaking down; he got the kerosene stove working but couldn't make it stop; the wood stove hissed and smoked with rotten wood. Meanwhile, his groceries were still under a tarp down at the bottom of the gully.

The steep southwestern gully and the hand-operated windlass used to raise supplies above it made Crater Lookout one of the toughest in the state to pack up to. Snyder remembers:

It took a full week of many trips for me to go down over the cliffs, load a box with food, come back up the cliff doing a third-class rock climb to get up again to where there's a winch, hand winch the box up from the lower platform to the upper platform along the cable, unload it, and

High on the Crater Mountain Trail, September 1998. "I asked the packer, 'Where does the trail go from here?' And he said, 'There isn't any trail from here. There'll be some marks painted on the rocks to show you which way to climb' . . ." Gary Snyder then in turn backpack all of that food load by load the last quarter mile to the lookout, including the batteries for the radio. Took a whole week to be entirely moved into Crater Mountain Lookout.

Now Gary understood the bemusement of the rangers at Marblemount when he had checked in back at the end of June. It had apparently been a big joke around the station, the fact that anyone was nuts enough to volunteer for a place like Crater Lookout.

Lucky McLeod, a Native American packer who worked for the Forest Service during the late '40s and early '50s, remembers Crater well: "Whoever put that lookout up there just must have been mad at the world," he says. "Else tryin' to prove something."

Gary had been to some high fire lookouts before on climbs in the southern Cascades. He'd seen the wreckage of the old L.O.s on Mount Saint Helens, Adams, and Rainier, but he'd never had to pack into or live in one. "I was sort of bemused myself by what they had put themselves to up there," says Snyder, reflecting on those first days in Crater Lookout. "But that was the spirit of the 'thirties for you. It was great. I hadn't realized myself that lookouts could be made in places quite that remote."

Yet despite the wicked weather, arduous packing, and feeling "filthy with no prospect of cleaning up," Gary was not unhappy in his hermitage. The sudden solitude after his weeks at the guard station was delicious, and although the lookout was totally socked in for the first three days, he thought the dense fog outside made the cabin's windows look like a *shoji* screen in a Japanese tea hut. In fact, said Snyder: "It was perfect. There was this blank white mountain fog light in this chilly, chilly little place, and I would be wrapped in my blanket doing my *zazen* or doing my calligraphy." In his journal, Gary took to calling the mountain "Crater Shan," the Chinese appellation for a peak, as in "Huang Shan" (Yellow Mountain) or "Nan Shan" (South Mountain). He even used "Crater Shan" as his return address on letters to his friends and by the end of the summer they were using it when writing him.

Deep as it was in the back country, Crater was not the most remote Forest Service lookout in the Skagit District — that distinction belonged to Desolation, twelve miles further north on Ross Lake. As for difficulty of access, there may have been a few other lookouts in Washington harder to get to than Crater, it depended on whom you asked. Several other lookouts in the state had hand-winched trams similar to Crater's for hoisting supplies where government mules would not be coaxed. Fixed ropes, iron handrails, footholds blasted in granite were not uncommon for Cascadian lookouts. On Three

Fingers Mountain, Forest Service crews had dynamited fifteen feet of pinnacle rock to flatten a tiny space for a lookout cabin and then installed fixed ladders across the deep chimneys leading to it.

But at 8,128 feet, Crater was definitely the highest fire lookout in the Skagit, and one of the highest ever built in all of Washington State. Only nine other lookouts had ever surpassed it in elevation, and by 1952 those nine were all in ruins or stood abandoned on their peaks. When Gary got to it, Crater was the highest operational lookout in the state.

Ironically, Crater was something of a failure as a fire lookout, precisely because of its elevation. It had been built during the flamboyant period of lookout construction in the early years of the Depression, when intrepid Forest Service teams, and later Civilian Conservation Corps (CCC) crews, cut new trails every season, packing up entire cabins in prefabricated pieces on muleback—and often on their own backs—to build a vast network of observation posts for the purpose of total fire suppression. Each year they created challenging new lookouts on ever loftier and more difficult perches. On the Okanogan National Forest, four other lookouts were built at elevations of 8,000 feet or more the same year as Crater (1932); every one was eventually abandoned.

Crater L.O. may have been a tribute to those builders, and to the hardiness of the lookouts who inhabited it, but in terms of fire detection, Crater was too high to be dependable throughout most fire seasons. True, on a clear day it had an unrivaled view of some three million acres of forest, but quite often the visibility was no more than three yards into the fog outside the windows, as it was on Snyder's arrival and for many days during his watch. Also, at 8,129 feet, the last snow melted out late and new snow came not long after—the year of Snyder's lookout, for instance, the time window between snows was only five weeks. The most reliable fire lookouts were lower down; six thousand feet—the elevation of lookouts like Sourdough and Desolation—seemed to be about optimal. More important than elevation was strategic location, good sight lines down major drainages, and a high percentage of days with good visibility.

If Crater Mountain Lookout was less than ideal for fire detection, it made for a perfect Zen hermitage, and Snyder had come loaded for Zen. "I took some good books up with me, basic Zen texts, and my black tea, some good Japanese green tea and some lapsong souchong, plus sumi brushes for doing Chinese-style calligraphy," remembers Gary. "I really kept myself busy. I had a daily schedule which included certain periods of meditation. I did *zazen* [Zen sitting meditation] certain hours, and then calligraphy practice, and then I would study a text, then zazen again, and then I'd go melt snow and bring it up and cook, and have tea and write some haiku and then do some more calligraphy practice and some more zazen, and the days just flew by."

From the guy wires of the lookout he strung Tibetan prayer flags inscribed with the Om Mani Padme Hum mantra and set up a low stone seat for doing zazen, on the lip of the precipice overlooking Jerry Glacier. Gary had tried zazen as far back as 1949 at Reed College but had practiced infrequently and somewhat self-consciously at first. Learning to sit had not been all that difficult, even in the near total absence of teachers. He had picked up the basic cross-legged sitting posture, hand positions, and so forth simply by copying the poses of statues of Buddhas he'd seen in museums in Portland and San Francisco. Developing regular practice was the hard part. On Crater Lookout he hoped to begin to do that.

"Crater Mountain was the first opportunity I had to really see if I could sit. That was one of the reasons I went on lookout," he remembers. "It gave me a chance to be consistent and to see if I could carry through and be comfortable with such a thing day after day. And I was quite comfortable. In fact, at the end of the season I didn't want to come down."

AFTER A FEW DAYS of being socked in, the clouds on Crater summit finally began to break apart, showing hints of the broad rugged back of Jack Mountain across the way, or brief glimpses of the green basin of Jerry Lakes down below. Then one morning the fog around the lookout was completely and suddenly gone, replaced by a nearly overwhelming panorama of mountains flowing to the horizons in every direction. No roads, no towns, no clear cuts, not even the dams were visible. At 8,129 feet, Gary was on one of the highest peaks around; the sense of space was tremendous.

From the northwest windows of the lookout Gary stared straight into the great grooved southern slopes and pocket glaciers of Jack Mountain, just three miles away. Crater and Jack were geologically quite similar, both monumental humps of ancient volcanic rock thrust up from the complex faults of Ross Lake. From Gary's L.O., Jack was the dominant presence on the horizon, a thousand feet higher than Crater and so close that it blocked out much of the view of the Big Beaver and Little Beaver country across the lake. But looking due north from the lookout, the horizon was wide and deep, marked by the intriguing cluster of Hozomeen Mountain and extending far up into the Hope Range of

British Columbia. The east window looked down the Crater Mountain saddle to the East Peak and beyond to Hart's Pass and a vast sea of mountains flowing to the far horizon—"Blue heaped upon blue," in the old Zen phrase. To the south, a dozen ridges ribbed the drainage of Granite Creek all the way to Rainy Pass. For a little human inspiration in the foreground of this staggering panorama, Gary tacked up a nude photograph of an old girlfriend from Portland in the west window—"her nipple just poking Mt. Challenger, Mt. Sourdough by her thigh." "Natural against natural beauty," he noted in his journal.

THE FIRST JOB of a lookout, according to the Forest Service handbook from those days, was to "Learn every peak, ridge, hill, road, trail, lake, creek, building and false smoke." The instrument for this was the Osborne fire finder. Extremely precise and easy to use, the fire finder was a stationary disc map with a rotating peep sight for pinpointing smokes in the surrounding mountains. It was mounted atop a steel shaft that went down through the center of the cabin floor and into the ground. Plumbed in summit bedrock and calibrated on the North Star, the Osborne fire finder was one of the greatest tools ever devised for learning terrain. Working from the center of the cabin, the lookout could scan the horizon in every direction through the Osborne's cross-hairs and identify any mountain or drainage in the surrounding country. The map charted an area twenty-two miles out from the lookout in every direction, for a coverage of 1,500 square miles. Beyond that, the Osborne sights could still be used to obtain azimuth readings as far as the eye could see. Smokes could easily be plotted to within a 160-acre "quarter section" on the map. With additional readings called in from a second or third lookout, smoke chasers could be guided to a fire with remarkable accuracy. To have that kind of coverage of the territory was one of the reasons so many lookouts were built in the days before aircraft overflights became common.

The fire finder was by far the most important piece of equipment in Crater, or any, lookout. It was the main sense organ of the lookout and central to the entire fire-detection effort. In a very real sense, fire lookout cabins were mostly just housings for fire finders. Indeed, fire finders predated fire lookouts; the first fire finder was designed in 1911, the first lookout cabins were not established until a few years later. The earliest fire "lookouts" in the Cascades were nothing more than seasonal sites for a fire finder, with a tent for the fire watcher and perhaps a telephone nailed to a tree and several miles of phone wire running down the mountainside—"rag houses" they were called. In 1929, three years before construction of the lookout, the Forest Service had a rag house on Crater without even a phone. In those days, if the fire watcher spotted smoke, he had to take a reading with the fire finder then hike seven and a half miles down to Frank Beebe's cabin, where there was a phone line out to the fire office twenty-five miles away in Marblemount.

During those first days of good visibility, Gary spent many hours squinting through the sights of the Osborne, pinpointing the hundreds of mounts and drainages surrounding him, identifying and savoring the evocative North Cascadian names: Three Fools Peak and Freezout Mountain, Devil's Dome and Hell's Basin, Grizzly Creek and Cutthroat Peak, Deception Pass, Last Chance Point—hard-luck names, given by the early miners. To the west the peaks had been named by mountaineers—Fury, Challenger, Terror, The Barrier, The Chopping Block, Despair, Triumph—legendary names among climbers, but quite recent, some in usage less than twenty-five years. These were the Pickets, an awesome jumble of twenty summits of 7,500 feet or more in a compact seven-mile range, then as now the wildest and most undiscovered country in the whole North Cascades. Indeed, the entire Upper Skagit region of the North Cascades was a climbers' Eden in the early '50s, still with plenty of unascended, nameless rock and ice.

Mountaineering in the region had grown indirectly out of the work of hardcore government surveyors like Sledge Tatum and Walter Reaburn, who made many of the first ascents in the region in the early years of the century; or the ubiquitous Lage Wernstedt, who climbed scores of summits in his cartographic work for the Forest Service in the 1920s and named many of them, including "the Pickets."

When Snyder was on Crater Mountain in 1952, climbing as sport was still a recent phenomenon in the North Cascades. The first alpine ascent of a summit in the Pickets had been made only twenty years before, when William Degenhardt and Herbert Strandberg climbed the Chopping Block. Fred and Helmy Beckey ushered in the modern era in the North Cascades beginning in the late '30s and early '40s, with climbs on Despair, Inspiration Peak, McMillan Spire, and Fury.

From his vantage point on Crater, Gary could see it all spread out before him in the low rose light of dawn, from stubby Luna Peak at the top of the Pickets south to the vast glaciers of Boston-Buckner ridge, all with a quarter turn of his head. Beyond, on the most distant horizons, he could see the snows of Komo Kulshan, Shuksan, and Glacier Peak—all three of which he would eventually climb.

Osborne fire finder, Desolation Lookout, July 1995.

Oil the saws, sharpen axes,
Learn the names of all the peaks you see and which is highest —
   there are hundreds —
Learn by heart the drainages between
Go find a shallow pool of snowmelt on a good day, bathe
   in the lukewarm water.

         Gary Snyder, "The Lookouts"

"I'd been in the South Cascades, down around Mount Saint Helens, and in the Olympics, but I wanted to see the North Cascades," recalls Snyder. "There's a lot of ice up there, lot of nice rock. . . . I was not disappointed."

IN THE SUMMER of 1952, Snyder had been climbing for more than eight years. He had made his first snow peak climb when he was fifteen — on Mount Saint Helens, in the summer of 1945, during the final week of World War II. As it happened, Japan surrendered the day after he came down. Hiroshima and Nagasaki had been atom-bombed during the week leading up to the climb, but Gary, at the Portland YMCA camp at Spirit Lake, had been only vaguely aware of the blasts before making his ascent. The first photographs from Hiroshima did not appear in *The Oregonian* until Sunday, August 12. That same day, his climbing party set out, camping at tree line that night in order to be on glacier ice at dawn. On the morning of the 13th, he summited—"an eerie, rigorous initiation and transformation . . ." he would later write, "above all the clouds with only a few other high mountains also in the sunshine, the human world still asleep under its gray dawn cloud blanket . . ." When he came down, the first thing Gary saw was a newspaper posted on the camp bulletin board with the boldest headlines he had ever seen and a photograph of the strange, towering Hiroshima bomb-cloud, accompanied by a story suggesting that nothing would grow in that devastated landscape for another sixty years. The next day, the war, which had been going on since he was eleven, was suddenly over.

Gary would always remember the old mountaineer who guided his party to the summit that morning as a figure from a bygone world: the man wore stagged-off logger's pants, caulked boots, and a black felt hat. He climbed with an iron-pointed alpenstock and smeared his cheeks with white zinc paste for protection. Snyder never again saw anyone in gear like his on any climbs.

The following year Gary did Mount Hood and joined the Mazamas mountain club in Portland, where he fell in with a fanatical bunch of like-minded teenage climbers whom he dubbed The Young-steigers (from *Steiger*, German for "climber") ". . . a large and loosely knit brotherhood of youthful mountaineers that believe in the gospel according to David Brower, Shipton and Tilman . . . a group that measures all mountains by the Himalayas, that combines its mountaineering interests with skiing, and takes both seriously."

In the ensuing years, Gary climbed eight to ten peaks a summer; by 1952 he had been to the top of Mount Hood—the nearest of the big snowcapped Cascades volcanoes to his home—fourteen times. "We never climbed anything just once," Gary says, remembering those times. "We did as many mountains as we could as many times as we could. You get to know them that way."

The new postwar mountaineering that the young Snyder got hooked on went far beyond traditional summer climbing. It was a year-round passion that included snow camping, skiing, and winter ascents and came about largely under the tutelage of young veterans of the 10th Mountain Infantry Division who had joined the Mazamas after World War II. "Those guys, I remember them well," says Snyder, "became my generation's—the sixteen-year-olds—teachers in that era's state-of-the-art snow and rock climbing. So we all went out climbing together with these twenty-five-year-olds who were very sharp. . . . It was a very good time to learn mountaineering, and the Mazamas hosted it."

Snyder and the Youngsteigers mixed military skills and discipline with their innate animism to develop a fresh mountaineering ethic that was totally opposed to the notion of "peak-bagging." "I and the circle I climbed with were extremely critical of what we saw as the hostile, jock Occidental mind-set that thought to climb a mountain was to conquer it. I'm not quite sure where we got that from, other than from our own sort of respect and pantheist affection for the mountains, but it became a very strong thing for me. . . . I always thought of mountaineering not as a matter of conquering the mountain, but as a matter of self-knowledge."

In those days, Gary would hang out after school at the Mazama's clubhouse on the top floor of the Power and Light Building in downtown Portland, spending hours among the maps, books and framed photographs of snow peaks and famous climbers, absorbing the tradition of Pacific Northwest mountaineering. The Mazamas was not only an alpine club, it was one of the earliest and most far-sighted conservation groups in the Pacific Northwest. As far back as 1906, the club had called for the creation of a national park in the North Cascades, touching off what would become a sixty-year debate over the use of public lands in the region.

When Snyder was on Crater in 1952, practically all of the enormous territory visible from his lookout had been under the administration of the U.S. Forest Service for a half century, going back to the creation of the first national forests from the former Washington Forest Reserve. The Forest Service had been established in 1905; the National Park Service in 1916. From that time on, the question of which agency would administer the wilderness, and to what end, would be a theme running through the history of the North Cascades.

During the 1920s, new national parks were created in the Arkansas Hot Springs, the Shenandoah, Bryce Canyon, and the Grand Tetons. To the Forest Service, these parks were felt as jurisdictional losses. In large part to prevent further slippage of lands to their new rival, the Forest Service adopted preemptive internal regulations setting aside "wilderness," "wild," and "recreation" areas in some of the more remote or scenic sections of the national forests — areas that, if not provided some sort of protection, might likely become candidates for national park designation.

At the same time, enlightened voices within the Forest Service, such as Aldo Leopold and Robert Marshall, argued for the maintenance of "primitive areas" within the national forests. Leopold and Marshall envisioned these as core wilderness areas that would remain forever roadless and unlogged, not merely as bureaucratic checks against the Park Service, but, in Marshall's words, "To preserve a certain precious value of the timeless, the mysterious, and the primordial."

In the North Cascades, the new Forest Service designations resulted in the creation of the Glacier Peak Recreation Area of 230,000 acres (1931) and the North Cascades Primitive Area of 800,000 acres (1934). The problem with these classifications from a conservation standpoint was that they carried no statutory weight; they were only departmental guidelines and could easily be redrawn or lifted entirely. Even commercial timber executives could get behind them, since keeping public logs off the market in loosely regulated "wilderness areas" helped maintain prices for their own trees. And since the protections were not backed up by any binding legislation, they could always be rescinded if the industry needed to feed their mills with public logs, as would happen following World War II.

Meanwhile, in the late 1930s, the idea of a national park in the North Cascades resurfaced in a big way with an official Department of the Interior study of the region and a subsequent recommendation for a huge "Ice Peaks National Park" running from Mount St. Helens north to the Canadian border and including all five Washington volcanoes and their surrounding wilderness. This proposal barely received any public discussion before being roundly defeated by a combination of timber and mining lobbyists and chambers of commerce from all over the state, afraid to lock up the ranges resources while the country still battled the Great Depression.

During the exact same period as the Ice Peaks proposal, the Forest Service was submitting its own ambitious plans, less grand, but quite significant. Robert Marshall and USFS director Ferdinand Silcox toured northwest Washington and recommended establishing an 800,000-acre Glacier Peak Wilderness Area adjacent to the already existing North Cascades Primitive Area to form a contiguous wilderness of a million and a half acres. With such creative propositions being floated by both Park and Forest services, conservationists were for a time divided over which department—Interior or Agriculture—might ultimately be the most appropriate custodian of the public lands.

This situation did not last long. In the 1940s, things changed dramatically. Robert Marshall and Ferdinand Silcox died within months of one another in 1939, suddenly depriving the conservation movement of its two most effective advocates within the Forest Service. Five years later, the post–World War II housing boom set off an unprecedented demand for lumber just at the moment when the timber industry's private holdings had become depleted to the point of near exhaustion. Now began heavy pressure to open up the national forests, to road and log the Limited Areas and Primitive Areas, to "get out the cut." The postwar Forest Service, without Marshall and Silcox, complied wholeheartedly, setting up a timber sale program to feed the mills of Weyerhauser et al. for decades to come.

Almost immediately following the deaths of Marshall and Silcox, the Forest Service reduced the size of their Glacier Peak proposal by more than half and classed it not as wilderness but as a "limited area." "A Limited Area means we haven't figured out yet just where to put the logging roads," a Forest Service planner was reported to have quipped at the time. For ten years the Marshall-Silcox area remained in that temporary status, while timber and mining companies nibbled away at the forests of the great snow peak's watershed. The logging trucks Snyder had seen barreling by on the Skagit Road when he'd first hitchhiked into the country back in June were still hauling out the bounty of those reclassified acres.

In the crosshairs of his fire finder sights on Crater Lookout, Gary could see the dome of Glacier Peak beckoning in the far mists behind the foreground snows of Mount Logan, but he was not yet aware of the conservation battle brewing lower down in the gateway valleys of the volcano. Eventually all the ground between would be in national park and fully protected wilderness areas, but that was years away. In the summer of 1952, Crater was safe in the North Cascades Primitive Area, fifteen miles from the nearest roadhead and seemingly impervious to any major commercial logging for at least another twenty years. Meanwhile, the Forest Service in the Upper Skagit "seemed like a very worthy and somewhat quiet and conservative agency that was taking care of public lands," as far as Gary could tell. The worst that could be said of it was that it fostered a "shopkeeper's view of nature" whereby "Forest equals crop / Scenery equals recreation / Public equals money. . . . Treat it right and it will make a billion board feet a year." What he was actually seeing, he later realized, were "the last years of righteous forest management in th United States."

By the end of his first week in the lookout, Snyder was still having problems with the old two-way Motorola PT 300 radio. Finally it got so bad that the dispatcher told him to come down to the guard station at Ross Dam and pick up a new one. The three-day round-trip hike gave Gary a chance to reflect on the fragility of the whole fire lookout and guard station network, which could be shut down by a single blown radio tube. The situation provided the impetus for "The Lookouts," his ironic ode to those elite mountain watchers, like himself, who were "Equipped by Science with the keenest tool / A complex two-way radio full of tubes" and were the envy of the lowly valley folk. But,

> . . . if that complex radio should break down —
> Taught how to use, but not to fix, its tubes —
> For all their artful watching, they are dumb.
> Totally useless, lost to human speech,
> They mutely have to make the long hike down.

A strange sight greeted Gary on his return to Crater — a sharp-shinned hawk lying dead at the foot of the lookout wall, where it had slammed as it came soaring up on a draft from the lake basin. It was a short-winged bird with a barred, squared-off tail and small, light-feathered body. Sharpies were characteristic birds on Crater. Gary had noticed them from his first days, seen them flapping and cackling after ravens twice their size out over the crags, right on the bigger birds' tails. "Fierce, compact little bird with square head," he noted in his journal.

He had lately been thinking of the poet Robinson Jeffers and Jeffers's "Inhumanism"— and now here was this bird that seemed to have blown straight out of the pages of *Cawdor*—"The broken pillar of the wing jags from the clotted shoulder." The dead hawk got him to musing ever more deeply about Jeffers. Jeffers adored hawks — also condors, eagles, vultures, herons, all the wings that sailed the cliffs and river

The view looking south down Crater Ridge from site of the old lookout, September 1998.

. . . a Jeffers landscape, with evocative rockheads jutting up along the ridge, hardy old map lichens splotching their sides and the daintiest alpine plants thriving for a brief season in the cracks. At that elevation there was nothing to tempt bear or deer; it was the realm of ravens and eagles. But for a pounding sea at its base, Robinson Jeffers would have felt perfectly at home on Crater.

mouths of his Big Sur coast, but hawks most of all. In poems like "Hurt Hawks," "Shiva," "Give Your Heart to the Hawks," "Winged Rock," "Rock and Hawk," "De Rerum Virtute," and many others, they dove and circled.

Snyder was a great admirer of Jeffers's work, which he had discovered in high school and read with great excitement. Jeffers, Gary felt, was the only poet to write with any real strength about the landscape of the West or the life of other-than-human Nature. Jeffers could sit by a campfire at the foot of a mountain wall and see ". . . through the flame-lit surface into the real and bodily living rock." His poems were a corroboration of Snyder's own feeling, from an early age, for the sentience of supposedly inanimate objects. At the same time, Jeffers was classically trained and grounded in the tradition of Greek tragedy, which Snyder also admired. Jeffers's vision even made reference to Native American and Asian myths, if only in a peripheral way—myths that were already central to Snyder's work and of which he would soon become an authority in his own right.

For Snyder, Crater Lookout was a fitting place to consider the necessary questions of poetry, nature, and humankind raised by Jeffers's work. The main problem with Robinson Jeffers as far as Gary was concerned that summer was the man's enormous bitterness towards humanity. While Jeffers could write with profound love for individuals—his family mostly—toward humanity as a whole his attitude verged on the misanthropic. "Boys," the poet warns his sons in "Shine Perishing Republic," "be in nothing so moderate as in love of man . . ." For Jeffers, a hawk perching on a treeless pinnacle of stone— "Fierce consciousness joined with final disinterestedness"—was an apt emblem of the future. In his letters, Jeffers called his philosophical attitude "Inhumanism"—"a shifting of emphasis and significance from man to non-man," but in his verse, his indictment of humanity was scorching and near total.

In "Fawn's Foster-Mother," a nursing woman gives one nipple to her baby and with the other suckles an abandoned deer fawn: in her old age she reminisces, "I had more joy from that than from the others." In "Hurt Hawks," the narrator, before shooting a broken-winged hawk to end its suffering, claims "I'd sooner, except the penalties, kill a man. . . ." For Jeffers, non-human Nature was imbued with "a transhuman intrinsic glory" while Man was but a "sick microbe," his civilization "a transient sickness." In "Original Sin," he writes: "As for me, I would rather/Be a worm in a wild apple than a son of man."

Ultimately, though he would always love Jeffers's poetry, Snyder couldn't buy into his Inhumanism.

I was wondering if, to take as strong a stance in and around nature as Jeffers does required such an alienated attitude towards human beings. He made a choice there to value nature over humanity, and on Crater I was reflecting on that.

There is a way which I think is clear in Eastern thought—in Taoism and Buddhism—to truly see human beings as part of nature, beings that are amusingly overdone in some ways and excessive in their capacities but ultimately as vulnerable as anything else. And there is no need to place blame, which is what Jeffers did.

BY THE TENTH of August Snyder had not seen another human being since returning from the Ross Lake Guard Station with the new radio two weeks before. Each day alone since then had built on and deepened his solitude until it had become a palpable ambience inside the cabin. Now the human silence was broken for only an hour in the evenings during the lookouts' nightly talkaround on the two-way radio.

The talkaround was supposed to provide fire watchers a nightly opportunity to stave off stir-craziness; but in fact, the scratchy, disembodied voices coming out of the Motorola only seemed to accentuate the sense of their remoteness. As the weeks of solitude wore on, you could hear the distraction and boredom creeping into some of the radio voices. By mid-August there wasn't much to say; lookouts were using up their radio time reading magazine pieces from old left-behind *National Geographics* and *Reader's Digests,* just to fill the dead air. "The poor lonely lookouts, radioing back and forth," Gary jotted in his journal.

After the talkaround, the mountains would be dark as the men lit their kerosene lanterns and set their candles to read, write letters, clean up the dinner dishes, play solitaire. On Crater, Gary brewed a pot of tea and dipped his pipe bowl into the tobacco can for a smoke. Outside the northwest window, the last magenta and orange streaks of the sunset glowed behind the dark hump of Jack Mountain until well past ten P.M. Thirteen miles due north across the dark Pasayten Wilderness, Gary could see the faint beams of Jack Francis's lantern on Desolation Lookout; nine miles to the west, Shubert Hunter's lamp in the windows of Sourdough. No other lights were visible anywhere. It was just the three of them—Gary, Jack, and Shubert—keeping watch over the entire Upper Skagit.

Shubert Hunter was a nineteen-year-old Native American kid from the Makah reservation at Neah Bay, in his first summer working for the Forest Service. Shubert hadn't intended to go on lookout; he was in the Marine Reserves and thought he might be heading for Korea, but Blackie Burns had talked him into taking Sourdough when the scheduled fire watcher bailed out at the last minute.

Jack Francis, the Desolation lookout, was an Army Air Corps veteran who taught high school down in Bremerton and worked for the Forest Service during his summers off. He was thirty-two. He had radioed from Desolation on Gary's first freezing day on Crater and welcomed him to "the community of lookouts." Since then they had spoken every night during the talk-around. Jack had grown up in Carbonado, a coal company town near Mt. Rainier. At sixteen he had moved up to Bellingham, where he worked alongside his father in a bituminous mine, drilling and shoveling twenty tons of coal a day. In World War II, Jack had been a waist gunner on a B-17, first over North Africa and later over occupied Europe. Like a character out of Heller's *Catch-22*, Jack had flown twenty missions over North Africa and was on his way home when he was transferred to the Eighth Air Force in England and had to fly twenty more.

Both Jack and Shubert had been in their lookouts a couple of weeks longer than Gary, and neither of them had had any visitors at all since packing up. Such unbroken solitude is almost unimaginable nowadays, but in the summer of 1952, the Ross Lake country was far from the National Recreation Area it would become. At that time, only a few intrepid mountaineers had ventured into the Upper Skagit. Fred Beckey had made a first ascent of South Hozomeen in 1947, but postwar mountain sports were still in their infancy. Even backpacking and camping were only beginning to achieve mass popularity; what vacationers did come to Ross Lake were mostly there to fish, and did not venture far from the shoreline camps. From his 6,000-foot lookout on Desolation Peak, Jack Francis could peer down at night and see the fishermen's tiny campfires at the mouths of Little Beaver and Silver creeks, but no one ever came up.

Even Sourdough Mountain, which had a public road and the small settlement of Diablo at its trail-head, was largely unhiked in those days. Shubert Hunter remembers no one coming by during his 1952 lookout. "I kept expecting people to come up because in our orientation the instructors prepared us for meeting the public, but I was up there the full summer totally by myself—just me, the chipmunks and deer."

Not everyone could handle being that cut off. Compounding the isolation was the fact that there was not all that much to the fire watcher's job description. You had to keep an eye out for smokes—twenty minutes out of every hour supposedly—and take certain weather readings and call them in each afternoon, but days on the Cascadian mountaintops were long, with seventeen hours of sunlight in high summer. Calling in the fire weather took only twenty minutes. How to fill the rest of the time could be a problem for some.

For Snyder, however, such complete and lengthy solitude was exactly what he had come to the mountains hoping to find. To him, solitude was not a thing to be endured, but savored. For an extroverted type, Gary had not only a high tolerance for being alone, but a strong need for it. Even as a boy growing up on the edge of the forests outside Seattle, he had often sought privacy and would build secret hideaways for himself in the woods. "When I was eleven or twelve even, I would sometimes make up a pack and go out for a night or two and camp in the woods by myself, just walk from our house out into the forest. I had a couple of campsites out there that I would go to, that I'd fixed up, and I'd stay there by myself. I liked solitude. . . . That's the way you learn, by sitting still and being quiet in nature. Then things start happening around you."

One of the things about lookout life was the way that the mundane essentials—things one took for granted in the cities, water for instance—could only be procured with time and conscious physical effort. By early August there was no snow to melt for drinking water anywhere close to the lookout. To get his water Gary had to go down over the steep north side of the summit to the top of Jerry Glacier, break off chunks of ice and pack them back up to the lookout to melt slowly in a washtub in the sun. It took a long time to melt the glacier ice to water; to maintain a constant supply for drinking, cooking, and washing meant continually adding new blocks to the meltwater. The daily ice trip became part of the round of his hours. It was harsh, but in times to come Gary liked to remember himself as he was on Crater, stubble-bearded and shave-headed, sunburnt and scrambling over the rocks like a hardcore maniac "in nothing but a jockstrap and boots, following veins of quartzite through cliffs."

On lookout there was ample time to simply be present in nature, to watch and listen to the buzz of the flies, the lazy flap of the prayer flags, the sudden scream of a hawk piercing the blue valley air over Devil's Creek. Over it all the ever-gliding clouds advanced, incessantly shifting shape and dragging their fluid shadows across the ancient hides of the mountains. Sitting still with eyes half open, or lean-

Osborne fire-finder shaft, all that remains of Gary Snyder's lookout

on the west peak of Crater Mountain, September 1998.

ing in the lookout door, observing this vast spectacle of change across a visible mass of three million unbroken acres became an art for Snyder — the art of mountain watching, as he called it in his journal. Out of his solitude came a new sense of time encompassing butterflies, Vaux swifts, chipmunks, map lichens, as well as cycles of change in the stratified metamorphic rock — "more than enough time for all things to happen" — even to the mountains, whose rumpled flanks were mottled with old burns and brilliant meadow greens, grooved with avalanche chutes and red fans of talus, pocked with snow, bristling with vast stands of conifers. In such a landscape — "a chaotic universe where everything is in place" — the lookout's task of scanning the ridges and drainages for smokes slid easily into the zazen of mountain watching.

"Aldo Leopold uses the phrase *Think like a mountain,*" remembers Snyder. "I didn't hear that until later, but mountain watching is like mountain being or mountain sitting. How do you watch a mountain? Nothing's going to happen in any time frame that you can consider — except the light changes on it. And so that was my mountain watching. The changing light on the mountain was like the changing thoughts in my mind, just these little shifting shadows, that's all that it is."

By mid-August, Gary's Zen adventure on Crater was beginning to draw to a close. Before long the early fall storms would begin rolling down from Canada, putting an end to the fire danger. Every afternoon, it seemed, there were more and more birds making their way down the Skagit — goshawks and Cooper's hawks, red-tailed hawks, osprey, occasionally a pair of golden eagles. At night the wind gusted against windowpanes while he lay propped in his bunk — "eyes tired, teapot empty, tobacco damp" — reading the Diamond Sutra by lantern light in Suzuki's *Manual of Zen Buddhism.* Outside the lookout windows, the Northern Lights rippled like a fine iridescent curtain high over British Columbia.

Ever since first reading the story of Hui-Neng down at the guard station, Gary had been curious about the Diamond Sutra, this apparently magical text, a single sentence of which had touched off Hui-Neng's first enlightenment experience. The Diamond Sutra was already more than a thousand years old even when Hui-Neng first heard it recited in the Kwangchow market. The Buddha himself was said to have delivered it as a sermon, and named it *Vajracchedika* — the "Diamond *Cutter*" — with emphasis on the diamond's incisive properties more than its clarity or preciousness as a gem. "It is the scripture that is hard and sharp like a diamond that will cut away all arbitrary conceptions, and lead one to the other shore." With his discovery of Hui-Neng's Platform Sutra, and then the Diamond Sutra, Gary was engaging the numinous Prajnaparamita, or "highest wisdom" texts of Mahayana Buddhism. D. T. Suzuki believed that the Diamond Sutra in particular was "the one of all the sutras of the Prajna-paramita literature in which the doctrine of Prajna is most concisely expounded." Concisely perhaps, but boggling to minds habituated to what Suzuki called the intellect's "ordinary dualistic groove." The Diamond Sutra, as Gary learned that August on Crater, was a masterpiece of paradox, ruthlessly absolute in its negation of all forms, even its own. It preached an unpreachable doctrine that was not to be adhered to — "neither a dharma nor a no-dharma" — while describing itself as a mere raft to get one to the "further shore," then left behind.

"Those who are not accustomed to this kind of reasoning may wonder what is the ultimate signifi-cation of all these negations," wrote Suzuki in his *Manual.* "The Prajna dialectic means to lead us to a higher affirmation by contradicting a simple direct statement. It differs from the Hegelian in its direct-ness and intuitiveness."

Suzuki's contention that the Diamond Sutra was the principal scriptural authority for the teachings of Zen echoed thousand-year-old opinions of some of the most famous T'ang Dynasty Zen masters. One Te-Shan [in Japanese, *Tokusan*], who wrote many commentaries on the sutra — his nickname was "Diamond Chou" — went so far as to say that "Unless one gains a certain insight into this dialectic of negation-affirmation, one has no right to say a word about Zen."

Among the notions that the Diamond Sutra cuts away at are the concepts of a separate ego, individ-ual beings, and the soul. Yet for all its negation of these, the sutra has a distinct aura capable, like the oracular *I Ching,* of impressing its receiver with an uncanny sense of personal communication. "Wher-ever this sutra is kept," it promises the reader, "the place is to be regarded as if the Buddha or a venerable disciple of his were present." As Gary lay up late reading, his the last lantern still going in the million-acre dark, he could feel the sutra taking him as deeply into Zen as the written word could go. "Almost had it last night," he noted in his journal, "no identity . . . my language fades."

LATE IN THE THIRD week of August Jack Francis came over from Desolation, and with Harold Vail hiked up to pay Gary a visit. They found him sitting in the lookout door in his jockstrap and a pair of Japanese sandals, his hide brown from weeks of mountaintop sun, smoking his pipe, surrounded by rippling prayer flags.

Gary made tea and the three lookouts admired the view and compared notes on their cabins. Except for a couple of Boy Scouts who had hiked up on their way from Hart's Pass to Ross Lake, Jack and Harold had been Gary's only visitors the whole time. They had come up to say good-bye. Fire season was just about over, they all agreed; you could just feel it in the air. Even if a fire got started on the forest now, the rains would be along soon enough to wash it out. Harold was leaving the next morning to go back to college; Jack was also going to be packing down and returning to his teaching job in Bremerton.

Harold had brought mail for Gary: a letter from Dell Hymes and two from Phil Whalen — the first beginning "Dear Hemingway," the other "Dear Gaygo" (one of Snyder's college nicknames). When Harold and Jack had gone back down the mountain, Gary went back inside the L.O. and read his letters. The one from Dell and the first one from Philip were two weeks old. Hymes told of an anthropology conference back in Bloomington — "There are worthwhile things said, and some entertaining things said, but only a few things that have the touch of authority and weight," reported Dell.

Philip wrote to say that he had landed a job as equipment manager of the audiovisual department at San Francisco State College and that a friend of theirs, Matt Troy, was staying in the apartment until Gary got back. As ever, Philip was reading three books at once — Mann's *Magic Mountain,* Robert Penn Warren's *All the King's Men,* Scott Fitzgerald's *The Beautiful and the Damned* — plus assorted science fiction. Whalen complained that the news was full of Democratic and Republican convention reports from Chicago — "Demo & GOP crap," as he put it. The Democrats nominated Adlai Stevenson and the Republicans picked Eisenhower, with California's Richard Nixon as VP. San Francisco was hot. "Working is bad anytime," said Philip, "but especially nasty in summer in the city. By God, next summer I'm going to have a mountain of my own."

To Gary, it all seemed very far away. Soon, however, he knew he'd be right back in it. He began readying himself for the call to close up the L.O., which he knew would be coming anytime. He cleaned and oiled the various fire-fighting and woodcutting tools — the McCloud and Pulaski, the grub hoe and rock bar and fire shovel, the double-bitted axes and the six-foot falling saw and backup blades — and stowed them in the crawl space above the low lookout ceiling.

At night he continued reading the Diamond Sutra, and also Blyth's essays on haiku. Living among the rocks of Crater he had come to appreciate the "dry hardness" of the haiku poets. *Sabi* it was called in Japanese, from *sabishi,* lonely and solitary, but not barren. "One does not have a great deal to give," he wrote in his journal. "That which one does give has been polished and perfected into a spontaneous emptiness; sterility made creative, it has no pretensions, and encompasses everything."

On the morning of August 23rd it began to snow and Blackie Burns came on the radio telling him to close up the lookout and pack himself back down to the guard station. It didn't take long; he'd already swept the place and done the inventory. All he had to do was load his rucksack and he was ready to go. Outside, he took down the radio aerial, then lowered and bolted the wooden shutters over the windows, dragged out the big plank storm door from under the lookout and braced it over the front doorway. Finally, he dumped out the remaining meltwater from the water basin and stowed the basin upside down under the cabin. Then, he bowed a prayer of thanks to the L.O. — nothing but a box again — shouted good-bye to the pikas and chipmunks and tramped off under full pack in the cold driving snow.

Glancing around after the first few switchbacks, already he could barely see the lookout in the snow and fog; at a hundred yards it had vanished completely. From that August snow back to the last snow in July there had been but a five-week mountaintop summer. It had flown by and Gary wished that he didn't have to come down. He felt that he was just settling into it. He lowered himself by the handline through the southwest gully, then marched quickly down the switchbacks to the Crater Lake cirque, where the snow had become a light blowing sleet. On the slope above the tarn he knelt on all fours over a thin little spring and swallowed the pure, slightly coppery-tasting water straight from the rock. Crater Shan, he felt for sure, had been his teacher; the mountain was a teaching. He drank from it and thanked it and filled his canteen. Then he stood up and hooked his arms back into the loops of his rucksack and entered the sheltering trees for the rest of the long hike down.

III.

Ever, ever be on the lookout!

Daito Kokushi

All Along the Watch Tower

Sauk & Sourdough, 1953

IN JUNE OF 1953, Gary Snyder was back in the Skagit, this time assigned to the lookout on Sourdough Mountain. As he had done the year before, Gary hitchhiked up from San Francisco to Portland first, where he stopped off to visit his mother and catch up on old friends for a week before moving north. On a whim he bought a battered 1937 Model A Ford from a man in Portland and drove it up Highway 99 to Burlington and then out to Marblemount, where he sold it for $25 to Harold Vail's brother Roger.

At the Forest Service compound in Marblemount Gary saw several of the men from '52. Blackie Burns was there, of course, running the show as ever, breaking in the green kids, giving them quick lessons in the use of the various fire-fighting tools and showing them how to dig their fire lines. Gary watched Blackie closely. Blackie Burns was fifty-seven years old that summer and had been with the Forest Service for nearly thirty. Burns—perfect name—was the archetypal Northwest Fire Dog. Born in Bow, a sawmill town at the foot of Bow Hill, near Samish Bay, he had worked in the woods his whole life. In the First World War, when he was twenty-two, he'd gone to France in a battalion of army loggers, and spent his service felling trees for the bunkers and trenches of the Western Front. He had joined the Forest Service in 1926, the year of the last great fire on the Upper Skagit. Blackie's entire fire-fighting life had coincided with the era of total suppression; by 1953 he was considered the top fire-control officer on the Mount Baker Forest. "He was impressive," recalls Shubert Hunter. "All the rangers paid attention when Blackie was showing where to locate fire lines, or later on when he was teaching how to burn slash."

Blackie was "crusty," "gruff," "crude," according to those who worked for him. "He cussed *a lot,*" says Shubert Hunter. Blackie was "in that old mold of a Western person with a lot of grit and confidence and humor," remembers Snyder. "And he was very tolerant of me. He could sort of read that I was a subversive, but he had a sense of humor about it, and he was the boss."

A natural teacher rather than a bureaucrat, Blackie never reached the position of District ranger in the Forest Service; nevertheless, at Marblemount he was de facto chief. "Burns basically ran things," says Harold Vail. "He was never head ranger, but he kept things going." In the mid-1950s, Blackie was coming to the end of his career, making way for the new breed of postwar forester. In 1953, Frank Lewis had been appointed head ranger for the Skagit District. At Marblemount, Gary noted the jarring differences in the two men—"Blackie, the old-timer, speaking a rich and colloquial language—Frank Lewis, the educated youngster on his way up, talking in Government jargon." When Lewis tried to emulate Blackie's manner—"I'll *growl,* fellas. I'll chaw ass!"—it was laughable.

Back at Marblemount that summer were Shubert and Reggie Hunter, the Native American brothers, as were Jim Baxter and Jack Francis, and One-eyed Wilcox too, out-cussing even Blackie. Harold Vail had not returned, but his younger brother Roger was back, working trail crew with his high school pal Tommy Buller. And Dick Willey the cook was still there, whipping up huge breakfasts of ham and eggs and home fries for the whole crew.

Also at the ranger station was Philip Whalen, in the Skagit for his first fire season. Whalen had arrived in Marblemount separately from Gary, and probably no one would have associated the two if

Snyder had not introduced him around as his friend. Fleshy, bookish, physically lethargic, Whalen could only be a lookout. With his thick-lensed, dark-framed glasses and corpulent build, he didn't look like any of the Forest Service guys on the compound. He gave the impression of an intellectual and an epicure—"a big fat bespectacled quiet booboo," as Jack Kerouac would later describe him, "—a hundred and eighty pounds of poet meat." All Philip wanted to do was make it through fire school, pack up to Sauk Lookout, his assigned mountain, and get down to some serious summer reading.

"Philip was not an athletic or physical person," remembers Snyder. "But I was able to convince him [to apply for lookout work] by saying 'It's not hard to pack up there, once you get there you don't have to do much, you'll have plenty of time to read, and they pay you . . . and the view is lovely. And he discovered that he liked it."

Indeed, Phil Whalen's lookout stints—he would return to the Skagit in 1954 and 1955—turned out to be some of the best jobs he ever had. The pay was decent—$700 for the season, which allowed him to reimburse Gary for "a pot of money" he had borrowed during their year on Montgomery Street. Also, the Forest Service restored a sense of structure to his life—for a few months at least—which he had not had since leaving the army at the end of the war.

"It was a very funny feeling to go up there to Marblemount and sleep in an old army barracks, since I hadn't done that in many years. They were regular military barracks with concrete slab floors and double-decker bunks," remembers Whalen. "And then they had this great cookhouse right there, so that after you got up and washed your face you went to this grand cookhouse where they did real American boarding house-style cooking—lots of ham and bacon and fried eggs and hashed potatoes and black coffee for breakfast, the whole works. . . just marvelous, and I enjoyed that a lot. And then they would give us a bag of sandwiches or something to go with us 'cause we had to work on trail. . . ."

In those days, Snyder and Whalen often appeared an unlikely duo, at least on the surface. Their separate arrivals in Marblemount, despite identical itineraries all the way up from San Francisco, was typical of the autonomy of their friendship. Gary loved to hitchhike; not only was it the cheapest way to go, it felt like an existential act that put him in communion with the likes of Bashō and Whitman. For Philip, the open road brought nothing but desultory rides and road shoulder doldrums. He preferred traveling by train or bus. A window seat on a Pullman car with Pound's *Cantos* in his lap was Philip's idea of travel.

There were other obvious differences. Whalen, a few months shy of thirty, was seven years older than Snyder and had been in the Army Air Corps during the war; unlike Gary, however, Philip had little sense of direction beyond immediate appetites for literature and food, both of which he sampled widely and consumed with gusto. While Snyder darted about with energy and plans, the bearish Whalen liked nothing more than to hole up and read. He once remarked that he could actually "absorb vitamins out of William Blake." Given a finite amount of money—and for Whalen the money was always quite finite—and a choice between books and food, he often opted for the books. Food was a close second, but he found that sympathetic friends liked having him to dinner, and he would eat heartily then.

Gary never had much money in those days, either, but he could stretch his pay ingeniously, bartering his services for rent, buying his clothes at Goodwill, even eating cheap cuts of horse meat—a practice he had picked up while working at the Warm Springs Indian Reservation in '51.

Snyder was every bit the intellectual Whalen was, but it hardly showed through his woodsman-mountaineer-working-class persona. At twenty-three Gary liked to test himself against physical things and tasks, and he had a knack for finding jobs that affirmed his self-image and at the same time provided grist for his poems. By the time he was twenty-two, he'd already worked as a newsroom copyboy, ship's steward, laborer on an archeological dig, timber scaler, and trail-crew hand. For Whalen, most employment—especially physical work—was an absurd and distasteful means toward procuring more books and monthly rent. On the other hand, he labored seriously at his writing and by 1953 had produced a large amount, both prose and poetry, nearly all of which he eventually discarded as unacceptable to his exacting standards.

Despite their friendship's surface incongruities, Philip and Gary were drawn together by important mutual experiences and interests. Both had spent formative years in Portland, Oregon, during and after World War II. Philip was born there in 1923, although from age four he lived in The Dalles, a small town in the spectacular Columbia Gorge seventy miles upriver from Portland. In 1941 he came back to Port-

Gary Snyder, overlooking Pierce Creek drainage from Sourdough Ridge, summer 1953. ➤

"I like that boy Snyder on Sourdough.
He's a calm son of a bitch." Blackie Burns

land, age eighteen, with his father and younger sister Velna, following the death of his mother. In 1942 Snyder arrived in Portland, age twelve, with his mother and younger sister Anthea, in the wake of his parents' divorce.

Portland in the '40s was a wartime boomtown, with aircraft factories and shipyards going twenty-four hours a day. Whalen worked in both before eventually being drafted into the Army Air Corps in 1943. As for Snyder, his mother Lois Hennessey found work as a reporter for *The Oregonian*, Portland's daily newspaper. Gary went to Lincoln High School; summers he spent in Washington, at the Portland YMCA camp at Spirit Lake.

During World War II, Philip hadn't been sent overseas, but he'd been to some godawful Army towns in the U.S.—Biloxi, Mississippi; Sioux Falls, South Dakota; Yuma, Arizona. In the service he trained radio operators and in his spare time managed to read all of Gertrude Stein. After his discharge, he returned to Portland and in 1946 entered Reed College on the GI bill. The following year Gary Snyder graduated high school and won a scholarship to Reed.

The two met on campus in the fall of 1948. As it happened, they became aware of one another as dramatic characters in performances before actually meeting face-to-face. Gary first saw Philip in a Reed production of Shaw's *Pygmalion*, in the role of Eliza's ne'er-do-well father, Alfred Doolittle. After the play, Gary went backstage to visit the cast and introduced himself to Philip, who impressed him as "witty, articulate, engaging—a way cut above the style of Oregon kids, and very well read."

Philip at that point recognized Gary from a photograph he'd seen in *The Oregonian*. At election time that year, a group of Reed students had been doing some political theater, satirizing the local Progressive Party with a mock convention of a "*Regressive Party*." Gary played a caveman in the skit, wrapped in a bearskin, ranting the Regressive slogan, "Back to the Neolithic!" The *Oregonian* had reported the spoof and run a shot of Gary on the front page. (Not only was his mother a stringer for the newspaper, Gary also worked part-time as a copyboy in the *Oregonian*'s city room.) Whalen, a Progressive voter at the time, had taken note of the photo, thinking that Snyder was "sort of a wild-looking guy."

The following year, they found themselves living in the same apartment building at 1414 Lambert Street, about a mile off campus in southeast Portland. In 1949, the Lambert Street house was an early version of the quasi-communal group houses that later became fond fixtures of American university life, with one telephone, one refrigerator, two bathtubs—shared among sixteen to eighteen people. "We were probably the original hippies," recalls Carol Baker, the only single woman living there at the time. In those postwar days, males far outnumbered females on U.S. campuses. Lambert Street reflected that demographic: During any given semester there were fourteen to sixteen men, many of them ex-servicemen on the GI Bill, and never more than two or three women, everyone squeezed into a rabbit warren of apartments in the rambling old two-story house.

"By far the most socially and intellectually stimulating environment I had ever encountered," according to Michael Mahar, another resident. "These occupants of Lambert Street were older students, several of them combat veterans from World War II, with a serious interest in their studies and an awesome grasp of skills ranging from mountain climbing to Chinese calligraphy. Their spirit of sharing contributed as much to my education as the formal course work in which I dabbled."

The Lambert Street house was exceptional for the number of published writers and scholars it spawned. In addition to Snyder and Whalen, their mutual friend the poet Lew Welch also lived there for a time, as did some others who would become lesser known, but serious published writers such as the poet Bill Dickey and the novelist Donald Berry.

In early 1949 Whalen moved into Lambert Street to share an apartment with Roy Stillwell, an army friend and violinist for the Portland Symphony. Snyder was already there, rooming with Lew Welch, with whom he co-managed the building in exchange for reduced rent. Snyder would often come around to Whalen's room for conversation. Whalen and Stillwell, the ex-GIs in their mid-20s, would intellectually lord it over the inquisitive nineteen year old.

"I'm afraid Roy and I teased him a whole lot about being a kid, about not having read this and not having heard that," recalls Whalen today.

"Phil tended to sit back and dispense wisdom like a grandfather," remembers Lambert housemate Mike Mahar. "As a counselor and commentator on life, he maintained a steady calm that somehow seemed to balance Gary's intensity." In time, Snyder came to appreciate that counterbalance — Whalen's "indispensable astringency," he called it. Philip, for his part, was soon taking intellectual cues from Gary. "Actually, he's a lot smarter than I am," claims Whalen. "He was very smart, and got better with time. And I got worse . . . "

During their time at Lambert Street, they shared deep mutual interests in poetry, drama, mythology, and things Oriental — passions that would hold them together for the rest of their lives. Poetry was perhaps the strongest of those forces—their own in progress, plus the works of the then-still-living poetic champions Pound, Eliot, Jeffers, and Williams, each of whom Snyder and Whalen read and reread and discussed for years, extracting and absorbing what would be usable from these monumental influences. At Reed in the fall of 1950, they'd had the good fortune to meet with and show their work to William Carlos Williams when he came through Portland on a reading tour. Williams was then sixty-seven years old and had just received the National Book Award for Book III of his *Paterson* cycle. At a reception for Williams at the home of Reed professor Lloyd Reynolds, Gary, Philip, and Lew Welch had a chance to show and read their work to Williams—"a jam session," according to Welch.

"To have William Carlos Williams land in Portland was quite wonderful. I remember being enormously excited by it all," says Whalen. In later years, Williams's meeting with the student trio would be recorded as a near mythic event—the master's passing of the bardic fire to the tongues of a new generation. At the time, however, it was something even more important for the fledgling poets. Whalen: "To have someone who I thought was a very great writer treat us like we were friends, like we were writers or something, and not like we were some sort of hick students in the Far West—that was very valuable." Ultimately, Lew Welch would be the one most influenced by Williams, but in the years immediately following it, the meeting at Reed was a potent mutual experience for Gary and Philip as well.

IN ADDITION TO poetry, Asian cultures and religions also provided much of the joinery for the Snyder-Whalen friendship. At Marblemount that June, Shubert Hunter, for one, was impressed by the rapport between Gary and Phil and recalls their intensity as they huddled over some Chinese text in the cab of a truck on the compound. "We were in the rig down at the station and they were talking about it, really getting in depth into it. It was like their religion. I didn't pay much attention, but some of the other guys on the crew mentioned it, and then the cook, he told me—'Them guys're *Buddhists.*'"

On Crater Lookout the year before, Gary had proven to himself that he could sit zazen consistently and for long stretches. Crater had also convinced him of the need for a teacher and confirmed his desire to go to Japan for formal training. On his return from the Skagit in the fall of 1952, one of the first things Gary had done was to mail off a check to New York to join the First Zen Institute of America, at that time the only organization in the country even nominally teaching traditional Rinzai Zen to Americans. Earlier, he had written to Nyogen Sensaki, the Zen master in Los Angeles that his Reed friend Bob

Looking west down Sourdough Ridge, September 1998. "Two seasons on lookouts . . .
gave me full opportunity to watch the change of mood over vast landscapes, light
moving with the day — the countless clouds, the towering cumulus. . . ."

Gary Snyder, *"The Making of Mountains and Rivers Without End"*

Richter had told him about in 1949, but Sensaki had not responded to Gary's inquiries about taking training.

As it turned out, when Snyder joined the First Zen Institute in October 1952 the group was in a somewhat torpid state. Its founder, Sokei-an Sasaki, a true Zen pioneer in the United States for more than forty years, had died in 1945, leaving no "dharma heir" to continue his teaching, at least not in the usual Zen sense of a successor *(hassu)* who has reached the same degree of enlightenment as his/her teacher. Instead, Sokei-an's work was being carried forward by his American wife, the well-to-do and indefatigable Ruth Fuller Sasaki. However, when Gary joined the First Zen Institute, Mrs. Sasaki was in Japan, completing Sokei-an's last book and searching for an English-speaking Rinzai master willing to come to America to take on the teaching Sokei-an had begun. In answer to Gary's questions about entry to a Zen monastery, the New York office replied only that it "would depend on individual qualifications and prevailing conditions," and sent him a complimentary incense burner and a box of "Happy Omen" incense sticks.

Sokei-an had been just the sort of spiritual adventurer the young Gary Snyder could relate to. He was like a character out of Bashō: self-contained, supremely resourceful, artistic, physically hardy, solitary and mobile, equally at home in the zendo or on the open road. In Japan at the turn of the century, he traveled to all the famous Zen mountain temples, making his way as a dragon carver. In 1906, Sokei-an came to California as part of a group of Buddhist priests who established a first fledgling "Zen center" in the United States for the then-tiny Bay Area Japanese community. When the other priests returned to Japan two years later, Sokei-an remained behind alone and became a Zen wanderer in America for the next ten years, drifting up through California and Oregon to Seattle, over much of the same ground Snyder would cover a half century later — student life in Berkeley, farm-forest work in Oregon, even a sojourn living with Native Americans, when Sokei-an stayed for a time among the coastal Salish Indians on an island in Puget Sound. For several years he worked and roamed across the States, in 1916 reaching New York City, where he gravitated to Greenwich Village and found acceptance among the prewar bohemians. With the poet Maxwell Bodenheim, he collaborated on some Imagist translations of Li Po poems for the famous *Little Review*.

In the spring of 1953, Ruth Fuller Sasaki returned for a time to the United States and began corresponding seriously with Gary about his prospects for formal Rinzai training in Japan. In late June when he arrived at the Marblemount Ranger Station there was a letter from her, a great letter full of practical inside information on the current Zen situation in Japan, plus realistic encouragement of his own efforts to get there, saying:

> A young man with an assured income of fifty dollars a month, who is willing to come to Japan and spend a minimum of three years there, who will for one year devote himself to the study of Japanese language and to acquainting himself with Japanese culture and to learning to practice zazen, then to spend two years under a Zen teacher — living in or out of a Zen monastery — may reasonably well expect to pass his first *koan* at the end of that time.

Gary was already practicing zazen, studying the language diligently and familiarizing himself as much as possible with Japanese culture.

"He must be prepared to endure extreme heat and extreme cold," continued Mrs. Sasaki. "He must also be prepared to adapt himself physically and mentally to a culture which, though charming and containing many real values, is alien to himself and at times difficult to understand, and he must, last of all, be prepared to have swept away every illusion he has ever held about Buddhism and about Zen. For such a person it is not impossible to study Zen in Japan."

AFTER GUARD SCHOOL, Phil Whalen went on a trail crew to Ilabot Creek, a small stream that flows into the Skagit a few miles west of Marblemount. After that, he packed to his lookout on Sauk Mountain, a distinctive front-country peak overlooking the junction of the Skagit and Sauk rivers. Gary was sent up to Ross Lake Guard Station, then on to Sourdough Lookout. The two did not see each other again until they were back in San Francisco in September, although they were able to chat for a few minutes every night during the lookout radio talk-around.

It had been a heavy Cascadian winter — and it was mid-July before the snows on Sourdough had melted out enough to send a pack string up the lookout trail. As in '52, Gary spent the first weeks after guard school working on Ross Lake, Ruby Creek, and at the Granite Creek Guard Station. In the middle of the month he was sent down to the Diablo Guard Station to meet the pack string that would take him up to Sourdough. Jack Francis was forest guard at Diablo that summer.

The Diablo Guard Station was a comfortable bungalow on the edge of the Seattle City Light company houses below the dam. In the old days, the gravel bar below Diablo Gorge — Reflector Bar, it was

Sourdough Mountain Lookout, July 1997.

called — had always been considered a boundary between the lower river and the upper "Valley of the Spirits" by area Native Americans. In the nineteenth century there were no permanent Indian settlements north of it. In the 1920s, however, Reflector Bar exploded with activity as the Seattle City Light power utility made it the staging area for the building of Diablo Dam. A railroad line was laid from Newhalem to the foot of Sourdough, and a 300-foot "incline hoist" was built into the mountainside to haul up flatcars loaded with heavy dam-building equipment and supplies.

When the dam was completed, the powerhouse was built at the foot of Sourdough Mountain at Diablo along with a cluster of two dozen company houses for the power project workers. Seattle City Light called the little settlement "Camp Diablo," but with its identical cottages and blowing lawn sprinklers it felt more like a tiny suburban housing development.

In the 1930s, City Light ran elaborate public relations tours from King Street Station in Seattle to Diablo to promote its hydroelectric agenda in the Skagit. Tourist groups were trained to Diablo, given a ride up the incline hoist to view the dam, and taken for a cruise across the spectacular green glacial reservoir, serenaded by recorded music playing from shoreline speakers, while guides astounded them with the numbers of dishwashers, clothes dryers, and toasters the dam would power in the coming age of total electrification.

The Skagit Tour, as it was called, was very popular with Washingtonians — in the late 1930s, two thousand people a week visited Diablo. The Skagit Tour came to an end with the Second World War, but in the summer of '53 it was revived, although never again on the prewar scale. As the Diablo Guard, Jack Francis didn't have to deal with the tourists, but their presence was an irritant after the absolute back-country solitude he'd had on Desolation the year before. Plus, Blackie wouldn't permit him to go on trail from the guard station; he had to stay put. It was practically an office job — not what he had in mind for the summer after teaching school all year.

On the 16th of July, Gary packed up to Sourdough with Blackie Burns and another Skagit old-timer, Roy Raymond, the three of them on horseback, with a string of four mules — Tex, Barney, Myrtle and Bluejay. Gary's mount was "Willy the Paint" — "a pleasant white-eyed little horse that took great caution on rock and snow."

The lookout trail began inconspicuously behind some low-roofed Seattle City Light sheds along the rail siding at the foot of the mountain, then climbed abruptly up the southwestern flank in a repetitive series of long switchbacks, gaining 2,500 feet of elevation in the first mile. Except for an occasional glimpse of snow-capped Davis Peak through the trees, there were no views for the first hour or so on the trail as the horses plodded steadily up through monotonous stands of lodgepole pine, low-growing salal and fern.

At five thousand feet, they came onto the snow, packed in the draws of the Sourdough Creek basin, where a big snowbridge had thawed out and swollen the creek with surging meltwater. The spooked horses had to be led across the whitewater by their reins, while the mules stood kicking each other as they waited their turn, causing Gary to muse that "Horses look noble from the side, but they sure are silly creatures when seen from the front. Mules are just naturally silly. . . . Myrtle would commence kicking Bluejay & Bluejay would kick Barney, all with great WHACKS on the forkies."

After the creek, the trail climbed hard into south-facing meadows abloom with wildflowers and opening on steep views of sinuous green Diablo Lake and Thunder Arm 5,000 feet below. On the far side of the lake was a stunning array of glaciers, from the blinding white of nearby Colonial and Neve all the way down to Boston, largest in the range. The higher the horses went now the grander the views got. At the top of the ridge the panorama was a sweeping visceral hit as the country to the north suddenly opened in front of them, from Fury on the western horizon all the way around to the huge eastern anchor of old Nokomokeen-Jack.

Along the Sourdough ridge, a sensuous crest of hard packed snow perfectly divided the plunging snowfields of the north slope from the flowery southern meadows and trees. A half mile east along that line was the lookout, unobtrusively perched on a rough summit shelf of Skagit gneiss, red shutters still down for the winter. Blackie and Roy unpacked the mules and helped Gary open up the lookout, and by late afternoon were gone down the trail. Unlike the year before on Crater, the unloading went easily. They were able to bring the mules almost to the door of the L.O. and stack everything right at the foot of the wooden steps.

Like Crater Lookout, the interior of Gary's Sourdough cabin was dominated by the Osborne firefinder cabinet in the center of the room, and as on Crater, many hours of his first days in the L.O. were spent targeting all the nearby creeks and summits and checking their names against the Osborne's disc map. The nearest big mountain to Sourdough was steep-faced, 7,000-foot Davis Peak, four miles to the west. Davis Peak was named for Lucinda Davis, a diminutive but spunky single mother with three children who in 1890 had come out to the Skagit from Colorado and moved into an abandoned upriver Indian cabin, which she turned into a roadhouse and store supplying the miners on their way to Thunder and Ruby creeks. In the old days, the mountain was called Stetattle Peak ("Stetattle" an anglicization of a Lushootsheed word for grizzly bear); with the miners it came to be known as "Mrs. Davis". Later, when her son Glee made a name for himself, the mountain came to be associated with the whole Davis family. It was Lucinda Davis and Glee, when he was still a young boy, who had made the first trail for horses up the south side of Sourdough to the summit at the turn of the century and stacked a cairn on the platform-like outcrop where the lookout would eventually stand. For them it was a picnic spot.

At that time, there was no such thing as a "fire lookout" anywhere in the Northwest. There was no Forest Service, nor any "national forests." All the country the Davises could see from atop Sourdough was part of what was then known as the Washington Forest Reserve. In those days, if a lightning strike ignited a wildfire on the Upper Skagit, or if a blaze escaped from the mining camps, it raged until the rains quelled the flames and no one considered it a catastrophe. The whole Upper Skagit forest was mottled with old and ancient burns, a tapestry of vast conifer stands in various stages of succession, shaped by the ice and lightning of ten thousand years—"a perfection of chaos," as Snyder would later call it.

Great fires on the Upper Skagit were as old as the Cascadian east wind, a foehn wind that could keep a fire going for months with its bellows-like rise and fall. Many smokes were set off by lightning, perhaps even more by native people burning open the forest understory to drive game and clear trails. The Upper Skagit country was already smoldering underfoot when Henry Custer, the first Euro-American to leave a written account of his travels, came into it in 1859: "Our route lay through a portion of burned timber lately on fire. The ground was still intensely hot," he wrote. "Smoke was still arising in all directions from numerous footlogs & trees. Fires are very frequent during summer season in these Mountain forests and are often ignited purposely by some of the Indians hunting in these Mountain regions, to clear the woods from under brush & make travel easier. Once ignited, they generally burn the whole summer, and only the drenching rains of the fall are able to check their further spread."

In time, the Davis's scenic promontory on Sourdough would become the site of the first fire-watch cabin in the North Cascades, and Glee Davis would build it. By 1915, Davis had gone to work for the Forest Service, and his first assignment was to pick a spot to watch for wildfire on the Upper Skagit. He

The original cupola-topped Sourdough Mountain Lookout seen from Pierce Mountain Trail in a Forest Service photograph from the 1920s.

chose Sourdough and that year improved the old family trail to accommodate mules, spooled seven miles of telephone wire to the ridge above Sourdough Creek, and set up camp for the region's first official fire season—"Tent Lookout," he called the site. The following year, the lookout cabin—a "ground house"—was built on the summit.

Glee Davis wanted to keep the lookout at his rag house camp on the ridge slope above Sourdough Creek, where there was ample firewood and water and a break from the wind, but the regional Forest Service chief from Portland, "Bush" Osborne—father of the fire finder, no less—visited Sourdough and insisted the lookout belonged on the natural platform where Lucinda Davis had stacked her cairn. His brainchild targeting device would work better from there.

Glee Davis built the L.O. from blueprints of the lookout on Oregon's Mount Hood. It was twelve feet square with windows all around and a small observation cupola in the pyramid roof. Unlike subsequent lookout cabins, which were made of precut lumber and glass and bundled in mule kits, Davis and a local blacksmith named Harry Clouds built Sourdough L.O. from boards of fir and red cedar shakes hand-split on the mountain. That first lookout stood into the early 1930s, buried to its cupola in snow for half of every year. Photographs from its last years show it looking battered, windows boarded up, lightning rod bent.

Gary Snyder's 1953 L.O. stood on the same outcrop of rock, but had replaced the Glee Davis lookout twenty years before. The Civilian Conservation Corps built the new Sourdough Lookout (which still stands) during Franklin Roosevelt's "first hundred days" in the summer of '33; it was one of the CCC's initial projects in northwest Washington. Glee Davis's original building was knocked down and burned on the mountain, the remains scattered over the broken northside shale.

As Gary scanned the surrounding territory through the fire finder, he could see the logic of choosing Sourdough for the premier lookout site in the area. Although it was a full 2,000 feet lower down than Crater, its sight lines more than made up for what it lacked in elevation. Situated on a wide western turn in the Skagit, Sourdough Mountain provided commanding views down six major drainages, which radiated out like the spokes of a wagon wheel from the lookout hub. To the south was Thunder Arm, green with the milk of nine glaciers—Colonial and Neve, McAllister, Klawatti, Inspiration and Eldorado, Boston, Fremont and Douglas, Ragged Ridge. To the southwest, a clear shot down the valley of the Skagit all the way to Sauk Mountain—Philip's peak. Due west, the headwaters of Stetattle Creek, pulsing down from the double cirque of Mount Terror. Looking north, he could follow Big Beaver

Creek all the way to its source at Beaver Pass, with glacier-faced Mount Redoubt poking up beyond. Northeast, only a partial view of Ross Lake, from Roland Point to May Creek, but a fine prospect of the east side of the valley, from Jack to Desolation to the crags of Hozomeen. Finally, completing the three-sixty, he could see due east down Ruby to the hump of McKay Ridge, where Granite and Canyon creeks came together, and beyond to Mount Ballard and Azurite Peak. Wedged down in the shadows of McKay Ridge and the southeast flank of Crater was Granite Creek Guard Station. Though he couldn't see the cabin, Gary thought of Jim Baxter, down there enjoying his solitude and those three-pound rainbows from Canyon Creek.

Up on Crater Shan, Gary's old lookout was closed. From Sourdough he could see the L.O. with his naked eye, silhouetted at the tip of the peak. With binoculars he could focus in on its pitched roof and battened-down shutters, snow piled halfway up the north wall. The District had decided not to man Crater in 1953 — there would never again be a full-season lookout in Snyder's cabin — and every time he looked across from Sourdough he got the strange sensation that part of him was still over there. "Keep looking across to Crater," he wrote in his journal, ". . . and get the funny feeling I am up there looking out, right now 'because there are no calendars in the mountains.' "

Although Crater was close enough to see from his doorway, lookout life on Sourdough was quite different from what it had been the year before. If Crater had at times felt Tibetan in its austerity, Sour-dough was idyllic. "Sourdough was so mild in comparison," Snyder would remember years later. "It was like the suburbs." Drinking water was easy to come by — there were long fields of sun-softened snow well into August, a heather-ringed waterhole to wash his face each morning, and several ponds for swimming out along the ridge. There was plentiful firewood — mountain hemlock, Douglas fir and Alaskan cedar — and fragrant alpine flowers — paintbrush, lupine and phlox, and beds of pink and white and yellow-flowered heather. Deer browsed just outside the door, black bear rolled around in the southern meadows, mountain bluebirds balanced on the tops of slender alpine firs just outside the lookout windows.

"Sourdough Mountain is very sweet. . . . It's a beautiful alpine environment. Those wet North Cas-cades meadows, similar to the Olympics, so many alpine flowers in the summer, it smells so good, so rich — it's a wonderful landscape, it's heavenly," recalls Snyder. "And you can go on much longer walks, you can go way back up the ridge and explore around, whereas on Crater there's nowhere to walk to unless you went way back down."

Because of its closeness to the railhead and the road at Diablo, there were also more visitors on Sourdough. Gary had several over the course of the summer — Baxter came over from Granite Creek, Jack Francis hiked up from Diablo, old Roy Raymond returned for a visit, and Dick Brewer, a painter from San Francisco who was subletting Snyder and Whalen's North Beach apartment, hitched a thousand miles to see him. Dick and Janet Miegs, old friends from Reed College, hiked up in mid-August with enough beer and wine in their packs for a two-day mountaintop bender worthy of old Li Po. Gary's stretches of solitude on Sourdough seldom lasted much longer than a week.

From Sourdough, Gary could look down the Skagit and see Sauk Mountain — Whalen's mountain — a small dark hump in the milky blue afternoon haze of the valley, twenty-seven miles to the southwest. Like Gary, Philip had gone on trail crew for a couple of weeks after fire school but by mid-July was ensconced in his lookout and settling in for a relaxing six weeks during which he planned to reread all of Shakespeare, plus Chaucer in Middle English.

Sauk Mountain is not particularly high by Cascadian standards, only 5,540 feet, but it has character — "small but remarkable," according to Fred Beckey. It is the first notable mountain on the Skagit, and can be picked out on the horizon soon after heading east out of Sedro-Woolley. With its turreted summit ridge, Sauk stands like a gatekeeper at the entrance to the Skagit mountain country behind it. The Sauk River comes down to it gray with Chocolate Glacier ash from the Glacier Peak wilderness and joins the green waters of the Skagit at its southern base.

Sauk has had a number of names over the years. In the late 19th century it was briefly known as Mount Sutter, after the prospector John Sutter. (There is still a Sutter Creek due east of Sauk Mountain.) Before Sutter, it was called Mount Pontalomah. An 1858 map shows it as "Mount Gweht," probably an attempted transliteration of the Lushootsheed word "D'w-gua-ut."

To the native Skagits and Sauk-Siuattles, the mountain was an old man sleeping between three wives, a reference perhaps to the trio of snowcapped volcanoes visible from the summit — Mount Baker twenty miles northwest, Glacier Peak thirty-five miles southeast, and Rainier a hundred miles due south. To the Indians, Sauk was both an oracular mountain as well as a peak for spirit quests; the eroded pits of old sweat lodges are still found on the mountainside where native vision seekers purged themselves before approaching the summits.

Phil Whalen's lookout had been put on Sauk in 1928, during the first flurry of lookout construction on the Mount Baker Forest following the Upper Skagit fire of 1926. The L.O. perched in the teeth of the summit, its corner posts set in cement among angular blocks of 250-million-year-old breccia. It was one of the old-school cupola lookouts, like the original Sourdough, twelve by twelve with windows all around, a corner bunk, a wooden table and chair, and an ancient tin Yukon stove. The fire finder was up in the cupola, reachable by a pole ladder in the center of the room.

"I felt it was quite a romantic building," remembers Whalen, "with this turret on the top. You'd climb up the ladder into the tower, peer about . . . " Looking east from the cupola, Philip had an excellent view of the Pickets; in fact, it was from such a vantage that the range was probably named, their tight-packed pinnacles appearing in a fence-like row. The view north and west was equally dramatic, dominated by the chaotic southside glaciers of Mt. Shuksan, the cone of Mount Baker, the crags of Black Buttes, and the low red hills of the Twin Sisters further west. The Skagit flowed to Puget Sound in great serpentine loops, and the sun set hugely into banded clouds behind the San Juan Islands. At night Phil could see light houses blinking out on the Sound. Full-moon nights, the moonlight shone on the somber ice of the Boulder and Talum glaciers on Mount Baker. Baker: to the Lummi Indians along the coast, "Komo Kulshan"—"the Great White Watcher." On Sauk it was a nightly presence.

On hot, dry summer afternoons huge fogs would pour up the Skagit from Puget Sound, sending mist racing up the verdant couloir of Sauk Mountain and turning it suddenly into a scene from a Chinese silk painting. With its steep cliffs, shaggy firs, and wriggling switchback trail, Sauk Mountain in the fog has to be one of the most Zen-looking landscapes in the North Cascades.

Philip Whalen's Zen in those days was for the most part literary and aesthetic. "Since 1946 I had been sitting very sporadically, and never consistently and with very long periods of nothing in between," he recalls, "and I don't remember now doing anything while I was up there on Sauk. I was mostly just reading heavily and looking at things, not terribly concerned about Buddhism."

Philip had originally been drawn to Eastern religions not by Buddhism anyway, but by Vedanta, the Hindu philosophy of the Upanishads:

When I first got out of the army in 1946 I was still thinking about what do you do about religion, and decided that what really suited me was Vedanta. So I finally got up enough courage to go and actually attend a meeting of the Vedanta Society in Portland where there was a man from the Ramakhrisna Ashram in India who was called Swami Devattananda — very good man, very

Site of Philip Whalen's lookout on Sauk Mountain, Mount Baker in the distance. To the Lummi Indians on Puget Sound, the mountain was Komo Kulshan—"the Great White Watcher."

well-trained. And it turned out they had an ashram way out in the country someplace, but attending it was very expensive, so I thought, 'Well, that's the bunk," and said, 'I just better sit by myself and see what I can do.' And I began getting some sort of flashes about how your mind would change, or your feeling or something would change from the experience of sitting . . . I was trying some breath-control kind of number that's in Patangali's *Yoga Aphorisms.*"

He had also been intrigued early on by Tibetan Buddhism, but ultimately could not get past its perplexing philosophy and hierarchies of deities, at least not as he found it in those days in the works of W.Y. Evans-Wentz. Whalen's mother had been a Christian Scientist — a religion that impressed him as "unnecessarily complicated . . . like Yeats and his bent gyres and cones and pulleys and belts and geary numbers," and turned him off to any over-elaborate spiritual systems.

Then, on Montgomery Street in 1952, Philip read Gary's D.T. Suzuki books on Zen, and thought, "Wow, this is great, because a.) it's uncomplicated; and b.) it's something that poets and painters and lunatics of all sorts did, and so certainly it's the right place for me."

"But the thing is," says Whalen now, remembering those days, "the people who we think of as being crazy poets and painters and all were really very well-trained practicioners I'm afraid. The stories are really quite interesting, but their 'craziness' was a licensed dottiness, not the freewheeling hippie number." It would be many more years — not until the late 1960s — before Philip began an every day sitting practice.

Knowing beforehand that packing to Sourdough would not be as arduous as getting to Crater had been, Gary loaded his rucksack with an eclectic slew of books for the summer of 1953. Again, he brought Suzuki's *Manual of Zen Buddhism,* ever the source of inspiration for his dharma studies with its solid selections from the Blue Cliff Record, Matsu, Huang Po, and Daito Kokushi. Gary also packed Thoreau's *Walden* and a collection of the prophetic books of William Blake, along with Faulkner's *Sartoris,* plays by Brecht and Artaud, Margaret Mead's *Coming of Age in Samoa,* a Japanese grammar, and Michener's *Tales of the South Pacific,* which had recently been adapted by Rodgers and Hammerstein to become the hugely popular Broadway musical *South Pacific.*

William Blake was the presiding bard that Sourdough summer. The unedited pages of Gary's lookout journal contain his lists and notes attempting to organize Blake's elaborate cosmology and astonishing cast of mythic characters, such as Oothoon, Urizen, Orc, Los, and Mother Enitharmon. In Blake, Gary also thought he saw a kindred prophet to Robinson Jeffers, who still exerted a strong influence on him. "I vaguely sense certain similarities between Blake & R. Jeffers. Voices of Prophecy, prophecies of doom. . . . "

To Blake's startling and seldom understood dictum "Sooner murder an infant in its cradle than nurse unacted desires," Gary appended this commentary:

Discipline of restraint is an easy one; being clear-cut, negative, and usually based on some accepted cultural values. Discipline of following your desires, *always* doing what you want to do, is the hardest. It presupposes self-knowledge of motives, a careful balance of free action and where the cultural taboos lay — knowing whether a particular "desire" is instinctive, cultural, personal, a product of thought, contemplation or the unconscious.

Finally, from *The Marriage of Heaven and Hell,* Snyder copied into his notebook Blake's famous "doors of perception" passage — lines that would become one of the key psychedelic aphorisms of the 1960s counterculture. "If the doors of perception were cleansed, everything would appear to man as it is, infinite. For man has closed himself up, 'til all he sees is through narrow chinks of his caverns." To which Gary added simply: "Ah."

Then there was Thoreau. Surprisingly, Snyder had never read *Walden,* or anything else by Thoreau, before going on lookout in 1953. If the old log-cabin guard station on Granite Creek had been the perfect setting for his encounter with Hui-Neng the summer before, then surely Sourdough Lookout was the place for Henry David Thoreau. Few backdrops could be more fitting or employments more compatible with a first reading of *Walden.* Had there been lookouts in Thoreau's day, it is hard to imagine him not doing at least a fire season or two. Even without lookout cabins per se, Thoreau clearly had seen glimpses of the lookout's mountain world — on Maine's Katahdin, and especially from Massachusetts' Mount Greylock. In July 1844 he spent a night in the perch of Williams College observatory on Greylock's summit and awoke to find himself in "cloud-land" — alone in his tower just above a vast, smooth-topped sea of ground-fog that had rolled in during the night. For Thoreau, it was one of the grandest mornings of his life — "a favor for which to be forever silent."

"The most interesting dwellings in this country," wrote Thoreau in the opening chapter of *Walden,* "are the most unpretending, humble log huts and cottages of the poor commonly." What could be more unpretentious than an L-4 fire cabin? Gary's L.O. was only slightly wider than Thoreau's Walden cabin, and with the exception of the fire finder (a device Thoreau surely would have appreciated, and probably improved somehow) the Spartan furnishings—low rope-webbed bunk, single chair and table, woodstove—were basically the same.

Gary was drawn to Thoreau's economy—the notion that "a man is rich in proportion to the number of things he can afford to let alone." Snyder had done without by necessity all through his boyhood and adolescence until it had become his habit. He jotted down Thoreau's famous admonition to "beware of all enterprises that require new clothes." In a more poetic vein, he also recorded the exultant and promissory closing lines of *Walden:* "Only that day dawns to which we are awake. There is more day to dawn. The sun is but a morning star." This last line—one of the most famous in nineteenth-century American letters along with "Call me Ishmael" and "I sing the body electric"—Gary played with until he made it his own. "The morning star is not a star" became the opening line for *Myths and Texts.*

It was all fitting together: the Zen, the Blake and Thoreau, lookouting, poetry. It was about seeing, "being open to what is about," as he had noted in his journal after reading Hui-Neng at Granite Creek the year before. Gary had entered into one of those periods of creativity wherein even the books he was reading became numinously charged and alive in his hands, their authors seeming to speak directly to him, "heart-mind to heart-mind," in the old Zen expression. "Ever, ever be on the lookout!" he read in the admonition of Daito Kokushi, one of the great medieval Rinzai masters. "You monks, who are in this mountain monastery, remember that you are gathered here for the sake of religion and not for the sake of clothes and food. . . . Let, however, there be just one individual, who may be living in the wilderness in a simple hut and passing his days by eating the roots of wild herbs cooked in a pot with broken legs; but if he single-mindedly applies himself to the study of his own spiritual affairs, he is the very one who has a daily interview with me. . . ."

ALL THAT SUMMER on Sourdough Gary bristled with various writing plans, his notebooks exploding with ideas for short stories, articles, novels, plays, even sketches for a two-projector, double-screened "Buddhist experimental film." Other than his journal writing and his poems, none of the other writing projects panned out, but the notes he jotted are indicative of his creative intensity at the time. One of his more intriguing ideas was for a play he was calling "Lookout," which would have been set in the interior of a fire-watch cabin and on a knoll of snow, rock, and pine, "reminiscent of Noh stage." The personae were to be the lookout, two guests, a passing fisherman, and the disembodied voices of other lookouts coming in periodically over the Motorola radio. There would be lightning strikes and a wildfire. "String together all this grunge for Lookout," he noted to himself. He wanted to do something dramatic à la Jeffers—"here man is sterile & hostile to nature; nature is fertile, but hostile to man."

The play itself never materialized beyond his notes, but the dramatic possibilities of solitary lookout life, lightning, and wildfire—"human history set agin [*sic*] the immensely greater timeless present of nature"—would be worked into *Myths and Texts* and ultimately provided the culmination for it.

On Crater the year before, Gary had not spotted any smokes. Nineteen-fifty-two had been a rather wet fire season on the Upper Skagit. The only burn belonged to Shubert Hunter, over on Sourdough. That was how the lookouts thought of it: whoever called in the first fix on a smoke owned it. So that one had been Shubert's fire: a lightning strike far up the Thunder Creek drainage, south of Fourth of July Pass. From Crater Lookout Gary had been able to see the thin blue smoke blowing up from behind Red Mountain, but the ridge line prevented him from getting an azimuth on the base of the fire. All he could do was sit in the lookout doorway, listening and scribbling down scraps of the squawking radio conversations as Shubert had struggled to guide two smoke chasers to the burn.

> *"you're practically there*
> *you gotta go up the cliff*
> *you gotta cross the rock slide*
> *look for a big blaze on a big tree"*

In '53, however, Gary saw more lightning almost from the beginning of the season. He became a connoisseur of storms, savoring the different kinds of lightning as it moved "from Hozomeen slowly west into red clouds turning gray, then black. Sheet lightning pacing over Little Beaver, fork lightning striking Beaver Pass . . . "

In early August, there were a couple of small lightning-caused fires on Thunder Creek, which finally provided the drama he'd been looking for. In the twilight a storm broke out on the Pickets, with jagged bolts shooting down behind mounts Terror and Fury. Standing on his lightning stool with his hair

Glass-footed "lightning stool," Sourdough Mountain Lookout, September 1998. "Snyder came off that lookout and said to me, 'Boy, if there's a lightning storm, make damn sure you get on your stool, because it'll blow your cook stove all apart and everything else. Make sure you have your radio antenna down; if you don't you're gonna fry.' Anyway, I got up there and got in a lightning storm and it happened just like he said it would." Tommy Buller

tingling with static, Gary watched the storm roll down the range into Thunder Arm like a huge bombardment, lightning raking the ridge tops "and then two fires: right after the strikes, red blooms in the night." The fires were soon obscured by drifting clouds, then it was dark.

In the morning, Gary spotted smoke "up Thunder Creek, high on a ridge," and called it in. It took two smokechasers eighteen hours to hike to the site of the burn: a smoldering snag and about an acre around it in flames. From Sourdough Gary stayed in contact with the two fire fighters while they dug their lines and then felled the snag—"It fanned sparks down like shooting stars over the dry woods, starting spot-fires . . ." Most of the night they worked, finally going to sleep in the mud and ashes, waking at dawn to see "the last glimmer of the morning star."

He didn't know it at the time, but this incident would provide Snyder with the ending of *Myths and Texts.*

> *The black snag glistens in the rain*
> *& the last wisp of smoke floats up*
> *Into the absolute cold*
> *Into the spiral whorls of fire*
> *The storms of the Milky Way.*

The nights were getting colder, and every dawn the valley was filled with a level ocean of churning fog from far up in British Columbia all the way down the Skagit, with tributary arms reaching far up into all the drainages so that only the highest peaks and ridges were visible, looking exactly like islands floating on the rising mist. If he rose before the sun, he would see Venus, low in the east, first over Jack, then over Crater Shan. "The morning star is not a star," he thought.

During his last week, things had slowed down to the way he wanted them, and like the year before Gary didn't want to come back down. But he knew it was coming. Each day he cut a little cordwood to build up the woodpile for next year's lookout. One afternoon while splitting, he saw a figure ambling along the ridge, coming towards the L.O. As he got closer, Gary saw it was Roy Raymond, the old fellow who had helped pack him up back in July, coming up for a visit on his day off. Roy had a postcard for Gary, from Diane Scott, an old girlfriend from Reed. The card was from an exhibit of Japanese painting that had come through Portland that summer; it was a fourteenth-century picture of Kanzan ("Han Shan") —"famed for his eccentric behavior and his carefree poverty," quoted Diane.

Roy stayed the afternoon and night. He and Gary played horseshoes in the afternoon, using some old muleshoes from a box under the lookout. In the morning they played five-card draw, huddling close by the woodstove. Roy was a lonely old guy, whose wife had died a few years before, and now he spent his time in the mountains, working for the Forest Service, doing a little carpentry, even panning the creeks now and then. "I sold the house and the furniture," he told Gary. "I got it down now to where I can get everything into a footlocker. My friends ask me What you sell that for, but hell, what use did I have for it? I'll never marry again."

When Roy went back down, Gary settled into his final days of solitude, extending his zazen sittings, chanting, doing calligraphy, sitting up late in the doorway looking up at the Milky Way stretching like a wisp of smoke from Jack Mountain across to Pyramid Peak. On the morning of August 30th it started to snow and Blackie radioed to close it up and pack on down. By noon he was ready to go. While the snow whirled outside, Gary took a few minutes to finish a short poem he'd begun a few days before in preparation for leaving. He ended it and hung it on a nail on the side of the fire finder cabinet:

> *I the poet Gary Snyder*
> *Stayed six weeks in fifty-three*
> *On this ridge and on this rock*
> *& saw what every Lookout sees,*
> *Saw these mountains shift about*
> *& end up on the ocean floor*
> *Saw the wind and waters break*
> *The branchéd deer, the Eagle's eye,*
> *& when pray tell, shall Lookouts die?*

He hiked off down the ridge, through all the familiar humps of gneiss and wreckage of basalt and incredible quartz-veined boulders. He turned to look uplake to Hozomeen one last time, but it was socked in, and by the time he turned into the first switchback of the south meadows, so was Sourdough Lookout.

Sourdough Mountain Lookout, September 1998.

GARY STAYED IN the Upper Skagit for another few weeks, working trail crew from the Ross Lake Guard Station with Andy Wilcox, old Ed Wyman, and Kim Oelberg, the Desolation lookout. They went deep into the back country along Big Beaver Creek, up past Thirty nine Mile Creek between Mount Prophet and Elephant Butte, where the sun filtered down in bars through dark stands of old growth red cedar. They spent ten days bucking gigantic blowdowns on the pack trail with two-man crosscut saws. It was up there that Gary performed his first sweat lodge.

"God, there's some trees up there, big cedars," says Snyder. "That was when I first made a Native American style sweat lodge. We heated rocks, threw an old packer's tarp over a framework, and rolled hot rocks in there and made myself a little sweat lodge. The other trail crew guys thought it was great, but too hot they thought. One of the guys was an Indian. There were always some Native American guys that were working on those crews, because they were the locals. That led into something I did for a number of years when I was out, which was to make sweat lodges, do that kind of Native American purification. Then I started doing it when I worked on trail crews down in the Sierra."

While Gary was up on Big Beaver, Jack Francis left Diablo Guard Station and headed back to Bremerton for another year of high school teaching. He took the train from Diablo back to Marblemount. Nineteen fifty-three was the last year for the train. The rails had been laid to Diablo during the construction of the dams, and now that Ross Dam was finished and running, all the rails and ties were scheduled to be pulled up from Diablo back to Newhalem as part of the dam's licensing agreement. By 1954 only the rails of the incline hoist at Diablo would be left in place.

Jack rode out on one of the last trains of the year. At Newhalem, Blackie Burns got on the car with a couple of other Forest Service men. Jack was reading a newspaper he'd found in the train and Blackie didn't notice him, but Jack recognized Blackie by his voice. Soon Blackie and the others were talking shop and gossiping about the various men in the district. Eventually the talk got around to the lookouts, and someone asked Blackie who he thought was the best on the forest. Jack perked up, eager to hear Blackie's judgment. "I like that boy Snyder on Sourdough," said Blackie. "He's a *calm* son of a bitch."

Although mountains belong to the nation,
mountains belong to people who love them.

Dōgen, *Mountains and Waters Sutra*

Highway 99

Fall 1953 – Summer 1954

O N HIS RETURN from the Skagit in the fall of '53, Gary left Montgomery Street and moved across the bay to Berkeley, where he began taking Japanese and Chinese language classes at the University of California to further prepare himself for his eventual Japanese journey. His new place was on the ground floor of a building on the corner of Benvenue and Ashby, ten blocks south of the UC campus. The tiny space, as Snyder described it to Whalen, was "small for human beings, but like Vimalakirti's ten-foot-square hut, it will accommodate ten thousand Bodhisattvas." Whalen, not wishing to take on the Montgomery Street lease, again drifted down to Los Angeles, where he stayed with friends until the spring of 1954.

Between Berkeley and Hollywood Gary and Phil kept in touch with a stream of weekly letters. In November, Snyder wrote Whalen full of excitement over his discovery of the poetry of Kenneth Rexroth, who lived in San Francisco and did a weekly talk show on cultural topics for radio KPFA. "REXROTH is the one. Get hold of *The Dragon and the Unicorn* at your neighborhood library right away & read it through," Snyder exhorted Whalen. "He has Jeffers, Williams & (less) Pound in his blood, & he's HONEST & INTRANSIGENT in a way that makes the rest of this modern crowd look puke-sick . . . I mean I'm really knocked out. . . ."

Kenneth Rexroth was indeed one of America's leading poets at mid-century. At forty-eight, he was in the prime of his powers; *The Dragon and the Unicorn,* which had so impressed Gary, was the latest volume in a prolific career that had established him as the dean of West Coast poets.

In late November, Snyder engineered a meeting with Rexroth through a connection at UC Berkeley and was invited to dinner on December 4th. At Rexroth's spacious apartment on Eighth Avenue, out by the Presidio, Gary was even more knocked out by the man than he'd been by his poetry. The two hit it off immediately over Chinese and Japanese poetics, with Snyder even managing to get Rexroth to show him some of the translations he was working on. Soon the conversation was veering back and forth from Tu Fu and Po Chü-i to William Carlos Williams, Ezra Pound and T. S. Eliot. Rexroth knew Williams and Pound well, calling them Bill and Ezra. When Williams came through San Francisco on his 1950 reading tour of the West—the same tour on which he'd met Snyder, Whalen, and Welch at Reed College—he stayed at Rexroth's. Rexroth's prestige was international. When poets such as Dylan Thomas, Spender, and Auden visited San Francisco, they contacted Rexroth, who would cook gourmet dinners for them, arrange readings on KPFA, and fete them at his Friday night salon.

As that first evening progressed, it turned out that Snyder and Rexroth shared many interests. Both were avid skiers and mountaineers and skilled back-country cooks. Besides his home on Eighth Avenue, Rexroth also had a rough, secluded cabin in Marin County at a place near Lagunitas called Devil's Gulch—exactly the kind of private place Snyder envisioned for himself one day. Gary understood perfectly Rexroth's need for a get-away like Devil's Gulch; they both agreed: contemplation and solitude in nature were not Romantic niceties but biological necessities. To Gary, Rexroth was the embodiment of many things that he himself hoped to attain. Here was a poet equally at ease in the metropolis and the wilderness, capable of living an exciting, cultured life in each. He was political as well, in a way that

Snyder admired: he was able to bring politics into his verse naturally, without being doctrinaire. Rexroth was an anarchist, with roots stretching back to the days of the Industrial Workers of the World (IWW), or Wobblies, as they were called. In the early 1920s Rexroth had soapboxed for the Wobblies on Seattle's Yesler Square—just as Gary's own grandfather had. Rexroth was also, like Gary, a pacifist, even during the Second World War, when he had made the highly unpopular move of declaring himself a conscientious objector.

Without doubt the most synchronistic connection of the whole evening came when Gary learned that Rexroth had once worked as a Forest Service trail-crew hand, cook, and packer in the North Cascades—out of the Marblemount Ranger Station, no less! This was back in 1924, when Marblemount was the dead end of the Skagit Road and the space beyond it on maps was unsurveyed white. Rexroth, a Hoosier by birth and Chicagoan in his adolescence, had been nineteen then and had never been in the Western mountains, but he talked his way into a job working ahead of the first pack string of the season on the route from Marblemount to Stehekin. Telling of his Cascadian adventures in his 1966 *An Autobiographical Novel*, Rexroth draws a Paul Bunyanesque portrait of himself as a young man—single-handedly doing the trail work of a twelve-man crew, exuberantly tipping boulders into mudholes, axing and sawing through blowdowns on the trail or blasting them apart with sticks of dynamite. On one of his weeks off, he hiked up the Skagit into British Columbia, climbing, he said, a snowpeak every other day along his route. The fire lookout era was only beginning in the early 1920s, and Rexroth had been part of it. Even Blackie Burns had not yet gone to work for the Forest Service. One of Rexroth's jobs during his Skagit summer was to help pack up the precut lumber and glass for the construction of the lookout on 8,100-foot McGregor Mountain—"the Siberia of lookouts." When Rexroth regaled Snyder with such stories, Gary could match him with his own tales of equally high Crater Mountain and how from his lookout he had been able to see the blue summits of McGregor in the far mists beyond Rainy Pass. It was a powerful and auspicious connection between the two poets.

To follow up on that first meeting, Snyder in January 1954 sent Rexroth "A Berry Feast," his best finished poem to that date. Along with the poem, Gary included a letter telling Rexroth:

My own generation is completely cowardly: there is need for poetry that cuts and slashes, that points to the existence of a non-human Nature in this world, that can talk about contemplation without falling into the rose-water and incense burners. . . . If American poetry has any future it lies in your direction — on a large cultural scale, too: the orient, the western half of this country, the non-European cultural traditions of America and the Pacific. . . .

The meeting with Rexroth filled Gary with pride in his own experience and a huge flood of self-belief in his powers. To Whalen he wrote to say that he'd been "favorably imprinted": "The Frontier-type Wobbly-Thoreau anarchism is in my blood, i.e., that's my own tradition, I was raised up in it. So put it with the Oriental historical depth, & I got a fulcrum to tip the whole damn civilization over with. Watch & see!"

IN ADDITION TO his Japanese and Chinese courses at Berkeley, Gary also studied *sumi* brush painting and T'ang-era Chinese poetics. His sumi instructor was Chiura Obata. Obata taught Gary how to grind sumi ink sticks in a stone *suzuri* and to make strokes with the various sumi brushes. Unfortunately, Gary never got to know Chiura Obata very well. Obata's influence was subtle, and not apparent for some time. When Gary studied with him, Obata was sixty-eight and only one semester from retirement from the Berkeley faculty. Their time together was short. "[He] was an intense, diminutive Japanese man . . . a naturalized citizen who had been in an internment camp — I learned little else about him," Gary would remember. "We learned by trying to match his fierce, swift strokes that made pine needles, bamboo stalks, eucalyptus leaves appear as if by magic on the white paper."

While conceding Obata's "consummate skill with the brush," the young Snyder thought that his instructor was something of a hack. After seeing a three-paneled screen that Obata had painted on commission, Gary wrote to Philip Whalen, ". . . no Zen, consequently no taste, and he absolutely PROSTITUTES himself (for very good money) to certain rich bay area buyers."

Had Gary gotten to know Obata and his art, he would have discovered a remarkable man whose accomplishments were very much in the spirit of what Gary himself was hoping to achieve creatively. In fact, Obata was already then an exemplar of the bioregional Pacific culture that Snyder would champion in years to come. His work was a potent reflection of twentieth-century California from the Japanese-American perspective, beginning with his sketches of the 1906 San Francisco Quake and Fire through to his heartbreaking paintings of wartime internment and the devastated atomic landscapes of Hiroshima.

What Gary would not discover for many years was that Obata also had a large body of landscape work from the Yosemite and that he, like Gary, had been decisively influenced by the writings of the great mountaineer-naturalist John Muir. A six-week backpacking trek in the Sierras in the summer of 1927 had been the turning point of Obata's creative life. Obata concocted his own inks and pigments from bits of rock, flowers, and the soot from down wood gathered on his back-country trips. He made a life's work of depicting many of the same mountains and rivers to which Snyder would dedicate much of the next four decades. It would be years before Gary would make the serendipitous discovery of Obata's real work.

Gary's other exceptional teacher at Berkeley that fall was Ch'en Shih-hsiang, his instructor in T'ang poetics. Ch'en was a renowned Sinologist and a calligrapher and poet in his own right. Still, Gary and Ch'en Shih-hsiang did not see eye-to-eye at first, as Ch'en rejected Gary's initial translations as too wildly experimental.

"I am engaged in a bitter fight with my teacher of Chinese poetry at the moment," Gary informed Philip Whalen. "I simply have exploited *a la* Williams, Pound, *et al* the breaking-of-lines & uneven indentation, & a few more tricks of language. I'll carry this fight to the Supreme Court if necessary. He's a nice man but he just doesn't understand English poetry." Within a couple of weeks however, Professor Ch'en began to appreciate the spirit underlying Snyder's formal idiosyncrasies, while Gary's respect for the old T'ang masters deepened under Ch'en's instruction. To Whalen Gary admitted: "Chinese poetry is indeed more complex, obscure, allusive, than I ever dreamed . . . tranquil, peaceful, sublime, and full of charming & accurate observation of nature." It was in Ch'en Shih-hsiang's classes that Gary made his first translations of Wang Wei, Meng Hao-jan, Liu Chang Ching, Yuan Chen, and the lines of the Tu Fu poem that begins "The nation is ruined, but mountains and rivers remain."

At the end of January 1954, Gary spread out his pale green quad maps of the North Cascades across the floor of his Benvenue Street apartment in Berkeley and savored his lookout prospects for the upcoming summer. After his genteel season on Sourdough, he was looking for something further "back," so crouching over his maps he zeroed in on the big country north of Nooksack Ridge and the Chilliwack drainage. On Copper and Winchester mountains he saw the tiny triangles denoting fire lookouts; these he applied for, and a few days later wrote Phil Whalen in L.A. to urge him to get his own applications in, too.

Sourdough Mountain Lookout from the north slope, September 1998.

Whalen, pleasantly unemployed and basking in the midwinter warmth of Hollywood, did not share Snyder's enthusiasm for getting back on lookout. He replied: "The thought of climbing another mountain appalls me, not to mention the week of fire-school. I am old and very fat. [Whalen was thirty-one.] Yet I may apply anyhow — I always take your advice."

On February 11 Snyder wrote again to inform Philip that he had heard back already from the ranger at Glacier. Winchester Mountain was taken; the only unoccupied L.O. in the district was at Copper Mountain — a short-season lookout, which Snyder declined. Gary's new plan was to try the Darrington district, and if no good lookouts were available there, then the Chelan National Forest. He had decided that the only "civilized" lookout areas were the Baker, Chelan, and Wenatchee forests, Rainier and Olympic national parks, and parts of the Gifford Pinchot. The only problem with the Olympics, he said, was the lack of lightning storms, hence "no Gothic fun." He told Philip that he was taking pleasure in being picky about where he worked now that he had two summers of lookouting under his belt — "telling them what I won't take, i.e., low lookouts." On the 14th Whalen wrote back to say that he too had applied for lookout work, again out of Marblemount.

Then came the bombshell. On February 10 in Bellingham, the Forest Service Supervisor turned down Snyder's application for lookout work. "Because of instructions from Washington, D.C. we are unable to offer you employment in any capacity," the letter said. Even the supervisor who wrote it seemed confused and somewhat embarrassed by the situation, since Gary was clearly so highly qualified. "We are unaware of the reasons for those instructions," the Supervisor explained, "but we must comply." Without further process or clarification, Gary Snyder was blacklisted from the U.S. Forest Service.

IN HIS EXHAUSTIVE chronicle of the McCarthy years, historian David Caute has called 1954 "the high summer of the great fear." Certainly it was a time when red baiters were riding high, although Joseph McCarthy himself, whose face and bullying manner came to personify the era, would be censured by his own fed-up Senate colleagues before the year was out. McCarthy, of course, was really only part of it. It was the time of the security index and the subversive list, the non-Communist affidavit, "blind memoranda" and "sympathetic association," Loyalty Review Boards, the Senate Internal Security Subcommittee, the Senate Subcommittee on Investigations, and the House Select Committee on Un-American Activities (HUAC).

As a seasonal worker in the Forest Service, Gary was not an incumbent employee; therefore, his application could be rejected—as it was—without explanation or appeal, no matter his qualifications and past performance. Gary's situation was not unique. Thousands of people had their jobs "phased out," were fired, forced to resign under pressure, or discouraged from even applying for work because of such security checks.

On what grounds would an unknown and unpublished twenty-four-year-old poet applying for a summer fire-watching post have been considered a threat to national security? Gary had never made any secret of his radical political opinions, which were vocally anti-Stalinist and critical of the Communist Party, despite his many Marxist friends. He considered himself a pacifist and anarchist in the mold of Thoreau, Kropotkin, and Gandhi, and was a member of no organization more revolutionary than the Portland Mazamas or the Wilderness Society. Anyone watching Gary closely in those days—and somebody *was*—would have been aware of these distinctions.

"I'm disloyal, & they figgered it out. So what," wrote Snyder to his friend Dell Hymes. "Of course, they will never take into account the fact that I feel nastily disloyal about ALL governments, that Russian dungheap or the foul British stew, or whatever peculiar mess of ideological pottage (in advanced decay) you can dream up. . . . I am coming more and more strongly to an Anarchist position, seriously, & with full cognizance of its philosophical silliness & general impracticality—I still don't see anything better around. . . . So maybe I'm a Confucian Anarchist: I believe in a non-state governed by Rites & Music."

Two days after receiving his rejection, Gary wrote Whalen in a philosophical mood. At the head of the letter he typed: "A SHAFTLESS ARROW SHOT FROM A STRINGLESS BOW WILL SPLIT THE ROCKS." He knew he could always get work at his old standby, the Warm Springs Lumber Company, or some other job in the woods. He figured he could probably even get hired by the Forest Service, if he played his cards right—just "walk in on a district station cold & get on the trail crew, by the time they've checked back my record half the summer will be gone."

To Philip he tried to brush off his blacklisting as merely "annoying," and joked that it would give him a chance to put together "a nostalgic & bitter article, with photographs, for *The Nation*." He laughed to think "about how the whole Baker forest is scandalized right now & burning with desire to know what I've done. Ho ho."

But Gary had gotten not only a whiff of Joe McCarthy's waning venom but also a foretaste of the creeping paranoia that would become a fixture of American life in the '60s. "They have likely got me blackballed all over," he guessed. "I'm going to make a stab at the Chelan forest straightaway & see how closely I'm netted."

On March 1st he contacted Frank Lewis, District Ranger at Marblemount, and asked if Frank had received orders to refuse him employment. Lewis wrote back sheepishly, "Yes, we have been instructed not to rehire you as you say. Please understand, Gary, that as far as your work here on the Skagit was concerned, it was entirely satisfactory."

In snyder's poem "Night Highway 99"—which contains one of the few published references to his 1954 blacklisting—he hints that his firing had to do with his outspoken Wobbly sympathies at the time, but Gary's political troubles really began years earlier with his membership in another radical union— the National Union of Marine Cooks and Stewards, an outfit far less known but just as storied in its own way as the legendary IWW.

In the summer of 1948, between his freshman and sophmore years at Reed, Gary had hitchhiked from Portland to New York City, where he shipped on a Grace Line passenger-freighter to the Caribbean, with a trip card from the Marine Cooks and Stewards. Four years later, that brief 1948 stint in the MC&S landed Gary on the Coast Guard's blacklist, barred from working at sea, and "tainted" as a poor security risk.

Despite the grief it later caused him, the summer of 1948 had been a great time for Gary, then eighteen years old: his first transcontinental road trip, his first time in New York, his first ship—even if his job was the rather inglorious one of a dishwasher in the passengers' mess. His hitchhiking partner on the trip across had been Carl Proujan, a fellow Reedie. He and Carl took a full two weeks to hitch coast-to-coast, following back roads mostly, camping out all the way. (Gary had a choice epithet, remembers Carl, for certain drivers who blew by them on the road: "You should shit 10,000 miles of barbed wire!")

Carl's mother was a maritime union official in New York, and would help Gary get his ship. It was she who suggested he get his seaman's papers through the Marine Cooks and Stewards, a union famous at the time for its racially integrated rank-and-file, and its unapologetically left-wing leadership. Its members included stewards, chefs, cooks, bakers, butchers, messmen, waiters, bartenders, porters, pantrymen, scullions, laundrymen, telephone operators, yeomen, even gym instructors.

It was no secret even then that gay men were a majority in the stewards' departments on most passenger lines. The Marine Cooks and Stewards, therefore, had gays at every level of its membership. MC&S fundraisers were notorious for outrageous drag-acts, and some of those flamboyant queens were among the union's toughest organizers. Many of the friends Gary made on that first trip were gays; in fact, on his return from the Caribbean, he stayed for a while at the Greenwich Village apartment of a group of gay stewards from the ship.

The MC&S was also thoroughly integrated ethnically and racially, having been built on the solidarity of its multi-ethnic rank-and-file, which included many Chinese, Japanese, Filipino and Latino members. In 1938, when most American labor unions still refused workers of color, the MC&S had integrated itself with 1800 black stewards from a private union. In 1950, the union went on strike to force the hiring of the first black stewardess on a Pacific luxury ship. When Gary went to the Marine Cooks local on Whitehall Street in Lower Manhattan, he would have seen on the wall the MC&S admonition: "No Race-Baiting! No Red-Baiting! No Queer Baiting!"

These policies were largely the influence of the Communist Party, which became a leading force in the MC&S years before, when the union had been in the thick of the great Pacific coast maritime strikes of the mid-1930s. In fact, one of the three men killed in San Francisco's "Bloody Thursday" was an MC&S cook, Nick Bordoise. Forty thousand workers followed his casket down Market Street in July 1934. When Gary shipped in the MC&S in the late 1940s the union was at its peak, with 12,000 members. Together with its sister union, the International Longshoremen and Warehousemen, the MC&S made up the far left wing of the CIO (Congress of Industrial Organizations).

With the passage of the 1947 Taft-Hartley Act, however, the MC&S's days were numbered. Taft-Hartley required all labor leaders to swear non-Communist affiliation to maintain their union's collective bargaining certification, and Hugh Bryson, the union's president, had been a well-known Communist Party member and refused to sign the mandatory affadavit. In 1950, the CIO expelled both the Marine Cooks and Stewards and the ILWU, leaving them vulnerable to raiding by rival unions and blacklisting by government agencies. Then, with the outbreak of the Korean War, the Coast Guard began screening all ships' crews for security risks. Membership, past or present, in the MC&S, could be cause for blacklisting. The FBI also zeroed in on the union, interviewing rank-and-file members about their political beliefs, pressuring them, with assurances of anonymity, to name union fellows as Com-

A portion of the old Highway 99 elevated above the Skagit flood
plain north of Burlington, Washington, August 1998.

"Hitched north all across Washington
Crossing and re-crossing the passes
Blown like dust, no place to work."
Gary Snyder, "The Late Snow &
Lumber Strike of the Summer of Fifty-four"

munists. In this way, the Marine Cooks and Stewards was decimated. Finally, union president Bryson was indicted in 1953 for his defiance of Taft-Hartley (he was convicted in 1956, and served two years in jail). By 1954, the National Union of Marine Cooks and Stewards was defunct.

When Gary came to San Francisco in the spring of 1952, he unwittingly walked right into this bitter waterfront purge. In early May, hoping for work on a ship, he applied with the Coast Guard to renew his merchant seaman's papers from 1948, and was promptly rejected as a "poor security risk." In the fall of 1952, after returning from Crater Lookout, Gary underwent another security check when he applied for a Customs Service job on the San Francisco waterfront. While he was given clearance for that position—it was in Export Customs, a lower security classification than Import Customs—the screening led to his father (a federal employee of the Veterans Administration) being interrogated by the VA's loyalty board in early 1953.

The VA board's letter of inquiry to Harold Snyder indicated that Gary had been under watch by FBI informers at least since returning from his summer job with the Marine Cooks and Stewards in 1948. "The Board is informed that your son, Gareth Snyder, reportedly has been closely associated with members or supporters of the Communist Party during the past several years; that these individuals reportedly include Carl Proujan and Dell Hymes . . ." The letter showed detailed knowledge of Gary's movements and even conversations while at Reed—"its remarkable accuracy caused us to ponder the identity of an informer in our midst," Gary's Lambert Street housemate Mike Mahar later recalled.

Someone must have traduced Gary, but he would never know for sure who, how, or exactly why. He had been caught in the government's Cold War purge of the Civil Service, but how was it that he had been able to work for the Forest Service in the summers of 1952 and '53 without any problem? It should be pointed out that in those years, the government's consolidation of information on citizens was only beginning; "the Blacklist" was really several blacklists, kept by separate departments and agencies, and the ability to cross-reference was limited by available technology. President Truman's 1947 executive order that established a loyalty yardstick for employment originally only applied to certain critical government offices. Each year thereafter, however, new departments came under scrutiny until by midway through the first term of the Eisenhower administration, every employee and applicant for government work was being screened by the FBI. Also, during the early and mid-1950s the criteria for "loyalty" and "security" within already-screened offices were tightened yearly: employees who had been determined loyal one year might be reinvestigated and dismissed as security risks the next. In October 1953, Eisenhower broadened the risk criteria to include "any behavior, activities or associations which tend to show that the individual is not reliable or trustworthy." Ultimately, it was this directive of Eisenhower's that cost Gary his 1954 lookout job. When finally pressed for an explanation, the Department of Agriculture admitted to Gary that he had been dismissed, not on "security" grounds, but for his "general unsuitability."

IN EARLY APRIL Gary mailed out a far-flung series of applications for summer work — to Oregon's Warm Springs Indian Reservation, to five national forests in northern California, and to the Gifford Pinchot National Forest in Washington state, where he had worked on trails in the summer of '49. With his extensive back-country resume he soon had three offers. Warm Springs said it would be glad to have him on its fire crew; Stanislaus National Forest in California wanted him for trail-building work; and even the District Forest Service Ranger at Packwood, Washington, tentatively offered him a fire-watch at Lost Lake Lookout on the Gifford Pinchot National Forest. Apparently, Gary's "net" was not all that wide, or there were holes in the mesh.

His troubles had happily not damaged Phil Whalen's prospects for Forest Service work. In late February, just two weeks after Gary's rejection, Philip received a reply to his application from Blackie Burns, saying: "We certainly would be glad to have you as a L.O. — will be figuring on you. Pretty sure Sourdough will be vacant."

Gary wondered if his Lost Lake assignment might yet somehow be vetoed, but supposed that he had outsmarted his blacklisters when he was notified in late May to report for guard school at Packwood on June 22. He also learned that Lost Lake Lookout was a hip-roofed cabin from the '30s, built on the same plan as Sourdough, sitting atop a 6,300-foot mountain in the Goat Rocks Primitive Area. The L.O.'s main attraction was a spectacular view of Mount Rainier, twenty miles to the northwest. Lost Lake even had something of a literary tradition: it was the lookout where Martha Hardy had written *Tatoosh* in the summer of 1944. So, in mid-June, Gary once again loaded his old rucksack and headed for a new mountain top, migrating north up Highway 99, a lone goose on a now familiar flyway.

He arrived in Portland on June 19, just as the House Select Committee on Un-American Activities opened two days of televised hearings into Communist subversion in the Pacific Northwest. Chaired by

Congressman Harold Velde, Republican from Illinois and himself a former FBI agent, the Committee had been conducting investigations on the West Coast all through the fall of 1953 and into 1954. Velde had taken over as chairman of HUAC in 1953, promising to expand the Committee's investigations into the field of higher education. In 1954 the Committee honed in on Reed College, or as some people called it, "the Red College."

Two witnesses friendly to the Committee testified. One was Homer Owen, a Reed alumnus and former Communist Party member who had graduated the same year as Snyder and Whalen. While at Reed, Owen had been on the central committee of the Oregon Communist Party; by the time of the Velde hearings, he had left the party and was living in Virginia. He had been flown to the hearings from Washington, D.C., where he worked for an unidentified "private business." The other Committee witness was Barbara Hartle, a twenty-year Communist Party member who in 1953 had been convicted under the Smith Act, and was cooperating with the Committee in Portland and also at hearings in Seattle. Together, Owen and Hartle named forty-two Portland-area people as communists in two days of testimony.

Gary was neither subpoenaed by the Committee nor named by any witness, at least not publicly. From his friend Bob Allen's house Gary watched the hearings on TV while Homer Owen "ratted and ratted and ratted." Owen named Gary's old buddy Lew Welch a Communist, for attending meetings of the John Reed Club five years before. That must have gotten a laugh — Lew was in Chicago at the time, working as an ad exec for Montgomery Ward & Co. Owen also named Marshall Kolin, Gary and Lew's Lambert Street roommate in 1949, and Carl Proujan, whom Gary had never seen again after their cross-country trip in 1948. Professor Lloyd Reynolds — inspiration to a quarter century of Reed students and co-advisor to Gary's senior thesis — was subpoenaed by the Committee; he appeared with an attorney but refused to answer any questions relating to his political beliefs. For this he was suspended by the Reed administration from teaching for the summer, until his case could be reviewed. (He was reinstated by the fall term.) Another popular Reed faculty member and friend to both Snyder and Whalen — Stanley Moore — was also subpoenaed. Moore had been a Communist Party member in the '30s and during the war, but had dropped out in the late 1940s. He was a renowned Marxist scholar and had been hired by Reed with the assurance of complete academic freedom. He had been tenured and promoted to full professor within five years. Moore was on sabbatical and so appeared earlier in the month before HUAC in Washington, D.C., where he took the Fifth Amendment. (Moore was fired from the Reed faculty that August for his refusal to testify.) Also at the Washington, D.C. hearings, Mrs. Homer Owen named Lloyd Reynolds's wife Virginia as a Communist for hosting parties of the John Reed Club. Such was the atmosphere as Gary thumbed it out of Portland on the summer solstice, heading for Lost Lake Lookout.

AT THE SAME TIME, Phil Whalen was making his way to the Skagit, from Newport, Oregon, where had had been staying for two months with old army friend Ben Anderson. At the end of June, Philip arrived in Marblemount in time for fire school. Not surprisingly, Gary's blacklisting had caused quite a buzz around the ranger station. G-men had come to Marblemount that spring and questioned various people about Gary, including Blackie Burns. "FBI plagued hell out of Blackie, who said hell, he'd hire you again & 6 more like you if they'd let him," wrote Philip. "*He* don't believe you are a communist & wouldn't care if you was on account you did your job so good." Several of the Forest Service men came to Philip to convey their best wishes to Gary. Blackie, Roy Raymond, Ed Wyman, Clarence O'Brien — all the old-timers sent their regards.

The winter and spring of '54 had dumped more snow on the North Cascades than anyone could remember, and the summer was getting off to a rainy start as well. The fire danger was extremely low, and Blackie did not feel pressured to get his lookouts onto their peaks. Phil was assigned to Sourdough, but was first sent up to Ross Lake Guard Station to wait for the trail to melt out, and to work on the lake in the meantime.

About the same time that Phil Whalen had arrived in Marblemount, Gary was heading to his lookout job on the Gifford Pinchot forest, following the Cowlitz Valley north, with the dome of Mount Saint Helens off to the east; then on to Mossyrock Dam, then Randle, and finally the ranger station at Packwood, where he checked in and attended an orientation. The next day was the beginning of guard school at the Forest Service compound in Randle. Gary bought six weeks of groceries for his lookout at the general store, happy to have made it after all. The following morning he was fired.

Outraged and nearly broke after selling off his food at a loss, Gary doubled back to Portland and took up the matter of his blacklisting with the powers that be. "I have spent several entertaining hours hassling with the FBI in their Portland office, to say nothing of a visit to the Regional Forester in Portland," he wrote to Phil Whalen. "Suffice it (for now) to say that my days of Government work are over."

> *Got fired that day by the USA*
> *(the District Ranger up at Packwood*
> *thought the Wobblies had been dead for*
> *forty years*
> *but the FBI smelled treason*
> *— my red beard)*

The Wobblies may not have been exactly "dead for forty years" in the summer of 1954, but they were certainly a moribund outfit. By the time Gary reached college in the late '40s, IWW membership was down to 1,500 nationwide from an estimated high of 18,000 just before the First World War. In Washington State, their last meaningful action had been a 1933 strike of hop pullers in the Yakima Valley.

Once, however, they had been the hope — the scourge, thought others — of the timber belt, the harvest circle, the rails, and the waterfronts of the Pacific Northwest. As both Wallace Stegner and James Jones later pointed out, the IWW was not so much a labor organization as it was a quasi-religion, replete with its own hymns, martyrs and holy places. The IWW's idealistic slogans — "One Big Union" — "An injury to one is an injury to all" — "The Union makes us strong" — "Building a new society within the shell of the old" — had once embodied the labor aspirations of the new century.

The Wobblies had been crushed in the Red Scare following World War One — an anti-radical purge far bloodier than Joe McCarthy's tedious mid-century inquisition. Particularly in Washington and Oregon, the IWW had been put down with extreme frontier brutality: deputized vigilantes flogged Wobblies with thorns of Devil's Club, tarred and feathered them, and killed more than a few. The anti-IWW hysteria in the Northwest reached a climax in 1919 not far from Packwood in the town of Centralia, where American Legion marchers attacked the Wobbly hall and after a gunfight (in which three Legionnaires were shot) lynched Wesley Everest from the Chehalis River railroad trestle. The bitter memories of class battles like the Centralia and Everett massacres lingered in Washington State for decades.

At the time of his firing, Gary had never been a member of the IWW, but he was proud of his radical bloodlines, which connected him to the One Big Union through his grandfather. Forty years earlier, he would no doubt have been a card-carrying Wob himself. As it was, his allegiance to the IWW during his college years took the form mostly of singing old songs from the Wobblies' "Little Red Songbook," educating his friends about the rich IWW history that was all around them, and paying an occasional nostalgic visit to the Seattle Wobbly Hall. That such sympathies could have been a factor in Snyder's blacklisting from the Forest Service as late as 1954 is an indication of the smoldering passions elicited by the Wobblies in the Pacific Northwest.

After his firing at Packwood, Gary contacted Warm Springs to see if the spot on the reservation fire crew was still open. It had been filled, but the Warm Springs Lumber Company said they would take him on to set chokers. Grimly, Gary accepted. Choker setting, he well knew, was the most dangerous work in any logging show. You could almost be sure if you saw an ad for choker setter in the newspaper that if you turned to the obituaries some unlucky logger would have just been waked.

As it was, Gary could not start work immediately. The week before, a lumber strike had been called throughout the logging camps and mills of the Oregon and Washington fir belt on the west side of the mountains, and had spread to the "short-log" pine country on the east slope, where Warm Springs was located. Seventy thousand loggers were on strike in the Northwest—"Chainsaws in a pool of cold oil / On back porches of ten thousand / Split shake houses," as Gary would later write—and for the time being he had to wait. In the interim, he decided to head up to Washington.

Gary began hitchhiking north, looking for day work, visiting with friends along the way for a night or two, then moving on, "a drifting gull," as he described himself in a letter to Philip. There were no jobs anywhere; the lumber strike had shut everything down. Gary spent the Fourth of July weekend in Seattle with Dick Meigs and his wife Janet, his old friends from Reed.

From Seattle, Gary hitched up to the Nooksack Valley, almost to the Canadian border, where Miegs had a cabin Gary could stay for a while—an old cedar-walled berry picker's shanty outside the village of Glacier on the Nooksack's north fork. Komo Kulshan was just eight miles south, all 10,700 feet of it, "burning in sun glare." Gary had now seen the White Watcher from all the directions; from the south, along the Skagit; from forty miles east when he was on Crater two summers before; from the west on 99; now from the north. That week he climbed it.

At Dick's cabin, Gary was less than forty miles from Sourdough. Of course, that was forty miles of unroaded wilderness. Anyway, Gary guessed correctly that Philip wasn't on the mountain yet, and figured it would probably be better to stay out of the Skagit. He didn't want to mess things up for Philip, or anyone else in Marblemount. Meanwhile, Gary began a new poem — "The Late Snow & Lumber Strike of the Summer of Fifty-four." He climbed both Shuksan and Kulshan, "alone in a gully of blazing snow" and was back in Portland by mid-July.

ON THE 18TH, Phil Whalen wrote Gary with an update from the Skagit. Philip had been living on the floating barge at Ross Dam with three rangers and two other seasonal men ever since fire school. Jack Francis had been stationed at the Diablo Guard Station again, but couldn't stand being cooped up, and quit the outfit when Blackie wouldn't let him go out on trail. Baxter had also recently disappeared, as he was apt to do, but not before giving Philip fifteen dollars to pass on to Gary. "All in Marblemount remember you kindly & wish you well," wrote Philip, slipping ten dollars of his own into the envelope along with Baxter's, and signed off saying "Do not give up hope. You will be showered with gold."

The Ross Lake Guard Station, or the "Ross Float" as it was called, was a large covered raft moored to a floating dock at the head of Ross Dam, near the southeast base of Sourdough Mountain. The floating guard station was the Forest Service's main staging area on the Upper Skagit. From it, lookouts and trail crews were ferried to all the other guard stations and trail heads along the lake. In 1953, Gary had worked at the float for a few weeks and described it in detail in his Sourdough journal:

> A floating dock with crosscuts, falling saws, spikes, wood, in't. At one end the green landing
> barge moored alongside. The main raft, with a boat-size wood door; inside a tangle of tools,
> beds, groceries. A vast Diesel marine engine-block in the middle of the deck with a chainsaw
> beside it. . . . Shelves on the unpainted wall with rice, coffee, pancake syrup. Cords, vices, wires
> on the workbench. A screen cooler full of bacon and ham. And this enters, under the same
> roof, into another dock-room in which the patrol boat floats, full of green light from the water.
> Around the edge bales of hay and drums of Diesel. Moored alongside outside, the horse raft.
> Covered with straw and manure. . . .

Squeezed in among all the guard station gear were cots for up to six men, all filled. "I've been living on the Ross float under the tutelage of Volley Reed, Fred Berry & Ed Wyman," Philip wrote Gary in

National Park Service "Float" on south bank of Ross Lake, July 1995. The Forest Service maintained a floating guard station much like this one at the head of Ross Dam during the 1950s. Phil Whalen, Gary Snyder, and Jack Kerouac all spent time on it before and after packing to their lookouts.

mid-July. "There are two other seasonal employees besides me, a couple of squirts who are reasonably easy to get on with." But there was no privacy. After three weeks, Philip complained that he could not read or write or even think straight while in such "concentrated association."

It rained every few days, keeping the woods wet and the fire danger low. Philip remained at the dam all through the month of July and into early August, doing various jobs around the float, hauling hay to Ruby Landing, cutting the boredom with quick swims in the cold waters from the guard station deck. To Gary he wrote: "The season is nearly over and I haven't a notion in my head about anything to write down even if I had the chance." Later, however, memories of those days would surface like the heavy logs that still occasionally floated up from the old submerged riverbed. An unfinished manuscript of Whalen's from early January 1956 shows that Philip had tuned in finely to his guard station mates and felt the creative possibilities of the situation.

There was certainly no lack of setting. The Ross Guard Station was situated dramatically on the lake, surrounded by the shaggy conifer slopes of Ruby, Sourdough, and Jack mountains on three sides and open to a spectacular view of Pyramid and Colonial peaks to the south. "Across the lake toward Ruby Creek the water was smooth and blue, reflecting the trees and rocks along the shore," wrote Whalen in his Skagit story. "The big snow ranges to the east and south sparkled; the glaciers on Colonial Peak looked cold and close over the head of the dam." The guard station itself was a tiny human outpost set against this vast natural splendor and the huge, silent, impersonal beauty of Ross Dam and its futuristic control tower, set in the cliffs on the Ruby Mountain side.

As for the Forest Service men Philip shared the float with, they were part of:

the great tribe of Tarheels that had begun moving into that country about forty years before, mountain people who had left the tired ground of North Carolina for the rich silt and volcanic loam of Skagit County. They brought along their rifles and their whiskey stills and their Elizabethan dialect (complete with the aspirate *h* before words beginning with *i*) to farm a little, log a little, and cook a little moon, but mostly to hunt and fish and trap among the mountains and the tall timber.

They wore themselves down against the mountains, against the trees (either as loggers or fire fighters), against each other, against their women & children, and finally against their own desires for all the things that other people want and have — the cars and trucks, farm and / or logging equipment, household appliances, sporting goods, movies, liquor — the works. Although they lived hundreds of miles from the city, there was nothing of the classical rube about them. . . . The chief thing distinguishing them from ordinary suburbanites was that they had not yet taken up psychoanalysis, but that would only be a question of time — in a little while some enterprising young analyst would decide to move into the country to practice among them, bringing the final blessing of civilization.

At one point in this unfinished 1956 Skagit story, Whalen's character "Red" is lying on the guard station deck with two of the other men, peering far down into the wavering depths of the clear reservoir waters after a cold swim.

Junior said, "Boy, you can't see the bottom anywhere near here. How deep is hit, do you figure?"
"I don't know for sure," I said, "Jim always says three-hundred feet, but I don't know."
Ryder said, "You can see from the slope of the bank that it could be — the pictures I've seen of this valley before the Dam was built make it look pretty deep."

In fact, the water beneath the Ross Float was considerably deeper than Whalen's characters imagined — 500 feet at "full pool." At the bottom lay the ancient bedrock steps of the Skagit gorge known as the Ripraps — a series of canyon falls and rapids that, in the days before the dam, marked the end of downstream navigation.

This was where Henry Custer and his Indian boatmen had ceased their southward canoeing in late August 1859, after paddling down from the boundary station at the 49th parallel in the first U.S. government reconnaissance of the Skagit. "The river flows here between rocky banks, with a swiftness and impetuosity which even makes my expert Indian canoe men feel more or less uncomfortable. From the anxious looks they cast around, I conclude that it is about time to look out for a secure harbor for our canoe," wrote Custer in his report. "We had stopped our onward course not a moment too soon; for within a distance of only 100 yards from our harbor, we found the River forming a perpendicular fall, which . . . if we had dashed over it, would have engulfed the whole party & sent us inevitably to our last accounts."

Henry Custer was certainly not the first white man to see the Ripraps of the Skagit — fur trappers no doubt had come to them fifty years before from forts in British Canada, or east from Fort Okanogan. But those early trappers were few in number, and left no mark or chronicle of their Skagit exploits. Custer, the topographer for the U.S. Boundary Commission that surveyed the international border along the 49th parallel in 1859, was the first Euro-American to provide a written description of the Upper Skagit. Custer traveled with two other government men and a party of ten porters and guides recruited from native Nooksack and Chilliwack bands living west of the Skagit. His mission was to explore the Skagit for ten miles above and below the 49th Parallel. At the boundary station a canoe was built for the river trip; it took three days for the Nooksack man who was Custer's chief guide to build the boat from scratch. The same man was his steersman when the canoe was launched on the river. Custer sat amidships, behind two teenaged Chilliwack paddlers.

One senses from his narrative that after weeks of hiking through burnt-over woods, and days portaging around huge snag jams on the river, Custer succumbed to the southward pull of open water. Near Dry Creek, where he should have come about according to his orders, Custer wrote: "Nothing can be more pleasant than to glide down a stream like this; the motion is so gentle; the air on the water cool and pleasant, and the scenery, which is continually shifting, occupies the eye and mind most pleasantly."

At the foot of Jack Mountain ("Nokomokeen" on his map), Custer caught sight of the mouth of Ruby Creek, which he called the Skagit's "East fork," and continued on, with his paddlers singing and shouting as the looping river straightened and the current gathered velocity. Custer followed the Skagit south to Ruby Creek, which he surveyed at its mouth, but did not follow further. From a vantage point at the foot of Sourdough, Custer looked across to Ruby Creek and wrote:

> . . . the East fork [Ruby Creek] . . . joins the Skagit by breaking through a high rocky ledge in a similar way as already observed at the junction of two of these mountain streams. Its high rocky banks are bridged over by a small fir tree, from a foot to 6 inches in diameter; its height above the stream may be about 150 feet. Over this primitive bridge one of the Indians was rapidly crossing and recrossing, looking with perfect coolness in the dizzy chasm below where the waters were dashing and roaring in their onward course. He invited each of us to join him in turn, but with little success.

When Henry Custer journeyed down the Skagit in 1859, he found no evidence of Native Americans along the river. The old trails that his party followed on foot had grown faint from disuse, and the younger Indians guiding him had little firsthand knowledge of the country. Custer does mention one elder—"Chinsoloc, a Samona Chief [who] had the most extended geographical knowledge of any Indian I ever had to deal with"—who was able to draw from memory a map of the territory, which Custer found to be "most minute and reliable." It was from Chinsoloc's map that the aboriginal names we still use, such as Hozomeen, were passed on.

The apparent absence of native people in the Upper Skagit in the mid and late nineteenth century is now thought to have been the result of a combination of catastrophic floods—evidence exists of a record flood in 1809 that would have destroyed any settlements on the Skagit plain—and also, about the same time, epidemic smallpox spreading ahead of the first Euro-Americans.

The archeological record now shows that there were native people in the Upper Skagit, both traveling through the valley and also occupying seasonal sites for a variety of uses in the generations immediately before Custer's explorations, and indeed, for several thousands of years before. Scatters of stone tools and weapons have been found on Sourdough less than mile from where Phil Whalen spent the month of July 1954 at the Ross Float, indicating that native people had followed trails along the flank of the mountain as a way through the steep Skagit gorge as long ago as 6,000 years.

On August 11, Phil Whalen finally packed up to Sourdough Lookout for what was left of the fire season. There were two trails to the summit: the steep, switchbacking southern one that Gary had taken in 1953, and an eastern route, the Pierce Mountain trail, more gradual but longer, beginning on the shore of Ross Lake near Cougar Island. Philip and Volley Reed were ferried to the trailhead in the old green World War II surplus landing craft, which had a front end that dropped down and let them ashore in a two-man parody of MacArthur's Philippine Return. They had no mules with them, just Phil and Volley Reed, backpacking Philip's personal effects; his food would be coming along by mule in another day or so.

The Pierce Mountain trail followed the moderate roll of Sourdough's long eastern slope for more than four miles without a single switchback. It was an old trail, not much used, with worn, healed-over axe blazes on the tree trunks along the way. The woods were silent and spacious, dominated by great pillars of two-hundred-foot Douglas fir sheltering a lower story of mountain hemlock and other smaller trees all bearded with pale green lichens. On the ground there were down trees everywhere in various states of decay: recent blowdowns with giant root wads clawing the air, old logs totally coated in green-gold moss, lying sedately in cool beds of deer fern, others cracked open nursing long rows of sapling fir. At 4,000 feet the trail came to an overlook high above the cold white vein of Riprap Creek, which pulsed soundlessly down the south of the mountain and emptied into the Skagit just below Ross Dam. The trail then rimmed the high Riprap drainage, climbed a tight series of switchbacks, and came finally into the open on Sourdough Ridge, three quarters of a mile east and a thousand feet below the lookout. It was Philip's first view of the Upper Skagit. From the ridge he could see both lakes—long, dark blue Ross running north to Hozomeen; sinuous Diablo and Thunder Arm to the south, green with the milk of a dozen glaciers—"the lakes in two lights green soap and indigo," as he would describe them in "Sourdough Mountain Lookout."

On Sourdough, Philip saw much more wildlife than he had the year before at Sauk. A large deer herd had grown up on the Upper Skagit following the great fire of 1926, but was later decimated when its winter yards in the river plain were flooded by Ross Lake. In the mid-50s, however, there were still large numbers of deer roaming the ridges—both blacktail and mule deer, and also an interesting cross between the two. The big bucks of this breed were like Arthurian stags: rough, majestic smoke-colored beasts crowned with five- and six-point antler racks. Whalen stumbled into a pack of about a dozen of them one evening. "I was going around the building up to that little rise that's to the southwest and I walked right into a herd of them. It was a real *frisson;* they jumped and I jumped," he recalls. "They reminded me of the Tibetan demons that have a deer's head, and I thought 'My Goodness!' Anyway, they all ran off."

Then as now, Sourdough was a good habitat for black bear. As Philip remembers,

So here's this bear sitting around on the rocks just outside the window, and I have a house full of honey and bacon and all this good stuff. And if that bear had wanted to he could have just walked right through that glass and it wouldn't bother him a bit. But he just sort of sat out there in the sunshine fooling around and I was inside yelling and howling and beating on tin pans trying to get him out of there. I didn't want him loitering around there, but he wouldn't go, and I was having all sorts of terrible apprehensions about what he could do if he wanted to. Finally he did go away, but only at his own speed.

By August, the lumber strike was over, and Gary was at work on the Warm Springs Indian reservation, seventy miles southeast of Portland, in the dry lava plateau country between mounts Hood and Jefferson. The Deschutes River ran along it on the east, and the Warm Springs River flowed through its heart.

The Warm Springs Lumber Company logged the old-growth Ponderosa pine forest under contract

Philip Whalen on the steps of Sourdough Lookout, August 1955. ". . . And I was trying to think about what else I knew about all that lookout business, and well, a real cornball description would be 'Cutting Wood and Hauling Water,' which is what Zen itself is supposed to be about in one of the old stories, but it happens to be true, so if anybody asks you what a lookout is like, that's what to tell them." Philip Whalen

with the tribal council, with the proceeds going to the reservation, and the cutting was planned for a truly sustained yield. "Unlike the thick-growing Douglas Fir rainforests west of the Cascades . . . the drier pine forests are perfect for selective cutting," wrote Snyder in an essay thirty years later. "Here [at Warm Springs] the slopes were gentle and they were taking no more than 40 percent of the canopy. A number of healthy mid-sized seed trees were left standing. The D8 Cats could weave their way through without barking the standing trees."

At Warm Springs in '51, Gary had been a scaler on the cold deck, that is, he worked at stacking already cut logs and sized the loads for the logging trucks. Scaling was part of the relatively safe "yarding" operation. Choker setting, by contrast, was part of "skidding"—rife with accidents. To Philip, he wrote from Warm Springs: "Am unmashed only by failure of natural law and percentages to wreak expected damage, as I (and all other chokersetters) am/are daily subject to falling pecker-poles, snapped jill-pokes, toppling snags, rolling logs, giant caterpillars which the driver cannot see over the hood of (to know and avoid you), tripping cables, swinging butt hooks, the idiocy of the man running the show, and other horrors too numerous to mention. . . ."

As it turned out, Gary, lightweight and wiry at twenty-four, was built for setting chokers and dancing over fans of huge felled pines in steel-pointed logger boots. The job was a far cry from the contemplative peace and quiet of a lookout; on the other hand, it gave him the chance to toughen up after nine months in Berkeley, and perhaps to sweat out some of the rage he must have felt at his screwing by the FBI. Such fundamental work was good for his writing, too. The Warm Springs rez had been fertile poetic territory before—in the summer of '51 it had inspired "A Berry Feast"; in '54 it provided further grist, as the men he labored beside, like Ray Wells, the Nisqually Indian, or Ed McCullough, the old Wobbly "knot-bumper," now lent their voices to the burgeoning tapestry of speech taking shape as *Myths and Texts*. His choker-setting experience also provided background for one of Gary's finest later essays, "Ancient Forests of the Far West." Ultimately, his second summer on Warm Springs would only strengthen his credibility on forest management issues, lending an edge of redneck practicality to his loftier ecological writings. Certainly no one would ever accuse a former chokersetter of being a tree hugger.

PHILIP PACKED DOWN from Sourdough on August 27th, and worked one final week on the Ross float before leaving. When he left, Blackie invited him to come back in '55 and man Sourdough again; he also told Phil to let Gary know that if things changed, he too was welcome back.

By September 7th, Phil was in Seattle, tanned and trim from another Skagit summer and happily plunging into a book-buying smorgasbord with his Forest Service paychecks, picking up everything from works by Apollinaire and Thomas Mann to *The Tale of the Genji,* an Oxford Life of Johnson, de Tocqueville, a Renaissance Italian history by Jacob Burckhardt, and a collection of medieval poetry by Helen Waddell. To Gary, who was still setting chokers at Warms Springs, Philip wrote: "My imagination is in great shape. Goodness knows what will happen next."

GARY REMAINED AT Warm Springs into mid-October, working hard, "writing extravagantly" during his weeknights in the Camp A bunkhouse, and drinking just as extravagantly on the weekends in the logger bars of nearby Madras. He hadn't shaved his entire time at Warm Springs, and now had a full pointed beard that made him look "like a cross between D. H. Lawrence and Fu Manchu." He even found time to write a short essay for the First Zen Institute newsletter, good-naturedly recommending fire lookout work "for anyone with yamabushi tendencies and some physical and mental toughness."

In the end, his blacklisting from the Forest Service had not been a huge catastrophe for him. Unquestionably his rights had been egregiously violated — as were those of many thousands of others — but in Zen fashion Gary managed to make the latest obstacle part of his journey. On the rez he made far more money than he would have on lookout — twice the Forest Service scale — and the chokersetter work put him in touch with perhaps more agile and harder parts of himself. In retrospect, it seems possible that Gary had already gotten what there was to get from lookouting; another fire season might have been merely redundant for him from a creative point of view. There would be plenty of mountains and rivers to come, and solitude for books and zazen. On a crate beside his bunk at Warm Springs that summer, Gary kept a small altar with a postcard of the sword- and book-wielding Bodhisattva of Wisdom, Manjusri. If Wisdom was, metaphorically, a balance of book and sword, or contemplation and action, then perhaps that was what Warm Springs was about — more blade than book.

My life has been spent in the midst of heroic landscapes
which never overwhelmed me and yet I live in a single room in the city—
the room a lens focusing on a sheet of paper.

Philip Whalen, "Since You Ask Me"

Cold Brilliant Sun

Sourdough Mountain, Summer 1955

I N 1955, Philip Whalen was back in the Skagit for his third fire season, once again manning Sourdough Mountain Lookout. In what was becoming a seasonal ritual for him, he arrived at Marblemount toward the end of June and spent his first week at guard school at Komo Kulshan station. Afterwards, he was sent up the Skagit to the guard station at Ross Dam for a week of hay hauling and trail building along Ruby Creek.

Surprisingly, lookout work had turned out to be a perfect job for him—almost the plum of a government post Gary had imagined for Philip in his 1951 poem "A Sinecure for P. Whalen." Despite Philip's initial reluctance and his occasional grousing about mean mules and bugs, where else could he get paid to read all summer in a landscape such as Sourdough?

For his part, Philip did good work for the Forest Service. Blackie Burns was glad to have him back on Sourdough since Whalen was probably the most reliable and accurate radio man the district had ever had on lookout in the Upper Skagit. In those days, it was impossible for trail crews and lookouts in the back country to directly radio the ranger headquarters in Marblemount. All radio messages had to go through Sourdough, and whoever was lookout there had to jot down the incoming message, then forward it — verbatim, ideally — to Marblemount. Finally, the lookout had to receive the response from Marblemount and radio it back to the original sender. Messages were often garbled in transition, and serious miscommunications were common.

Not so with Whalen as the repeater. Philip had tinkered with radios since he was a boy and, during the war, because of his poor eyesight, had been assigned to the Air Corps radio school in Sioux Falls, South Dakota, where he learned Morse Code and radio repair and became a radio mechanic and instructor of mechanics. Tommy Buller, who worked as a trail crewman on the Upper Skagit and was often in radio contact with Philip on Sourdough, recalls Whalen's reliability and accuracy as an operator to this day. "You could talk for ten minutes and have it all wrote down what you said, and he could repeat that and he would not miss a word. It was amazing. I don't know if he just wrote fast or had good shorthand, or what, but it would be word for word. And it seemed like he had that radio on 24 hours a day. It didn't make any difference what time of day you called, he would answer it. I don't know if he ever slept."

In early July, Philip sent Gary a newsy letter from the barracks in Marblemount. Jack Francis had not returned to the Skagit, wrote Whalen, nor had anyone seen or heard anything of Baxter. (Jim Baxter had actually paid a visit to Gary in Berkeley that spring.) Old Roy Raymond was in the hospital after a heart attack. Another old-timer, Ed Wyman, who'd been on the Big Beaver trail crew with Gary the year before, flunked his physical and had not been rehired. Then during guard school, Shubert Hunter's wife Dorothy gave birth to a seven-pound boy. In further news, a bear had gotten into the Granite Creek Guard Station and ransacked the kitchen. Construction continued on the new Crater Lookout, lower down on Crater's east peak; Crater West was closed for good. Tommy Buller had nailed down the fire door for good and packed off the fire-finder dish on his back, leaving Gary's old L.O. to the wind and the pikas. Mostly, though, things on the Skagit were more or less the same. Frank Lewis was "all charm and smiles," Blackie Burns and Clarence McGuire asked kindly after him as always, and whenever Gary's name came up old Andy Wilcox still hooted, "I packed fifty pounds of rice up that mountain for that god damned Chinaman!"

By the 12th of July, Philip was back in his old bunk at the Ross float, waiting for Wilcox to bring up the pack string to take him to Sourdough. While the faces and routines and landscape of the Skagit had become comfortably familiar, in the summer of '55 Philip looked on it all with newly sharpened senses. Earlier that spring he had taken peyote for the first time, and still felt subtly under its influence.

It had happened in Seattle. In March Philip had moved from the Oregon coast at Newport to a large apartment in the basement of an old Victorian house on Roosevelt Way, just off the University of Washington campus. His roommate was Harry Lamley, an old Reed College friend doing graduate work in Chinese studies. On April 22, at a party given by a friend of Lamley's, Philip ate three chopped-up peyote buds and went on an exultant twelve-hour voyage of initiation that "acted on my spirit and mind and body and everything else as a great cure," as he would later recall. In June, two weeks before coming up to Marblemount, he took a second trip that left him energized as never before —"Great fun reaching from a position in deep space to touch various suns & receiving great charges," he wrote to Gary. Even after the pyrotechnics of these trips had subsided, a healthy feeling of heightened awareness and vitality remained. By the time Philip arrived at Ross Lake Guard Station, the mountains around the dam looked positively "Byronic."

ON JULY 13TH, Andy Wilcox arrived at Ross Dam with the pack string. The plan was to tow the horses and mules on a raft to the lake-shore trail head of the Pierce Mountain Way, and pack Philip up by the same route he had taken in '54. The night before they were to go, Andy corralled the animals — three saddle horses and four mules — on the straw-covered horse raft lashed to the guard station dock. That night while the crew slept in their cots in the hold of the float, one of the horses — a one-eyed mare named Mabel — tripped overboard, startling everyone awake with a terrific splash. Philip got to the panicked, snorting animal first and kept her afloat by hooking one arm under her head while Andy the Packer stomped off cursing down the dock to bring around a boat to tow Mabel in to shore. The whole scene was pure slapstick, but as Philip looked up and saw the moon tilting over Jack Mountain and felt the huge horse pumping like Poseidon in the crook of his arm, he felt suddenly socketed-in to the moment and flooded with crazy grace. "I was kneeling over the edge of this raft in my underwear, hold-

Sourdough Mountain Lookout interior, September 1998.

"Then I'm alone in a glass house on a ridge
Encircled by chiming mountains
With one sun roaring through the house all day
& the others crashing through the glass all night
Conscious even while sleeping.

Philip Whalen, *"Sourdough Mountain Lookout"*

ing this horse under the chin," he would recall. "It was two o'clock in the morning and it was a beauti-
ful summer night, and the mountains were all around, and the lake, and this horse, and me—and I
suddenly had a great weird kind of *satori*, a sort of feeling about the absolute connection between me,
and the horse, and the mountains, and everything else. And you can't describe it very well—the feeling
—because the feeling is a feeling. But it was . . . a big *take* of some kind."

THE NEXT MORNING Whalen and his packers headed up the mountain, Philip riding on one-eyed
Mabel, who seemed now over her madness as she negotiated the trail with subdued expertise. Once he
was set up in the cabin, Whalen took out his writing notebooks and books and set his writing desk in
the south window facing the high Neve and Colonial glaciers across Diablo Lake. On the side of the
fire-finder cabinet, Gary's poem from two seasons before, now yellowed and fading—"I the poet Gary
Snyder / Stayed six weeks in fifty-three"—still hung on its nail. Philip looked at his friend's familiar cal-
ligraphic script and wondered where Gary *was*. All through the month of June, Snyder had been stuck
in Berkeley, deskbound, unable to land a job in any mountains, working as a proofreader strictly for
rent money, sounding depressed over being so far removed from the woods.

Despite his bravado in the face of his 1954 blacklisting, lookout work had been ideal for Gary, and
being deprived of it hit him where he lived. In fact, in February 1955 Snyder had made a final appeal to
the decency of the Forest Service, writing directly to Washington, D.C., to demand an explanation for
his firing at Packwood the previous summer and also to clear his record for possible future work.

In March he had received a maddening and sinister bureaucratic response: "Instructions were issued
that you were not to be reemployed on the basis of information available to this office which indicated
that you do not meet the general suitability requirements for employment in this Department. This
determination was made on general suitability grounds rather than security grounds."

In April, finally giving up on the Forest Service, Gary shifted his efforts to the National Park Service,
applying for summer work at Kings Canyon and Sequoia national parks in the Sierras. By early June,
however, he had not heard from them, and must have feared that his blacklisting had now extended to
the Department of the Interior as well. To Philip he complained: "I am physically sick for wanting to be
in the mountains so bad. I am forced to admit that no one thing in life gives me such unalloyed pleasure

as simply being in the mountains." Again a week later he wrote to say: "Everything feels all wrong: I just can't adapt to not packing up & traveling this time of year & my rucksack & boots hang accusingly on the wall."

At solstice, Gary was still in Berkeley, feeling desperate at the prospect of being trapped in the city all summer. Then at the last minute, the Park Service suddenly came through with a trail crew opening — in the Yosemite, no less — and by early July Gary was laying riprap in Pate Valley. To old friend Dell Hymes he wrote: "I am suddenly wafted off to Yosemite to be a trail crewman, for how long I cannot tell. But my old pattern has asserted itself & once again I am surrounded by boots, packs, food-bags, living in a tent & rising early." On Sourdough, Philip did not get this news until late July.

Meanwhile, Whalen organized the lookout, set up the radio, and settled in for another fire season. Unlike his short Sourdough stint in '54 or his time on Sauk in '53, which had been bracketed by weeks of trail-crew work, Philip's mountaintop solitude in 1955 would be long and uninterrupted — a full nine weeks.

Over the course of the summer, Philip had ample time to think about and integrate the experiences of his spring peyote trips. At the party where he had first taken it, he had eaten three buds — not dried buttons, but three fresh buds from whole, still-living plants that had arrived in a cardboard packing case from a mail-order botanic company in Texas — "an enormous shipment of the divine green," as he described it to Gary. On Sourdough in July Philip still had a vivid recollection of the dreadful taste — like eating soap — but surprisingly he hadn't thrown up, even though he had eaten some slices of pepperoni pizza and a couple of beers on top of it, according to the morning-after account he wrote to Snyder. After nearly two hours without any discernible effects, Philip had gone back alone to Harry Lamley's subterranean apartment, feeling "generally depressed and dissatisfied," but no sooner had he gotten by himself than he noticed "the shadows began to glow faintly."

Instinctively, Philip had headed for his bed "and was immediately rapt away." For most of the next twelve hours he had lain on his mattress, not exactly hallucinating, but going forth and returning from an intense "identification" with the mighty Hindu god Vishnu, "enormously powerful but divinely, consciously resting." To Gary he wrote: "I was the giant Vishnu on the waters, while in my belly there was a cold, brilliant sun." To feel this recurring identity with Vishnu, the great worker and sustainer and guardian of the dharma, seemed highly auspicious. Also, it took Philip back to his first serious interest in Vedantist philosophy ten years before, and even earlier, back to when, as a boy in The Dalles he had first read Lin Yutang's accounts of the Vedic heroes.

Philip's peyote trip had lasted from midnight April 22 until noon the following day, although it was difficult to say exactly when the drug completely wore off. During that time, Whalen had slept, awoke, and slept again; at times he felt himself dreaming yet remained consciously self aware. At other points he lay awake, sweating profusely while watching vivid projections of himself in the midst of various ceremonial rites. "Sometimes I was a pillar of the temple, sometimes one of the priests, sometimes the idol of the god before whom the ceremony took place. A couple of times I was the bound & mutilated fertility god, high on the oak while the priests circled round, wailing and doing the limping dance —

"Then I was born several times. I was a great tortoise, then I was Ganesha."

Although his body had jerked and tremored uncontrollably at times during his trip, reminding him of descriptions he'd read of insulin shock therapy, Philip's experience with peyote, both in April and again in June, had been remarkably positive. Despite his periodic depressions over the years and his always self- deprecating remarks about his grip on reality, Philip's psyche actually seemed to have been quite sound. If nothing else, he had proven on Sauk and Sourdough that he was at least capable of sitting still and watching his mind for long periods.

Responding to his friend's account of his trip, Gary wrote: "There's no doubt about it, Peyotl is pure magic. But what it does for you, I'm convinced, depends, just like the Indians say, on how pure your heart is. You must have a very pure heart. I never doubted it."

Gary had already taken peyote himself a few months before Philip, on New Year's Day, in San Francisco. "An astonishing experience," he reported to Whalen at the time. "Almost terrifying, one that takes you into an entire world which is left-handed, baroque, dripping with jewels, & where I for one, met Baudelaire, Rimbaud, Aleister Crowley . . . & a host of others, to whom the Peyote (almost a distinct personality) introduced me, as a sort of initiation. It is Jung's Unconscious, with trimmings, history, etc. all scrambled in." Gary had at once offered to share some buttons with Whalen, but Philip at the time had declined, writing back: "Don't need no more hallucinations than I got already."

On the West Coast, 1955 was *the* year of peyote on many college campuses. The word "psychedelic"— literally "mind-manifesting"— was coined that spring. Legal, non-toxic, dirt-cheap, easy to obtain, and heralded by the eminent Aldous Huxley the year before as having the power to open Blake's "doors of perception," peyote found many eager initiates among grad students and young professors, especially those in the burgeoning fields of anthropology, religion, and psychology. From Berkeley, Snyder summed up the prevailing feeling about the plant in a letter to Dell Hymes: "If you're *really* interested in shamanism, mythology, the imagination, here's the quick way to find out." At schools like USC, UC Berkeley, Reed College, and the University of Washington, there was a steady influx of peyote from the mid-'50s on. "Peyote flows in (through sources unknowable) in ever greater quantities," wrote Snyder to Hymes in April.

Peyote of course was hardly new: first mention of it in Western literature was by the Spanish friar Bernardino de Sahagún, who witnessed its use among the Aztecs in the 1550s. Archeological evidence shows it had already been in widespread shamanic use in Mexico for at least five centuries before Cortés, and probably much longer. The Spanish invaders suppressed the plant; records of the Inquisition in Mexico list hundreds of cases in which peyote use was punished, driving it into the western Sierra Madres. By the nineteenth century only a few mountain tribes still kept the old peyote rituals, namely the Tarahumaras, the Huicholes, and the Nayarit. Then, in the 1880s, peyote emerged suddenly from its long exile, on one hand making its way north to become a cult sacrament among many Native American tribes in the United States and, on the other, becoming of pharmacological interest in Europe. The plant was first studied scientifically in Germany in 1888. Ten years later, the Victorian psychologist Havelock Ellis ingested some peyote buttons, and wrote the first subjective description of the plant's effects, duly noting the "thick, glorious fields of jewels." Yeats is rumored to have experimented with peyote; his fellow Golden Dawn occultist Aleister Crowley certainly did.

In 1936, the French surrealist Antonin Artaud journeyed to Mexico's Sierra Tarahumara and took part in peyote rites that left him badly shaken but spiritually renewed. "Once one has experienced a visionary state of mind, one can no longer confuse the lie with truth," he wrote in the aftermath of his encounter. "There is no emotion or external influence that can divert one from this reality." In 1950, the San Francisco surrealist poet Philip Lamantia, then twenty-three, followed Artaud's example, seeking his own vision in the peyote ceremonies of the Washo Indians of California. With Lamantia, peyote arrived on the Bay Area literary scene. As early as 1951, he and a half dozen friends had "a sort of little Berkeley peyotl cult of our own . . . taking peyote weekly for several months." In February 1952, Laman-

Sourdough Mountain Lookout, September 1998.

tia gave Jack Kerouac — whom he'd known in New York in the late 1940s — and his friend Neal Cassady (hero of *On the Road*) their first peyote. Kerouac reportedly fell asleep. (Kerouac was living in San Francisco with Cassady and his wife and two children from December 1951 until late April 1952.)

One of the notable aspects of Philip Whalen's initiation was that both of his trips had been undertaken solo. "Everyone who had had peyote before marveled that I had my visions in solitude — all claimed that it was too frightening to be alone with it all." Indeed, in 1955 few people had the nerve to venture by themselves into the labyrinth of peyote. Aldous Huxley had had the clinical support of Dr. Humphrey Osmond; Artaud had his Tarahumara shaman, and Lamantia had taken the drug within the structures of Washo Peyote cult rites — "a sober ritual," he says, "as precise as the Roman Catholic liturgy, or the Byzantine." On Western college campuses in the mid-'50s, peyote quickly evolved into a party scene. "I'm going to a big peyote party Saturday night in SF," wrote Snyder. "With drums and flutes and many people. BYOB=bring your own blanket. Host will provide vomit-pans for guests. Everybody sit around the next day smoking & telling what they saw." By contrast, Whalen's psychedelic vigils in Harry Lamley's basement that spring had been lone encounters with the self and its symbols, more like the mountaintop quests of native vision seekers.

Whalen had not taken peyote without considerable skepticism. When the cactus had first begun to make its appearance, he initially suspected it might turn out to be little more than a form of "low grade samadhi" for campus hipsters and cautioned Gary to "Stay out of Beulah-land." At the same time, he had also been fearful of how it might affect his own psyche. "I had been apprehensive about taking the stuff; as I've told you before on various occasions, I consider myself dotty enough without doping myself — I was afraid of seeing only horrors," he admitted. "But. . . the few horrors weren't horrifying — I knew them only as things that had once frightened me but which now seemed somehow pointless, or as ordinary things again — no longer horror symbols."

By late June, with two extraordinary trips under his belt, Philip was himself extolling the curative powers of the shamanic succulent, at least in his own case. "Maybe I'm being simple minded about all this, but I think the junk has had a certain therapeutic effect on my psyche . . . nowadays I feel that I can sort out the realities & unrealities of this particular world more distinctly than I ever have before. I am more conscious of being conscious — that sounds literary, but take it literally — more aware that here I am with a lot to do. Best of all I find that I can work on things now, & that I am working."

EVEN BEFORE HIS peyote trips, Philip seemed to be experiencing a breakthrough in his poetic practice. For one thing, his poems had gotten longer, outgrowing the seven- or eight-line Imagist architecture in which he had been working for several years. As early as February he had been adding lines to a poem first begun at Montgomery Street on his return from Sauk Lookout in 1953 — the droll "'Plus Ça Change. . . ,'" about a married couple helplessly morphing into a pair of caged parakeets. "Improved from an older piece by addition and correction," he had written to Gary in February; adding, with typical self-deprecation, "The whole is probably worse, but it is whole." The newly finished work was not worse; in fact, "'Plus Ça Change. . . ,'" with its wicked sarcasm wrapped in deceptive casualness — "Just what *shall* we tell the children?" — would become one of Philip's signature poems.

"The Martyrdom of Two Pagans," a new poem written on his arrival in Seattle in March, was another indication of his creative change. "It has all kinds of crackle and vigor," thought Snyder on his initial reading. "Write some more like it," he urged. "I'll probably hammer on it some more at a later date," replied Philip. "This is the place it has reached & will stay awhile. I can't see it any more."

At the beginning of April, with spring coming gradually to Seattle, and summer looming on the horizon, Philip began thinking of the mountains again. A sharp memory of the avalanche lilies on Sourdough boring up through the thin snowdrifts above Riprap Creek the year before touched off a short naturalistic poem with a twist:

> *Now and then they ask me*
> *To write something for them*
> *And I do.*

The next day, Philip tossed the *I Ching* coins for a reading on the coming season and with typical synchronicity drew two hexagrams composed of the Taoist images for "Mountains" and "Waters" — "Chien (Obstruction)" and "Meng (Youthful Folly)." From these images Philip fashioned "For K.W. Senex," a poem of decaying snowpack and "shallow pools over matted duff" and the cold, slow trickle of water seeking its own level at the foot of mountains. "Poultry of some kind keeps happening," Philip joked to Gary, as the longer lines and scraps of lines for new poems continued to flow in on him. "I am just susceptible, that's all."

After his April peyote trip, Whalen's creative susceptibility became even more pronounced, with "If

You're So Smart, Why Ain't You Rich?"—"A new poetickal effusion," as he described it to Gary—which had come to him nearly in one piece over a twenty-four-hour period. "The weather is much warmer and the evenings lighter and the Muse slowly and graciously stirs my aging animal spirits so I sing—in broken quavering measure, to be sure, but a stave is a stave nonetheless."

Perhaps a more immediate prod than the weather, or even his recent loosening up by the peyote, was the appearance in Seattle of William Carlos Williams, who had come to read at the University of Washington in middle May. UW faculty poet Theodore Roethke introduced Williams. To Philip, Williams—now seventy-two—appeared "much enfeebled physically . . . but mentally and poetically sound." In the five years since Philip had met him at Reed, Williams had been battered by a number of strokes. Yet, despite his medical problems, the tough old Doctor had managed to publish five books since Whalen had seen him last. In '51 Williams had completed his long *Paterson* cycle, written his autobiography to his sixty-eighth year, then a novel (*The Build Up,* 1952), plus a book of *Selected Essays* (1954) and a collection of his early poems. Williams was mesmerizing, but heart-breaking as he read from *The Desert Music,* published the year before. "It was painful to watch," Philip would write in a later *homage,* ". . . you not quite articulate, and your hand terribly crimped, yet delivering yourself, your love, to us. . . ."

Williams remembered Phil from their meeting at Lloyd Reynolds's home in 1950 and was friendly and gracious in the short time they had to speak afterwards. "Seeing him set us all up enormously," said Phil. The day after Williams's reading, Philip sat down and wrote "If You're So Smart, Why Ain't You Rich?" The title, like "What *shall* we tell the children?" in "'Plus Ça Change. . . ,'" was a borrowing from a popular expression of the day. Indeed, the saying "If You're So Smart, Why Ain't You Rich?" practically encapsulated the bumper-sticker cynicism of the period's affluent anti-intellectuals. Whalen's poem reverses the proposition. While admitting that he's "squandered every crying dime" in pursuit of beauty, he in effect asks: "If You're So Rich, Why Can't You Be Even a Little Smart?"

"If You're So Smart, Why Ain't You Rich?" was a breakthrough poem for Whalen, and a point of demarcation in his work. As the poet Michael McClure would later point out, "Whalen was using the American speech that William Carlos Williams instructed us to use, but he put it to a different use. Whalen's poems were not only naturalistic portrayals of objects and persons . . . they also used Ameri-

Original Sourdough Mountain Lookout in a Forest Service photograph from the 1920s.

can speech for the naked joy of portraying metamorphosis." Gary, when he saw the poem, thought that it was "an elegant thing." It confirmed again Snyder's belief in Philip's work, which he had stated the year before:

> Your poetry has a consistent tone, style, & a very HIGH style (i.e. elegant) which is closer, to my mind, to T. E. Hulme's idea of really classical poetry than anything I can think of right off — I mean the really CONTROLLED understatement, tremendous focusing & concentration on immediate and particular doings — like haiku — but with a body of useful & intelligible symbols working that make the associations & perceptions more acute and (to a western reader) more useful. I've watched what you've done in revising your stuff: paring away all rhetoric or excess of any sort, without losing the exuberance & as a pure metric that doesn't seem — to me — derivative of anybody, but entirely recognizable as you.

By the summer of 1955, Philip had written more than 120 poems, dating back to the early 1940s when he was in his late teens, living in Portland. All but a handful of these he would now leave behind him as artifacts of a long apprenticeship.

LIKE WHALEN'S WORK, Gary's poetry had also risen to a new level in early 1955. The poems that would become *Myths and Texts* (though he had not yet conceived that title) were adding up and taking shape in clusters. That spring in Berkeley, Gary lived in a tiny one-room cottage in the back yard of a house at 2919 Hillegass, just around the corner from his former place on Benvenue. It was the first place Gary looked at on his return from Warm Springs in the fall of 1954, and after four months of bunkhouse living on the rez, he hadn't been picky. Also, the price was right — only $10 a month. To Phil Whalen he described the place as "A real *hojoki*," the sort of wayside hut where a Bashō might lay up for a night or two on his narrow road to the deep north. Gary had use of a wash basin and a toilet on the back porch of the main house, and hauled in his own water for drinking and cooking. The wiring in the shack was no good, so he cooked on a hibachi just outside the door. It was as if Sourdough Lookout had blown off the mountain and landed on Hillegass Avenue: austere, yet not without charm —"a *cunning* little one-room thing," according to Jinny Hubbell, an old girlfriend of Gary's, and the life-model for Kerouac's character "Princess" in *The Dharma Bums*.

Snyder's "hojoki"— or, more accurately, his *hojo*— was a good place for a poet to work. Soon after moving in, he sent Whalen a piece of a "new huge odd poem, the Bear Mother," hearkening back to the woman of "A Berry Feast," "whose breasts bleed/From nursing the half-human cubs," and based in his research into A. Irving Hallowell's "Bear Ceremonialism." The "huge, odd poem" he wrote in December '54 would go into the "Hunting" section of *Myths and Texts* under the heading *"this poem is for bear."*

The day after New Year's, still on a roll, Gary sent Philip another hunting poem, which would become *"this poem is for deer."* Throughout January Snyder continued to work on material drawn from the previous summer at Warm Springs, as well as from memories of treks in the Olympics when he was in his teens. Describing what he was reaching for in these new poems, Gary wrote to Dell Hymes in April: "I suggest you read up on bees, ants, the Fulmar, stars, geology, Camellias, breeding and migrating habits of Canada geese; if you wish to comprehend the cycle of poems now being begun; I mean to refer to nothing that does not exist in this saha-world, tangibly."

At the same time he was working on the sprawling cycle taking shape as *Myths and Texts*, Gary also continued to write single poems as they came to him — the bitter "Song to Be Sung Later," "Alysoun," "For a Stone Girl at Sanchi," and "For a Far-Out Friend"—"inspired," he told Whalen, "by Greta Garbo in *Camille* & consummated by Heinrich Zimmer-Joseph Campbell monograph 2 vol Bollingen *Art of Indian Asia* which I sneaked a two-hour look at in a local book-peddler's alley."

ON THE ZEN FRONT, Gary's long-held plan to go to Japan for formal training had picked up inexorable momentum that spring. In April, after two and a half years of cross-country membership and sporadic correspondence with the First Zen Institute in New York, Gary was finally able to meet in person with Sokei-an's widow, Ruth Fuller Sasaki, who was stopping over for one day in San Francisco on a flight from Japan to New York. Their meeting at the Fairmont Hotel proved to be quite propitious. With Mrs. Sasaki was the Zen master Miura Isshu, on his way to New York to deliver a series of lectures on koan study at the Zen Institute. Miura, the first *roshi* Gary had ever met, appeared "straight, clear, firm, somewhat aloof, no nonsense . . . like one of the old-time guys." In another fourteen months, Miura Isshu Roshi would be Gary's teacher at Shokoku-ji Temple. Their meeting was a pivotal juncture on the long road to Kyoto that Gary had set upon when he ditched grad school in '52 and headed west out of Bloomington with the notion of somehow doing Zen in Japan.

So much had happened since Ruth Sasaki had first written Gary at Marblemount in June '53, impressing upon him the rigors of formal Zen training. Back then, she had adjudged that a young man such as himself might "reasonably well expect to pass his first *koan* at the end of that time."

Gary of course had his own time table. Before ever hearing of Ruth Fuller Sasaki or the First Zen Institute, he had already set about learning Japanese, and Chinese as well. After her letter, he had shifted into higher gear, filling his Sourdough notebooks with Japanese characters and vocabulary that summer, and beginning his formal language program at UC Berkeley in the fall of '53. Since then, he had immersed himself in Japanese culture as much as one could while still living in the States, reading voraciously, taking up calligraphy, becoming a regular at Alan Watts's Academy of Asian Studies in San Francisco, as well as Berkeley's Buddhist Church of America, a Japanese-American congregation of Jodo-shin, or "Pure Land" Buddhists. As for zazen, he had by the spring of 1955 been practicing more or less regularly for over three years, including his extended retreats on Crater and Sourdough.

Nor would Gary wait for a Zen master to begin working on *koans*. He had already learned a bit about the theory of koan study from his readings of D. T. Susuki. He knew, for instance, that *koans* had been systematized for centuries in Japan in classic collections and the first one given to students was traditionally "Chao-Chou's Dog," a.k.a. the koan "Mu.":

> *A monk asked Chao-Chou:*
> *"Does a dog have Buddha nature?"*
> *Chao-Chou answered:*
> *"Mu" (no; without; nothing)*

There wasn't any "answer" to a koan in the Western sense; it was not a puzzle to be figured out. The idea was to saturate one's consciousness with the koan-Mu situation and not let it go until something happened. In the late winter of '54 Gary had assigned himself the koan and after several weeks with it, had "gotten it." To Dell Hymes, he wrote: "Twenty minutes *zazen* a day on this ('The meaning of Chao-Chou's *Wu*' [Japanese, "Mu"]) got my poor feeble brain to a point where (in this very basic attack on the whole roots of Buddhist theory, since if a dog has no Buddha nature, nothing has a Buddha nature, & the monk & Chao-chou are rendered utterly superfluous, but . . .) I suddenly could look around without a single myth or theory or notion of any sort sloshing around my skull. Just see. This didn't last, of course."

Looking south from Sourdough Mountain, September 1998.

"Morning fog in the southern gorge
Gleaming foam restoring the old sea level"

Philip Whalen, *"Sourdough Mountain Lookout"*

When Gary and Ruth Fuller Sasaki finally met, Mrs. Sasaki was clearly impressed — so much so that, on her arrival in New York, she wrote him with a tentative offer of a one-year scholarship from the First Zen Institute, with travel expenses paid and a monthly stipend for a year of Zen training in Kyoto. Miura Isshu had also seen something in Gary. Without elaborating, Mrs. Sasaki concluded her overture to Gary by saying, "It has been suggested that your Zen studies might well be under his [Miura's] supervision."

Now, however, a new problem presented itself. In late December 1954, Gary had applied for a passport, and in February 1955, it had been rejected. "In your case," read the letter from the State Department, "it has been alleged that you are a Communist." The letter was signed by Ruth B. Shipley, the notoriously dictatorial head of the Passport Office in John Foster Dulles's State Department. Shipley was an entrenched anti-Communist crusader who proudly testified to a Senate committee in 1947 that her office maintained a blacklist of individual Americans whom the police and various federal agencies wished to restrict from foreign travel for political reasons. "It is believed that it is not in the best interests of the United States for you to travel abroad at this time," had been the Shipley mantra for twenty-seven years.

Weirdly, Snyder's fate now seemed in the balance between these two matronly figures — the good Ruth Sasaki, who offered world travel and the possibility of spiritual enlightenment, and the wicked Ruth Shipley, who seemed bent on grounding Gary for life. Meanwhile, no appeal could be initiated with the State Department without first swearing a non-Communist affidavit. Of course, Snyder wasn't a Communist and never had been, but it galled him to have to knuckle under to a bureaucratic schoolmarm like Ruth Shipley. In the end, though, he held his nose and wrote the requisite words "I am not now and I never have been a member of the Communist Party."

In a defiantly truthful three-page affidavit, Snyder summarized the rejection of his seaman's papers by the Coast Guard in 1952, his 1948 job with the Marine Cooks and Stewards Union, and his anti-draft sentiments, stating, ". . . I would rather go to a concentration camp than be drafted. This is a perfectly legitimate expression of opinion, and one which I still support." He proudly recounted his youthful intellectual Marxism, but added, "I never accepted Russian Communism as the full flowering of the Revolution" — a distinction surely lost on the Passport officers. In conclusion, Gary defended himself and his ideas, saying, "It is clearly the record of an independent and flexible mind, and not that of a

Communist. I am still critical of this and every other government. But it is not my intention to go abroad to run down the United States, or work for some other government. Either notion I find abhorrent."

By early May, he had not heard back from the Passport Office. At first, thinking that his passport situation might soon be favorably resolved, he made no mention of it to Ruth Sasaki. But in mid-May, as their discussions of his traveling to Kyoto on a First Zen Institute scholarship began to take shape, Gary felt that he should apprise Mrs. Sasaki of the circumstances. His revelation did not alter her high opinion of Gary; however, she wished to keep the First Zen Institute separate from his current problems. She rescinded the institute's scholarship, but offered a new plan that would still bring Gary to Kyoto to study Zen on the same terms—as her employee. She also consulted about his situation with her attorney, who advised Gary to enlist the help of the U.S. Senator from Oregon, Richard Neuberger.

Meanwhile, Ruth Shipley had retired from the Passport Office, only to be succeeded by the equally severe Miss Frances Knight. On June 24 Knight rejected Gary's appeal, despite his sworn affidavit and the efforts of Neuberger in his behalf. Once again, Ruth Sasaki was unflappable in the teeth of Gary's setback, urging him to "keep up the Japanese," and assuring him that "the time intervening between when we think things should come about and when Nature does, usually can be used to excellent advantage."

"She must be quite a one," wrote Philip Whalen when he heard news of Mrs. Sasaki's involvement, "being willing to take on the State Dept., senators McCarran & McCarthy & all the other dragons." Meanwhile, a District of Columbia Court of Appeals, in an entirely different case, had dealt a blow to Frances Knight's "Petticoat Empire" at the Passport Office, ruling that a passport was a citizen's right, not a privilege, and could not be denied without due process. Now it would only be a matter of months until Gary would have his passport.

"I am sure, with the general loosening up of the State Department in all kinds of ways, the passport will eventually come through," wrote Mrs. Sasaki from Kyoto. "I shall be looking forward to your being here." It had been three years since he had departed Bloomington, and would be yet another before he actually landed in Kyoto, but he was now definitely on his way. To his old grad school roommate Dell Hymes, Gary could finally write, "I am off to Kyoto to study—Zen. Splendidly ridiculous—but practical—notion."

PHILIP'S ZEN WAS ALIVE and well on Sourdough, where he described the cyclorama of surrounding peaks as a vast *mala*—a Buddhist rosary—with himself, a void, in the middle of it—"an empty figure containing all that's multiplied."

> *I'm surrounded by mountains here*
> *A circle of 108 beads, originally seeds*
> *   of* ficus religiosa
> *   Bo-Tree*
> *A circle, continuous, one odd bead*
> *Larger than the rest and bearing*
> *A tassel (hair-tuft) (the man who sat*
> *   under the tree)*
> *In the center of the circle,*
> *A void, an empty figure containing*
> *All that's multiplied;*
> *Each bead a repetition, a world*
> *Of ignorance and sleep.*

While on peyote, Philip had encountered mainly Hindu figures—Vishnu particularly, and elephant-headed Ganesha, remover of obstacles; however, at one point he had also found himself identifying profoundly with the Buddhist myth of Sakyamuni's last temptation. "Sometimes I was Sakyamuni under the Bo tree being tempted by Mara, but resisting effortlessly—impossibly easy because, like Sakyamuni, I knew Mara had mistaken me for someone else, while knowing at the same time we were both relatively unreal. . . ."

After his trips, Mahayana Buddhism seemed to provide the best handle for keeping things in perspective, not getting carried away by the visuals. Philip was careful, for example, to avoid the word "visions" for the things he had seen, preferring instead the term "identifications." Alluding to the often used Zen image of the "pointing finger," Philip wrote Gary: "Peyotl is another finger pointing some-place."

Philip Whalen at Sourdough Mountain Lookout, August 1955.

"Personally, I feel the need for the Mahayana kind of deal—coming back to the village with gift-bestowing hands, as differing from the Vedantist and Hinayana kind of solipsism. But I don't say that their kind isn't needed; the world needs more sages than anything else right now. More prayer wheels, more visions, more poems, more magic." Philip Whalen to Gary Snyder

Anybody can have dreams in the ordinary course of things — during illness, childbirth or what not, which would be enough to send folks along the twisty path of the one and the many, the relativity of reality, &c &c. I can see how a cult could grow up around any drug which can produce dreams at will, once the value of dreaming has been established. Peyotl is only one of these. . . .

"But," he concluded, "as the old original rice-bag said, 'Meditate. Smarten up.' And so we must."

Philip's sitting practice was still rather sporadic in 1955, but his Zen spirit had been aroused to a new level with the jolt of the peyote and his moonlight epiphany on the Ross Lake horse raft. All through the summer he felt numinously under the influence of the horse-falling-into-the-drink, not unlike the accounts he had read of American Indians who had met with particular animals in their spirit quests and afterwards identified with the animal, or seen the animal as a totemic protector or ally. In the same way, the "Horse in the Water" became a powerful archetype for Philip, and would be for several years. He played with the images and names all through the summer. The most obvious association was his own name, "Philip"—"a lover of horses" in Greek, a name spread across the ancient world by Philip of Macedonia, father of Alexander. For the Greeks, the horse had always been a fertility symbol: Demeter, Poseidon, Athena, Aphrodite, Kronos—all had horse aspects. The flying horse Pegasus was the steed of the Muses, the wingéd horse of poetry — certainly an auspicious animal for a writer.

"The horse was very important to me and I made up a poetical, secret name for myself out of that incident, and had a seal made for it [when I lived] in Kyoto," remembers Whalen.

"The experience meant a great deal to me, because of my own name; and also, the Chinese *Ma* had very heavy connections: Su Ma Chien was the historian who was castrated for not changing his history; and Ma-tsu, one of the greatest Zen Masters —'Master Horse' he was called."

On August 14, Philip was visited on Sourdough by Ed and Jean Danielsen, old Reed College friends. Ed was a painter and Jean had family money; they were on their way to live in Denmark. The Danielsens brought Philip a letter from Gary, forwarded via Harry Lamley. Gary's trail crew was deep in the Yosemite Wilderness north of the Grand Canyon of the Tuolumne, on Piute Creek — rattlesnake country. At night by the campfire he was reading *Paradise Lost*. While Jean sunned herself on a table-like slab of rock outside the lookout and Ed made pencil sketches of the surrounding peaks, Philip composed a reply for them to take back down. He wrote Gary that Blackie had been transferred out of the Skagit and into the Glacier District. Up on Sourdough, it had been impossible to pick up any scuttlebutt about what had happened. Frank Lewis was apparently consolidating his position. Also, Tommy Buller had had an attack of appendicitis while at the Granite Creek Guard Station and had to be rolled down to Ruby Landing in a wheelbarrow by his friend Roger Vail. Roger went all the way back to Marblemount with Tommy until he could be put on an ambulance to Sedro-Woolley, and when Frank Lewis docked Roger for a half day for coming all the way in, Roger quit. That was about it from the Skagit District.

The next day, after the Danielsens had hiked back down the southern meadows toward Diablo, Philip began writing the first sections of "Sourdough Mountain Lookout," though what he came up with would not have that title for some time, and was not even yet in the shape of a poem, just some seed-lines that felt alive—"scattered fragments and pebbles and slobber and God knows what," as he later described them.

> I had a lot of bits and pieces that came in different moments and it wasn't until much later that I started figuring out what to put in between. It was just like any other poem, you get certain things down. . . . I just kept writing stuff that was all about the mountain, and it wasn't until I watched Allen [Ginsberg] getting the poem ["Howl"] ready for printing—he was busy nailing this thing together, and I think that that got me started looking at this "Sourdough Mountain" material to see what I could do with all that.

As August faded slowly to September, Philip was still in the lookout, with no immediate prospect of coming down. The mountains by then were all tawny grays and parched tans and the fire danger was very high, although in the end no fires broke out on the Upper Skagit. Philip hadn't been in the mountains this late in his other years. September had a different feel. The blossoms were gone from the wildflowers and the vast humming insect life of the mountain had finally ceased to throb. The heather had died back to a bloomless brown. The snow that had persisted on the ridge until late August was nearly gone and he had to hike quite a ways out to the last shrinking ponds to draw his water. He was seeing a lot of migrating raptors, which he hadn't noticed so much in other years—goshawks and Cooper's hawks swooping and tumbling in pairs over Diablo Lake, or diving down straight off a head wind after prey in the valley of Sourdough Creek. Reading in his bunk in the morning with his head even with the window sill he might turn to see a hawk hovering just thirty or forty feet out from the lookout ledge, close enough to watch its individual feathers rippling as it adjusted its wings in the air current.

Philip savored these final days, lying naked on the rock outside the lookout, feeling the mountain sun burning into him from head to toe as he lazily read the cosmologies of Heraclitus and Empedocles, reading and snoozing alternately in a pleasant intellectual trance.

At sundown on Sourdough, Philip could look down the Skagit and see his old mountain from two summers before, Sauk, a tiny hump in the Western mist. At night on Sauk, there had been many signs of human activity, lonely but alive, from the plaintive car headlights moving along the Skagit Road at the foot of the mountain all the way out to the town lights of Anacortes and the lighthouses and flashing buoys on the Sound. On Sourdough there was none of that. Diablo, at the steep southern base of the mountain, was not visible from the summit, only the crescent of lights along the top of the dam.

North of the lookout there had been, during July and August, campfires twinkling at the fishing camps at the mouth of Big Beaver Creek, or across the lake at Roland Point, but no more. The only other light besides his own was the fragile pinprick of light in Desolation Lookout; Crater L.O. was empty, the mountain dark. The night sky was dazzling with the cold blue winter constellations on the rise, and the aurora borealis "shimmying" hugely over British Columbia. Philip had to admit that after all his mountaintop solitude, he was still somewhat afraid of the dark, and didn't like to stray too far from the lookout. He could hear his father's voice, driven by "Ireland's fear of unknown holies," telling him: "Remember smart-guy there's always something/Bigger something smarter than you."

Philip thought a lot about his father on Sourdough, and his mother also. Lookout solitude was always conducive to memory; never more so than in '55. He experienced long reveries of growing up in The Dalles and his childhood visits to Portland. All night long the wind blew down from Canada, pounding on the north side windows. Philip sat close by the woodstove and worked by candles and lantern on an autobiographical prose piece called "Visiting," about a young fellow named Sam Rafferty (Whalen thinly disguised), who was "always traveling and never felt that he belonged anywhere in particular." From August 29th until September 5th he wrote 7,000 words of "Visiting," full of vivid detail of his childhood and adolescence in The Dalles and Portland.

As for the present, Whalen planned to leave Seattle and move down to the Bay Area once again.

Diablo Dam at Night, August 1998.

Twice before he had tried to make a go of it in San Fran; with the exception of the time he'd lived with Gary on Montgomery Street, he had not been able to establish himself there. He hoped this time would be different.

A week after Labor Day, Philip was still in the lookout. He had been on the mountain for two solid months, longer by more than two weeks than either he or Gary in any of their other fire seasons. It was cold. At night he lay in his sleeping bag fully dressed, listening to the ticking feet of mice scampering across the lookout floor with some tiny flake of captured food. In the mornings, making his way to the privy, which was hidden away in a clump of alpine fir on a ledge below the lookout, Philip saw his boot-prints in the outhouse trail, the tread-pattern stamped in the dust along with the hooves of deer and paws of bear and marmot. On the 12th, Marblemount finally called, telling him to pack out the next day. In the morning he was ready to go. A rosy, mile-thick fog ran down from Hozomeen to Gorge Creek—"The gorgeous death of summer in the east." A half inch of ice slid from the storm shutters when he dropped them down to close the lookout. A coyote yipped out along the ridge. Before heading off, Philip picked up a rock from outside the cabin door and stowed it in his pack—a rough, hand-sized, honey-colored flake of gneiss with a vein of quartz running in it.

> *. . . some of the quartz*
> *Stained by its matrix*
> *Practically indestructible*
> *A shift from opacity to brilliance*
> *(The Zenbos say, "Lightning-flash & flint-spark")*
> *Like the mountains where it was made*

He packed down the steep, switchbacking southern trail, the fog burning off ahead of him as the sun climbed over Sourdough. Four hours later he came down steeply out of the woods onto the suddenly flat ground at Diablo, walked past the great humming Diablo Powerhouse and its futuristic transformers and cable stanchions, over to the City Light bungalows with their ratcheting lawn sprinklers and finally to the gray Forest Service Guard Station. He dropped his rucksack and, as soon as he checked in and picked up his mail, stretched out on the cool, soft grass outside to wait for his ride back to Marble-mount.

There was a letter from Gary waiting for him, postmarked Berkeley and beginning "Cher Maitre." Gary had just recently returned to Berkeley after his summer in Yosemite. Philip read the letter sprawled out on the guard station grass with his head propped against his rucksack, while he waited for the Forest Service truck. Gary said that after his job with the Park Service trail crew had ended, he had trekked solo for ten days along the Pacific Crest, mostly off-trail, from the Minarets in the Ritter Range down to the headwaters of the Kern River in Sequoia. Now, he was home from the Sierra, pleasantly ensconced in his Hillegass hojo. Having heard rumors that Philip might be moving back to the Bay Area, Gary offered him the floor of the shack when he hit town. ("Gary's tiny doghouse," Whalen later described it.)

"Now if this is true, and I hope it is," wrote Gary, "you must come as soon as possible, because you are scheduled to read some of your own poetry at a reading to be given at the Six Gallery on the first Friday in October."

Philip did not hang around the ranger station once he got to Marblemount. He cleaned up at the barracks—first hot shower since the Fourth of July—and picked up his back pay at the fire office. Because he had been on lookout for so long, no one asked him to stay around for any trail work, and by the next afternoon Philip was in Seattle, clearing out his few belongings from Harry Lamley's place on Roosevelt Way and shipping them on to Berkeley ahead of him. By the 19th he was in downtown Portland, staying two nights in the Congress Hotel, visiting with old friends from Reed, raiding Powell's bookshop with his Forest Service pay. From his hotel window he could see the black iron of the Burnside Bridge spanning the Willamette, but he still felt "on the mountain." From the hotel he wrote Gary that he would be arriving in Berkeley on the twenty-first. He read Gary's letter about the upcoming poetry event over again with keen interest and amazement. "There will also be poets Philip Lamantia, and a person named Allen Ginsberg whom I met recently," Gary said, "—and others & me, & Kenneth Rexroth will do the introductions and such. I think it will be a poetickal bombshell."

Philip wrote Gary that he would be arriving around midnight. "Unroll the velvet carpets," he said in closing.

Who came to the reading?
Millions of people.

Philip Whalen to Anne Waldman

A Remarkable Collection of Angels

San Francisco and Berkeley, Fall 1955

A T THE SAME TIME Phil Whalen was packing down from Sourdough, Jack Kerouac—3,500 miles south—was pulling out of Mexico City on a *segunda clase* bus, to begin the dusty, thousand-mile ride north to the U.S. border at Juárez. He too was on his way to Berkeley. Kerouac had been in Mexico City since the end of July, living in a small adobe washerwoman's shanty atop a two-story apartment building at 210 Orizaba Street in Colonia Roma, a quiet residential neighborhood south of Glorieta Insurgentes. This 1955 sojourn in Mexico was Kerouac's fourth since first discovering the country in May 1950, on a visit to his friend William Burroughs. Since that 1950 trip, Mexico City had become the southern node and way station on the "immense triangular

William Burroughs's apartment at Calle Orizaba, 210 Colonia Roma, Mexico City, 1995. Much of the Beat Generation passed through these doors in the early and mid-1950s: Burroughs and his wife Joan Vollmer, Kerouac, Neal Cassady, Lucien Carr, Gregory Corso, Allen Ginsberg, Peter and Lafcadio Orlovsky. Kerouac wrote Doctor Sax *here in 1952 and the first part of* Tristessa *in 1955. Burroughs wrote his first two novels,* Junky *and* Queer, *while living here.*

arc" of Kerouac's back-and-forth wanderings between New York and San Francisco. Now for the eighth time in as many years, he was headed for California, this time to see his old friend Allen Ginsberg.

In his backpack on the seat beside him as he rolled north out of Mexico City, Kerouac had two fresh manuscripts—the first half of the novella *Tristessa,* based on his recent infatuation with the drug-gaunt but beautiful Esperanza Villanueva; and 150 poems of the "divine and divinely strange" *Mexico City Blues,* written during a two-week stretch in mid-August.

Mexico City had always been a productive environment for Kerouac the writer, providing him with both literary material and what was, for him, a conducive working atmosphere: creative solitude, anonymity, a highly favorable exchange rate for his limited U.S. dollars, cheap rent, accessible drugs, sex when he felt like it, for a few pesos. His rollicking 1950 visit to the city had furnished the perfect backdrop for the culminating action of *On the Road*—"the great and final wild uninhibited Fellahin-childlike city that we knew we would find at the end of the road," he called it.

William Burroughs—Jack's Mexico City host for his early visits—snorted that Kerouac was laboring under "some staggering misconceptions" about Mexico and Mexicans. In a 1951 letter, he informed Jack: "Mexico is not simple or gay or idyllic. . . . It is an Oriental country that reflects 2000 years of disease and poverty and degradation and stupidity and slavery and brutality and psychic and physical terror-ism. Mexico is sinister and gloomy and chaotic with the special chaos of a dream. I like it myself, but it isn't everybody's taste. . . . And don't expect to find anything like Lowell down here," added Burroughs, referring to Kerouac's hometown of Lowell, Massachusetts.

But Kerouac *did* find reminders of Lowell in Mexico (as he did almost everywhere he ever went). For one thing, he saw in Mexico a brand of Catholicism more uninhibitedly devout than any religion he had encountered since the French-Canadian parishes of his New England boyhood. Mexico's popula-tion was more than ninety percent Roman Catholic: for Kerouac, it was like being back in St. Louis de France grade school in his old Centralville neighborhood. Mexicans crossed themselves and even gen-uflected on the street when passing the always open doors of a church; inside, *penitentes* wept openly before statues of patron saints or followed the Stations of the Cross on their knees, conjuring for Kerouac memories of the French-Canadian women who did the same thing at the Grotto of Our Lady of Lourdes on the banks of Lowell's Northern Canal. In Mexico, images of the Virgin of Guadalupe—

La Patrona—were everywhere: posters of her leaned over the grilles of every *fonda,* to bless the food and protect the cooks; her scapulars swung with rosary beads from the rear-view mirrors of buses and careening taxicabs, votive candles flickered before her icons from the lonely roadside *capillas* of the Sierra Madres to the crib cells of the whores on Panama Street.

Despite Burroughs's admonitions about Jack's faulty Mexican notions, Kerouac had turned such images and associations to good creative use in *On the Road, Visions of Cody, Doctor Sax, Tristessa,* as he would later in *Desolation Angels, Orizaba Blues,* and *Cerrada de Medellín Blues,* all composed wholly or in part in Mexico City's Colonia Roma—one of the most fertile locales in Kerouac's artistic life. Now, with *Mexico City Blues,* he had, in this most Catholic of countries, produced his first full-fledged Buddhist work.

Rolling north through the "hard Durangos and impossible Chihuahuas" on his Mexican bus ride, Jack soared with the elation and almost orgasmic self-belief that always surged in him with the completion of new work. He was enormously proud of *Mexico City Blues.* Though the three small breast-pocket notebooks containing the new poems fit easily in the palm of one hand, Jack felt giddier than if he'd been hefting the Treasure of the Sierra Madre. "I have just knocked off 150 bloody poetic masterpieces," he informed Allen Ginsberg. To his agent in New York, Jack confidently predicted: "*Mexico City Blues* . . . will do for poetry what my prose has done, eventually change it into a medium for Lingual Spontaneity. . . ." Finally, on his last day in Mexico City, he wrote to Malcolm Cowley, his editor at Viking: "I'm not doing a pitch for Kerouac," he said, referring to himself in the third person, as though he had somehow gone beyond himself, "he doesn't need it anymore, he is walking around in ecstasy because his entire life-work is beginning to shape up and he knows that all of it . . . is holy and was a well done thing."

Though banged out in a spell of only two weeks, Kerouac's new blues were the culmination of years of working to make himself into a poet, an identity he had secretly assumed for himself as far back as his late teens. In 1941, not yet twenty, he had told himself: ". . . all poets like to kick, and this one here, Jack Kerouac, wants to kick in an original manner," but it would be another dozen years before he began to find his own "original kick" in the spontaneous and fleeting form of the blues, beginning with "Richmond Hill Blues" in September 1953, with its succinct credo:

Say what you mean

A poem is a lark

A pie

For two years he practiced—"woodshedding" like a jazzman in obscurity—building up his stamina and style through "Richmond Hill Blues" and "San Francisco Blues" until he could be as spontaneously deliberate as a saxophone soloist "blowing a long blues in an afternoon jam," as he described himself in his prefatory note to *Mexico City Blues*. All the while he expanded his themes and consolidated his expression until he found the fourteen pale blue lines of a single spiral notebook page to be the concisest canvas for his poetic statements. "My ideas vary," he explained, "and sometimes roll from chorus to chorus or from halfway through a chorus to halfway into the next."

Though the poems of *Mexico City Blues* must have been composed fairly quickly—about ten a day for two weeks—and were all written under the influence of one drug or another, they exhibit an extraordinary control. In the notebooks in which he composed *Mexico City Blues,* Jack's choruses are hand-lettered line by line, precisely, without erasures, outcrossings, or marginal additions.

Tucked down in his rucksack along with his precious stash of new writings was another sort of trove —three months' supply of Benzedrine, codeine, and Seconal from Mexico City *farmacias*—"for excitement, for sleep or for contemplation and when in Rome . . ." In addition to being a creative locale for him, Mexico had increasingly become a place for Jack to indulge his proclivity for drugs; that many U.S. prescription drugs could be bought legally over the counter in Mexico—not to mention the availability of marijuana, peyote, and hard drugs—was one of the main draws of the country.

For years, Kerouac had used drugs to summon the Muse, but nowhere more so than in Mexico City. In 1952, staying with Burroughs at 210 Orizaba, Jack had smoked pot nonstop while composing *Doctor Sax;* he also took peyote during the same period, which gave him "a charge like a high Benny drive," as he reported to his old New York friend the writer John Clellon Holmes. "I have now an irrational lust to set down everything I know . . . when I am an old man or ready to die, will be calm like the center of whirlpools and Beethoven's quartets . . . but at this time in my life I'm making myself sick to find the wild form that can grow with my wild heart. . . "

Bill Garver's room at Calle Orizaba 212, where Kerouac wrote Mexico City Blues *in August 1955.*
Colonia Roma, Mexico City, 1994. "His room had windows opening on the very sidewalk of
Mexico. . . . From the street you saw his pink drapes, looking like the drapes of a Persian pad, or
like a Gypsy's Room — inside you saw the battered bed sinking in the middle, itself covered with
a pink drape . . ." Jack Kerouac, *Desolation Angels*

Increasingly, Jack turned to drugs to supercharge his natural spontaneity. He stayed high on marijuana—"Miss Green" as he affectionately called it—the whole time he was in Mexico. But along with Miss Green there were the "other maids of honor"—his various uppers and downers, and occasionally even an injection of morphine. More and more, Jack was willing to ignore the physical dangers of his drug use for the sake of the potent creative states they fostered. Drugs and writing had become an accepted equation. "Came to Mexico to study Madame Green and dance with Mustapha Fustapha Fearcrow [morphine]," Jack wrote to Ginsberg. "Result: MEX CITY BLUES & Long Short Story." Years later, in an interview for *The Paris Review,* he would explain how he had written some of his Mexican poems, one line an hour, "high on a dose of M."

Kerouac wrote *Mexico City Blues* while sitting with Bill Garver, an elderly addict whom Jack had known from Times Square in the 1940s. Garver lived next door to Kerouac at 212 Orizaba, in a tiny street-level room, cool and dim, with one large sidewalk-facing window barred with ornate iron grilling and magazine prints of works by Orozco and Siqueiros taped to the wall above his bed. Garver, in his early sixties and a junkie for thirty years, had "retired" on a small family trust fund to Mexico, where morphine was cheaper and more easily obtainable than in New York and the police were uninterested in a reclusive old gringo such as himself. Garver spent his days lolling in bed, high, puttering about in his pajamas, or dozing over H. G. Wells's *Outline of History.* In two years he would be dead.

Kerouac ran errands for Garver, including scoring for him, and also kept the old man company in his frequent junk sicknesses. Jack did this out of compassion for a helpless character from the old days certainly; but also, Garver incongruously reminded Kerouac of his own cancer-dying father, whom Jack had tended in his last days. "I knew at my age, 34, were better to help an old man than to gloat in lounges," wrote Kerouac in *Desolation Angels.* "I thought of my father, how I helped him to the toilet when he was dying in 1946." Also, of course, there was Jack's literary curiosity. Sitting with Garver gave him a view of drug life that he knew would be grist for his own writing no matter how it played out. Moreover, Garver was a well-read man, who spouted snatches from *The Epic of Gilgamesh* and Herodotus along with junkie jargon. Now and then, bits of his conversation seeped into some of Jack's choruses:

Have to buy a couple needles
tomorrow, feels like
Shovin a nail in me

. . .

Nothin a junkey likes better
Than sittin quietly with a new shot
And knows tomorrow's plenty more

In 1955, Jack still had the physical constitution to absorb the various pharmaceutical ups and downs, not to mention prodigious amounts of alcohol. His inner systems would take it for several more years before capitulating. He was still functioning brilliantly, artistically at least, but the grueling routine of creative effort and constant drugging was taking its toll. Judgment Day was looming, and Jack could sense it. On the eve of his departure from Mexico City, he was startled by a glimpse of himself in the candlelit mirror on the wall of his rooftop hut, with "mad sick eyes, four or five of them swimming in a spectre. . . "

"I'm driving myself crazy Miss Greening," he admitted to Allen Ginsberg in a letter just before he left town. "I don't know what I'm doing or where I am."

AT CIUDAD JUÁREZ, Jack crossed back into the States, trudging over the bridge spanning the muddy Rio Grande with his bulky, low-slung army rucksack, passing through customs and onto the hot streets of El Paso, no longer even a gringo, but a perfect nobody—"the greatest unpublished writer in America." Indeed, by September 1955, Kerouac had completed six novels (nine counting his earlier "juvenilia"), but only one book had seen print, *The Town and the City,* published five years before in what seemed like a previous creative life, before he'd fully hit his stride with "Spontaneous Prose." Since then, he'd completed *On the Road, Visions of Cody, Doctor Sax, Maggie Cassidy,* and *The Subterraneans,* all at that point languishing on various editors' desks back in New York. *On the Road* alone had been rejected at Harcourt, Brace, Farrar-Straus, Dutton, Knopf, and Viking—although Viking was taking a second serious look at it, and would eventually publish it, but only after much prodding by Malcolm Cowley.

Glass Casket Christ, Church of Santa María la Redonda, Colonia Guerrero, Mexico City, 1994. "The last day I'm in Mexico, I'm in the little church near Redondas in Mexico City . . . and there He is, they've put on Him a handsome face like young Robert Mitchum and have closed His eyes in death tho one of them is slightly open you think and it also looks like young Robert Mitchum or Enríque high on tea looking at you thru the smoke and saying 'Hombre, man, this is the end." Jack Kerouac, *"Mexico Fellaheen"*

Making his way out to the Southern Pacific railyards, he hopped a westbound freight train, 800 miles to Los Angeles. From L.A., he caught another train north, the Zipper, on which he shared a car with an old hobo whom he later immortalized as "the little Saint Theresa bum" in *The Dharma Bums* (because the man had shown him a Saint Theresa prayer card). Jack rode the Zipper, or "Midnight Ghost," as the old tramp called it, as far as Santa Barbara, where he camped overnight on the beach. The next morning he switched to hitchhiking on nearby Highway 101, almost immediately landing one of the greatest rides of his life: a road rat's dream ride in a top-down Lincoln convertible, driven by a gorgeous blond California girl in strapless bathing suit—another scene made famous in the opening chapters of *The Dharma Bums*.

When he arrived in San Francisco, Kerouac spent his first night relaxing in a Skid Row hotel. The next day he caught the train to Berkeley, to move in with Allen Ginsberg, who, at twenty-nine, had recently enrolled at UC Berkeley. Ginsberg's place was a small brown-shingled bungalow, secluded behind a larger main house on Milvia Street, a few blocks north of University Avenue and the old F Train line to San Francisco. It was separated from an adjacent schoolyard by a high wood plank fence overgrown with blackberry brambles, string beans, and daisies. The saggy wood porch had vines curling up the posts and a rocking chair waiting to be rocked in. Kerouac immediately fell in love with the place, calling it "my hermitage" and a "rose-covered cottage"—his inner codewords for an archetypal home place. There were even fruit trees growing in Allen's yard, bearing apricots and plums. In his journal, Jack vowed, "Someday I'll buy that cottage at 1624 Milvia." Ginsberg was out when Kerouac first arrived, but Jack made himself at home, blasting Bach's *St. Matthew Passion* on Allen's Webcore Hi-Fi and pulling down a copy of Céline's *Guignol's Band* from the well-stocked bookshelves. So began the new season.

At that time, Kerouac and Ginsberg had known each other for twelve years, since meeting at Columbia University in late 1943. Like Snyder and Whalen, they were fellow writers, occasional housemates, ardent and prolific correspondents. Already by 1955 Ginsberg peopled four of Kerouac's books: as the "curiously exalted" Leon Levinsky of *The Town and the City*, "the sorrowful poetic con-man" Carlo Marx of *On the Road*, the horn-rimmed hipster "Irwin Garden" in *Visions of Cody*, and the lecherous Adam Moorad in *The Subterraneans*. Ginsberg and Kerouac had been bound for years in a powerful homoerotic Shadow-Brother relationship in which they wrestled like biblical siblings for one another's blessing. At their best, they were true Whitmanesque *camerados,* sticking by each other no matter what; at their worst, they were petty and sickeningly envious of each other. In September 1955 they had not seen each other for two years, though they had been in regular correspondence concerning their adventures, mutual friends, Buddhism, and writing.

Ginsberg had first come to California in the spring of 1954, carrying a glowing letter of introduction to Kenneth Rexroth from William Carlos Williams, Allen's mentor since 1950. As early as 1952, Ginsberg had sent Rexroth some of his poems at the suggestion of Williams, so Rexroth was not entirely unfamiliar with him. By June 1954 Ginsberg was attending Rexroth's Friday night readings, where he met the poets Robert Duncan, Lawrence Ferlinghetti, and many others, and reacquainted himself with Philip Lamantia (he'd met Lamantia four years before in New York).

During the same August weeks of 1955 that Kerouac was writing *Mexico City Blues* in Bill Garver's room on Orizaba Street, Ginsberg composed the first part of "Howl." He wrote the first draft while living at 1010 Montgomery Street in North Beach, just two blocks south of Snyder and Whalen's old apartment at the foot of the Montgomery steps. Shortly after, Ginsberg moved from San Francisco to Berkeley, where he enrolled in a master's English program with the Yeats scholar Tom Parkinson, a friend of Rexroth's from the 1940s. When Kerouac arrived at Milvia Street in mid-September, he had already seen "Howl." Ginsberg had mailed a first draft to him in Mexico City as soon as it was finished. Jack thought it was "great wild poetry . . . like Jewish prophets of Old." But Kerouac did not yet know about the Six Gallery event that was brewing.

On September 2, Ginsberg had moved to his Milvia Street cottage. On the 8th, he called on Snyder at the suggestion of Kenneth Rexroth, and recruited him for the upcoming gallery reading. Snyder accepted the invitation, and at the same time showed Ginsberg some of Philip Whalen's recent poems; on the basis of these, Whalen was added to the roster along with Ginsberg, Snyder, Philip Lamantia, and Michael McClure. Gary also suggested that Rexroth should be Master of Ceremonies, in recognition of his position as San Francisco's elder poet, and Allen agreed.

"A bearded interesting Berkeley cat name of Snyder," wrote Ginsberg in his journal after meeting Gary, ". . . studying oriental and leaving in a few months on some privately put up funds to go be a Zen monk (a real one). He's a head, peyotlist, laconist, but warmhearted, nice looking with a little beard, thin blond, rides a bicycle in Berkeley in red corduroy and levis and hungup on indians . . . "

Ginsberg and Snyder met again a few days later to further plan the reading and share some more of their poems. Allen also told Gary more about his friend Kerouac who was by that time en route to Berkeley from Mexico City. At that point, Ginsberg, having heard from Jack about *Mexico City Blues,* was hoping that Kerouac would read some of his work at the Six Gallery. Snyder in turn told Ginsberg more about Whalen, who was also on his way and would soon be arriving. Both Allen and Gary agreed that they should all go to the first possible soirée at Kenneth Rexroth's as soon as everyone was in town.

The quartet of poets first got together on September 23rd, a Friday evening, the regular night for Rexroth's salon. Gary was bringing Philip to Rexroth's for the first time, and Allen was bringing Jack. They met in San Francisco, outside the Key Terminal, on First and Mission, where the old F train came into town across the Bay Bridge. "Jack and Allen had just come over from Berkeley, and I was with Gary," remembers Whalen, "Jack was wearing a red windbreaker jacket, smoking a cigarette, looking very James Dean, handsome and gloomy. He liked me right away, because I reminded him of somebody from Lowell."

Before heading out to Rexroth's they first went for some beers at The Place, the epicentric watering hole of the North Beach scene, above Union Street on Telegraph Hill. From the station, their route took them up through Chinatown, under the green-tiled Bush Street gate with its auspicious golden serpents and copper-scaled fish. It was the first night of the fall. The autumnal equinox had occurred just that afternoon. They walked up the long grade of Grant Avenue, under red-and-green flying eaves and red iron balconies and a hundred flashing Chinese neon signs. At every cross street, the view was the same up and down the hill for blocks on end—people swarming, bakeries wafting the aromas of lotus buns and moon cakes on the early evening fog, restaurants sending out whiffs of rice and beef, butcher shop windows with red-gold pig's heads and rows of glazed ducks hanging upside-down, tiny shops selling lichee jelly and ginger candy, deer's tail, shark liver oil, ginseng.

The four hit it off immediately, especially Gary and Jack. Gary liked Kerouac's "affable clarity, and funny little phrasings. I could see right away that he was smart and an original."

From The Place the four made their way out to Rexroth's. "There was a great room, great chambers with high ceilings and a very luxurious feeling of space, and a lot of chairs and tables and a vast library," recalls Whalen. Snyder and Ginsberg had been frequent participants in Rexroth's Friday gatherings for more than a year. Somehow their paths had never crossed before. Now everyone was coming together so smoothly, as though under the gathering influence of a literary force majeure.

Although Rexroth had never met Kerouac or Whalen in person before that night, he had been made aware of their works through the enthusiasms of Snyder and Ginsberg. Earlier in the year Gary had read several of Philip's poems to the salon, and as far back as 1954 Allen had been showing Jack's work to Rexroth, including large chunks of *Visions of Cody*. Rexroth was tremendously impressed with Kerouac's writing.

That night at Rexroth's, Jack gave a mesmerizing reading of a section from "October in the Railroad Earth." As Kerouac read aloud, the rhythm of the prose reminded Snyder of something he had come across back in the spring, a piece in the *New World Writing* anthology called "Jazz of the Beat Generation." It had been the first time Gary had ever heard the term "Beat Generation," and the writing stuck in his head for its energy and evocation of people. "Jazz of the Beat Generation" was indeed Kerouac's but had been published under the nom de plume "Jean-Louis" (his French-Canadian given name, without surname). As Jack read on, it dawned on Gary that Kerouac must be the author from the *New World* collection. "I flashed that *he* was Jean-Louis," says Snyder. "And then I knew he was a truly gifted writer with a new kind of language sense that would change how we wrote prose . . . I really did think all this on first hearing him read."

THE SIX GALLERY was a funky co-op exhibit space, fashioned from the former workbays of an old car repair shop in the Marina of San Francisco by six young painters from the nearby Art Institute. At the time, Ginsberg referred to it as "a rundown second-rate experimental art gallery." For the reading, Michael McClure remembers that "someone had knocked together a little dais" and that on the wall behind the platform were "pieces of orange crates that had been swathed in muslin and dipped in plaster of paris to make splintered, sweeping shapes like pieces of surrealist furniture."

Six battered upholstered chairs were arranged for the poets in a semi-circle about ten feet behind the podium, which, like the wall sculptures, was also constructed of fruit crates, and was not quite high enough. Kenneth Rexroth—in a cutaway Goodwill tux—walked up to it as the night began and remarked that it looked to have been built for "a midget who was going to recite *The Iliad* in haiku form." "Purely amateur and goofy," Ginsberg would later write. Kerouac sat alone on the edge of the stage, back to the readers, his finger crooked in the neck-hook of a gallon jug of Casanova Red.

To Lawrence Ferlinghetti, the Six Gallery seemed like a tiny space; McClure remembers it as "a huge room." Estimates of the attendance vary from a low of seventy-five to upwards of 250, but everyone agrees that the place *felt* packed. "A surprisingly large number of people had showed up," says Gary Snyder. "Far more than we had expected, and the mood was excellent, so it turned into a real social event as well as an artistic event."

"The Six Gallery reading was open to the world and the world was welcome," wrote McClure. "There were poets and Anarchists and Stalinists and professors and painters and bohemians and visionaries and idealists and grinning cynics." Taken together, the crowd comprised a remarkable cross section of the burgeoning Bay Area counterculture, a fitting audience — and constituency — for the "remarkable collection of angels on one stage" that Ginsberg and Gary had promised on the invitation.

THE SIX GALLERY reading has sometimes been called the first synthesis of the East and West Coast factions of the Beat Generation. Certainly, the event was significant for the merging of regional energies, which at the time were experienced much more keenly than today. Recall that less than two years before the reading, Snyder, in his first letter to Kenneth Rexroth, had predicted a dominantly West Coast future for American poetry, saying "I doubt much good poetry will come from East the Rockies." Until the Six Gallery event, Kerouac and Ginsberg, for all their travels, had felt equally chauvinistic, only from a New York perspective. "We thought the *West* Coast was dead!" their characters say in *The Dharma Bums.*

In geographical terms, Ginsberg was clearly the urban, East Coast figure among the readers, Snyder and Whalen the exemplars of the West. McClure, although a Kansas native, had acquired an abiding love of Pacific Northwest nature from living six years of his boyhood in Seattle. Philip Lamantia, of the five readers, was at that point the only truly bi-coastal character, and had been so for more than a decade. He was a native son of San Francisco's Mission District, but Surrealism had taken him to New York when he was only sixteen years old. Turned on to the paintings of Miró and Dalí in exhibits at the San Francisco Museum of Art when he was but fourteen, he had begun to write poems, and had been accepted for publication in the prestigious Surrealist magazines *View* and *VVV.* André Breton — the

"Pope" of surrealism — had anointed him "a voice that rises once in a hundred years." Young Lamantia had then gone to New York to meet Breton, Max Ernst, Yves Tanguy, and other European Surrealists who had fled to New York to escape the Nazis. With Charles Henri Ford and Parker Tyler, American poets influenced by Breton, Lamantia eventually coedited *View,* and by the age of eighteen was considered "among the finest non-French Surrealists."

So Lamantia led off the reading. It seemed appropriate that Philip should be at the top of the order. After World War II when the Surrealists in New York exile had returned to Europe, Lamantia had come back to San Francisco and, with Rexroth and the poet Robert Duncan, helped found the Anarchist "Libertarian Circle"— one of the earliest expressions of the Berkeley–San Francisco Renaissance of the late 1940s. With Duncan out of the country at the time of the Six Gallery Reading, and Rexroth taking the role of the evening's "Master of Ceremonies," Lamantia was the only reader on stage representing that Renaissance.

There were other reasons why Lamantia made a fitting initiator for the night's reading. For one thing, he knew more of his fellow poets on stage, and had known them for longer, than anyone else. He had first met Allen Ginsberg in 1950, when they were introduced by Carl Solomon at the San Remo Bar in New York. Five years before that, Ginsberg had taken note of Lamantia's poems in *VVV* and been astounded to the point of envy. He would include Lamantia in the dramatis personae of "Howl"— as having seen "Mohammedan angels staggering on tenement roofs illuminated"— a reference to a 1953 vision Lamantia had related to him.

Lamantia also knew Michael McClure from the poetry soirées of both Rexroth and Robert Duncan, and shared a deep interest with McClure in the physical mysticism of Antonin Artaud. Lamantia had even once met and talked, albeit briefly, with Whalen outside North Beach's Black Cat Café, around 1952. Only Gary Snyder was completely unknown to him on the night of the reading.

Yet it was with Snyder that Lamantia shared the most common ground. Of the poets, they were the only two native San Franciscans (the hospital where Gary was born was just eight blocks south of the Six Gallery), and, despite their greatly differing poetic styles, Snyder and Lamantia were also the only two of the readers who really considered Rexroth a mentor. Lamantia, at age seventeen, had been Rexroth's earliest protégé. In those days, Philip not only attended Rexroth's Friday night poetry salon but often stayed on at Rexroth's house for whole weekends. "I used to have endless conversations with him. Rexroth was, I tell you, a whole academy," says Lamantia. Fifty years later, Philip would still call him "Rex"— King. Gary also acknowledged Rexroth as "a great mentor, a great, *driving* mentor."

Snyder and Lamantia shared other interests as well — anarchism, pacifism, peyote, Native American folktales and anthropology, and the outdoors. As a teenager, Philip had often backpacked in the San Bruno hills south of San Francisco where he sensed the ghosts of the Ohlone (Costanoan) people who had venerated the owls in the redwoods before the Spanish came. No less so than Gary, Philip had delved into the texts and myths of native peoples, ultimately taking part in "the Tipi Way" of the Washo tribe near Lake Tahoe and the tobacco ritual of the Cora Indians of Mexico's western mountains.

For all of this, Lamantia on the night of the Six did not read from his own work, but from the poems of his friend the late John Hoffmann — a postwar Boho legend rumored to have died in Mexico from a rare overdose of peyote. Almost nothing is known now, or was even then, about John Hoffmann. What immortality has attached to his name is largely the result of Lamantia's reading of his poems that night. But who was Hoffmann, and what were his poems that led off the famous reading? In the late 1940s and early 1950s in New York, Hoffmann had been something of a mythic underground character. Burroughs had mentioned him in his 1953 novel *Junky,* and he was also a minor character in Kerouac's *The Subterraneans.* Hoffmann's shade hung in the smoke of the Six Gallery, one of Ginsberg's "best minds" destroyed by various madnesses. In "Howl," John Hoffmann was one of those who "got busted in their pubic beards returning through Laredo with a belt of marijuana for New York," and it was Hoffmann who finally "disappeared into the volcanoes of Mexico leaving behind nothing but the shadow of dungarees and the lava and ash of poetry. . . "

Hoffmann was a Californian from Menlo Park who went east in 1949. In Greenwich Village he became friends with Carl Solomon, Gerd Stern, Gregory Corso, and other figures of what would soon be dubbed the Beat Scene. Allen Ginsberg had met him on a few occasions in New York and recalled that he was "reputed to be one of the most intelligent people, an apocalyptic, and poet. He said very little, was not surly, though, just very silent and too gone hipwise to talk." According to Carl Solomon, he was "blonde, handsome, bespectacled," and had a "spaced-out quality that amused many people." Though he had never published a single poem, in his lifetime or posthumously, Hoffmann was highly regarded as a poet by avant-garde connoisseurs.

Lamantia read from the twenty-nine short poems that Hoffmann had left behind under the title *Journey to the End*. Hoffmann's poems were laconic, metaphorical, surreal, like Lamantia's in their use of alchemical symbols and ornithological imagery, and so sounded good in Philip's "oracular style." Taken together, the poems had the tropical atmosphere of a shipwrecked beach with blinding sands, shrieking carrion crows, armies of ants carrying off a lime tree.

In October 1955 Lamantia had already published one book — *Erotic Poems* (1946) — and had finished most of the work for two other collections. He was considered by many to be one of the leading San Francisco poets. Why then did he choose to read the unknown Hoffmann's work, and none of his own? One explanation is that only a few months before the Six Gallery reading, Lamantia had nearly died in Mexico himself, from a scorpion sting while staying in the remote mountain village of Jésus-María in the western state of Nayarit. In his near-death delirium, Lamantia had cried out for the Virgin Mother to save his life. Ironically, this spiritual outburst shook the atheistic beliefs he'd held since his early teenage years, and over the next months called for a major reevaluation of his life assumptions. "I was going through a crisis of conversion and I couldn't write and I didn't want to read my old poems even though Rexroth said, 'Oh you should get out — All the poems that you wrote before, you can't go on thinking that they were all mortal sins!'" recalls Philip today. "But indeed, I *was* sort of thinking that way — I wanted to withdraw."

In the summer of '55 Lamantia went to a Trappist monastery in Oregon (dedicated to Our Lady of Guadalupe) in his effort to understand his seemingly autonomous reversion to his childhood Catholicism, but by October he was still grappling to make sense of what had happened to him. He had not yet incorporated his new vision into readable poems, and for the time being was unwilling to stand publicly behind his prior work.

Next to read was Michael McClure, the youngest of the poets, then twenty-two years old. Before launching into his own work, McClure first read a letter by the poet Jack Spicer to the painter Johnny Ryan, one of the founders of the Six Gallery. Spicer, also one of the original Six, had subsequently gone East, had run out of money in Boston, and was trying to get back to San Francisco. His letter was an open plea for a job that would allow him to return.

McClure was good friends with Spicer, who, with Robert Duncan, led another poetic salon, across the Bay in Berkeley. Duncan was, after Rexroth, perhaps the Bay Area poet most respected by his peers.

Rexroth himself thought that the San Francisco Renaissance owed "more to Duncan than to any other one person." McClure, although he often attended Rexroth's Friday nights, considered Duncan his foremost mentor.

At the time of the Gallery reading, Duncan was in Majorca, but his presence subtly pervaded the entire event, from the gallery space itself, which he had helped to establish, to the readers whom he had imprinted to varying degrees. While his influence had been decisive for the young McClure, he had also had a profound effect on Philip Lamantia, and made a strong impression on Gary Snyder as well. Certainly had Duncan been in the Bay Area at the time, he would have been invited to share the stage with the others. Whether he would have accepted is another matter.

McClure began reading his own poems, starting with "Point Lobos Animism," a poem "addressed to Artaud, and written from a tidal rock in Whaler's Cove south of Carmel, sinking into the animism of that extraordinarily beautiful and mystical place." McClure also read "Night Words: The Ravishing," "Poem," "The Breech," and "The Mystery of the Hunt"—all nature poems of one sort or another, including city nature. McClure called his words into the smoke of the crowd while prowling along the edge of the gallery stage like Jackson Pollock working with his bucket along the borders of a floored canvas. He closed out his set with a passionate reading of "For the Death of 100 Whales," his own howl at the machine-gunning of scores of killer whales by American soldiers at an arctic NATO base in April 1954.

PHILIP WHALEN NOW came shyly to the stand. Two weeks short of his thirty-second birthday, Philip was the oldest of the readers and the least known, even to the other poets, except for Gary, who had total confidence in him. "Funny and dry, his usual style," says Snyder. "His wit and learning both came across." Whalen followed McClure's Lawrencian cry for the slaughtered orcas with a mock-serious delivery of "Plus Ça Change. . . ," his poem about the couple stuck in a birdcage of a marriage. McClure, who had never seen or heard of Whalen before that night, was taken aback with delight by the contrast between Philip's work and delivery and his own. "As I watched him read," recalled McClure in his memoir of the event, "the meaning of his metamorphic poem gradually began to sink in. We laughed as the poem's intent clarified. . . . You can see them changing into parakeets."

"'For the Death of One Hundred Whales' is this broken ballad, this projective poem, pretty fucking mad," continues McClure. "So then, that was followed up with Phil's incision and depth comedy . . . "When Philip started reading his poetry, I was delighted because I could see it was coming out of Williams, but also out of other things I didn't know about," continues McClure. "It was coming out of a great deal of capriciousness, whimsicality, and scholarship, and also coming out of these cartoons that Philip probably knew even better than I did, being ten years older than me—like Toonerville Trolley, and Smokey Stover, and the Nutt Brothers, [Whalen also read "The Martyrdom of Two Pagans" and "If You're So Smart, Why Ain't You Rich?"] and those poems of his had that strange, strange American quality of humor and incision that those cartoonists of that period had. I loved it. I really enjoyed it a lot. Phil was completely engaging. Then there was the intermission."

AFTER A SHORT BREAK, Allen Ginsberg took the stage. Word had circulated during the break that the unheard-of poet from William Carlos Williams's hometown had a big poem, but Ginsberg's delivery at first was low-key. He had downed quite a bit of wine to take the edge off his stage fright, and as he approached the podium he was a bit drunk, as was a sizeable portion of the crowd, thanks to the Dionysian duo of Kerouac and his drinking buddy Bob Donlin, who, like a couple of Catholic ushers at Mass, had taken up a collection for wine, and made a big liquor store run and kept the jugs circulating throughout the night.

Ginsberg began slowly and carefully so that he wouldn't mess up. Even his soon-to-be-anthemic opening—"I saw the best minds of my generation destroyed by madness"—was tentatively and flatly delivered. Soon, however, Allen felt himself growing surprisingly clear-headed and verbally deft as his long Whitmanesque lines slowly picked up freight-train momentum. He began to breathe with the poem, inhaling like a saxman at the anaphoric head of each line, then projecting the words into the out-stream, the words rolling on until the breath carrying them was spent. Another quick gulp of air, another dive into the words. Allen could see Kerouac seated on the edge of the dais, back to him, facing the audience, nodding and swigging from his wine jug. At some point, Jack began muttering "Yes!" at this or that image; then began punctuating Ginsberg's every line break with an urgent "Go!" as at a jazz jam. Suddenly, Allen raised out his arms in the ancient gesture of the prophets, and felt himself possessed by a "strange ecstatic intensity." From the semi-circle of chairs behind Allen, Michael McClure watched in amazement. Unlike Gary and Phil Whalen, who had read "Howl" during the weeks leading up to the reading and listened to Ginsberg practicing certain passages of it aloud, McClure was totally unprepared for what he was hearing and seeing. On the other hand, Michael had known Allen much longer than they and could appreciate how Ginsberg had been changed by this poem. The last time he'd seen him, Allen had just enrolled at UC Berkeley and was bussing tables at Kip's hamburger joint. Now here he was sounding like the young Shelley reading *Queen Mab* and Michael realized he was witnessing the transformation of Ginsberg "from quiet, brilliant, burning Bohemian scholar trapped by his flames and repressions to epic vocal bard."

Many of Ginsberg's lines were so emotional for him that he had to fight back welling tears, but the electrified audience spurred him on. Not only Kerouac, but many other people also were shouting "Go!" now; by the end of the poem an exuberant chorus of it went up with every new breath Ginsberg drew.

> *. . . and stand before you speechless and intelligent and shaking with shame, rejected yet*
> > *confessing out the soul . . .*
> *the madman bum and angel beat in Time, unknown, yet putting down here what might*
> > *be left to say in time come after death . . .*

When it was over, Ginsberg broke down spent before his transported listeners, his tears now freely running down his face—"tears which restored to American poetry the prophetic consciousness it had lost," he later claimed. For a moment it was completely quiet in the room. Then, from out of the packed crowd Neal Cassady, whom Allen had just proclaimed "secret hero of these poems, cocksman and Adonis of Denver," materialized in his Southern Pacific brakeman's uniform with gold-buttoned vest and watch chain, saying "Allen m'boy, I'm proud of you!" Kerouac, still at the edge of the stage, beamed to see his two great friends basking in this moment of unabashed mutual approval:

"... and when Irwin [one of Kerouac's fictive names for Allen — actually, Ginsberg's real given name, meaning "friend"] had finished howling the last poem and there was a dead silence in the hall it was Cody [Cassady], dressed in his Sunday suit, who stepped up and offered his hand to the poet (his buddy Irwin with whom he'd hitch hiked thru the Texases and Apocalypses of 1947)—I always remember that as a typical humble beautiful act of friendship and good taste—"

Now Rexroth, fighting back tears himself, came over to congratulate Allen. Then everybody swarmed him—Jack, Donlin, Ferlinghetti, all the other readers, shaking Allen's hand, hugging him, pounding him on the back as though he'd just won the game with a towering home run. "Ginsberg . . . left us standing in wonder, or cheering and wondering," wrote Michael McClure, "but knowing at the deepest level that a barrier had been broken, that a human voice and body had been hurled against the harsh wall of America."

THERE WAS MORE to come. After things settled down a bit, Rexroth introduced Gary Snyder. Other than Kerouac, there was probably not another writer in the room who could have refocused the crowd's energies in Ginsberg's cathartic wake. But Snyder did, skillfully guiding his listeners from Allen's Passaic and Harlem river lamentations, to the myths and songs of the Deschutes and the Willamette. From killer Moloch to Coyote the unkillable, the irrepressible Native American anti-hero and survivor. Gary, looking a little like a young D. H. Lawrence in his pointed beard, read "A Berry Feast," and working sections from *Myths and Texts,* which he had titled just a few weeks before and had been adding to right up until the night of the event. He had spent the whole weekend before with all the then-existing pieces of it spread out on his tatami mats, fitting them this way and that, reading them to find their relationships, finally arranging them in the three groups that would become "Logging," "Hunting," and "Burning."

The transition from Ginsberg to Gary could not have been more jarring, beginning with Snyder's look and manner: Allen had read in the dark, rumpled sportcoat and loose-necked tie of an urban intellectual; as he rolled into his poem, his voice rose to carry the continental echoes of North Jersey shuls and Union Square labor rallies. After him, Gary had come to the microphone in Goodwill flannel, denim jeans, and hiking boots and read his lines in a laconic and resonant Northwest drawl—"with heroic firmness and a smile." Yet it was the unlikely blending of their styles on the same platform that was one of the most potent aspects of the Six Gallery reading, signifying as it did a joining of East and West Coast energies on such an unprecedented cultural level.

In the poems he read that night, Snyder conjured Ginsberg's Moloch in his Pacific Rim manifestation: the one whose yellow-snouted Caterpillars had leveled the groves of Cybele to build the suburbs, knocked down the sacred pines of Noh-master Seami, the cedar of the Haidas, and washed the clear-cut hills of old China down to the Yellow Sea—

the sawmill temples of Jehovah
Squat black burners 100 feet high
Sending the smoke of our burnt
Live sap and leaf
To his eager nose.

Coyote, the great trickster, would not only survive the onslaught of Weyerhauser, but would in time prevail. Gary ended his reading with an image of the grinning, panting, mischievous Coyote biding his time on a ledge in the foothills, overlooking a city in the plain:

Dead city in dry summer,
Where berries grow.

It was an apt ending to a night of prophetic verse.

"Save the invitation," Gary told a friend. "Some day it will be worth something."

Great things are done when men and mountains meet
This is not done by jostling in the street.

Blake, *Epigrams*

When Men and Mountains Meet

San Francisco & Berkeley, Fall 1955

THE INVITATION TO the Six Gallery reading had promised a "charming event"; instead, the night had exploded into the "poetickal bombshell" that Gary had predicted to Philip the month before. One of the first results of that bombshell was that all the poets, Rexroth included, were immediately booked for solo readings around town. "From that night on," wrote Gary Snyder many years later, "there was a poetry reading in somebody's pad, or some bar or gallery, every week in San Francisco."

The poets, already doing good creative work on their own in the months leading up to the reading, were now galvanized anew by mutual association and the novelty of an enthusiastic audience. Ginsberg, wildly inspired by the event and goaded on by Lawrence Ferlinghetti's offer to publish "Howl" in his new City Lights Pocket Poets series, went to work at once on the version he'd read, adding Parts II and III and the "Footnote to Howl." Other poems flooded in, all long-lined and memorable: "A Strange New Cottage in Berkeley," "A Supermarket in California," "America." One of Ginsberg's greatest poems, "Sunflower Sutra," was born and banged out in twenty minutes while Kerouac leaned in his doorway, waiting to go drinking.

Snyder too was busy, advancing on three fronts simultaneously. As the autumn progressed, he added more poems to the *Myths and Texts* cycle; he worked on translations of the T'ang Chinese poet Han Shan; and he completed several fine new poems based on his summer trail crew.

In the Yosemite that summer Gary's work had all been rock and dust: building trail and blasting huge granite boulders the size of small houses — it took a half a day sometimes to plant a single charge of TNT, hand-drilling and pounding the stick-hole with a four-pound singlejack hammer. But the brutal labor begat poems — more than a dozen eventually from that one six-week trail-crew stint. "Riprap" and "Milton by Firelight" alone were worth every drop of sweat he'd shed.

Whalen was prolific also. Even before the Six Gallery reading, Philip had been stirred by his initial contacts with Ginsberg, Kerouac, and Rexroth. Just off his nine-week sojourn on Sourdough, into the supercharged atmosphere of the Bay Area poetry scene, Philip had not been the least bit overwhelmed. It was as though he'd been saving himself for just such a historic moment. His poetic voice now rang with confidence and authority. One feels it in "Memorial to the Throne," written a week after his arrival, and dedicated to Jack Kerouac, whom he'd just met.

> *"If they ask you*
> *Whether I'm walkin',*
> *Tell 'em I'm flyin'"*
> *Standing fast in the middle*
> *of the Diamond Silence.*

When he had first come off the mountain, Philip was going around saying that "Poetry is Shit," that he was sick of it —"Let it all die and rot and stink." When Kerouac spoke of a new language, Whalen retorted: "Go to the ant!"

I don't want to hear about it
The Future of American Letters
Or anybody's Letters

But now here he was, writing a new poem every few days.

KEROUAC SUPPORTED the poets on the Six Gallery stage with boisterous cheers on the night of the reading, but his personal opinion of most of them and their works was actually quite ambivalent. Ginsberg had wanted Kerouac to be on the Six Gallery stand with him, but Jack had declined, certainly not from lack of poems or eloquence, for Kerouac was a superb reader with Sinatra-like tone and an innate rhythmic sense. "Allen Ginsberg has arranged for me to read before an audience, but I won't do it because I'm too bashful," Kerouac told his editor Malcolm Cowley shortly after arriving in Berkeley. "Poet ain't court jester, I say."

Stage-shyness was only part of the story. Kerouac was as haughty as he was insecure, and may not have wanted to throw in with the untried bards. At any rate, Kerouac's group portrait of the sextet in *The Dharma Bums,* written two years after the event, is a satiric caricature, brimming with condescension. Ginsberg's poem, which Kerouac calls "Wail" in his account of the reading, was obviously great, but Jack's personal feelings toward Allen were too tangled to allow much real objectivity. Lamantia, McClure, and Whalen he dismissed. Only Snyder, as "Japhy Ryder," stands out as a figure to be taken seriously—"earnest and strong and humanly hopeful" and "the only one who didn't look like a poet, though poet he was indeed."

"The other poets," wrote Jack, "were either hornrimmed intellectual hepcats with wild black hair like Alvah Goldbook [Ginsberg], or delicate pale handsome poets like Ike O'Shay [McClure] (in a suit), or out-of-this-world genteel-looking Renaissance Italians like Francis DaPavia [Lamantia] (who looks like a young priest), or bow-tied wild-haired old anarchist fuds like Rheinhold Cacoethes [Rexroth], or big fat bespectacled quiet booboos like Warren Coughlin [Whalen]." Zeroing in on their work, Kerouac continued: they were "either too dainty in their aestheticism, or too hysterically cynical to hope for anything, or too abstract and indoorsy, or too political, or like Coughlin too incomprehensible. . . "

Kerouac thought that Whalen's poems, which he had heard and read during the days leading up to the Six Gallery event, were "aridly unemotional", about the deadliest flaw a poem could have in Jack's

swer your question so that all the Brotherhood will understand.
As good and pious men and women come to you wishing to
begin the practice of seeking to attain highest perfect Wisdom,
they will simply have to follow what I am about to say to
you, and very soon they will be able to subdue their discrimina-
tive thoughts and craving desires, and will be able to attain
perfect tranquillity of mind.

The Practice of Charity
(The Dana Paramita)

(3) Then the Lord Buddha addressed the assembly. Every
one in the world, beginning with the highest Bodhisattva-Ma-
hasattvas, should follow what I am going to teach you, for
this teaching will bring deliverance to everyone whether hatched
from an egg, or formed in a womb, or evolved from spawn, or
produced by metamorphosis, with or without form, possessing
mental faculties or devoid of mental faculties, or both devoid
and not devoid, or neither devoid nor not devoid, and lead them
toward perfect Nirvana. Though the sentient beings thus to
be delivered by me are innumerable and without limit yet, in
reality, there are no sentient beings to be delivered. And why,
Subhuti? Because should there exist in the minds of Bodhisat-
tva-Mahasattvas such arbitrary conceptions of phenomena as
the existence of one's own ego-selfness, the ego-selfness of an-
other, self-ness as divided into an infinite number of living
and dying beings, or selfness as unified into one Universal
Self existing eternally, they would be unworthy to be called
Bodhisattva-Mahasattvas.

(4) Moreover, Subhuti, the Bodhisattva-Mahasattvas, in teach-
ing the Dharma to others, should first be free themselves from
all the craving thoughts awakened by beautiful sights, pleasant
sounds, sweet tastes, fragrance, soft tangibles, and seductive
thoughts. In their practice of charity, they should not be in-
fluenced by any of these seductive phenomena. And why? Be-
cause, if in their practice of charity they are uninfluenced by
such things they will realize a blessing and merit that is in-
estimable and inconceivable. What think you, Subhuti? Is it
possible to estimate the distance of space in the eastern
heavens?

No, Blessed One! It is im...able to estimate the distance
of space in the eastern heaven... limits of space in the
Subhuti, is it possible to... Or to any of the
northern, southern and w...
four corners of the univ...
No, Honored of th...
Subhuti, it is e...
merit that will...
tices charity...
This truth...
(19) The...
If a d...
treas...

estimation. Though he liked Philip personally and would come to admire his poetry, he did not yet appreciate the dry wit of a poem like "Plus Ça Change. . . ". The week before the gallery event, he had coached Whalen to bolster his own work with some more overtly humorous stuff by Lew Welch.

"Damn you, I told you to read that Welch's prose piece at the reading and you didn't," he wrote Philip three months later. "Listen to me next time, to break the monotony of serious verse you should read that amusing prose. . . ."

A FEW DAYS after the reading, Kerouac made a visit to Gary's Hillegass cottage, where he was amazed to find Snyder living in a style even more Spartan than Thoreau himself. In Walden, Thoreau had made much of his reduction of his cabin's chairs to an essential three —"one for solitude, two for friendship, three for society," but Gary had no chairs at all —"not even one sentimental rocking chair," as Kerouac observed in The Dharma Bums. Nor did Gary own a bed; he slept on a thin foam camping pad covered with a cougar hide. In a famous passage that became a sort of interior decoration guide in the late 1960s, Kerouac described the inside of the fictive Japhy Ryder's cottage based on Gary's hojo.

> In the corner was his famous rucksack with cleaned-up pots and pans all fitting into one another in a compact unit and all tied and put away inside a knotted-up blue bandana. . . . He had a slew of orange crates all filled with beautiful scholarly books, some of them in Oriental languages, all the great sutras, comments on sutras, the complete works of D. T. Suzuki and a fine quadruple-volume edition of Japanese haikus. He also had an immense collection of valuable general poetry. In fact if a thief should have broken in there the only things of real value were the books.

That afternoon, Snyder showed Kerouac the Han Shan poems that he was translating from the Chinese. Snyder was trying to finish his courses in the East Asian program at Berkeley before leaving for Japan, and his Han Shan poems were part of his class work. His instructor in T'ang poetics was, for the fourth time, Ch'en Shih-hsiang. The previous year in Ch'en's class, Gary had ambitiously blocked out

◄ *Kerouac's leather-bound copy of Dwight Goddard's* A Buddhist Bible, *the original scroll manuscript of* The Dharma Bums, *and one of Kerouac's rucksacks.*

translations of Po Chü-i's "Long, Bitter Song" and "Song of the Lute" and had spent many hours with his instructor both arguing and savoring the intricacies of Po's seven-character lines. They had become friends. When he went to Ch'en at the beginning of the fall 1955 semester, Gary was fresh from his solo trek in the Sierras and his summer job in the Yosemite. Ch'en, who had once written some T'ang style poems himself from a rock overlooking Vernal Falls, saw in that landscape the Chinese realm of the Immortals and suggested that Gary might try his hand at translating Han Shan, the legendary back-country hermit-sage of China's misty T'ien Tai mountains.

Han Shan was a T'ang Dynasty folk hero, the archetypal "Zen lunatic." He was said to have been an elusive character who scrawled his poems on precipitous basalt cliffs or the broken walls of forgotten mountain villages. There was a strong flavor of spiritual audacity in Han Shan. "Who can leap the world's ties and sit with me among the white clouds?" he dared; and "My heart's not the same as yours / If your heart was like mine you'd get it and be right here." According to legend, Han Shan would sometimes come down from his mountain hermitage for a meal of leftovers, hobo-like, at the back door of Kuo Ching monastery, where his sidekick, the equally ragged and silly Shih-Te, worked in the kitchen.

Though Han Shan and Shih-Te appeared destitute and perhaps simple-minded, people believed Han Shan to be a Manjusri—an incarnation of the bodhisattva of wisdom—and Shih-Te to be a Samantabhadra, bodhisattva of compassion. And while they are treated as the original Zen lunatic duo, in T'ang China there was already a long tradition of Taoist sage-fools stretching back through Lao Tzu, and beyond, to the mountain-dwelling shamans who periodically instructed China's earliest governors and emperors. Sometimes sage and governor were the same person at different life stages, for occasional solitude, far from society, was considered integral to developing the character of a ruler.

Once a government official came to Kuo Ching monastery, hoping to interview Han Shan, to find out if he was truly a wise man. But all he saw was Han Shan's back slipping out the door. Later, the governor sent messengers high up into the peaks of Cold Mountain, where Han Shan was said to have his hermitage. In the fog they shouted an offer of clean robes, rare incense, and a comfortable room if Han Shan would come down and become the governor's advisor. Han Shan kicked scree down at them, called them thieves, and disappeared into the upper mists.

So said the traditions. In fact, there may have been no historic individual named Han Shan. "He" was from the early T'ang period, but the dates of his life in the various accounts differ by a hundred years, from the mid-seventh to the mid-eighth century. The name "Han Shan" translates as "Cold Mountain," and refers not only to the poet (or poets) but also to a mountain and to the poems themselves. The cave where Han Shan is said to have had his hermitage is today called Hanyen ("Cold Cliff"), about twenty-five miles inland from the East China seacoast in present-day Chekiang province. Han Shan's writings, transcribed from rock faces, tree trunks, and crumbling walls, and the handed-down stories of his life, were quite possibly a conglomeration of works and legends of various hermits, poets, and wandering monks associated with that region.

At any rate, to Gary, Han Shan and Shih-Te suggested a couple of grizzled American railroad tramps. As a boy he had seen Chinese landscape paintings in the Seattle Art Museum — long scrolls depicting floating cloud and flowing mountain streams. Always somewhere in those paintings among the crags and dwarf pines and brooks there had been hapless human figures — the ragged Taoist and Zen hermits of old China. And if the misty peaks in those old scroll paintings looked for all the world like his own familiar Cascadian west slope, the vagabonds in them had their Pacific Northwest counterparts as well. "You sometimes run into them today," wrote Gary. "In the skidrows, orchards, hobo jungles, and logging camps of America."

Whoever Han Shan was, the three hundred poems attributed to him were written in a rough, fresh, colloquial style, unusual for his time, and for that reason had never made it into the Chinese canon along with his contemporaries Li Po, Wang Wei, Tu Fu, and Po Chü-i. In fact, English-language translators completely overlooked Han Shan until 1954, when Arthur Waley published translations of twenty-seven of his poems.

In his earlier semesters with Ch'en Shih-hsiang, Gary had already developed a knack for transmitting the bittersweet aloofness of solitary T'ang mountain men like Wang Wei and Meng Hao-jan. Now, fresh from his summer blasting rock and building trail, Gary knew he had the perfect vocabulary — and spirit — for translating Han Shan. He took up Ch'en's suggestion with relish, blocking out his translations character by character, like laying riprap, feeling himself — in Rexroth's phrase — in poetic "communion" with the gnarly old challenger-bard of Cold Mountain. Gradually, Gary created a tough, knowing, lonesome persona for a modern-day Han Shan.

Kerouac was hugely impressed that Gary was translating these poems from the Chinese and by

Gary's identification of the old Chinese hermits with American hobos, a connection that he too had made. Even before meeting Gary, Jack had come across Han Shan in his readings; earlier that year, feeling that the comforts of his family life were holding him back from more heroic, solitary spiritual adventures, he had noted in his Dharma journal, "Be like Han Shan." Now, in Gary, Jack had finally met someone who could understand what he meant when he called himself a modern-day American *bhikku*. ". . . I believed that I was an oldtime bhikku in modern clothes wandering the world," Kerouac would later write in *The Dharma Bums*, "in order to turn the wheel of the True Meaning, or Dharma, and gain merit for myself as a future Buddha (Awakener) and as a future Hero in Paradise."

Kerouac had first gotten into Buddhism in late 1953 in New York, following his breakup with Alene Lee, the woman who was the life-model for the "Mardou Fox" character in his novel *The Subterraneans*. The end of that brief but intense affair had been particularly painful for Jack, and in the wake of it he began to cast about for a way free of his recurrent love problems. Feeling betrayed not only by Alene, but also by his friend Gregory Corso (who'd had sex with Alene), Kerouac was in emotional retreat. "I don't want to live in this beastly world," says his character Leo Percipied at the end of *The Subterraneans*, no doubt echoing Jack's own real-life sentiments at the time. He first went looking in the writings of Thoreau—like himself, a Massachusetts loner, the greatest of them all—for instructions on the self-sufficient life. While reading *Walden*, Kerouac became intrigued with the many Oriental references and began following some of Thoreau's leads until his readings brought him to Ashvaghosa's *Buddhacarita*, a first-century verse biography of Siddhartha Gautama, the historical Buddha. At Columbia in the early '40s, Kerouac had become curious about the Asian religious classics. Later, he came across references to Shakyamuni as a Fellaheen hero in the writings of Oswald Spengler, but it was not until late 1953 that he seriously began investigating Mahayana philosophy.

Sauk Mountain Trail in the fog, July 1997.

"Han Shan could have lived here,
& no scissorbill stooge of the
Emperor would have come trying to steal
his last poor shred of sense."
Gary Snyder, *Myths and Texts*

During the week after the Six Gallery reading, Jack wrote a letter to Stella Sampas, his future wife, back in Lowell, Massachusetts, reflecting on the beginnings of his Buddhism:

> . . . in October [1953], sadly walking across the railyards by the full sad yellow moon I went
> to the library to pick up books on Oriental Philosophy and came up, idly, with Asvhaghosha's
> Career of Buddha, or Buddha-Charita, which I read with heavy heart, getting lighter every hour,
> rushing back to the library for more Buddhism, ending, with one night, complete enlightened
> realization . . . where I saw the words 'If a disciple will simply practice kindness he will immedi-
> ately attain Highest Perfect Wisdom' and I saw and realized and remembered and all in a flash
> the sad eyes of Sebastian [Stella's brother and Kerouac's high school best friend, who was killed
> in World War II] and why he had been born in the world to weep and to know . . .

In early 1954, Kerouac's Buddhist inquiry deepened further during a visit with his friends Neal and Carolyn Cassady in California. In the San Jose Public Library Jack found a book that would change his life — Dwight Goddard's *A Buddhist Bible*. *A Buddhist Bible*, like Suzuki's *Manual of Zen Buddhism*, was a solid anthology of key Buddhist sutras in some of the first English translations available.

Goddard's *Bible* turned out to be the great book of Kerouac's thirties. Jack made an immediate con- nection with the collection's difficult Prajna texts — the old wisdom classics of the Mahayana such as the Heart Sutra, the Diamond Sutra, the Lankavatara and Surangama sutras, and the Sutra of Hui- Neng — the same works that had been shaping Snyder and Whalen's understanding of the Dharma since late 1951. Drawn by the curiously beautiful symmetrical obversions and double negatives of these scriptures, Kerouac consumed them whole and by the end of 1954 could quote chapter and verse with the fervor (and sometimes the fanaticism) of a born-again Baptist spouting gospel.

Jack never returned *A Buddhist Bible* to the San Jose library. Instead he had a rough leather cover made for it and carried the book around with him all over the United States and Mexico, reading it nearly every day for the next four years. The Diamond Sutra especially inspired him — "the diamond that cuts through/to the other view," as he would call it in *Orizaba Blues*.

Concurrent with this immersion in the dharma, Kerouac began writing a new kind of poetry, and over the next few years the two things — Buddhism and "blues" — fed into each other and were inextri- cably joined. Kerouac had written verse much earlier, since at least 1940, but his initial attempts were at best brilliant imitations of Whitman and Wolfe. In the late summer of 1953, however, while living in

Richmond Hill, Queens, with his mother, Jack began writing quick, free-wheeling poems in the shirt-pocket notebooks he used for spontaneous prose sketching, and began thinking of them as "blues" in the style of Charlie Parker's pyrotechnic saxophone improvisations.

In the Buddhist scriptures Kerouac found a supporting aesthetic as well as an ethical system. "It's taken me all my life to learn to write what I actually think," wrote Jack in an effort to explain himself to his skeptical editor Malcolm Cowley in September 1955, "—by not thinking. Quote from Suragama Sutra: 'If you are now desirous of more perfectly understanding Supreme Enlightenment and the enlightening nature of Pure Mind Essence, you must learn to answer questions spontaneously with no recourse to discriminating thinking. For the Tathagatas in the ten quarters of the universes have been delivered from the ever returning cycle of deaths and rebirths by this same single way, namely, by reliance upon their intuitive minds—'"

Kerouac began working Buddhist ideas and allusions into his writing for the first time, very tentatively, in *San Francisco Blues,* then more overtly and with more assurance as his understanding and experience of the Dharma deepened. By 1955 the Buddhist influence was all-pervasive—with *Mexico City Blues,* poetry and Buddhism came together in the first formal expression of Jack's own original take on the Dharma as well as his first major book of poems. It was Kerouac's genius in those days to create fusions of remote cultural archetypes—to see, for instance, American jazzman Charley Parker as a blues-blowing Buddha, or Western boxcar tramps as latter day Zen lunatics. When it worked, it was inspired and totally original—a spontaneous, jazzy, druggy, visionary, American, catholic fusion of Mahayanist wisdom teachings and pop culture. For example,

Charley Parker Looked like Buddha
. . . And his expression on his face
Was as calm, beautiful, and profound
As the image of the Buddha
Represented in the East, the lidded eyes,
The expression that says "All is Well"
— This was what Charley Parker
Said when he played, All is Well.

. . .

Charley Parker, forgive me —

. . .

Pray for me and everybody

In the Nirvanas of your brain

Where you hide, indulgent and huge,

No longer Charley Parker

But the secret unsayable name

That carries with it merit

Not to be measured from here

To up, down, east, or west —

— Charley Parker, lay the bane,

off me, and every body

WHEN JACK FIRST MET Snyder and Whalen at the equinox, Philip had only been down from Sourdough a week and was full of funny stories about bears and pack horses and back-country characters like Blackie Burns and One-eyed Andy Wilcox, Uncle Jim Baxter and Shubert Hunter. Jack watched and listened intently to Gary and Phil cracking each other up with stories from "the Skagit." It sounded amazing: the huge hydroelectric dams and green lakes and the ranges of glaciers, mountains with names like Sourdough and Crater, Desolation, Hozomeen. From the start, Jack wondered if he could handle being a lookout.

Snyder, of course, was an experienced mountaineer, and eight years younger, but Whalen was nearly the same age as Jack, and certainly in no greater physical shape. If Philip could make it as a fire lookout, reasoned Kerouac, so could he.

"I think that both Gary and I were strange creatures that he had never seen the like of before, being from this part of the world, this West Coast and so on. Being people who spent a lot of time in the woods or outdoors or whatnot caught his attention," says Whalen.

It was true: Kerouac had never spent time hiking in the back country, although he had grown up just two hours south of the greatest mountains in the East — New Hampshire's White Mountains. Indeed, there was granite in Kerouac's very blood; over the generations, his French-Canadian forebears had worked their way down through the valley of the Merrimack, as he well knew. But hiking to his ancestral river's sources in the Pemigwasset Wilderness and Franconia Notch had never been a value for a milltown youth in Great Depression. Young Kerouac's aspirations had always lain south of Lowell, in Boston, and ultimately New York.

Even so, the idea of living alone in a little shack on a mountaintop had been a fantasy of Kerouac's since his teenage years, ever since he'd begun thinking of himself as a writer; but it had always been just a dream until he met Whalen and Snyder. Here were guys who had actually done it.

As Kerouac grew older, he broadened his teenage dream of the mountain shack into a more general concept of a "hermitage." Sometimes it was a mountain hut in Colorado, sometimes it was "a rose-covered cottage" along the banks of Thoreau's Concord River in South Lowell, where Jack had rowed with his high school girlfriend Mary Carney in her father's wooden boat. Even at the height of his frenetic road period with Neal Cassady in the late '40s, Kerouac had periodically craved solitude. While he was living in Denver in the summer of 1949, the long mountains west of the city beckoned him to become a "Thoreau of the Mountains." To Allen Ginsberg, he had at that time fantasized, "I'll buy a saddlehorse for $30, an old saddle on Larimer St., a sleeping bag at Army surplus; frying pan, an old tin can; bacon, coffee, beans, sourdough; matches, etc.; and a rifle. And go away in the mountains forever."

By his thirtieth birthday he began to talk of it openly as such: a hermitage. "Someday I'm going to be a hermit in the woods," he vowed to John Clellon Holmes in June 1952, ". . . very soon now I'll visit my site."

Kerouac's longing for a hermitage intensified at the same time he became seriously interested in Buddhism. "Go somewhere to limitless solitude in the tolerant open and where yr food is cheap, and devote all time to thought," he told himself early in the journal that would become *Some of the Dharma*. In the Lankavatara Scripture, which he discovered in January 1954, he underlined the notion that "one should have his abode where one can see all things from the point of view of solitude." And, in a prescient remark to himself, Jack wrote: "I don't want to be a drunken hero of the generation suffering everywhere with everyone — I want to be a quiet saint living in a shack in solitary meditation of universal mind. . . ."

Hang-glider's Gangplank, Sauk Mountain, July 1997.

"Who can leap the world's ties
And sit with me among the white clouds?"

Han Shan, "Cold Mountain Poems,"
trans. Gary Snyder

He decided the best place for his shack would be in Mexico, where the living was cheap and the earth was "an Indian thing." "I'll go down to Mexico someday and live my own kind of healthy life," he wrote in a journal entry around the time of his thirty-second birthday, "— in hot sun every day, good self-cooked food at night, early long sleep — a self-sufficient practicing Dhyanist in Mexico — a selfish religionist resting — a womanless man of Tao . . . "

As Kerouac continued his Dharma studies during 1954, he found support and corroboration for his notion of a hermitage shack in the traditional Buddhist *viharas* (literally, "sojourning places") — meditation huts built at intervals along the pilgrimage routes of old India for traveling monks — and quickly began to envision "My own little *vihara* in the Valley of Mexico — the first of many monk-shacks on the ground."

By the end of 1954, the hermitage concept had taken on the force of an imaginative imperative for Jack, then living at his mother's apartment in Queens. "Get to Thy Hermitage!" he shouted at himself in his journal that Thanksgiving, 1954. Typically however, Kerouac hadn't considered any of the practical details of living on the ground in his Mexican dharma shack. It was one thing to jot down reassuring sayings from Thoreau into his journal ("The woods are easier to live in than you've ever in your wildest dreams imagined"), but when Jack really thought about his chances for a self-sufficient life outside of consumer society, it scared him. "Dear Lord above I'm frightened tonight," he admitted to himself. "What do I know about deserts? Water? — Where shall I go to escape this civilization which at any moment may thrust me in jail or war or madhouse? A shack in the woods outside Rocky Mount, be near family? — what of the gnats, heat, tics, mosquitos, disapproval?"

During the first half of 1955, Kerouac lived at his sister Caroline Blake's place in Rocky Mount. His plan, while still in New York, had been to build some kind of shelter in the woods behind the Blake house soon after his arrival, with a stove and an outhouse, water to be packed in. But when he got to Rocky Mount, a heaped-up pile of dead grass and leaves to sit on while meditating in a little clearing in the woods was as far as he got — "Twin Tree Grove," he called the spot. It was the closest he came to any sort of hermitage until he met Gary and Phil. There he meditated every day. At night he slept in his sleeping bag on the unheated back porch-room of the main house, dreaming of his Mexican vihara.

The reality of his Mexico City sojourn was not one of healthy solitude and self-cooked meals and contemplation as he had envisioned it from the suburban woods of Rocky Mount but a grueling routine of blues writing and drugs, as we have seen. The Mexican hermitage-fantasy went up into Bill Garver's syringe, when Jack took a fix of morphine on his first day back on Orizaba Street. ". . . got sick first day on shit," he wrote to Ginsberg. "—Feel aimless, ephemeral, inconceivably sad, don't know where I'm going, or why—. . . All I want as far as life-plans are concerned from here on out, is compassionate, contented solitude — Bhikkuhood is so hard to make in the West—. . . "

And yet, in a strange sort of way, Jack's rooftop hut at 210 Orizaba in 1955 foreshadowed the Desolation lookout cabin where he would spend the summer of '56. It too was a "shack of isolation" in a fashion: up on the roof above the other tenants, with a view of the tops of the purple-flowering jacaranda trees and avenues of graceful date palms and the roosters crowing all morning from other rooftops of the *colonia*. As a gringo, Jack was separated definitively from the people he lived among, and to him, they were a backdrop as impersonal as mountains in a way. The rooftop was a sort of ideal Kerouackian retreat, in that he could have lengthy periods of solitude for writing, reading, and meditation but could also come down when he felt like it for conversation with the erudite Garver or a steak dinner at Kiku's or a visit to the girls of Panama Street. In fact, Mexico City was one of the few places where Kerouac was able to resolve, for a time, the perpetual conflict between his ascetic and sensual impulses — by immersing himself in both.

LISTENING TO GARY and Phil talk about their lookout cabins in the Cascades, with their wood-fed Yukon stoves, pure snow water to drink, writing poems by lantern light with deer browsing outside in the moonlight, Jack's hermitage-fantasy was reborn in its original form, the remote mountain hut. It was not only possible, but as a Forest Service lookout, the Eisenhower administration would even pay him to do it.

Gary and Philip both encouraged Jack to apply. Whalen said he would write him a letter of recommendation to Frank Lewis, the District Ranger. Gary stirred his imagination with the names: Komo Kulshan and Shuksan, Crater Shan and Hozomeen, Ruby Creek and Panther Creek and Fourth of July Pass — a T'ang landscape straight out of Han Shan, but right there in twentieth-century America, only a few hours northeast of Seattle. "Who can leap the world's ties/And sit with me among the white clouds?" Han Shan had demanded to know. Gary could, Whalen could; and, they said, so should Jack.

Meanwhile, for all his transcontinental questing, Kerouac had never really gotten into the back country. He had ridden in buses and cars over the Rockies and the Sierras and even once across the Cascades (Portland to Butte, '49) but those trips had all been on blacktop. He had never trekked in mountains, never measured himself, step-by-step, breath-by-breath, against the sweet, stubborn earth. Now, fired up by Gary and Phil, Jack wanted to head for the nearest mountains for a late-season camping trip with his new friends. Whalen had had enough of the high country for the year, but Snyder was game, and guessed there was still time for one last weekend in the Yosemite before the snows. And so, on the next-to-last weekend in October, Kerouac, Snyder, and one of Gary's mountaineer friends, John Montgomery, drove up to the town of Bridgeport and camped two nights on Matterhorn Peak in the Sawtooth Range. The trip turned out to be one of the high points of Kerouac's thirties and is commemorated in one of the most memorable sections of *The Dharma Bums*.

Gary had often seen the Matterhorn looming to the east when he was on trail crew on Piute Creek that summer. Piute Creek had its sources high up in the Sawtooths, not far from Matterhorn Peak. Now he was approaching it from the Bridgeport side, following the drainage of Horse Creek. For Kerouac, that October Saturday night camping on the great mountain was one of the grandest of his life, and his feelings for Gary were commensurate. The fraternal image of the two of them sitting zazen on the ledge at 10,000 feet, his eyes closed, Gary's open, would remain with him always. "Our rock dhyana," he called it. With the Matterhorn climb, Gary entered Jack's archetypal, inner hall of brothers that included Gerard, Sebastian Sampas, and Neal Cassady.

Snyder too was deeply moved, both by the awesome surroundings — "cold sky the color of Prajna's eyes (gray violet in the sunset, pale, pale)" — and his new friend, whom he described a few days later in his journal as ". . . Jean-Louis Kerouac, a Great Hero and Noble Buddhist of Literature and the Road." For many years to come, an October chill would remind him of Jack.

In late November in Berkeley, Kerouac and Ginsberg got into a "religious argument" over some point in the Heart Sutra.

> We were at a girl's house in Berkeley, G [Ginsberg], me and Bhikku Gary Snyder, discussing the Prajna-Paramita more or less, where I re-iterated that self has no reality but G said: "Well, I dont care, I'm gonna go right along and just be Allen G." and I yelled "O for krissakes I'm gonna leave

if you go on talkin like that" (I was getting drunk & surly on wine) and he yelled "Well then GO!" "Thank you," I yelled, "a most excellent idea!" and I stalked, left the house, went back to the cottage, packed up and left California eventually . . .

After leaving Ginsberg's Milvia Street apartment, Kerouac took the F train to San Francisco, where he checked in to his old Skid Row retreat, the Cameo Hotel.

Good old silence at last — nothing

but a tugboat out in the bay

of San Francisco

The Cameo was an oddly consoling place to Kerouac, with complex personal and creative associations. He had roomed there when he worked as a brakeman on the Southern Pacific in the fall of 1952. In March 1954 he had returned to the Cameo, also in a huff — after an earlier Buddhist religious argument, that one with Neal Cassady.

The Cameo was located around the corner from the Little Harlem honky-tonk where he and Neal had raved many a night in the late '40s. In the 1950s the streets north of the S.P. yards on Townsend Street were San Francisco's Skid Row: pawnshop windows full of wedding rings, Purple Hearts, and heaps of shoes; rank-smelling quarter-a-night flops, mattresses in alleys littered with Sterno canisters, wooden-fronted bars with planks knocked out showing men collapsed on the floor. For Neal, who grew up amid such scenes on Denver's Larimer Street, Skid Row held no allure. The unromantic reason people went to Skid Row, he told Jack bluntly, was because they hated life.

Paradoxically, the atmosphere of palpable self-annihilation stimulated Kerouac's creativity. Periodically he liked to get a cheap room and sit in the window, sip wine, write in his journal, and watch the desultory human drama on the street below as it slowly unfolded to a sound-track of hacking derelict coughs and curses coming through the hotel room walls. The Cameo had twice before been a great place for Jack's writing. In the fall of 1952 he had written "October in the Railroad Earth" while rooming there — one of his greatest successes in Spontaneous Prose — and during his 1954 sojourn had completed eighty "choruses" of "San Francisco Blues." Also during his 1954 stay, he had experienced the first breakthrough in his then-new Buddhist meditation practice — an hallucinatory aural buzz that he considered his "first intimation from Dharmakaya's Silent Realms that all the Tathagats are indeed there. . ."

"The beauty of the Cameo Hotel whether when as brakeman or now 1955 . . . I always had the quiet opportunity to remember my own mind—my own mind of Dharma-self," he wrote, remembering to add: "(which is in-existent)."

FOR KEROUAC, the season of poetry and dharma came to an abrupt and unexpectedly morbid dénouement with the suicide of Natalie Jackson, an artist's model and lover of Neal Cassady's. Jack was especially jolted by Natalie's death, having been the last person to speak with her before she killed herself. "I tried to tell her everything was empty," Jack confided to his dharma journal, "including her paranoiac idea that the cops were after her & all of us—she said O YOU DONT KNOW! then the next day she was found dazed on the roof and when a cop tried to catch her she jumped. . . "

Within a few days Jack checked out of the Cameo Hotel, and retreated to the Cassadys' home in Los Gatos, in preparation for another cross-country hitch—heading back east to spend Christmas and the winter with his family in North Carolina. While in Los Gatos, Natalie continued to fall in Jack's dreams. "Had a horrible dream—Frienda mine fell off a bridge and sailed naked and white down to the river rocks saying quietly 'o yes yes oh yes' as though he suddenly remembered something that his self was made to lose."

On December 4, Philip Whalen read at San Francisco State, delivering a poem he had written only the night before—"Unfinished," a tough, didactic Zen-whack of a poem that could not have been more finished. "A single waking moment destroys us / And we cannot live without / Ourselves," read Whalen to the small, subdued Poetry Center crowd.

> *You come to me for an answer? I*
> *Invented it all, I*
> *Am your tormentor, there is no*
> *Escape, no redress*
>
> *You are powerless against me: You*
> *Must suffer agonies until you know*
> *You are suffering;*
> *Work on that.*

In Berkeley, the winter rains soaked the old brown shingled houses south of campus. Swift clouds sheared the tops of the sodden eucalyptus hills above the Greek Theater; the Campanile tolled in fog. On Hillegass, Snyder's hojo leaked: a thin trickle stained one burlap wall, a slow drip through the roof boards plinked into a tin camp pot in the middle of the room. In a dry corner, Gary piled his blankets and wrapped himself to write:

> *Granite sierras, shelves of books,*
> *All my friends, scatter*
> *Aimlessly tumbling through*
> *Years and countries*
> *Aristotle's herd of formal stars*
> *stampedes:*
> *The diamond-point mercy*
> *Of this timeless rain.*

Jack Kerouac in smoky flame
Blazing bright at Buddha's name
    Gary Snyder, "Ballad of Rolling Heads"

Bhikku Hostel

Marin-an, Early 1956

IN MID-ĐECEMBER 1955, Kerouac headed east to spend the Christmas holidays with his family at his sister Caroline Blake's home in Rocky Mount, North Carolina, where he would remain throughout the winter. Two days after Christmas, he began writing *Visions of Gerard,* his "book of sorrows" about the death of his nine-year-old brother Gerard from rheumatic fever, in the summer of 1926. Kerouac was only four when Gerard died; the loss embittered Kerouac's parents and cast a pall of sibling guilt and grief over young Jack's formative years, and beyond.

    Indeed, thirty years after the event, Gerard's ghost still hung over Kerouac's typewriter. "The whole reason why I ever wrote at all and drew breath to bite in vain with pen of ink," he claimed, was "because of Gerard, the idealism, Gerard the religious hero." Kerouac's first creative treatment of Gerard was in

The Town and the City, where he split his dead brother's traits between the fictional twins Julian and Francis Martin (Gerard's baptismal name was Francis Gerard Kerouac). Two years later he introduced Gerard as a minor character in *Doctor Sax.* Earlier he had related Gerard's story in confessional and heartbreaking detail in a series of letters to Neal Cassady in 1950–51. Still, by 1956 he had not yet made the full-length expiation-portrait of Gerard that he knew he must.

Natalie Jackson's awful death in San Francisco in late November was the catalyst. In Kerouac's psyche any death inevitably conjured memories of Gerard's "pure and tranquill face." Soon after Natalie's death, while still in San Francisco, Kerouac began to sketch the shape of *Visions of Gerard* and to picture himself writing it. He already had the title and could feel his forces welling but would wait until he got back east under his family's roof to cut loose in "fast blowing sessions" of spontaneous "pops, tics, flashes, and blues."

Kerouac put a great deal of pressure on himself in *Visions of Gerard.* "If I cant handle this I'm lost," he told himself as he spread out his old notes and preliminary pages and popped some Benzedrine to get rolling. Gerard's story was to be the chronological beginning of his projected multivolume Duluoz Legend, the telling of which Kerouac by 1955 considered his "continual lifework." He had already begun the autobiographical Duluoz saga, albeit unsystematically, in *Doctor Sax* (1952) and *Maggie Cassady* (1953); with Gerard, the envisioned masterwork would take on uninterrupted sequential form. It would also be Kerouac's first novel-length Dharmic prose work, with saintly Gerard as the embodiment of "the Brotherhood Ideal propounded from afar down the eternal corridors of Buddhahood."

"O Lord, reveal to me My Buddhawork," prayed Jack, alone and high at his sister's Rocky Mount kitchen table, "and give me the great intense eager ecstatic excitement of the Holy Words, amen!" He finished the book in nineteen days, sometimes writing a torrential 3,000 words an hour. Indeed, during the entire winter of 1956 at the Blakes', Jack's pencil was almost never still. In addition to *Visions of Gerard,* he completed the final fifty pages of his Buddhist journal, *Some of the Dharma*—out of which many passages would eventually find their way verbatim into *The Dharma Bums.* Jack also revised the first half of *Tristessa,* continued to polish his current draft of *On the Road,* and began a new novel, tentatively called *The Martin Family,* a projected sequel to his first published book, *The Town and the City.* All the while he maintained a prodigious correspondence with friends, banging out thousand-word letters every few days.

During such manic writing times, Kerouac entered into a world of his own, an invisible private sphere peopled not so much by living family nor stocked with mundane objects but alive with poetry and the bardic presences of Shakespeare and Omar Khayyam. To Jack, at such peaks of inspiration, Emily Dickinson seemed closer at hand than his sister Caroline; poet William Blake far more real than his engineer brother-in-law Paul Blake.

During this creative burst, Kerouac also put the wheels in motion for the upcoming summer, applying to the Forest Service for a fire watch in the Mount Baker National Forest. Phil Whalen recommended Jack to District Ranger Frank Lewis, and by February 6 Jack had been accepted and assigned to man Desolation Lookout. Whalen would again be taking Sourdough. Jack thanked Phil for his support and began spinning plans: "Glad and surprised to hear you might be going yourself this summer. We could beat our way up together. . . . I told Krayer [the Assistant Ranger] I hoped I would be able to do that work every single year from now on, if I fill the bill." To Carolyn Cassady he was even more enthusiastic: "O boy, O boy, O here I go, I got the offer for the job watching fires . . . and I told the Forest Ranger I hoped he'd take me back next year, and the next, and all my life. It will be my life work . . . " And to old friend Lucien Carr: "If I don't get a vision on Desolation Peak, my name ain't William Blake!"

MEANWHILE, in the gray Big Easonburg woods behind his sister's house, Jack reestablished his dharma camp in "Twin Tree Grove," and began training his mind "on the emptiness aspect of things." With *A Buddhist Bible* propped in the twist of a pine root, he delved ever deeper into the Diamond Sutra, Hui-Neng, and the Prajnaparamita-Hyridaya (Heart Sutra), with its paradoxical dialectic, "Form is emptiness, emptiness is not different from form; neither is form different from emptiness, indeed emptiness is form." The Heart Sutra is the condensed "heart" of the Prajnaparamita teachings and the most succinct statement of the Buddhist doctrine of *shunyata* ["emptiness"].

Kerouac was fascinated by the irrefutable symmetry as well as the rhythm and poetic repetitions in such lines of the Heart Sutra, as he was by similar constructions in the Diamond Sutra. To his delight, he found that the word "form" could be lifted from the equation as though from a syllogistic template and that any noun at all could be dropped in its place to make a new statement. Jack called this template "the Prajna-paramita Wringer," and loved to play with it, substituting various random words or

"Il est beau le moissonner, cette fleur au matin de la vie, avant que le souffle impur du monde en ait terni sa blancheur".

—Soeur Antoine de Jesus.

phrases for the word "form" in order to surprise himself with new insights such as his "Money Prayer"—"Money is emptiness," he wrote in his dharma journal. "Money is not different from emptiness; neither is emptiness different from money, indeed emptiness is money." "I know it works," he wrote Gary, "because it's worked for me, alone, with dogs, in my Twin Tree Grove here, every night now for the past six weeks."

Back on the West Coast, Snyder and Ginsberg had embarked in late January on a hitchhiking trip through Gary's old haunts in Portland, Seattle, and Bellingham, and on up to the Nooksack Valley. On the way, they gave poetry readings at Reed College and at the University of Washington in Seattle. For Gary, who had finally received his passport—"No reasonable doubt exists as to Mr. Snyder's loyalty," the State Department had concluded in November—the trip was a last nostalgic swing through the landscape of his youth before his departure for Japan, now set for early May, less than four months off. For Ginsberg, it was an opportunity to deepen his friendship with Snyder and to learn more about Gary's Northwest, about Nature, and hitchhiking.

On January 24th, they hitched north out of Berkeley following Highway 99 to Mount Shasta, where they turned onto Route 97, which took them up into Oregon on the east side of the Cascades, through Klamath Falls and Bend and Madras to the Warm Springs Reservation in the snow all the way. Crossing the Deschutes and riding across the rez in the driving snow, Gary explained to Allen that this was where "A Berry Feast" and *Myths and Texts* had come from—five years before, gambling with the Wasco and the Wishram under Hee Hee Butte, watching the wild races between the Yakima and Puyallup horse-

"Gerard," Lowell, Massachusetts, 1993. "I see there in the eyes of Gerard the very diamond kindness and patient humility of the Brotherhood Ideal propounded from afar down the eternal corridors of Buddhahood . . ." Jack Kerouac, *Visions of Gerard*

Prayer card inscription: "The Harvester came for this flower in the morning of life before the impure spirit of the world tarnished his innocence."

men, listening to all the fantastic Coyote stories with his anthropologist friends Dell Hymes and the Matsons. He told how Joyce Matson, baby on her hip and breasts full after giving birth that summer, would each morning shoot a stream of milk into her husband Homer's coffee mug, then her own, then Gary's.

> *Her breasts, black-nippled, blue-veined, heavy,*
> *Hung through the loose shirt*
> *squeezed, with the free hand*
> *white jet in three cups.*

On the 26th they were in Portland, hanging around Reed, where they lined up a poetry reading at Anna Mann Cottage for mid-February. They poked around Portland's Skid Row, where Allen purchased a pair of two-dollar cork-soled logger's boots and almost immediately announced that he wanted to work in the woods. Gary paused on the 27th to write Phil Whalen back in Berkeley. "[Ginsberg] is reconsidering rhetorical poetry, sez it makes him feel foolish to shout MOLOCH! at fir trees," he said, adding that "Hoodlatch [Bob Allen, Gary's Reed College friend] has a quantity of [peyote] blossoms, we mean to walk rainbows tonight."

On January 29th they bused north to Seattle, where they stayed a week and gave a reading at Parrington Hall on the campus of the University of Washington—"Five old ladies ran out screaming," wrote Ginsberg to Neal Cassady. Gary took Allen on a walking tour of the old hard-luck, radical Seattle. He showed him the Colman docks, where forty years before the steamship *Verona* had brought back the Wobblies from the Everett Massacre: every last man had been arrested, and marched up Yesler Way to the King County jail. As Gary and Allen walked Yesler, Gary started singing "Hold the Fort," the song that the Wobs had sung on the *Verona*. He knew all the old IWW songs from *The Little Red Songbook*— songs like Joe Hill's "The Preacher and the Slave" and "The Rebel Girl," or "The Portland Revolution" by Dublin Dan. That was what he loved about the Wobblies: how they had brought song and humor to the class struggle, along with their blood and muscle.

Yesler Way was the original "Skid Row," the Seattle loggers' main skid road, where in the early 1900s the long bodies of the last old-growth giants had been skidded down the muddy hill to the docks of Elliot Bay. Those old trees, Gary explained to Allen, had become the two-by-fours and siding of all the turn-of-the-century wooden houses that they lived in back in the Bay Area. Coming to Yesler Square, Gary told him about his Wobbly grandfather Henry Snyder, who had made speeches there back in the day when Seattle was the great anarchist enclave of the Northwest. All of the legendary Wobbly orators had spoken, read poems, or sang to rouse up the "soldiers of discontent" in Yesler Square, everyone from Elizabeth Gurley Flynn and Charles Ashleigh to Joe Hill himself. Rexroth claimed to have soap-boxed there himself in 1924 on his way to the Skagit. Now the Square was full of broken-toothed Sterno bums and soup kitchen Bible jocks, with the mournful horn of the Bremerton Ferry sounding in the balmy mist.

The Seattle Wobbly Hall was at the top of the square at Fourth and Yesler. Gary and Allen went inside, where they found a half dozen blear-eyed old Swedes and Finns playing cards at a round table. On the wall above them were yellowing photographs of Joe Hill, Frank Little, and Wesley Everest, across whose image were scrawled his last reported words: "Tell the boys I done my best." Below these picture frames was the famous Wobbly motto: "Forming the New Society Within the Shell of the Old," still a damn good slogan, thought Gary. "Problem is," the old men said, "these young fellers can't see ahead and we don't have nothin' to offer." They told Gary and Allen to help themselves to the various pamphlets and broadsides on the counter and leave whatever they could afford.

Also on the wall was a poster of Karl Marx wielding a double-bitted falling axe, saying "Where I cut one off it will never grow again!" Gary jotted this down, later including it in *Myths and Texts*:

> *O Karl would it were true*
> *I'd put my saw to work for you*
> *& the wicked social tree would fall right down.*

After, in Russo's Bar on Yesler, Allen told Gary over ten-cent beers how the place reminded him of the dreary Communist Party hall back in Paterson, New Jersey, where his mother had taken him when he was only seven to hear William Z. Foster and Scott Nearing talking revolution. They wandered up to Pike Place and strolled through the market sharing a pound of hard smoked peppered salmon. Finally, Gary took Allen down to a curio shop on Alaska Way where a shriveled, cross-eyed mummy in a broad-brimmed prospector's hat was propped up surreally in the window. It was said to be the wizened corpse of Frank Little, one of the most effective IWW leaders, lynched forty years before in Butte, Montana, while organizing a strike of copper miners. Gulls wheeled overhead, to Allen "their bleak lone cries representing our souls." The strange Seattle afternoon ended up as a poem in Ginsberg's *Reality Sandwiches*.

FROM SEATTLE, they made their way up to Bellingham for five days with Dick and Janet Miegs. They walked along the docks below the red brick Victorian City Hall clock tower, looking out across the bay to Lummi Island. Gary recalled the afternoon he had gone out to the Lummi Reservation with his fellow lookout Jack Francis, before packing up to Sourdough in '53. Where was Jack now? This was Gary's last chance to see some of his Forest Service pals. He tracked old Roy Raymond to the run-down Helena Hotel in Bellingham, and Roy was able to locate Jim Baxter, who came down from Ferndale, and there was a little reunion in Roy's room one afternoon. Baxter was dressed in a black suit, having just been to a funeral. Roy sat in a stuffed chair by the window, looking as though he still hadn't recovered from his heart attack the year before. Gary reminded him of the time in '53 when Roy hiked up to see him on Sourdough and they spent the afternoon pitching muleshoes in the flat ground behind the L.O. "I couldn't make it up that hill now with this weak heart of mine," said Roy. "But when I get back on my feet I'd like to go back up there, fix up a shack up around Concrete or Marblemount, get a little part time job." "Why don't you go down to Mexico?" suggested Gary. "Weather's warm, and your money'll stretch eight or ten times more than here." "Oh no," said Roy. "Can't go to Mexico with this weak heart." Later, outside the hotel, Baxter said about Roy, "He'll never be any good again." It was the last time Gary saw Baxter, though they corresponded for several more years.

"Today in Bellingham talking with Gary's ranger and forester friends," wrote Ginsberg in his journal. "They see him as a little golden Dharma hero of Northwest Bull Durham woods — the agile mind outwitting theirs, the admissions of tobacco chawing humanistic fear ('danged if I want to lose my balls on that mountain') and 'Danged if that city slicker weren't afraid to lose his balls on that mountain.' Sometimes a snotty kid, sometimes a gazing Dharma hero with Aethereal Beard."

From Bellingham, Gary and Allen went to Dick Meigs's cabin on the Nooksack, where Gary had spent that week in the summer of 1954 after his firing at Packwood. Koma Kulshan was cut off by fog. "Impassive giant of ice & rock/Silent motionless being with eternal thoughts," wrote Ginsberg. After a couple of days, Allen continued on to Vancouver, BC, leaving Gary alone in the cabin. For Snyder, his impending departure for Asia loomed as an obvious turning point in his life.

All America south and east,

Twenty-five years in it brought to a trip-stop

Mind-point, where I turn

Caught more on this land—rock tree and man,

Awake, than ever before, yet ready to leave.

            damned memories,

Whole wasted theories, failures and worse success,

Schools, girls, deals, try to get in

To make this poem a froth, a pity,

A dead fiddle for lost good jobs.

SOON AFTER HIS RETURN from his Northwest trip with Allen, Gary closed up his Hillegass hojo and moved across the Bay to Marin County, settling into a rough, unfinished cabin in Mill Valley, on property rented by his friend Locke McCorkle. Gary had met McCorkle at Alan Watts's American Academy of Asian Studies in San Francisco and the two had taken to each other from the start. Locke was the same age as Gary, a carpenter, and had been a political radical in his late teens and early twenties, before getting into Buddhism as "a better means of Revolution." Locke was married to a woman named Valerie White; they had a year-old daughter, Tasha. In appearance and lifestyle, the McCorkles were a good fifteen years ahead of their time. In mid-1956 they already looked and lived like Marin hippies from the early 1970s.

They lived on Montford Road, a narrow tar lane that ran out of Mill Valley and into the hills behind the town. Their low, tin-roofed house was just above the road, nearly hidden by a dense stand of bamboo and the trunks of a half dozen pines. A hundred yards up the steep slope behind the house, surrounded by tall eucalyptus trees and a windrow of Monterey cypress, was the cabin that Gary moved into in mid-February 1956.

Locke and Valerie were happy to have Snyder staying in their otherwise empty shack on the hill. They loved what he did with the place—covering the plank floors with grass mats and the walls with burlap and quad maps and Chinatown scroll paintings and his own poems—and they didn't mind him having visitors. They shared Gary's vision of the place as a refuge for the wandering poets and way seekers of the burgeoning "rucksack revolution." Their rent for the entire five-acre property, house, and shack was only $25. In barter for his keep, Gary felled and corded a few trees for Locke and Valerie's main-house woodstoves.

In late February, Gary wrote Jack in Rocky Mount, inviting him out to share "McCorkle's high hermitage" with him before heading to Desolation. "The cabin on my friend's place in Washington—the Nooksack Valley place—and this cabin on McCorkle's land, are the first two bhikku-hostels in the country," he told Kerouac, "& I hope we can someday get more; a little shack or cave or pad, every one day's hitchhike (about 500 miles) apart all over the land."

Earlier, Kerouac had written to Snyder telling him the news of his Desolation assignment and asking for "any tips you may have about Fire Lookout preparations & routine." Gary replied with a long, information-packed letter about the Skagit, with advice on everything from where to buy his lookout groceries to how to behave around the District Ranger—"Just play it straight and do what he wants."

More important for Kerouac the writer than to Jack the Lookout, Gary dug into his own journals to paint a detailed panoramic portrait of the Upper Skagit, including fire history, background on the Ruby Creek gold rush, the Goat Trail, the Skagit dams, vignettes of his own fire watch on Crater, and vivid sketches of previous Desolation Lookouts like Jack Francis and Kim Oelberg. He even sent along a brush painting of Mount Hozomeen that he had made from Sourdough in 1953.

"Your human history of the mountains very useful to me," replied Kerouac. "I'll be careful to keep mum around Frank Lewis and to dig the good old logger characters." Kerouac would mine this letter heavily—and others from Snyder as well—for later use in *The Dharma Bums*. Not only did he use details, such as Gary's self-described appearance in 1952—"beard just started & a bare shaved head"; he would also lift several paragraphs whole from Snyder's letter and transpose them into the text of *The Dharma Bums* nearly verbatim—Snyder's description of the great Upper Skagit fire that gave Desolation its name, his description of his radio conversations with Jack Francis, his "greenest kid you ever saw" story about lookout Kim Oelberg.

WITH THE SPRING equinox, Kerouac set out from Rocky Mount for California yet again, busing across the South and Texas, making a quick trip across the border at El Paso to replenish his supply of

The peaks of Hozomeen seen acrosss a vast river of morning ground fog from a distance of twelve miles south at Sourdough Lookout, September 1998. From this perspective Gary Snyder made a brush painting of Hozomeen in the summer of 1953. In February 1956, after Kerouac was assigned to Desolation Peak, Gary sent the painting to him "I never dreamed Mount Hozomeen would have such a jagged sharp menacing look," replied Jack.

uppers and downers, then hitchhiking across the Southwest to LA, finally hopping a freight up the coast to San Francisco. He arrived in the Bay Area at the end of March and headed for McCorkle's.

By the time Kerouac appeared at Montford Road, Gary had already named the cabin "Marin-an"— Japanese for "Horse Grove Hermitage," for the adjacent hillside pasture with its grazing mares, and a punning reference to the county. The shack looked west across Marin's Homestead Valley to the steep leeward slope of the Panoramic Highway ridge, with Muir Woods just on the other side, and the wide Pacific a few miles further. Ocean fog constantly rolled over the ridge, then blew off. The April sun warmed the grove. Marin-an in April was like a huge aviary, loud with songbirds dancing in the trees.

When Kerouac arrived, during the last days of March, Gary was putting the final touches on *Myths and Texts,* capping four and a half years of poetic endeavor. Fresh new poems were coming to him as well, like spot-fires flaring off a larger burn — short, individual works like "Marin-An," "Migration of Birds," "All Through the Rains," "Makings," and "After T'ao Ch'ien." For a while he thought of gathering these under the title *The Marin Poems,* but they never came together as a collection and he dropped the idea. In the end Snyder's "Marin Poems" would find their separate ways into *Riprap, The Back Country,* and eventually, *Left Out in the Rain.* Meanwhile, no sooner had the ink dried on *Myths and Texts* than a new long poem much vaster in scope began to loom in his mind.

Shortly after settling in at McCorkle's, Gary had gone over to San Francisco with Locke to attend a lecture at the Academy of Asian Studies by a visiting Japanese artist and tea master named Saburo Hasegawa. Hasegawa inspired Snyder with the notion of landscape painting as a meditative practice, and compared Zen landscapes to the tangka and mandala of Tibetan Buddhism. Gary wondered if a poet could create an equivalent work, that is, achieve the same spiritual level with words — in a landscape-based poetics — that a painter could in the way of the brush. During the month of March, Gary attended all of Hasegawa's lectures, met him, and eventually raised the subject with him. Hasegawa invited Gary to tea.

> I still remember the day, April 8, 1956, because it was also the Buddha's birthday. He [Hasegawa] frothed up the tea with a bamboo whisk, we chatted, and he talked at length about the great Japanese Zen painter Sesshū.
>
> I asked him if he thought it was possible to do in poetry what was done in the great landscape paintings graphically, like the *Mountains and Rivers Without End* scrolls, and he said 'Of course,

you can write poetry that does the same thing! Why don't you just do it?' As I left that day I resolved to start another long poem that would be called *Mountains and Rivers Without End.*

So, just as "A Berry Feast"—in 1952 his longest work to that time—had provided a platform and foothold for the exponential creative effort of *Myths and Texts, Myths and Texts* would now be his new base for the monumental climb of *Mountains and Rivers Without End.* In painterly terms, if "A Berry Feast" had been a broad single canvas, and *Myths and Texts* a wider, three-paneled screen, *Mountains and Rivers* would be a long unfurling scroll. With only a few weeks to go before his departure, there wasn't much time for new work, but the seed-idea of *Mountains and Rivers Without End* was planted there on the slope of Marin-an.

KEROUAC TOO WAS preparing the ground for future artistic work while at Marin-an. He had already decided, back in the fall, to write a book with Gary as hero. *Visions of Gary* he was thinking of calling it, in the character-driven mode of *Visions of Cody* and *Visions of Gerard.* In fact, the situation at Marin-an was similar, in artistic terms, to his living arrangements in the winter of 1952, when he wrote *Visions of Cody* while staying with Neal and Carolyn Cassady on Russian Hill ["Cody Pomeray" was Kerouac's fictional name for Neal Cassady in the Duluoz saga]. Again he was living with his "main character" in a perfect creative incubator, learning and observing and sharing souls in the Now but ever attentive to those moments when a "vision"—an epiphany of the individual—might suddenly occur: Gary in the doorway of the shack, banging a frying pan and chanting the Triple Refuge; Gary cooking supper at the stove "singing like a millionaire"; Gary poring over his Japanese grammar by lantern light.

For Kerouac especially, Marin-an was an ideal situation: weekdays of leisurely reading, meditating, studying the sutras, writing, hiking over the highway ridge and down into Redwood Canyon, late nights talking literature and dharma—and death—with Gary; then big parties every weekend with people coming over from North Beach and Berkeley, with a bonfire throwing a magic circle in the eucalyptus grove and a few people walking around naked in the flame-light, jugs of Casanova Red circulating, couples slipping off into the darkness up the hill, then coming back, and all the time music—Indian ragas or Cal Tjader's vibes drifting up from McCorkle's booming hi-fi in the main house. For Kerouac, the alternation of weekday quietude and gregarious weekends was just right.

Jack Kerouac at Gary Snyder's going-away party in early May 1956. Kerouac remained at Marin-an

for another six weeks after Snyder's departure before leaving for Desolation Peak.

"I marvel at the calm of the Japanese haiku poets who just enjoy the passage of days and

live in what they call 'Do-Nothing-Huts' and are sad, then gay, then sad, then gay, like

sparrows and burros and nervous American writers." Kerouac to John Clellon Holmes

MEANWHILE, GARY WAS having his own poetic visions of Kerouac. One afternoon while Gary studied his Japanese grammar inside the cabin, a hummingbird hung buzzing at the unfinished open window, then shot off. When he looked up from his book, in the sudden stillness he saw Jack outside, stretched out on his sleeping bag in the mottled light of the yard, reading his Diamond Sutra, like a young Walt Whitman lounging with the Upanishads. "Jack Kerouac outside, behind my back / Reads the *Diamond Sutra* in the sun"—The snapshot line, from "Migration of Birds," captured the sun-splashed scholarliness and ease of their life at Marin-an. It also caught Kerouac in his contemplative aspect, and joined Jack's name with the Diamond Sutra in an abiding association.

Certainly, Kerouac aligned himself spiritually with the Diamond Sutra during those years. It was *the* book of his Buddhist period and probably one of the three or four most influential things he ever read. The Diamond Sutra is a condensation of the voluminous Maha-Prajnaparamita scriptures (Highest Perfect Wisdom or Great Transcendent Truth). It teaches the practice of the six *paramitas*, or Buddhist virtues—Charity, Kindness, Patience, Zeal, Tranquility, and Wisdom. In North Carolina during the summer of 1955, Jack had hit on the idea of dividing the sutra into seven days' consecutive study—one day for each of the six *paramitas*, and a seventh for the powerful concluding "Samadhi" passage of the sutra. It was as though Kerouac were going back to Catholic school, with the Diamond Sutra as his new catechism.

Read, as I'm doing, the Diamond Sutra every day, Sunday read the Dana Charity chapter; Monday, Sila Kindness; Tuesday, Kishanti Patience; Wednesday, Virya Zeal; Thursday, Dhyana Tranquility; Friday, Prajna Wisdom; Saturday, conclusion," he wrote to Allen Ginsberg. "By living with this greatest of sutras you become immersed in the Truth that it is all One Undifferentiated Purity, creation and the phenomena, and become free from such conceptions as self, other selves, many selves, One Self, which is absurd. . . .

The year 1956—the Easonburg Woods, Marin-an, then Desolation Lookout—marked the peak of Kerouac's Buddhism, as well as the high point of his relationship with the Diamond Sutra. In fact, in Kerouac's practice, the two things—the Dharma and the Diamond Sutra—were inseparable.

It has been said—even by Philip Whalen—that Kerouac's Buddhism was mostly intellectual, but Jack's encounter with the Diamond Sutra, though certainly literary—*everything* was literary to Kerouac—was far from merely bookish. It was a visceral, fateful wrestling. The Prajnaparamita doctrine of Emptiness embodied in the sutra—*shunyata*—was seductive and spiritually dangerous. In the 1940s

Sokei-an had called it "a poisonous word," and cautioned his American students against slipping into "the harmful view of Emptiness," warning them not to even approach the doctrine without a teacher. Likewise, D. T. Suzuki pointed out: "Hui-Neng's concept of nothingness (wu-i-wu) may push one down into a bottomless abyss, which will no doubt create a feeling of utter forlornness," warned Suzuki. "The philosophy of Prajnaparamita, which is also that of Hui-neng, generally has this effect. To understand it a man requires a deep religious intellectual insight into the truth of Shunyata."

GARY SNYDER LEFT for Japan on May 6, 1956, after a three-day going-away party described at length in *The Dharma Bums* and remembered to this day by those who were there. Philip Lamantia, in the crowd that saw Snyder off at the pier, recalls Gary boarding the ship under the hugest seaman's duffel he had ever seen. Kerouac remained at McCorkle's for another six weeks, writing *Old Angel Midnight* and *The Scripture of the Golden Eternity,* reading haiku and drinking with his friends Bob Donlin and poet Robert Creeley and getting himself in shape for Desolation by hiking up to Gardner Lookout on Mount Tamalpais. At night he slept outside the shack, looking up at the moon. Deer ventured down through the trees, "hooftrompling" his sleep. One night Jack had a numinous dream that would ultimately provide the culminating "vision of Gary" at the conclusion of *The Dharma Bums.* In the dream, the figure of old Han Shan became merged with Gary—not the twenty-six-year-old Gary as he was in the present but an older version of Gary, his face like "Dostoevsky's death mask."

"O what a vision or dream I had of Han Shan! He was standing in the marketplace in China on a Saturday morning, with a little peaked hat very much like yours," Jack wrote Gary, "and a seamed and weatherbrowned little face, and very short, and hopelessly tangled rags hanging from him all over, and a small bundle bindlestiff bundle, he looked very much like you but smaller and he was old. Cant you find someone like that in Japan?"

Gary was still at sea aboard the *Arita Maru* when Jack had this dream. His ship arrived in Kobe on May 21; he was in Kyoto on the 22nd. By the end of May, Snyder's first letters from Japan began arriving in the Bay Area—Kerouac, Whalen, McCorkle, Ginsberg all received dispatches about Gary's first week in the country. He was settled in at Rinko-in, a temple in the venerable Shokoku-ji complex, where Dwight Goddard and R. H. Blyth had sat before the war.

It had been decided that although Ruth Fuller Sasaki had herself put up the funds to bring Gary over, he would work with Miura Isshu. The roshi, who until that time had been abbot of Koon-ji Temple (near Mount Fuji), would relocate to Rinko-in, where he would prepare himself—learning English among other things—for his eventual move to New York. Gary would be his student and personal attendant, cooking and serving all the teacher's meals.

Meanwhile, during Gary's first weeks in Japan, Miura Isshu was still away at Koon-ji and Gary was free to investigate Kyoto on his own. Kyoto was hot, but the Rinko-in temple was cool and airy, dark, and saturated with the serene fragrance of three centuries of incense. He began visiting some of the other temples in the Shokoku-ji complex, marveling at the gold-gilt Buddhas and dragon-painted ceilings and the imposing Kasyapa figure in the main zendo, "his eyes real and piercing anyone who enters the main door." Outside the temple grounds in the streets of Kyoto, Snyder's first impression was of the jarring poverty of the ordinary people. "I went around all week wanting to throw bombs at whoever's responsible, it hit me so hard," he wrote to Philip Whalen. "But there's nobody to blame it on."

As was his habit, Gary immediately sought out the highest places in the area. Within days of his arrival in Kyoto, he hiked Mount Atago, at 3,000 feet the highest hill in the Kitano River watershed. On his fourth day, he went up Mt. Hiei, Kyoto's sacred "guardian mountain"—*Hiei-zan* in Japanese—a mountain about the size of Tamalpais, a few miles northeast of the city. [Northeast is an inauspicious direction in Japan—the "Devil's Gate" through which evil forces may enter.] Three centuries before, Bashō had lived in a hermitage on the slopes of Hiei-zan. At the top was a thousand-year-old temple—Enryuku-ji, surrounded by a grove of ancient cedars. Inside the temple was a shrine room to Kwannon, so ornate that to Gary it "looked like a peyote dream."

From the first, Gary formed strong opinions about Japanese Buddhism. Enryuku-ji, for instance, had been envisioned as a "center for the protection of the nation." But the Tendai monks—"the treasure of the nation"—had made strategic Mount Hiei a fortress from which to launch military raids on Kyoto. In his journal, Gary noted that "the only superstitions that are really dangerous to peasant Buddhist types are the superstitions of nationalism and the state."

"The center of this world is quietly moving to San Francisco where it's most alive," wrote Gary in his first Kyoto journal entry, after meeting the few other Westerners on the compound and getting his first glimpse of Japanese monks going about their daily routines. "These Japanese folks may be left behind and they won't recognize it when they see it."

"There's no need for anybody to come over here," he wrote to Whalen, on only his second day at Rinko-in. "Sincerity and beatness and humour — you people got 'em & these don't; especially that magical quality of beatness and what it does."

After all Gary had gone through to get to Kyoto, Philip Whalen wasn't having any of it, especially the part about the beat magic. "You sound dangerously near to indulging in a great maudlin fit of sentimentality and nostalgia," he responded. "Have your mental faculties decayed in that incense-laden air?"

Gary soon thanked Philip for taking him to task — "although I confess my addled mind scarsely recalls just what I wrote to warrant such Johnsonian calls for restraint," he said, adding, "*I have never proposed myself as beat.*"

IN THE END, Phil Whalen decided not to return to the North Cascades for another fire season. He had taken the rather humorous job of cleaning glassware for the Poultry Husbandry Department at UC Berkeley. It sounded goofy in a Whalenesque way — "The Egg Plant," he called it — but it was exactly the kind of reliable and undemanding work — it ended each day at noon — that Philip wanted to hold onto while working on his poems. He had also inherited Allen Ginsberg's cozy cottage on Milvia.

Kerouac, who had fantasized about hitching up to the Skagit with Philip and radioing back and forth between their lookouts, was on his own. Just as the four dharma bums — Kerouac, Snyder, Whalen, and Ginsberg — had come together in perfect synch to inaugurate a new season of poetry and Buddhism in September of '55, now Gary's departure seemed to signal the sudden end of something. Within a month of Snyder's leaving, the quartet was again completely dispersed — Gary to Japan, Jack to the North Cascades, Ginsberg on a sea voyage to the Arctic, with only Whalen remaining in the Bay Area.

On the 18th of June, a Monday morning, Kerouac set out for Desolation from McCorkle's, marching off down Montford Road under full pack. In Mill Valley he began hitching north, following Highway 101 through Sonoma and Mendocino and Humboldt counties to Eureka and up into the redwoods to Crescent City. There he turned east to join up with Highway 99 at Grants Pass, Oregon. Now he was in Snyder country, following Gary's well-worn path up into Portland, across the Columbia, north to Snoqualmie Pass, and beyond — to America's last and greatest wilderness.

The slope behind Locke McCorkle's house on Montford Road outside Mill Valley, where Snyder and Kerouac stayed in an unfinished cabin in the spring of 1956. Snyder named the place "Marin-an"— Japanese for "Horse Grove Hermitage," for the adjacent meadow with its grazing mares.

How the gravity of Nature and her silence startles you,
when you stand face to face with her, undistracted, before a barren ridge
or in the desolation of the ancient hills.

Goethe

Desolation Adventure

Desolation Peak, Summer 1956

JUST AS GARY always sought out the heights of any new locale—to scan the scene and meet the spirits of the place—so Kerouac was drawn to riverbanks. At Marblemount during his first week of fire school, Jack liked to walk into town after dinner in the Ranger Station cookhouse, to get a bottle of wine at the low, long-logged Marblemount General Store. He would drink it— a half-pint "poorboy" wrapped in a tight brown paper bag—on the banks of the Skagit, close down by the water so that he could smell the river and feel the rush and pull of its "heaving bulk." Jack liked to drink his wine in meditative sips, sitting cross-legged on the flat seat of a sawed-off stump or a rock, smoking his pipe and scribbling away with his nubby number-two lead pencil in his blue "Golden West" notebook.

The Skagit was a powerful, fertile *mountain* river — "the moving mountain" Kerouac called it — which made a hard swerve west at Marblemount, received the surge of the Cascade River and flowed onward, thick with rock flour and dully glowing green. During his fire-school week, Jack sometimes stayed along its banks until after midnight, "drinking to the sizzle of the stars," and mesmerized by the glittering moonlight on the speeding water.

Kerouac had always loved rivers. Growing up as he had in the great watershed of the Merrimack and Concord, he had from an early age been attracted to them as sources of mystery and experience. In Lowell, mountains had been "misty intimations," visible in the far north on the clearest days only, but the river was always right there, close enough, he liked to say, that he had been born to the sound of March ice cracking at the falls, and that he could remember hearing it. The Merrimack had been his first river, his first "road," leading him to his earliest adventures. Since then, how many times had he crossed the Hudson, the Delaware, the Susquehanna, the Ohio, the Mississippi? The Missouri and the Platte? The Rio Bravo and the Moctezuma? For Kerouac, crossing a river was always a significant act — "Now we must all get out and dig the river and the people and smell the world," as his character Dean Mori-arty says when coming to the Mississippi in *On the Road.* So enthralled was Kerouac with the romance of rivers that for a time in the late 1940s, he even considered calling *On the Road* "Rain and Rivers."

Jack wrote many haiku by the banks of the Skagit during that last week of June. When he had first begun playing with haiku — shooting them back and forth with Snyder and Whalen and Ginsberg in the fall of 1955 — he had thought of them as fun, but "small." By late spring of 1956, however, he had come to respect both the form and the old haiku masters themselves, "who just enjoy the passage of days and lives in what they call 'Do-Nothing Huts' . . ." Before 1955, Jack had apparently never written haiku; by the time he got to the Skagit, however, haiku had become a favored form of condensed imag-istic sketching. Kerouac could compose haiku very quickly. On a given evening by the Skagit he might knock off a dozen or more. Of those, only a few became finished haiku, after careful honing.

Later, he stretched out many of these haiku into the short, energetic single sentences of *The Dharma Bums,* sometimes with the addition or deletion of a word or two, but mostly verbatim. The energy of much of the description in *The Dharma Bums* is haiku energy, haiku rhythm — "almost as if he were writing a book of a thousand haikus," as Allen Ginsberg later noted. There are instances in *The Dharma Bums* of a half dozen and more of these flattened-haiku sentences in a single descriptive paragraph.

Skagit River North of Marblemount, July 1995. *"My pure little favorite river of the Northwest,*

by which I'd sat, with wine, on sawdust stumps, at night, drinking to the sizzle of the stars and

watching the moving mountain send and pass that snow—" Jack Kerouac, *Desolation Angels*

ONE AFTERNOON in Marblemount Jack returned from fire school to find a blue aerogram letter from Gary on the cookhouse table. The letter, written on the summer solstice, contained two new translations of eight-lined Han Shan poems, and was adorned with the small kanji characters for "Rinko-in" and "Shokoku-ji" in Snyder's neat calligraphy. Gary described the temple grounds with stands of forty-foot-high bamboo waving in the Kyoto summer heat and "a bunch of monks making quite a racket on their Jap flutes somewhere."

"When they recite sutras with a steady Kwakiutl-dance-drum beat & riffs on the bells & sticks it's something to hear—a big prehistoric coyote chanting," he wrote, adding, "There are things tucked away in Buddhism that go back to the days when men married bears & talked to the buffalo."

Gary recalled the Marblemount compound where Jack was, remembering the circling nighthawks and barn swallows chattering over the meadows surrounding the ranger station, even telling Jack where to look for the swallows' nests in the cross beams of the horse stables. He also suggested that Jack check out a lovely pass along the Cascade River Road, a place full of wildflowers and views of jagged ice pinnacles, where he himself had spent both of his Fourth of Julys when he was at fire school. He sent his regards to Blackie and Andy Wilcox, as ever, and signed off: "Keep your socks darned & your boots greased!"

At the time Gary wrote his solstice letter to Jack, he had been in Kyoto for a month, but had not begun serious training, since his teacher Miura Isshu had not yet settled in Kyoto. By the time this letter arrived in Marblemount, Miura had come to Rinko-in and taken Gary back with him to his former temple, Koon-ji, to help with his final move. Koon-ji was an old temple that had once housed twenty-five monks. Now there was only one man, barely keeping the place going. Gary was to help clean the place and assist Miura Roshi in his move.

Even after a month in Japan things still reminded Gary of America—the smell of the abandoned monks' quarters at Koon-ji put him in mind of the musty mining shacks along Ruby Creek, right down to the mouse droppings in the left-behind coffee mugs. The monk's drum in the courtyard thumped with the same steady shamanistic beat that he'd heard at Warm Springs. Even the gold-leafed statue of a world-weary Manjusri on the Koon-ji altar reminded him of Warm Springs and the little sword-wielding Manjusri he used to keep in the bunkhouse back when he was setting chokers.

In the dim light of the Koon-ji zendo, Gary looked at the row of statues of former masters, trying to discern their personalities from their sculpted expressions. Mopping the slate floor before them, he saw men "who had made it through will, effort, years of struggle and intensity." Others through "poverty, wandering, and simple-minded self-sufficient detachment." And what about Manjusri? Tradition said that Han Shan was an incarnation of Manjusri, the Bodhisattva of Wisdom. The Manjusri in the zendo had "the face of a man who did it with cool intellect and comprehension, cynicism, and long historical views."

The spring of 1956 had been dry, and Frank Lewis was anxious to get his lookouts on top early, so Jack was spared the two-to-three-week trail crew stint that usually followed fire school, and was sent directly up the Skagit to the Ross Guard Station, and then on to Desolation. The night before Kerouac packed up, a storm blew down the lake, rocking the guard station float so that he couldn't get much sleep at all, and in the morning when he shoved off it was pouring rain. After a breakfast of ham and eggs, he and his packers left the dam head at six A.M. — July 5th — in a small blue tugboat with the horse barge behind — past the cabins and dock of the resort, around Green Point, around Cougar Island and onto the open lake, between the steep foggy flanks of Sourdough and Jack mountains. Out the back of the tug, Jack could see the animals huddled in the barge — three horses and four pack mules with tarp-covered loads, all heads down in the rain. The shores of the lake were barely visible in the blowing mists. Andy Wilcox was Jack's packer; Marty Gohlke, the Assistant Ranger from Marblemount, was coming along also; Fred Berry was piloting the boat. The ride took two full hours to get to Desolation.

At the shoreline trailhead the horses clambered off the horse raft, Jack and his rangers mounted — Kerouac on the mare Mabel, Phil Whalen's "satori horse" from the year before — and began packing up the hill in the rain. Jack felt like "a shroudy monk" under the hood of his poncho. The Desolation Trail began steep and stayed steep for 4,000 feet as it switchbacked up the west-southwest slope of the mountain through a world of moss-draped and moss-coated conifers. The area traversed by the pack trail had been burned over many times in centuries past, creating a tight packed landscape of trees of varying ages, from stands of fifty-year-old lodgepole pine, to occasional Douglas fir and Western red cedar giants that first sprouted in the after-heat of great sixteenth-century fires. In the rain, Jack and his packers plodded on like Renaissance knights following their narrow human path through the huge chaotic order of the wilderness.

At 4,400 feet the trail came out into the open, in fields exploding with paintbrush and lupine. The view down the lake toward Sourdough was grand in clear weather, but on the day of Kerouac's packing up, visibility was not more than fifty yards at best. In the fog he began to see the bodies of fallen Douglas fir snags lying slantwise in the open southern meadows. Many of these old trunks had toppled in the 1926 fire that had burned over from the Little Beaver drainage and leaped the Skagit to race up Desolation. Now they lay, cracked open by the decades, nursing fragile saplings and rows of wildflowers. There were other trees from that same 1926 fire —"widowmakers" they were called by firefighters, to be avoided in a burn —thirty years dead but still standing, their bare gnarled limbs groping tortuously in the fog and rain.

DURING HIS FIRST week in the lookout, Kerouac tried to pursue a regimen of writing, meditation, and dharma studies similar to what he'd followed at McCorkle's shack or his rooftop hut on Orizaba Street or his "Twin Tree" grove behind his sister's place in North Carolina. But compared to Desolation, those scenes had been idylls, with friends, running water, and liquor stores nearby. Now he was completely alone in some serious back country, and the emptiness of vast nature —something he had never experienced —was just seeping in.

Jack approached his solitude in a writerly way, and planned on using its long stretches to produce new work. Somewhat paradoxically, he spent his first wilderness nights with his mind in New York, as he swallowed the last of his Benzedrine to jump-start a new novel based on his pre-road days in Ozone Park in the mid-1940s.

WHEN THE RAINS and fog of his first days blew off, the view from Desolation was everything that Gary had foretold —"hundreds of miles of pure snow-covered rocks and virgin lakes and high timber." Jack threw himself into learning the terrain, cleaning and leveling the Osborne fire finder, then aiming it at the adjacent mountains to fix their names in his mind. This was what every lookout did, of course; but for Kerouac it fulfilled far more than just his Forest Service job description, it was an exciting literary endeavor —background for the book he knew he would write eventually about his Desolation experience. It was also an act of poetic communion with Gary and Phil, who'd inspired him in the first place with those very Skagit names. Kerouac took to the fire finder like a kid with a brand-new

Desolation Lookout, July 1995. "Such places (where the Scripture is observed) however wretched they may be, will be loved as though they were famous memorial parks and monuments, to which countless pilgrims and sages will come (to Desolation Peak!) to offer homage and speeches and dedications. And over them the angels of the unborn and the angels of the dead will hover like a cloud."

Jack Kerouac, *Desolation Journal*

Christmas toy, targeting each neighboring peak in the finder's delicate sights, checking its name on the Osborne map, feeling himself more and more centered in his new, blue mountain world with each ID. Like Adam in the morning, Jack spent that first week bestowing names on the surrounding drainages and snows, delighting in the pure act of identification as well as savoring the incantatory litany of names—

> names Japhy had sung to me so often: Jack Mountain, Mount Terror, Mount Fury, Mount Challenger, Mount Despair, Golden Horn, Sourdough, Crater Peak, Ruby, Mount Baker bigger than the world in the western distance, Jackass Mountain, Crooked Thumb Peak, and the fabulous names of the creeks: Three Fools, Cinnamon, Trouble, Lightning and Freezout. And it was all mine, not another human pair of eyes in the world were looking at this . . .

Kerouac didn't need the Osborne fire finder to locate or identify Mount Hozomeen. It was the most distinctive thing in his three-sixty, and practically boomed its own name. From his earliest conversations with Gary and Phil the previous fall, Jack had been hearing about the big, two-pointed mountain, and there it was. Of course, Snyder and Whalen had seen it at a distance of twelve miles, from their Crater and Sourdough lookouts. Gary had made his brush painting of it from Sourdough in '53. Even from a dozen miles off, Hozomeen was conspicuous on the horizon—"unforgettable," in Fred Beckey's opinion—but Kerouac on Desolation was palpably within the great mountain's aura, only four miles from Hozo's north peak summit. Hozomeen's south peak, with its ragged col and sheer basalt cliffs, was even closer. From the beginning, Jack was mesmerized—"Hozomeen, Hozomeen, the most beautiful mountain I ever seen," was a rhyme that flowed like a natural mantra from his first awed glimpse of it. It was a line he would use more than once.

Hozomeen is more than just a twin-peaked mountain. Its two main 8,000 foot pinnacles are supported by an array of shouldering peaks and spur ridges packed together in a twenty square mile complex—the Hozomeen Range, as it is sometimes called. Ten of these clustered peaks are higher than Desolation. Hozomeen is, in Buddhist terms, a huge aggregation of *Dharmakaya*—"the body of the great order"—running with streams and bristling with forests, nurturing vast amounts of life, including gray wolves, secretive cougars, and even a few grizzly bear.

Desolation, with its gently rounded and treeless northern lookout yard, was a perfect platform for the contemplation of Hozomeen's "untouchable towers" and "inaccessible horns." Kerouac—like every Desolation lookout before or since—spent many days before it, drawn in by the immensity and complexity of its form, with the constantly shifting light and cloud show playing over its flanks and summits. After a few weeks Jack had seen Hozomeen in every light from predawn rose to full-moon silver. He had even stared at it upside-down while doing his yoga headstands, a point-of-view from which the mountain appeared as "a mess of double pointed rock/Hanging pouring into space."

When the last slash of orange sunset flared out behind the Hope Range of British Columbia—around ten P.M. during the month of July—the lookout windows became like black mirrors reflecting only the cabin's interior. In the darkened glass Jack saw the familiar sight of himself hunched over his writing table, working in his notebooks, a candle burning on the table and a kerosene lantern perched behind him on the fire finder stand. He couldn't see through these reflections to the scene outside, so it was easy to lose himself in his visions of a decade-gone New York, or to dream up elaborate outlines for the Duluoz saga. But when he stepped into the night outside the L.O., he was spooked by the sound of deer hooves clattering away over the rocks, and the jarring presences of the surrounding peaks, arrayed like silent watchers in a dark cyclorama around his tiny, lantern-lit cabin.

The night world of Desolation was nearly overwhelming—"a little too much for a city boy," he later admitted. During his first weeks especially, the darkness took some getting used to, as it did for most lookouts. At first he didn't stray very far from the lookout and the fragile realm of light it created. Twelve and fifteen miles south, the pin points that were the lookout lamps of Sourdough and Crater seemed farther away than the tilting stars of Scorpio and Sagittarius. The night mountains felt far more sentient than they did in the day, and not always benign. Skagit Peak, immediately next door across Lightning Creek, looked positively sinister, its pointy rock dome like a smoking black helmet in the clouds. But none was more potently suggestive than Hozomeen. Hozomeen at night, with lurid sashes of Northern sunset running horizontally behind it and blue-black clouds cutting off its summits, suggested a titanic blast furnace, or forge. Other times, with smoke-like clouds billowing around its peaks, it looked like a volcano about to blow up in the dark. It seemed alive inside, deep in its bowels, from which an almost tangible force seemed to emanate. For weeks Jack was afraid to turn his back on

Hozomeen in the night, fearful it would somehow morph into the Abominable Snowman and swoop across Lightning Gorge to devour him. Only later could he write, "You realize the ghosts are all friendly . . . you learn that all the myths are true but empty."

WHILE HOZOMEEN clearly presided over the upper Ross Lake country, there were other notable sights on Kerouac's horizon. Looking due south out the cabin door the first thing he saw was his synchronistic namesake—Jack Mountain, a magnificent peak as well, a full thousand feet higher than Hozomeen, with a mile and a half slab of glacier ice slanting down its northeast face. Jack Mountain was made of the same rock as Hozomeen, yet somehow it lacked Hozomeen's charisma. Together, both peaks had long ago been crunched up from the prehistoric ocean floor to form their parts of the same long, mountainous barricade running east along the Ross Lake fault—the Hozomeen Terrane, as it is known by geologists. Jack is one of the highest peaks in the North Cascades, and to mountaineers a far more difficult ascent than Hozomeen. Still, it does not dominate the imagination the way Hozomeen does. Jack impresses, but seldom startles. Only partially is it a matter of proximity—Jack is twice Hozomeen's distance from Desolation, certainly mitigating its impact, but even from Crater or Sourdough the eye tends to be pulled past Jack to Hozo.

Kerouac's writing table faced Jack Mountain, but the big peak never particularly inspired or frightened him. "Old Jack," he called it familiarly, as he sometimes referred to himself. Even the splendid Nohokomeen Glacier (which Gary and Phil could never see from their lookouts) didn't do much for him. "A thousand football fields of snow all raveled and pink," was all he had to say for it. Not being a mountaineer, he never got caught up in the slow spectacle of the glacier's subtle summer changes.

Looking farther south, Kerouac could see Crater poking up over the broad southeast shoulder of Jack Mountain, while on the other side of the lake was the long gradual east-west ridge of Sourdough, still with snow on the north side of the ridge. Through his binoculars Jack could see the L.O. on Sourdough, tiny, an exact replica of his Desolation cabin, with its pointed roof and out-propped shutters. He could see it perched up on the snowy ridge line, outlined against the gray backdrop of Pyramid Peak. Beyond Sourdough was the great range of glaciers: Colonial and Neve, Inspiration and Eldorado,

◄   *Desolation Lookout seen from the lookout trail, July 1995.*

Boston and Buckner and Logan. In the glasses Jack could also see Gary's closed-up old lookout on Crater summit; the new Crater Lookout, operational for the first time that summer, was on the East Peak, manned for the season by a college kid from Oregon.

THE SAME WEEK that Jack packed up to Desolation, Gary had returned to Kyoto from Koon-ji Temple with Miura Isshu, and his new life as a Zen trainee began in earnest. In early July Gary formally requested to become Miura Isshu's disciple; then, in a separate ritual he acknowledged himself a lay follower of the Buddha. At Rinko-in's main zendo altar, Gary prostrated himself on the slate floor before Miura Roshi and recited the gatha of the "Three-fold Refuge":

> *I take refuge in the Buddha, the incomparably honored one;*
> *I take refuge in the Dharma, honorable for its purity;*
> *I take refuge in the Sangha, honorable for its harmonious life.*

Then he took the Four Great Buddhist Vows.

> *Sentient beings are numberless; I vow to save them.*
> *The deluding passions are inexhaustible; I vow to destroy them.*
> *The Gates of Dharma are manifold; I vow to enter them.*
> *The Buddha-way is supreme; I vow to complete it.*

The ceremony closed with the Roshi and another monk chanting the Heart Sutra over Gary, with its great central line, "Form is emptiness, emptiness is not different from form, neither is form different from emptiness, indeed, emptiness is form." Afterwards they made a trip to the grave of Miura's own master, Nanshinken, who in his day had been known as the toughest sodo roshi in Japan. Gary laid flowers and burned incense in honor of his teacher's teacher. He was now officially Buddhist, a member of the sangha. The journey from his road shoulder revelation reading Suzuki on the Humboldt to these

Desolation doorway, looking south,
Jack Mountain in the distance, July 1995. ➤

vows taken on the cool temple floor of Rinko-in had lasted nearly five years. With typical understatement, Gary wrote to Phil Whalen back in Berkeley: "Well the way I figure now is that if enlightenment's a real thing it should be possible to get it in Japan just as easy as America, so I won't worry about it."

UNLIKE GARY and Phil, who had always packed up as many books as they could and used their lookout time to indulge in voracious reading programs, Kerouac took only one book with him to Desolation: his leather-jacketed *Buddhist Bible,* with its marker-ribbon set to the pages of the Diamond Sutra. Jack's reading on Desolation was aimed at one goal: to condition his mind to "emptiness," and, if possible, to actually bring on a vision. If any book could do that, he was convinced, it was the Diamond Sutra — the scripture that had sparked Hui-Neng's famous first satori. "Something will happen to me on Desolation Peak, as happened to Hui Neng on Vulture Peak," he had written to Gary earlier in the year. Now he was acting on Hui-Neng's thousand-year-old advice from the Platform Sutra to "just devote yourselves to the one volume of the Vajracchedika-prajnaparamita Sutra [Diamond Sutra] and you will, seeing into the nature of your being, enter upon the Prajna-samadhi."

Jack read the Diamond Sutra, following his practice of studying one paramita/chapter a day in a weekly cycle, as he had been doing more or less regularly since 1955. As Gary had learned on Crater in '52 when he'd also been reading the Diamond Sutra, there were few settings better than the vastness and solitude of a fire lookout for touching the spirit of such texts.

AFTER TEN DAYS all the novelty of lookout life had worn off. "Time drags," Jack wrote of the days that began at 4:30 A.M. with the sun blasting in over Freezout Mountain and didn't end until it sank slowly behind Mount Spickard eighteen hours later. He complained that he could hardly sleep because of mice running around the lookout all night; during the day he suffered plagues of blackflies, deerflies, mosquitoes, bees. Inside, the cabin was crawling with spiders and flying ants. Still, he wrote that he was feeling happier than he had in years.

Then his tobacco ran out. Jack had intended to quit smoking as part of his mountaintop asceticism, but when the last of the cigarettes that he'd brought was gone, he soon found that his solitary L.O. was not a good place to go cold turkey. First he tried to assuage his withdrawal by smoking some dried coffee grounds, which he claimed got him high at first, then sick. "Need tobacco, going nuts," he scrawled in his notebook. Finally, his cravings got the best of him, and he radioed down to the Ross Guard Station to send a boat to meet him at the shoreline trail head with a can of tobacco and some rolling papers. The Ross guards apparently took pity on him, and in fact had a boat waiting on the Desolation shore at the appointed time. They invited Jack on board, and took him with them on their rounds of the fishing camps up and down the lake. From north of Jack Point he could look up from the boat and see his little cabin perched at the rounded summit. That night he slept at the Ross Float, after a great ham steak dinner from the guard station meat cooler, and a couple of nips of white lightning out on the dock. The next day he was ferried back up to the lookout trail head, with a one pound tin of Prince Albert rolling tobacco tucked fondly under his arm.

He hiked back up the hill, alone again, over the same path he'd taken on horseback in the rain on his first day of Desolation. Now on foot, he had more of a chance to look around at the wilderness of rot and power that enclosed him, opening before him step by step, then folding shut behind him, the cushioning duff swallowing up even the sounds of his footsteps. Nothing but the sound of his own blood in his ears and the raw whoosh of his breathing as he plodded up the switchbacks. Unlike Gary, Jack could hardly name a single species in the all-thrusting chaos of lichen-bearded limbs and clawing rootwads, or the stands of perfectly straight blowdowns flattened and scattered like so many pickup sticks. But already he had come to understand Gary's saying that the mountains were their mind.

"Yes, for I'd thought, in June, hitch hiking up there to the Skagit Valley in northwest Washington for my fire lookout job 'When I get to the top of Desolation Peak and everybody leaves on mules and I'm alone I will come face to face with God or Tathagata and find out once and for all what is the meaning of all this existence,'" he would later write in *Desolation Angels*. "But instead I'd come face to face with myself, no liquor, no drugs, no chance of faking it but face to face with ole Hateful Duluoz Me."

Back in the lookout, Jack now resigned himself to at least another five weeks of solitude, diverting his thoughts from the inhumanity of Desolation with memories of Esperanza Villanueva, the woman who had inspired *Tristessa* and would be waiting for him—he hoped—in Mexico City when he got down from the mountain. He worked on long letters, never mailed, to Neal Cassady and Peter Orlovsky (Allen Ginsberg's lover), and a very long one to his mother, to which he added every few days.

To entertain himself, he drew up a goofy "List of Things for My New Life"—his post-Desolation life. "Have Fun!" "Make plays for women old and young!" and "Take money from homosexuals (that's a joke, son)" were a few of the entries on the list. One of the fantasies that consumed him was to purchase a tape recorder on his return, for voice-composing plays. For a few days he toyed with the image of himself spontaneously speaking "play action" Broadway hits onto reels of tape. "BROADWAY HERE I COME!" he wrote in his notebook, in caps. He read whatever random old magazines and moldy books he found lying around the lookout—a biography of John Barrymore, old Westerns, and *The God That Failed,* a collection of essays by formerly left-wing writers who had become disillusioned by Communism. He also spent many hours playing a solitaire baseball game he had invented thirteen years before with his friend Seymour Wise. It was an elaborate game, with two decks of hand-drawn cards forming countless combinations of strike-outs and walks, ground-outs and fly-outs, extra base hits and home runs. The game could be played for hours, and Kerouac also kept detailed scorecards in various notebooks. He had a whole league of teams, with rosters manned by players with names like Parker, Cassady, etc. Some of the old pitchers were thirteen-year veterans of Kerouac's league, with illustrious records and memorable games enshrined in the Cooperstown of his vast imagination.

MOSTLY, HOWEVER, Kerouac wrote. Even before his July 21 tobacco run to the Ross Guard Station, he had finished 15,000 words of the Ozone Park novel he had started on his first night. He also added to "The Martin Family"—the projected sequel to *The Town and the City* that he'd begun in the spring in North Carolina. Jack kept various notebooks as well. One was the small blue "Golden West" memo book of the type he always kept in his chest pocket, for on-the-spot sketching and spontaneous journaling. Another was a slightly more deliberate record of his lookout life, which he added to almost daily and called "Desolation Adventure." This book eventually would form the basis for the "Desolation in Solitude" section of *Desolation Angels*—"written up there in boredom and good health, a real gas of mountain prose done in full bloom of snowburn and windburn and Sourdough burn," as he later described it to Phil Whalen. Kerouac called it his Desolation Adventure because that's what he wanted it to become and was afraid it might not—he always worried that from a literary standpoint Desolation might only offer a chronicle of solipsistic tedium. Jack also kept two poetic notebooks: one of haiku, entitled "Desolation Pops"—for the "little Samadhi" packed into the three-lined form—and another of one-page blues choruses, which would eventually be published as "Desolation Blues" in his posthumous *Book of Blues.*

Snowpan and shovel, Desolation Peak, July 1995.

Another writing project that occupied him throughout the season was his ongoing "transliteration" of the Diamond Sutra, that is, his personal reworking of the sutra "from the English-of-the-Translators, to an English to be understood by ordinary people." From the beginning of his interest in Buddhism, Kerouac had attempted to render into his own words the unfamiliar Sanskrit, Chinese, and Japanese terms he came across in his readings. He also substituted what he considered simpler English words for the sometimes ponderous translations of the sutras in Dwight Goddard's *A Buddhist Bible.* These transliterations were to further his own understanding, but also to help explain the Buddhist concepts to other Westerners. There was a strong evangelical aspect to Kerouac's Buddhism. Jack took seriously the Diamond Sutra's promise of future merit to those propagating its message of non-attachment.

Jack had played with various alternate names for the Diamond Sutra over the years. He was aware that "Diamond Sutra" was a shorthand title. The more precise translation of its Sanskrit title, *Vajracchedika,* was "Diamond *Cutter*"—with the emphasis more on the incisive properties of a blade than the clarity or preciousness of a gem. "The Diamond Vow of God's Wisdom," "The Diamond Cutter of the Wise Vow," "The Diamond Cutter of Ideal Wisdom" were some of the names he gave it. By 1956, Jack was convinced—some of the time, at least—that it was the only book he would ever again need. He planned to create a small, hand-lettered version of his completely transliterated Diamond Cutter by itself, so that when traveling he would no longer have to weigh down his pack with the entire 600-page Goddard anthology, most of which he felt had served its purpose in his development. He called his Desolation transliteration "The Diamond Cutter of Perfect Knowing."

Despite his steady output on these various works, none of them save the "Diamond Cutter" really excited Jack. His Ozone Park and Martin Family manuscripts were never finished. As for Desolation, he seriously questioned whether high-country stillness and the daily interior life of a solitary modern man would provide enough juice for a book in the Kerouac style. He wanted to write "poems about hearts not just rocks." He complained to himself that he was "too bored here to write anything interesting," and fretted that he was losing touch with the sources of his old inspiration. "One thing's sure, I better start living adventurously again so I'll have something to write about," he told himself without apparent irony, little realizing that he was in the middle of one of his greatest literary adventures, one that would, in years to come, launch countless wilderness treks and vision quests.

Looking due west across Ross Lake, Jack's view was straight up the U-shaped valley of Little Beaver Creek, the route Henry Custer had followed into the Skagit in mid-August 1859, crossing over Whatcom Pass from the Chilliwack country to the west—the first Euro-American to do so. Custer called Little Beaver "Glacier Creek," from its origin in the glacial cascades he observed coursing over the precipitous ice cliffs of the Challenger Glacier—"Wila-Kin-ghaist" to his native guides. Glaciers had sculpted the valley 10,000 years before: what was left of the Cordilleran ice sheet could still be seen in an array of crevassed glaciers hanging from the east side of Whatcom Peak to the pinnacles of Crooked Thumb.

After Challenger, Custer had pushed further east down the Little Beaver drainage, following an ancient, half-forgotten hunting trail along the creek, and reached the west bank of the Skagit on August 14, 1859. The next day, Custer's party crossed the river and marched north to Hozomeen, skirting the base of Desolation as they went. Kerouac, peering down from his lookout a century later, knew nothing of old Henry Custer. The riverbank trail that Custer and his men had taken was all under the waters of Ross Lake in 1956, his adventures long forgotten by all but the most diligent local historians.

Desolation was a no-name peak when Custer passed by on that mid-August day in 1859 and would remain so throughout his survey. Custer was, however, the first white man to use the word "desolate" to describe the tawny mountains east of the Skagit. During his late August reconnaissance of the river, Custer hiked up an easy hill south of Hozomeen—probably Jackass Mountain—for a look around and in his journal noted the "desolate" character of the surrounding peaks. He would pass Desolation twice more on his travels that month but left it nameless on his map. It was not until the U.S. Forest Service map of 1931 that Desolation was finally named—by the ubiquitous Lage Wernstedt most likely, who made aerial photographs of the burned-over mountain in November 1926 following the great Upper Skagit fire of that year.

The fire of 1926 was a pivotal event in modern Skagit history. When Snyder and Whalen and Kerouac came to the country in the 1950s, some of the old Forest Service men who had been on the burn still talked about it. The smoke had been detected quite early in the season, on the Fourth of July, far upstream near the headwaters of Big Beaver Creek. From there it worked its way north and east into the drainage of the Little Beaver, then burned east toward the Skagit, stalling and surging with the wind

Hozomeen Mountain, July 1995. "Every time I thought of the void I'd be looking at Mt. Hozomeen (because chair and bed and meadow grass faced north) until I realized 'Hozomeen is the Void—at least Hozomeen means the void to my eyes'—Stark naked rock, pinnacles a thousand feet high protruding from hunch-muscles another thousand feet high protruding from immense timbered shoulders, and the green pointy-fir snake of my own (Starvation) ridge wriggling to it, to its awful vaulty blue smokebody rock . . .

Hozomeen, Hozomeen, the most
beautiful mountain I ever seen . . ."

Jack Kerouac, *Desolation Angels*

over many weeks, until it finally leaped the river (the Skagit was not damned then) and swept over Desolation, driving off the suppression crews with its fury and raging until it was finally blanketed by October snow.

In fact, the 1926 fire, though memorable, was not an unusual event in the long life of the watershed. It was actually more typical than not of the big burns that had shaped the Upper Skagit forest. Desolation and the area east of it in the Pasayten have always been particularly fire-prone, being in the rain shadow of the northern Pickets and 9,300-foot Mount Shuksan. The ridgetop of Desolation had been raked over by lightning and kept bald with periodic burns from time immemorial. Prior to 1926, fire had scoured Desolation's summit in 1919, 1880, and 1872. Earlier, a huge 1851 conflagration had scorched almost the entire mountain and burned far north into British Canada. Another enormous fire in 1648 had completely burned over Desolation. In between these "great" fires were many smaller ones. On average, a fire of one size or another occurs on Desolation about every fourteen years.

After the 1926 fire, however, there had not been another major burn on Desolation, and there was none on it, or nearby, during Kerouac's season on the peak. But in mid-August, after weeks without rain, lightning began striking the dry Upper Skagit. Kerouac had to stand on his little glass-footed lightning stool and felt the hair lifting on his neck as his rooftop lightning rod ticked with "a strand of electricity from a strike on Skagit Peak, great power silently and unobtrusively slithers through my protective rods and cables and vanishes into the earth of desolation." At night he lay in his rope-webbed bunk in the southwest corner of the L.O. (rope instead of metal springs, so as not to attract electricity) while heavy thunder pounded the mountains from the Pasayten to the Pickets.

Finally, on August 14 Jack saw a fire break out twenty-two miles south of him in the Thunder Creek drainage, not far from the 1952 and '53 burns that Gary had written about at the end of *Myths and Texts*. The smoke, which had ignited from a storm the night before and burned slowly throughout the morning, suddenly blew up behind Ruby Mountain at three in the afternoon. From twenty-two miles away Kerouac saw the black column churning up like an explosion in an oil refinery as the fire went from a three- to a twenty-acre burn in just two hours, fanned by a late-day wind blowing southwest up the Skagit.

Over the radio he heard his counterparts on East Crater, Sourdough, and Lookout Mountain scrambling to determine the coordinates. Finally Sourdough got an accurate read on the base of the fire, which was on a slope above the junction of Thunder and McAllister creeks. Jack, uninvolved in the drama and disinterestedly slurping noodles on Desolation, listened to the suppression efforts unfolding over his two-way radio.

Kerouac admired the courage and stamina of the smoke chasers who had to march to the burn carrying heavy fire packs for fifteen miles before they could even begin digging lines and felling trees, but he had to guffaw when he heard the Sourdough lookout refer to the smoke as though, by merely fixing its location, he now somehow owned it. "These guys being forestry careerists they are very religiously jealous of 'his' and 'my' fire," he noted in *Desolation Angels.*

Although Kerouac greatly admired the skills of old "Forestry Bodhisattvas" like Blackie Burns, in the end, he knew that the big fires were nearly always put out by rain or snow. As for wilderness fire suppression, he asked, "What American loses, when a forest burns, and what did Nature do about it for a million years up to now?" Mostly, Kerouac thought of the Forest Service as "a front for the lumber interests, the net result of the whole thing being, what with Scott Paper Tissue and such companies logging out these woods year after year with the 'cooperation' of the Forest Service . . . people all over the world are wiping their ass with the beautiful trees."

DESOLATION MAY HAVE gone nameless into the twentieth century, but the high gray crags of Hozomeen were held in awe and given title long before the first white men ever stepped foot in the Skagit country. They were Hozomeen to Chinsoloc, the Indian elder who drew the map of the Upper Skagit country for Henry Custer. In the language of the Lower Thompson natives, Hozomeen translates as "sharp, like a sharp knife," a seemingly obvious reference to the mountain's upjutting pinnacles. But the name may have originally derived from pure utility: in ancient times, we know now, good stone blades came from Hozomeen rock.

Not for centuries but for several millennia before Henry Custer led his 1859 party past Hozomeen, native people had been drawn to the area by its metamorphic chert, a rock that chips to a good cutting edge and rivals obsidian as a material for arrowheads, spear points, axes, and knives. Amazingly, ancient people had been quarrying Hozomeen chert on the Upper Skagit 8,000 years ago and supplying blades to a widespread region, from Puget Sound east to the Similkameen Valley, and from the Fraser River south to Lake Chelan.

Mount Prophet Moon, looking west from Desolation Peak, July 1995.

One of the largest of these old chert quarries was on the western flanks of Desolation. Kerouac couldn't have known of any of this. No one at that time did. The first chert quarries along the Ross Lake shore were not discovered until twenty years after his death. Not until well after Jack had left the Skagit had anthropologists begun to question the old Boasian model that the first peoples had stayed along the Coast and not ventured into the mountains. Gary, who had been trained in that school, was repeating the current anthropological belief at the time when he told Jack, "I don't think the Skagit Indians ever penetrated that far back into the mountains."

"DESOLATION WAS aptly named," says Jack Francis, who manned the lookout in '52. "No one came . . . and there was a guest book in the lookout that had been there for twenty years with only two signatures in it—and they were former lookouts themselves who knew how isolated the place could get and so came up to visit."

Kerouac, like Jack Francis before him, had no visitors in his entire sixty-three days on Desolation, a phenomenal stretch of solitude for a gregarious urban man like Kerouac, who despite his frequent and outspoken longings to be alone, had an even stronger need for the regular communion of his friends.

In the mornings he rinsed his face in a battered tin basin of pure mountain snow water, and in the evening, he "made his fire roar" and sat before it smoking—just as he had dreamed it when he was seventeen. Indeed, fifteen years before, back in New England, he had imagined himself in exactly such a scene, "with the mountains steeped in absolute silence and blackness." But when he looked up and saw his thirty-four-year old face reflected in the black lookout windows that now surrounded him, it sometimes seemed impossible that he had ever wanted this.

"How sad my great bronzed face in the windows with their dark backdrop, the lines in my face indicating halfway in life, middle age almost," Jack mused in the stock-taking of his final weeks on Desolation. He was well aware that at thirty-four many of his artistic exemplars had begun to see the waning of their powers. At thirty-four, Melville's greatest works were behind him. At thirty-four, Thomas Wolfe had finished his Eugene Gant trilogy and was dying. And Charlie Parker—Jack still couldn't believe it—was already dead, only halfway into his thirty-fifth year. Even the stoic Thoreau had to admit, a few days after his own thirty-fourth birthday, "I think that no experience which I have today comes up to, or is comparable with, the experiences of my youth. . . . I can remember that I was all alive, and inhabited my body with inexpressible satisfaction."

Other nights Kerouac was not quite so haunted. He could see a completely different image: "My hair was long, my eyes pure blue in the mirror, my skin tanned and happy." There was truth in both reflections. With his system clean of both alcohol and amphetamines for nearly two months, Jack at the end of August 1956 was leaner and healthier than at any time since his football days at Columbia.

On those nights he assured himself that thirty-four was not that old, and buoyed his creative hopes with images of his hero Dostoevsky, whose greatest works were of his maturity. At thirty-four, Dostoevsky was only just out of Siberian leg-irons. If Dostoevsky could write five masterpieces in the decade of his forties, Jack told himself, then such a creative outburst was not impossible to him. Shakespeare, another of Jack's literary gods, had also exploded with midlife genius — *Hamlet, Othello, Lear, Macbeth, Antony and Cleopatra, Coriolanus,* all written between the ages of thirty-six and forty-three. At thirty-four, Whitman had hardly begun to sound his voice. Joyce was in Zurich, finishing *A Portrait of the Artist as a Young Man,* with *Ulysses* and *Finnegans Wake* still to come.

"Where the top of this arch of life may be, it is difficult to know," wrote Dante. "I believe that in the perfectly natural man, it is at the thirty-fifth year." Hopefully, the dark woods of Desolation would lead Jack to Paradise, as they had for Dante. "Now I'll go on, into truly mighty work," Kerouac vowed to himself. "This will be my Desolation Testament." In fact, Desolation would be Jack's last great adventure; at thirty-four, Kerouac's life was almost three-quarters gone. There were still plenty of high times to come, of course. With the publication of *On the Road* in 1957, Kerouac would have all the excitement he could handle. He would have his "satoris" in New York, Big Sur, Paris, and other places, but nothing Jack would do again would ever be as worthy of his great literary exuberance as his two months on the mountain.

JACK'S BRAND of religious experience, from his French-Canadian boyhood on, had always been mystical and visionary, replete with the lore of miraculous apparitions, stigmatas, showers of celestial roses. Mexican Catholicism appealed to him for the same reasons, as did Buddhism, with its elaborate litanies of Bodhisattvas and flower-strewing devas. The contemplative side of Buddhism had a strong

Desolation Lookout under a full moon, July 1995.

"In the evening, with the mountains steeped
in absolute silence and blackness, I would make
my fire roar and would sit before it smoking . . ."

Jack Kerouac, *Atop an Underwood*

appeal for Kerouac as well, but a routine of Zen ordinariness — daily zazen without spiritual fireworks — went completely against his temperament. Jack could be a monk, but only for a few days at a time. What he wanted on Desolation, as everywhere and always, was "ecstasy of mind." By the end of August, he admitted to himself: "I'd rather have drugs and liquor and divine visions than this empty barren fatalism on a mountaintop."

Without the stimulation of a visceral "Desolation satori," Jack's longing for the realm of the senses grew ever more acute. From Day One back in Marblemount he had kept a running tally of his Forest Service earnings in his chest-pocket notebook; now he fantasized about how he would spend it in a riot of sensual pleasures once he got down. Mexico loomed in his mind, fragrant, sexy, hot with color, noisy, delicious. He would pick up a girl in the Zona Rosa, or quietly devour a box of incomparable Mexican chocolates in his hotel room while savoring Boswell's Johnson. More and more, he turned his back on Hozomeen and found himself standing in his south-facing lookout door, thoughts drifting 4,000 miles beyond Hart's Pass, to Mexico City, counting the days until he would lie in "the warm arms of Esperanza."

"Enough of rocks and trees and yalloping y-birds," he wrote. "I wanta go where there's lamps and telephones and rumpled couches with women on them. . . . I'd rather undo the back straps of red-heads dear God and roam the redbrick walls of perfidious samsara than this rash rugged ridge full of bugs."

Finally the rains came, soaking the Skagit, ending the fire danger on the forest. On the morning of August 26th, Jack's two-way radio crackled with the news that the season was officially over. He heard Blackie Burns calling down his Glacier District lookouts. Kerouac was ecstatic. "Yippiee I yelled and sang in my sack to hear it!" He could not pack out immediately, however. The Skagit, and the Desolation area particularly, had a higher fire danger than other districts in the region. It would be another twelve days before Kerouac could close up the L.O. and return to "the world."

All along the ridge now, the huckleberries were ripening black and dark red and purple-blue — "a mile-long patch of sweet blueberries all the way down to the timberline." Jack spent his last days combing the low bushes in his own private berry feast among swooping, squawking birds. When he looked back up to the cabin, the birds fluttering over it seemed to be rejoicing, as in a scene out of Saint Francis. Then one morning he saw bear sign — fresh, leaf-packed scat on the trail and a tooth-punctured tin can of condensed milk from the L.O. garbage pit. As Jack peered down the foggy ridge, an image came to him of Bear as Bodhisattva, and though he never saw an actual bear on Desolation, he wrote one of the most moving passages of *Desolation Angels* in honor of "Avalokitesvara the Bear."

"He wears on his might the seal of blood and reawakening—His toes are webbed and mighty," he wrote. "He will not show himself in the mystery of those silent foggy shapes, tho I look all day, as tho he were the inscrutable Bear that cant be looked into—He owns all the Northwest and all the Snow and commands all mountains."

AUGUST 29TH—a Wednesday—marked Kerouac's fortieth day since going down for tobacco to the Ross Guard Station, then hiking back up the Desolation Trail with his can of Prince Albert. Forty days and forty nights of uninterrupted solitude, forty days without any human contact other than the nightly talk-a-round hour on the radio (which Jack didn't usually participate in). Plus his first sixteen days in early July. And still another eight before he could leave. Few modern people had been put to such a solitary test. Thoreau said that he had felt lonely but one time at Walden, and then only for about an hour, and later realized that he hadn't quite been himself at the time. But Thoreau had never been as isolated at Walden Woods as Kerouac was on Desolation. Kerouac was running on scriptural time, topping Jesus's forty days in the wilderness, closing in on Buddha's forty-nine beneath the Bo Tree.

Kerouac had endured. He was not broken or shattered. He wrote that his "mind was in rags," but that was a literary exaggeration. In fact, his psyche had held. Furthermore, Desolation had not, as some have claimed, "ruined Kerouac as a writer." On the contrary, Jack's time on Desolation would furnish him with good literary grist for future works—the culmination of *The Dharma Bums*, the finest chapters of *Desolation Angels*, the long "Alone on a Mountaintop" essay in *Lonesome Traveler*, and the 12 Choruses of "Desolation Blues."

As August turned slowly into September, Jack's spirits soared. His last days on Desolation—once he was certain they *were* the last—were some of his best as he reaffirmed the spiritual quest that had brought him to the mountain in the first place. Perhaps he hadn't been given the vision he had sought—at least not the sort of Hui-neng Blakean pyrotechnics he had expected—but he *had* seen another world. For a time he had been privileged to dwell in the realm of the Immortals, where, as in the old Zen saying, he "whistled at the moon and slept in the clouds."

On the morning of September 5th, Marty Goehlke, the Assistant Ranger from Marblemount, woke Jack over the radio with the news that a boat would be coming uplake to get him the next day, and that he should close up the cabin. Unlike Gary, who had come off his lookouts with some sadness, Kerouac on his final day was more than ready to leave. "Last day of Desolation! I sang it as I woke up in my sweet sack — took down the anemometer & pole — All ready to fly down the mount to Old Mexico —," he wrote. Then, somewhat numbly, he closed out his impressionistic "Desolation Adventure," not so much concluding it as giving it up. "Desolation Adventure has power," he adjudged, "but it is not suitable for my potentialities."

That night was a Wednesday, Jack's night for studying the Virya Paramita of the Diamond Sutra. The Virya section of the sutra had always been one of the most poignant to him. Goddard translated Virya as "Zeal and Perseverance." Jack, in his transliteration, called it "Eagerness," a virtue he had always possessed in abundance and which he considered absolutely indispensable in the heart make-up of an artist, or any visionary. It was in that chapter that the scripture seemed to magically cut across the centuries to address its individual readers with the promise that "wherever this Scripture shall be observed and studied and explained, that place will become sacred ground." As Jack looked around the clean-swept shack — tools stashed, inventory done, his rucksack loaded and ready to go by the door, he thought of all the nights he had stayed up late in his bunk, studying the sutra by lantern light. "Such places," the Diamondcutter prophesied, "however humble they may be, will be reverenced as though they were famous temples and pagodas, to which countless pilgrims will come to offer worship and incense. And over them the devas and angels will hover like a cloud and will sprinkle upon them an offering of celestial flowers."

It was one of Kerouac's favorite passages. That last night on Desolation it must have seemed to Jack that the sutra was speaking to him, heart-mind to heart-mind. Before turning in, he worked the Virya passage into his transliteration, changing certain words for poetic effect, or to make them more understandable to Western readers. "Temples and pagodas," for instance, he changed to read "memorial parks and monuments." "Devas," a Sanskrit term meaning "shining ones," he dropped in favor of "angels of the unborn."

"Such places (where the scripture is observed), however wretched they may be, will be loved as though they were famous memorial parks and monuments . . ." scribbled Jack in the blue Golden West notebook he had carried in his shirt pocket all summer. Then, his mood swelling with self-belief, he went on, ". . . to which countless pilgrims and sages will come (to Desolation Peak!) to offer homage and speeches and dedications. And over them the angels of the unborn and the angels of the dead will hover like a cloud."

Then, as always, coming down, he added: "Tomorrow morning at 11 AM Fred will meet me with the boat and a pack of cigarettes at the foot of Desolation Trail—"

Religious Heros of America
practicing kindness & mindfulness . . .
Jack Kerouac

A Decent
Mad Narrative

1957–1959

EXACTLY ONE YEAR to the day of his leaving the Skagit, Kerouac's life changed forever with the publication of *On the Road* and Gilbert Millstein's *New York Times* review comparing Jack's book to Hemingway's *The Sun Also Rises* and declaring Kerouac the "principal avatar" of the Beat Generation.

Joyce Glassman, Kerouac's girlfriend at the time, was with him in New York on the eve of Millstein's review and recalls reading it with him as it hit a newsstand at Sixty-sixth and Broadway. "It was all very thrilling—but frightening, too. I'd read lots of reviews in my two years in publishing: none of them made pronouncements like this. . . . What would a generation expect of its avatar? Jack kept shaking his head. He didn't look happy, exactly, but strangely puzzled, as if he couldn't figure out why he wasn't happier than he was. We returned to the apartment to go back to sleep. Jack lay down obscure for the last time in his life. The ringing phone woke him the next morning and he was famous."

On Desolation, Kerouac had sometimes fantasized about what it would be like when *On the Road* was finally published. Although he hadn't yet signed a contract at the time of his lookout, the book had been verbally accepted at Viking, and Jack could be confident of its eventual publication. On Desolation his material expectations for the book had always been exceedingly modest — a new bathtub and refrigerator for his mother, perhaps an apartment for the two of them in Greenwich Village, so he wouldn't always have to be running out to Queens. His first novel, *The Town and the City,* hadn't caused any major changes in his life when it came out in 1950; that *On the Road* would be a life-altering event for him, he didn't suspect.

As soon as it became obvious that *On the Road* was a winner, Kerouac's editors — the same ones who had timidly dragged out the publication of the book for years — now wanted another work from Jack to rush into print before the "Beat phenomenon" crested and broke. They did not want one of the half dozen manuscripts he had already finished, however, but a quick sequel to the adventures of Dean Moriarty and Sal Paradise, something for the readers who had just put *On the Road* on the best-seller list. Unfortunately, Kerouac himself had done much to encourage such expectations, boasting to Malcolm Cowley in early March, "After ROAD comes out and we be able to ascertain the situation, I can quite easily write another just like it, that is, on a typewriter in 3 weeks time with cup after cup of black coffee . . . "

There was no doubt in Jack's mind what the follow-up to *On the Road* ought to be. Nor did he need any prodding from Viking to produce a book about Gary. He had been itching to do a full-length portrait of Snyder ever since their time together in the fall of 1955, and well before the publication of *On the Road,* Kerouac already had "The Dharma Bums" in mind as a possible title. In early April 1957, he told Snyder: ". . . was lying in bed contemplating next novel, THE DHARMA BUMS, which is mostly about you, my freight hop to Frisco in Fall 1955 and meeting you and the Gallery 6 poetry reading and our climb of Matterhorn with John Montgomery . . . " Throughout the spring and summer of 1957 Jack conceptualized the new work, sometimes as "Dharma Bums," other times as "Visions of Gary," or even "Avalokitesvara," in homage to the Bodhisattva of Compassion. In late May he started writing under the title "Avalokitesvara," but the narrative stalled within a week — "bogged down in metaphysical discussions," as he explained in a letter to Allen Ginsberg. Indeed, how to work his Buddhist ideas smoothly into the story was going to be one of the major issues he would have to deal with in *The Dharma Bums*. It was, after all, a major violation of William Carlos Williams's basic admonition: *no ideas but in things.* Jack wanted to do both: to tell his story, and tell some of the dharma at the same time. If nothing else, he was totally confident that he was on the right track with a picaresque narrative about Snyder. After Neal Cassady, Gary was one of the greatest men Kerouac had known. To Philip Whalen he wrote: ". . . he [Gary] is really the only character on any fullscale tragic-funny-wild level like Signor Cassady I can write a decent mad narrative about."

Kerouac finally began writing *The Dharma Bums* at the end of November 1957 in Orlando, Florida, where he had moved with his mother in July of that year after an unsuccessful and rather slapstick effort to relocate her to Berkeley. Jack and Gabrielle, his "Mémère," lived in the rear apartment of a bungalow on Clouser Avenue, a sleepy back street in Orlando's College Park. Their two-room flat was cramped and without air-conditioning, but shaded by a sprawling Florida oak draped with Spanish moss; Jack's workspace was on the screened-in, tin-roofed back porch off the kitchen.

For *The Dharma Bums*, Kerouac rented a heavy black Royal typewriter "with a good firm fast touch" and, preparing for a pounding marathon at the keys, cranked a ten-foot length of cheap yellow teletype paper into the platen, so as not to interrupt the hoped-for torrents of coming language with constant breaks for paper changes. He had done the same thing six years before, when writing *On the Road*, typing then on long, taped-together strips of architect's paper.

On November 26, Kerouac spread out his spiral notebooks from '55 and '56, his letters from Gary and Philip, and his Dharma journals, then popped some benny, and plunged into the story of *The Dharma Bums*, beginning with his own arrival in the Bay Area in late 1955 and his sudden coming together with Ginsberg, Snyder, and Whalen around the Six Gallery poetry reading.

Kerouac worked closely from life, extracting much of his narrative straight from his various notebooks of the time, and using his friends as life-models for "his characters." In his original draft of *The Dharma Bums*, Jack used their actual names; only later replacing them with pseudonyms—"Japhy Ryder" for Gary Snyder, "Alvah Goldbook" for Allen Ginsberg, "Warren Coughlin" for Phil Whalen, and so on.

From the outset, Kerouac did not attempt a historically accurate sequence of events, but focused in

DHARMA

(1956)
Desolation
Peak

①

DESOLATION

GOLDEN WEST

®

NO. W-730

19¢

1

on the character of Gary Snyder. "Started *Dharma Bums* + discovered that *discussion* of my subject leads me into pure narrative and dialogue, instead of preconceived purpose of blindly covering all chronological moments," wrote Jack in the journal he kept during the twelve-day composition of the book. "The subject is dharma bums, Gary, Zen lunatic poetry, mountains, solitude, patience, sex free-dom etc.—Gary mainly."

After a solid week of writing, Kerouac had covered all the material dealing with the Six Gallery and his Matterhorn hike with Gary and John Montgomery, the *yabyum* (tantric sex) scenes, and the death of Natalie Jackson. He felt that the story was about two-thirds told, an estimate that proved in the end to be almost numerically exact. After completing a "splendid chapter about Rocky Mount Devotions of early 1956," Jack wandered outside and "had a Satori in the moonlit yard eating, that is sucking ice cold oranges right off the tree, three of em." He spread his sleeping bag on his back yard lawn, and read *Don Quixote* and the Diamond Sutra by flashlight in his sack. By early December Kerouac was on such a creative roll that he sometimes worked until dawn, then unwound by shooting baskets, dribbling and hooking and singing Jackie Wilson's "Reet Petite" ("the finest girl you ever want to meet") until his mother called him in for breakfast. The few times his narrative hit a snag, he simply shifted his writing energies to the ongoing manuscript of "Old Angel Midnight," where he dissolved any word blocks in pure language play—"Wrote a little *Lucien Midnight* + then resumed on my magnificent *Dharma Bums* (after reading Wednesday Virya Zeal)—"

After ten days Kerouac came up against the biggest creative dilemma in *The Dharma Bums:* how to conclude it. Should he end the book with the departure for Japan of his protagonist, Japhy Ryder? Or continue the story, sending his narrator Ray Smith onto Desolation Peak? From Kerouac's journal, it appears that until his last two days of work on *The Dharma Bums,* he had not considered bringing his

◄ *The spiral-ringed, breast-pocket notebook Kerouac wrote in during his sixty-three-day lookout on Desolation Peak. From 1952 until the end of his life, Jack always kept a little book such as this at the ready to record his immediate observations on the life in and around him. "Secret scribbled notebooks . . . for yr own joy," he called them. Jottings from this book furnished material for both* The Dharma Bums *and* Desolation Angels.

Kerouac's shanty atop Calle Orizaba 212, where in the fall of 1956 he wrote the first

book of Desolation Angels and finished Tristessa.

"I came into town on the bus from Nogales and immediately rented a rooftop

adobe hut, fixed it up to my liking, lit a candle and started to write . . ."

Jack Kerouac, *Desolation Angels*

own lookout experience into the narrative. In fact, Jack had already written and submitted *Desolation Angels* to Viking earlier in the year—the detailed soliloquy of his lookout that he'd written on the mountain and later on Orizaba Street—only to have it emphatically rejected for its lack of characters and action. Now, Kerouac didn't know what to do. "Long day shooting baskets and knocking tangerines out of the tree and writing *Dharma Bums* and drinking whiskey," he brooded in his journal on December 5. "But I'm sad because there seems to be no climax in the story and all I got left now is Gary's hike to Potrero Meadow, with me, which ain't very dramatic—"

Sometime on the 5th or 6th of December, Kerouac decided to go ahead and end the book with his own sojourn on Desolation Peak as the climax, for better or worse. For Jack it was a creative gamble that flew straight in the stern face of Malcolm Cowley, who had not simply turned down his earlier Desolation story at Viking, but had gratuitously adjudged that no other house would be interested in it, either. "Duluoz seems to be moving through his own reflections almost in a world of ghosts," said Cowley in his rejection letter.

Jack himself had often doubted the literary suitability of his Desolation material. Still, he had always said that a writer *had* to believe in the dignity of his own experience, had to be in love with his own life, or all was lost. More to the immediate point, *The Dharma Bums* just didn't feel *done,* and Kerouac had nowhere to take his tale other than the plotless solitude of Desolation Peak. Jack spent two final days honing down his nine weeks on lookout into a tight, thirty-page capstone for the book, culling many of the same details from his journals that he'd used in *Desolation Angels,* but casting them now in a brighter light. He also mixed in chunks of text lifted straight out of some of Gary's letters to him in which Snyder described the Skagit terrain and various details of lookout life. Finally, for the book's culminating vision, Jack drew on the dream he'd had of Gary as Han Shan during his last weeks at Marin-an in '56. "And suddenly it seemed I saw that unimaginable little Chinese bum standing there in the fog, with that expressionless humor on his seamed face. It wasn't the real-life Japhy of rucksacks and Buddhism studies and big mad parties at Corte Madera, it was the realer-than-life-Japhy of my dreams. . . ." For two straight carriage-slamming days, Jack "swung and swung and swung" on his rented Royal— rapping out 9,000 words in forty-eight hours—pausing only to flip through his old Desolation notebooks or to dig through some letters, finally completing the book's elegiac final passages at midnight on Saturday, December 7.

"Japhy," I said out loud, "I don't know when we'll meet again or what'll happen in the future, but Desolation, Desolation, I owe so much to Desolation, thank you forever for guiding me to the place where I learned all. Now comes the sadness of coming back to cities and I've grown two months older and there's all that humanity of bars and burlesque shows and gritty love, all upsidedown in the void God bless them, but Japhy you and me forever we know—"

Spent and proud, Jack walked outside and lay down in his sleeping bag in his Orlando backyard and looked up at the stars. He had finished the book in just twelve days—a full week less than the three he'd vowed to Cowley that it would take him. By an odd coincidence (which Kerouac never mentioned and probably didn't notice in the heat of his work), it happened to be the "eighth day of the twelfth month"— December 8, the Japanese Rohatsu, traditionally the day of Sakyamuni's enlightenment. "I'm glad to just have it all unified in my possession on a 100 foot scroll," Jack jotted in his notebook, "—the story of *The Dharma Bums*." When he lay back and looked up, instead of the Buddha's Morning Star, Jack saw the moving light of the recently-launched Soviet Sputnik in its silent orbit across the Florida sky.

With *The Dharma Bums*, Kerouac felt that he had in significant ways surpassed *On the Road*. In his journal on the day after completion, he conceded to himself that the writing in his new book was perhaps not as dramatic or stylistically the equal of *Road*, but overall he felt *The Dharma Bums* to be the superior book because of the "explosive significance" of its Buddhist message.

"*The Dharma Bums*, for me, is better than *On the Road*," he told himself. "Because what Neal was, a mad holy hepcat, wasn't as great as what the dharma bums were—religious heroes of America practicing kindness & mindfulness (that's what Neal could have been)."

WHILE KEROUAC WAS in Orlando writing *The Dharma Bums*, his fellow poets were scattered across the continents, bursting with their own poems. Phil Whalen was on the other end of the country, living in a beach house amid the foggy pines of Newport, Oregon, working on the poems that would appear in his first book, *Like I Say*. Ginsberg was in Paris, writing the beginnings of "Kaddish"—his wrenching elegy for his mother Naomi, who had died the year before and had been buried without the traditional Jewish funeral lament for lack of a *minyan* at her grave. It would take Ginsberg another year and more to finish the entire thing—"Proem, Narrative, Hymmnn, Lament, Litany and Fugue"—his masterpiece —but it was begun. At the same time, Snyder was in the Arabian Sea—"the sea where the heroes sail"—

aboard the rusty-bellied tramp oil tanker *Sappa Creek,* in the midst of an eight-month voyage. On the night Jack completed *The Dharma Bums,* Gary was half a world away, deep in the tanker's engine room, "laughing covered with grease & loaded with silly wrenches & generally being a sort of Bodhisattva of machinery without any past or future." Although Gary complained at the time that the *Sappa Creek* was a Flying Dutchman sort of ship "just floating around in its own rust & ruin with its hoary white-bearded crew re-reading the ten thousandth time the same magazine & wondering when we'll ever get home," many good poems came of the voyage — the beautiful "A Stone Garden" and "T2 Tanker Blues," which went into *Riprap;* "Oil," "The Wipers' Secret," "Six Hells of the Engine Room," "Once Only," into *The Back Country;* and "A Seaman's Ditty," "Straits of Malacca," and "The Engine Room," which were included years later in *Left Out in the Rain.* Altogether, the fall of 1957 was an amazingly creative period for all the poets.

As the new year dawned, Kerouac proclaimed 1958 "the year of the Dharma." To Gary he wrote: "the dharma bums, my new novel, is all about you, your name is japhy ryder, make you famous, I can hear it now, folk songs about japhy ryder, of east oregon woods . . . gary, hang on, come home, this is your year, the year of the dharmy." From the *Sappa Creek,* Gary replied: "Maybe this is the year of Dharma. Now Arabian Sea heading in for last load & trip home. Tiger, if you like, join me in the mountains this summer. I mean to wander Sierras & Cascades both. Also, bhikku cabin around SF area — we'll look into it." Though they had not been together for two years, their old camaraderie felt as solid as ever.

Kerouac was tremendously excited. "1958 will be a great year, year of buddhism," he wrote to Phil Whalen, then still in Oregon. "With dharma bums I will crash open whole scene to sudden buddhism boom and look what'll happen closely soon . . . everybody going the way of the dharma . . . then with arrival of gary, smash! watch. you'll see. It will be a funny year of enlightenment in america. I dunno about 1959 but 58 is going to be dharma year in america . . . everybody reading susuki on madison avenue . . ." Then, suddenly striking a minor key, he added darkly, ". . . but I fear for Frisco, I fear for a coming silly stupid revolution with blood in the streets in that town of poetry and hate . . . "

Gary Snyder returned to California from his *Sappa Creek* oil voyage on April 15, 1958. He'd been at sea for eight months, gone from America for two full years. When the tanker docked in San

Pedro, the entire ship's crew was paid in cash. Gary disembarked with a sheaf of thirty hundred-dollar bills folded into a bandanna around his waist and immediately caught a midnight train north to Oakland, arriving at eight in the morning. From Oakland he took a ferry across to San Francisco. The first person he looked up when he arrived was Locke McCorkle. During Gary's time in Japan, Locke had broken up with his wife Valerie and moved from Marin back into the city with his brother Bob. Their apartment, Gary's first stop, was high on the steep Filbert Street steps overlooking the Embarcadero. Together they hit all the North Beach bars on Gary's first Saturday night — the Black Cat and Iron Pot, the Place, the Cellar, Gino & Carlos, Vesuvio.

North Beach had changed; indeed, San Francisco and all America had changed. On the day that Gary returned, San Francisco was still abuzz from the arrival two days before of the newly acquired Giants baseball team. Swiping the Giants from New York had been a huge coup for the city. The street crews were still sweeping up the ticker tape and orchids that had showered on the motorcade of Mays, Cepeda, Gomez, and company as Gary made his way up Montgomery Street to North Beach for the first time in two years. The movie marquees along Market Street were flashing with Lana Turner in *Peyton Place*, Brigitte Bardot in *And God Created Woman*, and Brando and Montgomery Clift in *The Young Lions*. Lenny Bruce was playing Ann's 440 Club on Broadway. In his journal, Gary noted that it felt like "a crazy new America." He'd noticed it right away, when Bob McCorkle had greeted him with a joint before he'd even dropped his duffel bag. There was a new looseness. For one thing, Joe McCarthy was gone from the scene. The scowling self-appointed Chairman of the Permanent Subcommittee on Investigations had died, discredited and suffering from liver disease, the year before — not that there weren't plenty of ogres to take his place. But America's energy level had definitely gone up a notch. The week of McCarthy's funeral, the country was bouncing along to Elvis Presley's "All Shook Up," latest in a phenomenal onslaught of hits that had only just begun at the time of Gary's departure in 1956. Gary had heard the new music in Japan, of course, but now he could feel and see the full force of it, even as Elvis was inducted into the army the week that Gary arrived back.

On North Beach, he'd never seen the streets thronging so. Unfortunately, he couldn't help noticing a new breed of phony hipster all too prominent in the crowds. To Jack he wrote: "I did see indeed the scene which jumps but where did the great love we put out for them go?"

Across the alley from Vesuvio, Allen's *Howl* was in the window of City Lights Books along with Jack's

On the Road and *The Subterraneans,* which had been published a few weeks before and was causing a stir with its Telegraph Hill setting. Gary was startled to hear Kerouac's name everywhere he went. "My, your name is being throwed about," Gary wrote to Jack on the Monday morning after his first weekend. "Whydn't you come sneakin' in & live here too? Or as a great triumphal hero through SF Mad North Beach nights streets of people just started swingin, looking for a leader — if you're pure enough — & you are . . . "

KEROUAC HAD ABSOLUTELY no interest in "leading" anyone. After nine months of fame, he no longer even felt safe in public. The "blood in the streets" he had foreseen in January had already been shed by early April — his own. Stumbling drunk outside New York's San Remo Bar at closing time one night, he'd been badly beaten by three men and left lying in MacDougal Street with a broken nose, head lacerations, and a concussion. While Kerouac did his best to shrug off the severity of the incident, the vicious pounding had taken a toll on both his body and spirit, and left him feeling emotionally numb. To Phil Whalen he described his condition: "Was drunk 2 weeks ago, got beat up by hoodlums, stopt getting soused, feel great," he said, but added: "Have changed a little, tho. No joy. No sorrow needer. Well, all I need is some more of you and Gary this summer."

At the time of Jack's beating, Neal Cassady — suddenly a minor celebrity himself due to Kerouac's portrayal of him as *On the Road*'s "Dean Moriarty" and Ginsberg's saluting him as "the Adonis of Denver" in "Howl" — had been set up and arrested for selling pot by narcotics agents in North Beach. (In July, Cassady would be sentenced to five years in San Quentin. He served two.) Taken together, Jack's San Remo injuries and his old friend's bust were a one-two punch that completely knocked the wind out of Kerouac's "year of the dharma" enthusiasm. For the first time in his life, Jack began to be wary of the street; a triumphal walk through North Beach now was the last thing on his mind.

In early June he expressed these fears to Philip Whalen. "You know, I'm afraid to come to Frisco this September, supposing an old junkey friend rushes up to me in the street & the cops swoop in?" A week later, he repeated his worries to Gary Snyder. "I told Whalen in a long letter the other day I'm genuinely actually no shit afraid of walking down North Beach and all of a sudden some old buddy rushes up with pockets loaded with shit and the cops swoop in. SF is absolutely silly with cops."

By May 8 — his twenty-eighth birthday — Gary was living once again in the old bhikku hostel at Marin-an. The main house on Montford Road had been taken over by Sandy Jacobs, a North Beach scene-ster and musician and his wife, Sumire Hasegawa, daughter of Saburo Hasegawa, the painter and tea-master who had served Gary his first "froth of jade" [powdered green tea] and encouraged him in his notion of a landscape-based poetics. Sandy and Sumire never used the shack, and didn't mind Gary reclaiming it, although the place hadn't been lived in since Kerouac's departure for Desolation two years before, and needed some fixing up.

"The Marin-an shack was so ugly dirty mistreated, and the poor ground all chewed up by horses," Gary wrote in his journal. He spent a few days cleaning the cabin and grooming the grounds Japanese style — trimming and sweeping under the pines as he had learned to do at Rinko-in, bundling up the down laurel and eucalyptus branches for kindling, until the old dharma shack ambience was restored, and he wrote happily: "Now tis clean & pure and California Quail come & the birds sing & everybody loves it."

Gary put down fresh grass mats on the floors, spread his old cougar hide on his sleeping pad, brought in a Coleman lamp to read by, a Coleman stove for cooking, and he was set. In the cabin he'd even found a pair of jeans and some T-shirts that Kerouac had left behind two years before. Gary pulled on one of Jack's old shirts, trimmed the lantern, and settled in to finally read *On the Road*. It was his first chance to do so; at the time of the book's publication, he'd just shipped out on the *Sappa Creek*, and no one had ever sent him a copy at sea. In his journal Gary noted simply: "Now reading *On the Road* . . . and beautiful rolling book it is." When he finished it, he wrote Jack, "You know, it's just fine — to the very limit excellent — & I can't imagine what bugs in their buddha-minds these people have who see destructiveness in it."

Gary had big hiking plans for the coming season, and wanted to reconnect with his old friends on back-country adventures. Lew Welch had come out to the Bay Area from Chicago finally; with Lew he went fishing off the rocks at Muir Beach. With Locke McCorkle he set out to reexplore his favorite Tamalpais canyons and ridges, all the while spinning plans for the grand summer hikes he'd fantasized from the deck of the *Sappa*. Gary wanted to see the Bubbs Creek country and the Kern River and the

Olympic Coast and the Washington Cascades all. He invited Jack to come out to hike in the Sierra again with him and Phil Whalen. "O there's no end of mountains & rivers!" he said, sounding like the "ever youthful" Japhy of Jack's visions. Finally, as though sensing Jack's needs from afar, Gary reiterated with comradely affection that Marin-an was once again ready for its poets. "There's bread, wine, bed & time waiting for you here."

WHILE KEROUAC AND Ginsberg had achieved huge notoriety with their works, Gary and Philip had also begun to be recognized. Also at City Lights were the *Evergreen Review* containing Gary's "A Berry Feast," and the Zen-oriented spring issue of the *Chicago Review* with Whalen's "Sourdough Mountain Lookout" and Snyder's essay "Spring Sesshin at Shokoku-ji"—one of the greatest firsthand descriptions of Zen practice ever written by a Westerner. The *Chicago Review* also carried a prepublication excerpt from *The Dharma Bums*—Jack's descriptions of his meditations in the North Carolina woods.

With the publication of *The Dharma Bums* scheduled for late September, Kerouac worried what his friends' reactions would be to his fictive treatments of them. He was especially concerned what Gary would think of Japhy Ryder. "Don't ever get mad at me for writing about you as I've done," Kerouac implored Gary in June, without, however, offering to show him any of *The Dharma Bums* edits. At any rate, Snyder trusted Kerouac's artistic motives and wasn't concerned. His only response to Jack's preemptive plea was to suggest, "Why not dedicate *dharma bums* to Han Shan?"—an idea that Jack embraced wholeheartedly, immediately inserting Han Shan into the dedication page of the galleys.

PHILIP WHALEN WAS the first of the gang to see *The Dharma Bums* in published form. Jack sent him an advanced reading copy in Newport, Oregon, at the end of September. Philip opened the book in the afternoon mail and didn't put it down until he finished it, near midnight, then immediately wrote Snyder to say: "I don't know if this is on the open market yet or not—if it's on sale now in San Francisco, let me (in the words of our mutual friend, Mr. G. Graumann Sales, Jr.) advise you (effective immediately): KATY, BAR THE DOOR!

"Book is beautiful, but god only knows how the young of the Bay Area (or elsewhere) will understand it & how they'll react (not to mention the Luce organisation). Be brave."

Gary read the book later that week. Jack had been anxious about how Gary would react to his portrait, but Gary's initial reaction to *The Dharma Bums* and his characterization as "Japhy Ryder" was gracious and brotherly.

"*Dharma Bums* is a beautiful book," Gary wrote Jack, "& I am amazed & touched that you should say so many nice things about me because that period was for me really a great process of learning from you, not just your vision of America and of people but your immediate all-embracing faith. & thank you for sending me a copy. Philip forwarded it to me. Everyone is reading it."

On an aesthetic level, however, Snyder was troubled by what he felt was Jack's hasty workmanship. This feeling would grow in time to eclipse Gary's positive first impression of the book. Spontaneity was one thing, but *The Dharma Bums* looked sloppy, as though it had been rushed into print. To Whalen he wrote, "I do wish Jack had taken more trouble to smooth out dialogues, etc. Transitions are rather abrupt sometimes." In *On the Road,* despite all its editorial changes over the years leading to its publication, the prose had always coursed as seamlessly as river water, but *The Dharma Bums* was in places an obvious cut-and-paste job. Gary could see where paragraphs of his own letters to Jack and sections of Jack's dharma journal had been slapped into the narrative like swatches of a poorly thrown-together quilt. To Gary, such carelessness was inexcusable. Still, the book had an undeniable energy and was, as he said to Philip, "quite a chronicle," adding, "I hope we all won't get arrested."

Whalen, getting ready for a visit to San Francisco, sighed: "I expect by the time I get to the city, Grant St. will be quite a scene, millions of brown-robed bonzos marching around collecting begging bowls full of beer, wine, bagels, spaghetti, etc."

Jack now had three books in the window of City Lights, all published within the previous twelve months. Philip also wrote to congratulate Jack on his amazing trifecta, but was noncommittal about *The Dharma Bums,* preferring to focus on *The Subterraneans.* "Jack . . . now I've read DHARMA BUMS & am nearly through re-reading paper back ROAD, big literary decision: SUBTERRANEANS is the greatest. In there you make it on the big Dostoevsky confession scale like you said you wanted to . . . "

IN 1958 GARY had hoped to renew his bond with Jack in another wilderness trek like their Matterhorn climb of three years before. In May, Kerouac had said he would be out in late summer: "We can take off to Northwest jaunt with Phil [Whalen] and Locke [McCorkle] maybe, four dharma bums." As the year progressed, however, a California trip became less and less likely for Kerouac. In June he pushed it back to September, and in July he postponed it further into the fall. By October, it became clear that Jack wasn't coming west, as he assigned it to the indefinite future, saying, "I'll see you probably in Fall or Winter, or mebbe even reach you in Japan in 1959."

For Kerouac, who continued to worry that his life no longer was providing the stuff of future narratives, it was a missed opportunity. Also, with Gary set to return to Japan for the foreseeable future, it was a passed-up chance to revivify their friendship face-to-face. Then again, Jack was no longer in physical condition for the kind of ambitious trekking Snyder had in mind. In August, Gary and Locke McCorkle did a ten-day backpacking trip in the Sierras, camping at Cedar Grove and hiking a week in Kings Canyon and across to the upper Kern River and back, a hundred-mile loop that would inspire Gary's poem "Bubbs Creek Haircut." In September, Snyder reunited with Philip Whalen in Newport, Oregon. They went up to the Olympic Peninsula, camping on the Pacific beaches north of the Quinault Indian Reservation along Highway 101. "NW trip was great & Whalen is too beautiful & penetrating to believe," he reported to Jack. "Slept on Indian Olympic beaches of the ocean—Queets, Kalaloch." Finally, in mid-October, Gary squeezed in a last late-season hike in the southern Sierras, a five-day trek to climb the Black Kaweah—"a dreadful ragged confusing & tortuous looking peak"—with Claude Dalenberg and Bob Greensfelder.

In addition to new back-country adventures, Snyder had also wanted to share with Jack some of the Zen he had learned in Japan. Right around the time *The Dharma Bums* was published, Gary had turned one of the rooms at Marin-an into a tiny zendo for a small group of sitters. Gary was intent not only on his own Zen training, but in sharing it with his friends. He still believed in the Rucksack Revolution, and rooting the dharma on America's West Coast was an integral step in that process. "Week nights people come & silently sit to the bell & clackers, real zendo style," he proudly informed Jack. "About six cats regularly turning up." The "six cats" included Locke, Claude Dalenberg, Bob Greensfelder, Lew Welch, and Albert Saijo. Gary's new girlfriend, the poet Joanne Kyger, whom he'd met in early June at a Poetry Center reading in San Francisco, also came to sit occasionally.

During the first week of December, Gary organized a *Rohatsu sesshin*—two hours of nightly zazen for a week, culminating in dusk-to-dawn sitting on the seventh night. The Rohatsu sesshin, especially important in Zen, commemorated Sakyamuni's enlightenment. Gary did his best to conduct a traditional sesshin, with certain Snyderesque embellishments — such as running *kinhin* through the woods at night. Kinhin, or "walking zazen," is practiced at the end of sitting, or in alternation with longer rounds of sitting during sesshin, to restore circulation to the legs. Generally it is performed with a measured gait, walking in a circle around the zendo, "calmly and steadily, with poise and dignity." "Gary would have us crashing through the underbrush and jumping over boulders," recalls Kyger. "It was more like the Marines or something — in the dark!"

Toward the end of the sesshin week at Marin-an, a letter arrived for Gary from Jack. "I haven't written because five thousand sillinesses have kept me from it," he told Gary. "If you only knew how horrible it is to be 'famous' you wouldn't want it, in fact you dont want it." Kerouac then went on to catalog a few dozen of the thousands of impositions on his energies, concluding "No wonder Hemingway went to Cuba and Joyce to France." Then, ominously, he signed off by saying, "I was in love with the world through blue purple curtains when I knew you and now have to look at it thru hard iron eyes."

As the "year of the Dharma" that he had prophesied drew to a close, Kerouac felt his own Buddhism slipping away. He had been quite prescient about 1958; it had been "a funny year of enlightenment in America" — right alongside the new cultural awakening were the beginnings of the "coming silly stupid revolution" Jack had foreseen, complete with Madison Avenue types reading Suzuki, and college boys with "Dharma Bums" frat jackets at his door. As for "blood in the streets," the beating he had taken outside the San Remo Bar in April felt like a portent of worse things to come.

The Dharma Bums had been hammered by the reviewers. All of a sudden, it seemed, every book critic in the country was an expert on the Mahayana and was taking him to task for his spiritual crudity and lack of seriousness. Worse, people like Alan Watts and Ruth Sasaki — Gary's friends — had shown little or no solidarity, Jack felt. Ruth Sasaki claimed that *The Dharma Bums* was a good literary portrait of Gary, but that Kerouac knew nothing about Buddhism. Watts singled out Kerouac's writing (while exempting Snyder's) as being exemplary of what he termed "Beat Zen" — "a shade too self-conscious, too subjective, and too strident to have the flavor of Zen." "Even Susuki [D. T. Suzuki, whom Kerouac had met in New York in October 1958] was looking at me through slitted eyes as tho I was a monstrous impostor of some kind (at least I feel that, I dunno)," he later complained to Snyder.

Thoroughly demoralized, Kerouac admitted to Phil Whalen the real reason he hadn't come to California in "the year of the Dharma." "I'd be ashamed to confront you and Gary now I've become so decadent and drunk and dontgiveashit," he confessed. "I'm not a Buddhist any more, I'm not anything, I don't care. I do care about hearts."

Soon enough, however, Jack was back at his Diamond Sutra—"nodding my head decisively over D Sutra again and fuck Susuki, fuck Sasaki, fuck em all!" he ripped. "They think Buddhism is something apart from Transcendentalism, well they're not Buddhists, they're Alan Watts social philosophers and glad-to-meet-yas. They want 'group meetings' to 'discuss' 'Zen' that's what they want, not the sigh."

"Why doesn't Gary just get a cabin in the Sur woods? Fuck Japan, it's all words. Fuck religion, it's all words . . . Bang your gavel, jedge, I'se guilty. I'se guilty of no-more-a-yogi. . . . It was all prophesied on Desolation."

NINETEEN FIFTY-EIGHT turned out to have been one of the last opportunities for Jack and Gary to cultivate their friendship in person in the midst of their accelerating life changes. During Snyder's ten-month stay in California, he didn't travel east of the Sierra range — in fact, he never had since returning from Indiana University in early 1952. More and more Gary saw himself as a citizen of a developing Pacific Rim bioregional culture, with little reason or desire to venture east of the Great Basin. Kerouac, for his part, was settling more deeply into his East Coast life with his aging mother, moving up and down the seaboard between Northport, Long Island, and Florida every year or so. In Northport, Kerouac lived only a few miles from the Huntington homestead of the young Walt Whitman; as for Whitman's Open Road, Jack was becoming less fit by the month to follow it. Nothing was ever said, but when Kerouac did not follow through on his plans to come to California that fall, something went out of the relationship.

In February 1959, fretting that Gary's feelings for him had cooled, Jack wrote: "Since *Dharma Bums* came out I feel that you've been silent and disappointed about me. . . . I don't think the book was as bad as you think; when you look at it again in future years, when the world will have gotten worster, you'll look back and appreciate the job I did on 'you' and on Dharma Bumism." Then, conjuring up their 1955 Matterhorn hike: "I don't understand your cold silence after our rock dhyanas together, really don't."

By the time Kerouac mailed this letter, Snyder had already left California to return to Japan. He'd

U.S. Geological Survey summit marker, in the rock outside the door of Desolation Lookout, July 1995. Kerouac,
immersed as he was in the vast time frame of the Diamond Sutra, would not have been surprised to learn that
the hump of chert his lookout perched on was more than 300 million years old and had been forged and heaved
up from the bottom of the prehistoric Methow Ocean. "Even Hozomeen'll crack and fall apart," he knew.
"Nothing lasts, it is only a faring-in-that-which-everything-is, a passing-through . . ."

shipped on February 21, 1959, aboard the Japanese *Hiyeharu-maru* ("Spring on Mt. Hiei"), on a sixteen-day voyage to Yokohama. Jack's letter, which had been forwarded to Japan via air mail while Snyder was still slowly crossing the Pacific, awaited Gary on his arrival in Kyoto in early March. Gary replied immediately: "I told you I liked it [*The Dharma Bums*], but that doesn't make it right." In particular, Gary took issue with the book's misogynist interpretation of Buddhist attitudes. "Nobody ever said anything against love or entanglement with women but you," he told Jack.

In his letter, Kerouac also confessed that he had not been in any shape to come out to California during Gary's recent ten-month sojourn in the Bay Area. "I've become soft and have abandoned my rucksack bummism." To this Gary slapped, "If you come here I'll put you to work hoeing my vegetables & cutting firewood on the hill — far kinder than hell, where they pull out the writer's tongue with red hot pliers."

Stung by the violence of Gary's image, Kerouac made no direct response. Instead, he wrote to Philip Whalen, "Well I guess he's done with me . . . he thinks Dharma Bums not great book. It better than any of em as will be proven when those Sierras turn to dust."

ON HIS RETURN to Kyoto, Gary moved to a cottage by the Kitano River in the northeast suburb of Yase, and bought a motorcycle, a black Honda Dream 250, to make the daily run into town. The road outside his door was dusty, and whenever Gary took off or pulled in on his bike, clouds of it rose in his wake, so the place became "Jinchu-an" — "Hermitage in the Dust." Despite the flurry of epistolary temper between Jack and him over *The Dharma Bums,* when Gary received a copy of Kerouac's newly published *Doctor Sax* in early May, he sent warm congratulations and an open invitation to visit. "This house is five miles from downtown Kyoto but it could be a hundred. I am right at the foot of Mt. Hiei where the Tendai temples are," he told Jack. "Come stay in my cabin which has many mats on the floor & a nice tile roof & a bath that heats with wood."

In his February 23rd letter, Jack had also blasted organized Zen, saying "There are no Hui Nengs around there, left, I'll bet." Kerouac was right, of course — to a point. Snyder, as an American outsider on the Kyoto scene, was well aware of the "snobbish aristocratic & insular self-esteem" of the average Zen bonze. But that was nothing new: the master Ikkyu, the fifteenth-century abbot of the Daitoku-ji Temple where Gary now sat, had said more or less the same thing five hundred years before.

Daitoku-ji had been built in 1319 to accommodate the large number of students who had gathered around the Zen master Daito Kokushi, "Great Teacher of the Nation," the same Daito Kokushi whose famous admonition—"Ever be on the lookout!—Gary had first read back on Sourdough in the summer of '53. Now he heard it, chanted in Japanese, before every *teisho*-lecture. For most of its history, Daitoku-ji had been a bastion of both the warrior class and the Zen arts, which were intertwined in Japanese culture. After Japan's defeat in World War II, however, Daitoku-ji could barely attract new monks for training. The Japanese postwar generation shunned Zen. And so, what had been one of the most orthodox Rinzai temples—in fact, the temple specifically charged with praying for the health of the Emperor—now became the temple most open to foreigners.

Ruth Fuller Sasaki was the first American to study at Daitoku-ji after the war, with Zuigan Gota, "Dharma brother" of Sokei-an. When Gota Roshi retired, Oda Sesso Roshi became the new abbot of Daitoku-ji, and in 1959 Gary became Oda Roshi's first foreign disciple. There may not have been any Hui-Nengs in Kyoto in 1959, but Gary found Oda Roshi to be "an extremely subtle man, by far the subtlest mind I've ever been in contact with"—nothing like the bullying Zen masters Kerouac had imagined in *The Dharma Bums*, "throwing young kids in the mud because they can't answer their silly questions."

Recalling Oda Roshi several years later, Gary would remember him as "an especially gentle and quiet man . . . and a marvelous teacher whose teaching capacity I would never have recognized if I hadn't stayed with it, because it was only after five or six years that I began to realize that he had been teaching me all along. I guess that's what all the roshis are doing: teaching even when they're not 'teaching.'" Gary would remain Oda Sesso's student until the roshi's death in September 1966.

At the end of April 1959, Gary began regular *sanzen*—private interviews—with Oda Roshi and was given the famous koan, "Listen to the sound of the Single Hand!" "So I get up at 3 A.M. nowadays go down at 4 A.M. for *sanzen* & crack my haid on a *koan* he laid on me," he wrote to Jack. The Single Hand koan is one of the three main *hosshin* koans, or "eye-openers," believed to be best suited to get beginning students to their first enlightenment experience, but some mornings after sanzen with "the Old Man," Gary would barrel off on his bike, up into the green hills northwest of the city to blow off steam, "gunning the cycle around steep gravelly curves and bouncing on the ruts & boulders." In the evenings he returned to Daitoku-ji for zazen. "An amazing process," he wanted Kerouac to know. Snyder was twenty-nine years old, and he felt "Dumb as a newborn baby." "I sit here below Mt. Hiei," he wrote in his journal, "alongside the Kitano River, Kyoto city just downstream, working on a *koan*, recalling friends, and gazing across the steep mountain slopes."

You may think that in mountains many wise people and great sages are assembled. But after entering the mountains, not a single person meets another. There is just the activity of the mountains.

Dōgen, Mountains and Waters Sutra

Fire on the Mountain

Epilog

ON OCTOBER 2, 1968, the North Cascades National Park was established, transferring 700,000 acres of the Mount Baker National Forest from the Forest Service to the Department of the Interior. The same act also added 10,000 acres to the Glacier Peak Wilderness Area and created the half-million-acre Pasayten Wilderness east of Desolation.

With the creation of the Park, all the country that Snyder, Whalen, and Kerouac had watched over from their lookouts in the mid-fifties was now protected, either by National Park or Wilderness Area designations. Robert Marshall and Ferdinand Silcox's vision from three decades before—of a huge, contiguous, permanently protected Cascadian wilderness—had, after many years of conservationist effort, largely been realized.

At the time of the signing of the North Cascades Act, Kerouac was in his hometown of Lowell, Massachusetts, packing for yet another move to Florida, this one his last. Philip Whalen was in Bolinas, California, readying the manuscript of *On Bear's Head* for publication in early 1969. Gary Snyder was in Japan, preparing to return to California after ten years of back-and-forth journeys between Asia and North America.

During the 1960s, Gary had forged a fully bi-cultural identity in a way few Western — or Japanese — writers before him had. By 1968, he was fluent, culturally engaged, and artistically productive in both Japan and the United States. In 1967 he had married Masa Uehara, a vivacious Japanese woman he had met the year before in Osaka. Nineteen Sixty-eight was eventful and pivotal. In April their first son, Kai, was born. In December, eight months after becoming a father, Gary's own father died. Not only was his father gone by 1968, some of his most important teachers had passed on as well. Oda Roshi had died late in 1966, Ruth Fuller Sasaki in 1967. Even old D. T. Suzuki, whose words had given Gary "the push of his life" back on the Humboldt in 1951, had died, at ninety-six, in July 1966. Gary had met him once, in 1961 at Daitoko-ji. "I got to bow my head to Dr. Suzuki and say a few stumbling things, and I almost wept," he later wrote.

Snyder's Zen training did not end with the death of his teacher Oda Sesso. Under Oda, Gary had received the precepts, put on Zen robes, and been given his Dharma name — *Chofu* — "Listen to the Wind." He had even lived for times as a de facto monk at Daitoko-ji, but had never registered in the lineage of the temple to become a priest. He was then, and remains, a "koji" — a lay adept. After Oda Roshi, Gary's life in Japan moved into a new phase. "In Zen they tell you, 'Nobody ever finishes their practice,'" he points out. "'Even the Buddha is still working on himself.'"

During 1967, Gary continued his practice at Daitoku-ji with Nakamura Sojun Roshi and Morinaga Roshi, but he was more and more out of Kyoto, as he became increasingly involved with a group of Japanese "cultural radicals" around the poet and wanderer Nanao Sakaki, whom he had met in 1963. Like a modern-day Han Shan, Sakaki had emerged from the ruins of postwar Tokyo a homeless but unvanquished twentieth-century Japanese Dharma Bum. In fact, Sasaki's tribe originally called themselves the Bum Academy. By 1966 the Bum Academy had established a communal farm in Nagano prefecture, and in the spring of 1967, they began a satellite ashram at Suwanose, a volcanic island in the East China Sea off Kyushu. In July, Gary and Masa joined the Suwanose communards in creating the

Banyan Ashram, or Banyan Dream, named for a huge tree whose spreading branches and hanging roots provided a living shelter for zazen or napping in the midday heat. On August 6, 1967, Gary and Masa were married in a dawn ceremony on the rim of the Suwanose volcano.

In April 1968, the same month that Masa gave birth to Kai, *The Back Country* was published, Gary's first book with New Directions, the house of his poetic fathers Pound, Williams, and Rexroth. (Gary dedicated the book to Rexroth.) He also received the Levinson Poetry Prize and a Guggenheim. *The Back Country* was a hefty and complex volume, one hundred poems long, opening with "A Berry Feast." The poems embodied Snyder's bicultural synthesis, ranging from the Skagit to the Ganges rivers, from Sourdough Mountain to Hei-zan, from North Beach to Tokyo and Calcutta. There was also a section entitled "Kali," poems for and about the women he'd known, loved, married, lost. Finally, the book concluded with Gary's translations of twenty poems by Miyazawa Kenji, the schoolteacher-poet, Buddhist, and ecologist, whose poems, born of the rugged landscape of his native Iwate prefecture, shared the feeling of Snyder's mountain poems.

In December 1968, now with Masa and Kai, Gary returned to California to reconnect with "Turtle Island," his "old/new name for the continent," beginning again with the plants and soils and waters. During a 1966 visit to the States, Gary had gone in with Allen Ginsberg, Richard Baker of the San Francisco Zen Center, and Swami Kryananda [J. Donald Walters], to buy a hundred acres of black oak-ponderosa pine-manzanita land twenty-five miles north of Nevada City, California, in the old gold-mining area of the Sierra foothills. Gary's plan was to eventually establish a homestead on his parcel — "Kitkitdizze" he would call it, for the low-growing aromatic shrub that covered much of the ground — but in December '68 it would be another year and a half before he could begin building. In the interim, Gary, Masa, and Kai settled in Muir Woods, on Redwood Creek, just west over the Panoramic Highway ridge from Marin-an.

For their first few months, from December 1968 until March 1969, Gary and Masa were very near to Phil Whalen, who was staying just a few miles up the coast road, on the mesa in Bolinas. In the mid-1960s, Philip had followed Gary to Kyoto. With the help of a grant from the American Academy of Arts and Letters and a job teaching English for the Kyoto YMCA, he had sailed for Japan in April 1966 and lived there until the end of 1967, when he returned to California to edit his upcoming book of collected poems, *On Bear's Head*.

At forty-five, Philip was uncomfortable with the idea of such a retrospective. "I'm still writing more and I'm not really satisfied with the ones which appear here," he complained in his preface, with typical Whalenesque self-effacement. But he had been so prolific in the seventeen years since leaving Reed (and his publications so scattered) that his output demanded such a collection. There were also many recent poems that had not been published previously, including those collected under the title *The Winter*—forty poems written during his 1966–67 stay in Kyoto.

On Bear's Head was a large volume—three hundred twenty-five new and collected poems—and his first with a major house (Harcourt, Brace). He had thought it would be too difficult to prepare the manuscript by overseas mail, so had come back to the States, but by the time Gary and Masa saw him, he was "homesick" for Kyoto and eager to return as soon as his proofing was done.

During his 1966–67 sojourn in Kyoto, Philip had first stayed with Gary in Shichiku, in Kyoto's North Ward, a ten-minute walk from Daitoku-ji Temple. Then he moved to a place of his own in Shinkyogoku, near the Shirakawa, Kyoto's "White River." Philip did no formal Zen training while in Japan, but he did begin to sit regularly on his own—"no matter how late, no matter how drunk, get up and do it." But his real practice was simply roaming Kyoto, visiting the temples and stone gardens and Buddhist shrines, taking in the Zen that permeated the city, turning it back out in elegant poems like "White River Ode" and "Sanjusangendo." From the very outset, the city had inspired him to poems. On one of his first nights in town in 1966, walking the streets feeling high after a bath and some sake, Philip heard the haunting melody of a Noh song along the Kamo, reminding him suddenly that he was actually living in

Philip Whalen at the Hartford Street Zen Center, San Francisco, 1997.

In 1972 Whalen took up residence at the San Francisco Zen Center, where he became the student of Richard Baker, the dharma heir of Soto Zen master, Shunryu Suzuki. In 1973, at the age of fifty, Philip was ordained a Buddhist monk. So began his "life of elegant retirement in the character of a Zen Buddhist priest at the Hossen Temple in San Francisco and at the monastery of Zenshinji at Tassajara Springs, far in the mountains east of Big Sur." In 1987, after fifteen years of practice, Philip received transmission from Baker Roshi at Crestone Mountain Zen Center in Colorado. His Dharma name is Zenshin Ryufu, meaning "Zen Heart, Dragon Wind." In the 1990s Philip was abbot of the Hartford Street Zen Center in San Francisco, until ill health forced his retirement.

the town of Noh master Seami. The haiku poets Buson and Bashō had also lived in Kyoto, and, of course, Lady Murasaki. Whalen relished moving through such a heady cultural landscape, not only rich in past literary associations but redolent with the here-and-now aromas of fantastic foods and scents of exotic flowers, two of his greatest pleasures. "It's wonderful to be there and read *The Tale of Genji* on the spot, as it were," Philip remembered in a later interview. "Lady Murasaki had a real eye for the look of things and for weather. Her accounts of what it smelled like and felt like and looked like were really marvelous." By the mid-1960s there was also a strong whiff of pot in the Kyoto air — "a great deal of goody to be had," according to Whalen "— best place in the world to get loaded because it's so beautiful to see, just to look at, and walk around in."

Philip did a lot of writing in Kyoto during his 1966–67 visit, both poetry and prose, working every morning in a little coffee shop across from Kyoto University. He finished the forty poems of *The Winter,* later collected in *On Bear's Head,* as well as his second novel in four years, *Imaginary Speeches for a Brazen Head.*

Kenneth Rexroth, who visited Snyder and Whalen in Kyoto during 1966, was impressed with Whalen's "authentic joy" in those days, writing: "When Philip Whalen, in his red whiskers, looking like a happy Ainu bear-god, walks down Omiya-dori in Kyoto's weavers' quarter, every face lights up with that old-time Buddhist joy, even though most of the inhabitants are Left Communists, militant atheists, Koreans and Untouchables. . . . I have in fact seen Philip ambling past the market stalls and running into a march of demonstrating strikers, and everyone smiled and waved and he waved back."

Kerouac in the fall of 1968 was dying. He had been for a long time. In 1960, after three years of post–*On the Road* notoriety, he had written in desperation to Gary in Japan, "I'm fat, dejected, ashamed, bored, pestered & shot. Living at home with my mother, open to invasions of all kinds. . . . I'm slowly going mad." Kerouac's old hermitage fantasy, dormant since Desolation and forgotten in the whirl of fame, had begun to reassert itself with new urgency — no longer as a place to cultivate his soul, however, but as a last-ditch shelter to save his hide. "I must get a cabin or die," he told Gary flat out early that year. "I'm really in bad shape & in danger right down the line & *must do it* This Spring." Gary urged him to find a place soon. "A cabin in the hills is what you need — one room and a woodshed's plenty."

Clearly, it was not enough. By 1960, Kerouac's drinking and drug dependencies had progressed far beyond the geographic panacea of "a cabin in the hills." When, for a month that summer he tried taking refuge at his friend Lawrence Ferlinghetti's rustic shack in Bixby Canyon on the Big Sur coast — "This coast crying out for tragedy like all beautiful places," as Jeffers once described it — he didn't last two weeks before falling apart with soul-sickening paranoia and delirium tremens.

So cataclysmic was his Big Sur crash that Kerouac didn't even know what to call it. He knew that he had at least temporarily lost control of the "peace mechanisms" of his mind, but in the aftermath he wasn't sure if he'd had a bona-fide nervous breakdown, or some kind of horrible but necessary ego-shattering satori. Existentially confused, he wrote Gary: ". . . never knew *satori* could be so painful — yet if I had HAD a true *satori* I wouldn't be writing this letter to you — just sending *samapatti* telepathic messages — let me know what the masters say, for God's sake, I'm at the end of my rope —"

IN 1964, KEROUAC'S SISTER Caroline, whose homes had sheltered Jack so often in the 1950s, died suddenly of a heart attack, leaving him alone to look after his mother, Gabrielle. "Jack's Zen is taking care of his mother," he had joked to Phil Whalen in the early '60s. That sardonic comment took a profound and frightening turn in 1966 when the woman suffered a massive stroke that left her paralyzed and in total need.

A month later, Jack was rescued from the burden of her care by the intervention of Stella Sampas, who had heard of the Kerouacs' misfortune and traveled from Lowell to Cape Cod to help out (Jack and his mother had moved to Hyannis, Massachusetts, in April 1966). Throughout all his travels Jack had remained in correspondence with Stella, periodically checking in with her, never wanting to lose that living link with the old days and his old friend Sebastian. Stella had never married, never moved from family house on Lowell's Stevens Street where he had hung out with Sebastian before World War II. She was an old-school, good-hearted, dutiful Greek daughter, and when Jack asked her to marry him, she willingly accepted. They were married in November 1966, and in early '67 they moved back to Lowell.

For years Jack had said that if he ever returned to his hometown, he wanted to retire to a ramshackle "rose-covered cottage" on the banks of the Concord River, where it skirted the southern part of town on its way to join with the Merrimack. But in the end, he bought a new split-level home in the Highlands, the neighborhood of choice for Lowell's nouveau riche.

Kerouac's return to his hometown was not the genteel writerly retirement he had often fantasized,

THE SCRIPTURE OF THE GOLDEN ETERNITY

When you've understood this scripture, throw it away. If you cant understand this scripture, throw it away. I insist on your freedom.

Scripture 45

Inscription on the Kerouac Commemorative, Jack Kerouac Park, Lowell, Massachusetts, 1989.

"Someday this town will put up a monument to me," Kerouac wrote in a letter to an old friend before leaving Lowell for good at the end of 1968. Perhaps thinking along the lines of Rodin's Balzac, he added, "I'll even pose naked for it if they want me to." Twenty years later, the city of Lowell did in fact honor him with a monument, but it contained no sculpted representation of Kerouac the man, only his words — passages from his works carved into the polished facets of eight granite columns arranged in a mandala.

but a monumental twenty-month binge remembered in Lowell to this day. By all accounts, it was a roaring, cursing, vomiting, excruciatingly public yet bitterly lonely drinking death on a par with those of Dylan Thomas and Brendan Behan. Though his final collapse didn't actually occur in Lowell—that would happen in St. Petersburg, Florida—anyone could see that Jack was a dead man waiting to drop. He was forty-five.

Somehow, he still managed to write, doggedly completing *Vanity of Duluoz* in the grip of his sickness. Kerouac liked to say that he could see the tops of the pines at Walden Pond from the second-story window of his house in the Highlands, a distance of twelve miles. If so, it was as close as Jack ever came to Walden in those last years of his life. He might still pay a tangential homage to Thoreau as a literary neighbor from the Concord-Merrimack watershed, but at the end of 1968 Kerouac was philosophically farther than he'd ever been from Thoreau. "Who's going to come out and say that the mind of nature is intrinsically insane and vicious forever?" ranted Kerouac at the anguished end of *Duluoz,* the last book published before his death. He had become fixated on the archetype of Kali, "that horrible Mother Kali of ancient India and its wisdom aeons with all her arms bejeweled, legs and belly too, gyrating insanely to eat back thru the only part of her that's not jeweled, her yoni, or yin, everything she's given birth to. Ha ha ha ha she's laughing as she dances on the dead she gave birth to. Mother Nature giving you birth and eating you back."

WHEN WORD CAME WEST that Jack had died—"dead of a gastric hemorrhage in the old folks capital of the world," said the *Berkeley Barb*—Snyder was living at Camino del Cañon in the Muir Woods, not far from the junction of Redwood Creek and the Dipsea Trail—the same path he and Jack had hiked together in the days before Gary's first trip to Japan in 1956. "I wonder which one of us'll die first?" Kerouac had speculated back then. "Whoever it is, come on back, ghost, and give 'em the key."

"It was very sad to hear of Jack's death," remembers Gary. "I lit a candle and incense, sat in zazen for a long time, and then chanted some sutras and the 'Dharani of the Great Compassionate One' [a magical text invoking the Bodhisattva Avalokitesvara] to help send his spirit off on its journey, to reawaken his eye to emptiness, and fearlessness and non-attachment."

"When I think of Jack now, I remember him as a dear friend and comrade, and a man from whom I got a new sense of writing, an eye on prose that was really refreshing," said Snyder at age seventy. "But

Kerouac's Grave, Edson Cemetery, Lowell, Massachusetts, 1989.

The earth, the earth!
It is the heart.
Do, do the work!
Hold fast, hold fast!
O great victor!
Hold on, hold on!
Dharani of the Great Compassionate One

also there's the sadness of a somewhat lost and wasted talent — not that he didn't produce a lot, but if he had had better physical and psychological health, it would have been interesting to see what else he might have done, because there was still obviously more maturing possible there, and what people do in their maturity can be kind of interesting. So, there's a certain sadness about Jack's life. But what he did was certainly remarkable."

Kerouac's body was flown north from Florida for burial in his native ground of Lowell, Massachusetts. His requiem mass was in the granite-walled Franco-American cathedral of St. Jean-Baptiste — the church from *Doctor Sax* and *Visions of Gerard*. Allen Ginsberg was one of Jack's pall bearers. Photographs at the cemetery show bare-branched October beeches against an immaculate blue Merrimack sky. For Kerouac, October had always been the magic month, the "top prince" of his private religion. "October to me is more than a month," he once wrote, in one of his periodic, self-addressed letters to his soul. "It's an ecstasy. I can reach a fuller understanding with this immense prince than with people." He had died on October 21 — the anniversary of the day he and Gary had headed off with John Montgomery to hike the Yosemite Matterhorn, exactly fourteen years before. Jack's body was laid in the Sampas family plot, a few feet from his friend Sebastian's. Of his old literary compatriots, Ginsberg, Peter Orlovsky, John Clellon Holmes, Gregory Corso, Robert Creeley were at graveside to see the casket down. Gary decided to remain in California. Philip Whalen was in Kyoto.

It had been eight years since Philip had seen Jack, but they had remained in friendly correspondence, albeit infrequently, nearly to the end. Earlier in the year, while preparing for his return to Japan, Philip had been picking through his stateside belongings, looking for items to sell for traveling cash, or just throwing things out. Among his books, he found Jack's old copy of Blake's *Jerusalem* from 1957, when they were in Berkeley together, and returned it to him. Kerouac had been tickled to receive it and sent Philip his thanks, joking, "In a previous lifetime you were Benjamin Franklin trudging the Bradford Road in the mud and rain with letters for log cabins."

"Well, I can't say that my opinion of Jack has changed in the last thirty years," said Whalen in our 1998 interview. "I thought that he was a terrific writer when he was around and what he wrote was exciting and marvelous. And *he* could be exciting and marvelous some hours. When he was in a mood to be sociable, he could be wonderful, and when he was not, he was a stone drag. But that's the way folks are, at least literary folks, I guess."

THE PILGRIMS THAT Kerouac in 1956 predicted would one day come to Desolation Peak—"to offer homage and speeches and dedications"—began to show up within a year of his death. Gerry Cook, the Park Service lookout who manned Desolation that summer of 1970, still remembers Jack's first post-humous acolytes: two East Coast college dropouts laden with technical gear and a notion to climb Hozomeen, then to skip across the border into British Columbia. They'd hitchhiked all the way from New York—"on the road" and on the *run*—a couple of Vietnam war draft resisters heading for Vancouver. All the way across the U.S., they confided to Gerry, they'd planned on doing this—to stop off at Kerouac's lookout to say good-bye to America before they left it.

"Even then there were Kerouac worshippers," says Cook. "Those two that came—I remember them really well because they were coming *because* of Kerouac."

Jack's lookout had become a shrine, as he had foreseen. Cook, himself a college student at that time, had been well aware of the Kerouac connection prior to being assigned to Desolation. He had begun working for the Forest Service in 1967, before the Park had been created, and in those days, there was always a copy of *The Dharma Bums* or *Desolation Angels* floating around the station, and even a few old-timers who had gone to guard school with Kerouac or worked trail with Snyder or Whalen. He had read Kerouac and Snyder before, and he packed their books with him when he went on lookout.

"In 1970 the job they offered me was Desolation Lookout," Cook recalled in 1998. "I didn't ask for that job, but I was certainly intrigued by the romanticism of it. . . . Of course I was aware of Kerouac—I loved being in those lookouts and reading what Kerouac and Snyder wrote right there. I really got off on that. It added a tremendous amount to that experience. It gave me direction right when I was there. And I used that to get more out of those places than I would have otherwise, I know that."

Maxine Franklin, an Athabascan poet from Wasilla, Alaska, who, like Cook, has spent several seasons on lookout at both Desolation and Sourdough, also recalls being drawn to fire-watching by the "romanticism."

"The thing that makes it so special," she says, "is that it's actually a *job*. They actually pay you, yet you get to live in a way that's almost like a Chinese hermit. Civilization never has its complete, total appeal or control over you once you've had that solitary experience. You can meditate, you can have a mystical or spiritual orientation and still be able to do your job. It's one of the very few non-productive jobs our culture allows. . . ."

As Gary Snyder's poems and books of essays began to receive wide distribution in the late 1960s and early '70s, some favoritism — much of it regional — toward Snyder's works over Kerouac's began to build among Park workers, and Northwest readers in general. The perception developed that Kerouac had been a poor lookout, a clueless East Coast hipster, too lazy to learn the differences between the conifers or the names of wildflowers and stars; that he was a sloppy, out-of-shape hiker, not "hardcore" enough. Those who actually spent time in Desolation Lookout usually modified their opinions of Jack after a time.

"Ever since I've been here I've heard people slashing Kerouac for being lazy," says Gerry Cook, who went on from his lookout summers in the early seventies to become a field supervisor for the North Cascades National Park today. "There's this image that Kerouac was a bum and that he wasn't into being a lookout much and that he wasn't a hard worker. But you don't have to be to be a lookout. A lookout is a perfect place for a guy like that. The guy lived life, he was on a different kind of mission, and this is a great place to come do that mission.

"Snyder — he's got our respect because he was a hard worker, and he wouldn't bullshit you. My image of him is that he'd look you right in the eye and tell you what he thought, and he wouldn't back down from a challenge and he worked his ass off — and that's how you gain respect among certain people here. But both of them were very meaningful to me."

Maxine Franklin, whose first lookout was on Desolation in 1976, had some problems with Kerouac's writing in the beginning. "When I first read Kerouac, I couldn't identify with him very well because he wasn't interested in the same things on the lookout that I was. He was interested in what was going on in his own head, and at that time I was really interested in what was happening in nature, what plants were there, what birds were there. . . . I was interested in the natural history, the geology, the things that *weren't* me. And he did spend an awful lot of time thinking about what he was going to do when he got down off the lookout, where I spent the whole summer just totally immersed in being there. He felt that it was kind of a scary place — that Hozomeen was very threatening. I felt that Desolation was an extremely gentle, almost tame place. Compared to the ruggedness of the rest of the Cascades, Desolation is *very* gentle, a very rounded mountain. To me, it just felt like it was not the same place that he described. . . . I've learned to appreciate him a lot more since then. But I was always a Gary Snyder and Philip Whalen fan."

Gary Snyder at Kitkitdizze, his home in the Sierra foothills

near Nevada City, California, October 1997.

AFTER HIS BLACKLISTING in 1954, Gary had never again gone back to the Upper Skagit country. He did, however, make one important trip to the North Cascades in the late summer of 1965, to climb Glacier Peak with Allen Ginsberg. That year, Ginsberg had gotten a Guggenheim, and with some of the money bought a VW microbus and headed west.

In late summer of 1965, Gary and Allen took off for a month-long camping trip in the Oregon and Washington Cascades, culminating in a six-day trek in the newly designated Glacier Peak Wilderness Area. It was Gary's first visit to the North Cascades since his 1956 trip to the Nooksack, also with Allen.

Glacier Peak, the 10,500-foot volcano that Gary had first glimpsed as a boy growing up north of Seattle and later sighted in his fire finder from Crater Mountain, had been the primary regional battle-ground between conservationists and the Forest Service all during the 1950s and early '60s. The Glacier Peak Wilderness Area had not come about until 1960, and then only by decree of the Secretary of Agri-culture, after a decade of Forest Service intransigence. The designated Glacier Peak wilderness of 1960 was still only half the size of the area originally proposed by Robert Marshall and Ferdinand Silcox in the late 1930s, and well into the 1960s the Forest Service fought tooth-and-nail to keep the Glacier Peak wilderness open to logging, mining, and road building. Not until the passage of the Wilderness Act of 1964 was the Glacier Peak Wilderness Area finally and fully protected by statute.

Their summiting morning on the glacier was one of the finest Gary had seen, from any mountain-top, ever. "So many mountains, on so clear a day, the mind is staggered," he wrote in his journal. From the top of the 10,500-foot snowpeak they could see more than a hundred miles in the pristine Septem-ber air—south to Oregon's Mount Jefferson, east across Puget Sound to the blue Olympics, north to the Selkirks of British Columbia, and west across the Columbia Plateau, even to the distant peaks of the Colville Indian Reservation, where Chief Joseph was buried. "You mean there's a Senator for all this?" asked an awe-struck Ginsberg, as they drank in the magnificent three-sixty. Gary later seized on Allen's question, putting it at the center of a key environmental essay, "The Wilderness." "Ultimately," wrote Gary, "there *isn't* a senator for all that."

On the surface, of course, there was. Washington's congressional delegation had gotten behind the Wilderness Act, which had provided Glacier Peak and its adjacent surrounding wilderness with impor-tant legislative protections. But the Wilderness Act, important as it was—"the climax of preservationist environmentalism," in the opinion of Wallace Stegner—was only a beginning. Many conservationists were unsatisfied with the nine million acres of wild lands set aside in the National Wilderness Preservation System the act set up. The original bill had called for a system of 160 million acres. It was not simply about numbers of acres; the acres could, and would be increased in time. The Wilderness Society's Howard Zahniser had fought hard—to the death, some said—for the definition of wilderness incorporated in the act: ". . . an area where the earth and its community of life are untrammeled by man, where man himself is a visitor who does not remain." Zahniser's original draft, written and introduced to Congress in early 1956, read "where man himself *is a member of the natural community,* [italics added] who visits but does not remain. . . ." Somewhere in one of the many revisions that the bill underwent in the nine-year struggle for its passage, the philosophic notion of humankind as a member-species of a natural community was dropped.

"I would like to think of a new definition of humanism," wrote Snyder, hearkening back to Ginsberg's question, and further, to old Robinson Jeffers, "and a new definition of democracy that would include the nonhuman, that would have representation from those spheres. This is what I think we mean by an ecological consciousness."

OVER THE YEARS the Skagit remained part of Snyder and his poems. In 1959 when *Riprap* was published, among the dozen working-class heroes of the book's dedication page were the names Roy Raymond, Jim Baxter, and Blackie Burns. Baxter and Raymond also show up in the opening lines of "Night Highway 99," included in *Mountains and Rivers Without End.*

Old Roy Raymond, who with Blackie Burns had packed Gary into Sourdough Lookout in 1953, never worked in the woods again after his 1955 heart attack. The last time Gary saw him was in 1956 at the Helena Hotel in Bellingham—the meeting alluded to at the beginning of "Night Highway 99." A couple of years after that Roy disappeared, last seen checking out of his hotel under full backpack. Perhaps he was finally going up into the watershed to fix up an old miners' cabin for himself, up on Thunder or Ruby, as he often said he would. A few weeks later, a body was found floating in the Skagit; people assumed it was Roy's, although no positive identification was ever made.

Gary learned this from Jim Baxter, who kept in touch for several years, even writing him in Kyoto. Although he'd always liked Gary, Baxter clearly had little understanding of what his old Forest Service pal was up to in Japan. "Don't let those old Buddhist priests lead you astray," he admonished in his last letter in 1960. "I like Christianity best because Christ is still alive and all the leaders of all other religions is dead." Baxter had lived the outdoors life to the end. In the mid-'60s he canoed and portaged from the Canadian border all the way to the Arctic Ocean. His end was sadly ironic. For all his woodsmanship and wilderness travels, Baxter died in his bunk, of exposure, after catching a chill rounding up some boats in a storm, at a boy scout camp at Silver Lake, Washington.

As time passed, Gary's last personal contact in the Skagit District was with Jack Francis, his fellow lookout from 1952. When *Earth House Hold* was published in 1969, Gary sent inscribed copies to Francis and asked him if he could track down Blackie Burns and pass along a copy to him as well. Jack found Blackie — then seventy-four years old — living with his wife, Edna, in Wickersham, a tiny village north of Sedro Woolley. Blackie had suffered a couple of heart attacks and had to take it easy, related Jack. "Blackie says he regrets now, more than anything else, his inability to get out and hike around the mountains. He said he had hauled too many heart attack cases out of the mountains in the past, and didn't want to force others to have to do the same for him."

Blackie Burns died in late August 1974, at the age of seventy-eight. Jack Francis sent Gary the obituary from the Bellingham paper and recalled the day Blackie had picked him up in the Ross patrol boat at the foot of the Desolation trail when he'd packed out of the lookout in late August 1952. "After I got aboard Blackie gave me a drink from a flask he took out of his vest. I saw him looking at me as I took a swallow — and that stuff really burnt its way down. When I reacted he chortled and was happy. It was moonshine he picked up down in Marblemount, white lightning."

A few months later, in October 1974, Jack Francis drove up to Ruby Creek on the recently opened Cross Cascades Highway, with the intention of revisiting Crater Mountain Lookout. The road passed within a hundred yards of the old Granite Creek Guard Station, by then boarded up and just about forgotten in the dark woods away from the road. What had once been a full two-day trip from Marblemount by truck, boat and mountain trail in the old days had been reduced to a smooth one-hour drive. The back country had become front country.

Jack hiked up the Crater Lookout trail, remembering the day he and Harold Vail had gone up to see Gary, and found him sitting in the doorway in his jockstrap, puffing on his pipe. At the western summit, however, the lookout was gone. Only the steel fire-finder shaft remained protruding from the bedrock chert, still straight, but covered with a fine coat of rust. Gary's L–4 cabin, Jack later learned, had been declared an "attractive nuisance" and was torched by the Forest Service in the summer of 1968. Scattered around the site were various scraps of fire-blackened metal and molten window glass left over from the burning. Some of these fragments Jack scooped up and later mailed to Snyder, then in his fifth year at Kitkitdizze.

"A box of junk—but a rather special box of junk," wrote Jack. "A farmer with a barn can always find use for nails, clevis bolts, shutter hinges, and old parts for door locks. The molten glass—well, that's different—maybe you can mount it, then while sitting in front of your wood fire you can pretend it's a glass ball—look in it and perhaps see visions of your lost youth."

True, Gary's twenties were well behind him when he received Jack Francis's letter in the late fall of 1974. By then he was forty-four, a world-renowned poet (*Turtle Island* was published that week. It would win the Pulitzer prize the following spring), a householder, thrice-married, with two young sons, Kai and Gen. But Snyder's Cascadian lookout days—which is what Jack had surely meant by "youth"—were far from lost. They were alive in his poems and essays, dog-eared copies stashed in the packs of thousands of hikers around the country and on the bookshelves of hostels from Amsterdam to Kathmandu.

THE YEARS THAT Snyder, Whalen, and Kerouac worked in the Skagit were the heyday of the lookout era. In 1953, when Gary was on Sourdough and Philip on Sauk, there were 5,000 fire watch cabins on public lands across the United States, mostly on the great conifer forests of the Northwest. Oregon had eight hundred, Washington State had more than six hundred. On the Mount Baker Forest alone there were forty-three.

As the Forest Service began to rely more heavily on aircraft for fire detection in the late 1950s, many lookouts were decommissioned. As time passed, the L.O.s, one by one, began to disappear. Left unmanned, they slowly gave way to the mountaintop elements, or were picked apart by vandals. The Forest Service eventually burned down many of them, to avoid possible "attractive nuisance" lawsuits. Of the poets' lookouts, Sauk was first to go. The old cupola-topped cabin, where Philip Whalen spent the summer of '53 reading Shakespeare and watching the martens flow across the snowdrifts, was burned down by the Forest Service a few years after he left. Following his season there, the slopes of Sauk Mountain had begun to be heavily logged. A switch-backing haul road was built up the mountain

One of Snyder's axes, with Kitkitdizze brand, October 1997.

> *". . . Pound was an axe,*
> *Chen was an axe, I am an axe*
> *And my son a handle, soon*
> *To be shaping again, model*
> *And tool, craft of culture,*
> *How we go on."*
>
> Gary Snyder, "Axe Handles"

from the Skagit Road to timberline. High school kids from the nearby town of Concrete liked to drive up it and party on the peak; eventually Whalen's lookout was trashed to the point that the Forest Service torched and built a newer, supposedly more secure, flat-roofed model on the same spot. That building, too, was vandalized, and was finally taken down in the mid–1980s. Today, only the charred corner posts of the original lookout and a heap of broken foundation stones mark the site.

Fittingly perhaps, the last two operational fire-watch cabins on the Upper Skagit today are Kerouac's on Desolation and Snyder's and Whalen's on Sourdough. Despite the latest in aircraft and satellite fire detection technology, first spottings of smokes on the Upper Skagit are still routinely called in from these Spartan seventy-year-old structures by lookouts sighting down the same fire finders that Gary, Philip, and Jack used fifty years ago. It turns out that the old lookouts, once written off as obsolete, still have a viable role to play in fire detection, often working in tandem with aircraft spotters and fire-fighting planes.

The lookouts—not just Sourdough and Desolation, but all of the still-standing L.O.s around the country—have also come to be valued for less utilitarian reasons. Hikers have always loved to see them beckoning in the breaking clouds at the top of a trail. Now, too, as solitude, self-reflection, and plain silence have become ever more fleeting and rare in our lives, the lookouts have emerged as symbols of a nearly lost and longed-for American simplicity and integrity—Thoreau's cabin transferred to the mountaintop.

In 1989, both Desolation and Sourdough lookouts were added to the National Register of Historic Places, not so much for their literary significance, however, as for their importance in the history of forest protection. Kerouac was mentioned in passing on Desolation Lookout's nomination citation; no reference to Snyder or Whalen was made in Sourdough's. Inside the door of Sourdough's fire-finder cabinet, however, their names are written on a yellowing roster, along with those of all the subsequent lookouts.

Today, thanks to National Park and Wilderness designations, the North Cascades that Snyder, Whalen, and Kerouac saw look much as they did a half century ago when the poets went on their lookouts, though there are a few notable exceptions.

The panorama from Kerouac's old lookout remains the same, with great Hozomeen, ever changing aspect in the clouds and light, anchoring the view, commanding all attention. Desolation is still a remote place — eighteen miles south to the nearest road, or a half-hour boat ride from Ross Dam. To the north, on the Canadian side, there is still only a single gravel road coming down from the town of Hope to the border crossing at Hozomeen.

From Sourdough, the northern vista is absolutely unchanged from the day of Snyder and Whalen. The same astonishing one-eighty that greeted them at the top of the ridge in the fifties — the northern half of Whalen's *mala,* from Davis Peak in the west all the way around to Jack and Crater in the east — is what one sees today. The view to the south is significantly different, however, changed permanently by the Cross Cascades Highway that skirts the flanks of Ruby Mountain on the far side of Diablo Lake. On a summer's day the distant throg of a Harley chopper can carry across the valley; weekends, RV headlights flicker all night as they climb the grade from Panther Creek. Sourdough Mountain, despite its awesome three-sixty of surrounding wilderness, is hardly wilderness itself; cars can drive right to the trailhead in Diablo. Were it not for the daunting gain of the lookout trail, Sourdough L.O. might well have suffered the same fate as Whalen's cabin on Sauk by now.

What the poets saw from their lookouts may appear intact, but *how* they experienced that landscape over the season is probably not possible today. They came to the Skagit, after all, not for scenery, or to "do" a mountain, but to be changed themselves by the sublime uneventfulness of lookout life. Hozomeen on Day One is not the same mountain as on Day Fifteen. (Kerouac lived completely alone with it for sixty-three days.) The kind of absolute solitude that Snyder enjoyed on Crater or that Kerouac toughed out on Desolation can only be tasted in three- and four-day draughts at most these days, in part, ironically, *because* of them. Over the years, as the fame of Kerouac and Snyder (and to a far lesser, but growing extent, Whalen) has spread, their lookouts have become destinations for increasing numbers of hikers wishing to see firsthand the little shacks and vast surrounding landscapes that inspired their works. Rare now is the summer's day that doesn't bring a literary pilgrim to one of the poets' peaks in the Upper Skagit.

For all that, the peaks certainly do not disappoint, not even Sauk, the lowest and most overrun, with its logging road leading to a timberline parking lot. On the old vision-peak nowadays, one more likely crosses paths with daredevils seeking satori on a snowboard or paraglider than a poet reading Shakespeare on the summit, but with luck one can still camp in solitude among the rocks of Whalen's perch for a night: under a full moon the light still glimmers on the glacier ice of Komo Kulshan, as it did for Philip a half century ago.

Crater too has become a destination for hard-core Snyder enthusiasts looking to lay their own eyes on the landscapes that inspired *Myths and Texts* and *Mountains and Rivers Without End* fifty years ago. Despite the difficulty of access—the fixed ropes that once ran through the southwest gully are long gone—and the absence of any shelter on the summit, people do come. A tin-can "summit register" tucked into the rocks at the base of the fire-finder shaft contains their scribbled homages to Snyder and his works. And from that rusty Osborne pole, still plumb as the day it was driven, one turns and sees what the poet saw on those transparent mornings fifty years ago, when Desolation called to welcome him, for then and ever, to the "community of lookouts."

Prayer Flags at Desolation Lookout, July 1995.

Annotations

The following are the main archives referred to in the text, preceded by their shortened forms used in the annotations: UC Davis. Gary Snyder Papers, Department of Special Collections, Shields Library, University of California Library, Davis, California; Reed: Philip Whalen Collection, Special Collections Library, Hauser Memorial Library, Reed College, Portland, Oregon; Columbia: Philip Whalen Papers, Rare Book and Manuscript Library, Columbia University, New York, New York; Kerouac Estate: John Sampas, Stella and Jack Kerouac Estate, Lowell, Massachusetts; American Philosophical Society: Dell Hymes Papers, American Philosophical Society Library, Philadelphia, Pennsylvania; Sierra Club: Sierra Club Papers, Bancroft Library, University of California, Berkeley, California; Norman Leonard Collection, Labor Archives and Research Center, San Francisco State University, San Francisco, California; North Cascades National Park Service Complex, Marblemount Curation Facility, Marblemount, Washington.

CHAPTER 1: AFTER THE GOLD RUSH

P. 1. *"The miners' lives were bold":* Gary Snyder, *A Place in Space,* p. 57.

P. 2. *all-male milieu:* Gerry Cook, interview with the author, Marblemount, Washington, September 14, 1998. "The Forest Service was definitely a male-oriented society. You take a whole bunch of young males—it was mostly a red-neck, male-oriented, macho society, but these lookouts even then weren't that way, they were definitely different."

P. 2. *first fire watcher . . . Mabel Gray:* Ray Kresek, *Fire Lookouts of the Northwest,* p.69.

P. 2. *directive to discourage:* ibid.

P. 2. *Martha Hardy . . . Tatoosh:* Ira Spring and Byron Fish, *Lookouts: Firewatchers of the Cascades and Olympics,* pp. 118–120.

P. 3. *Bonnie St. Aubin:* Harold Vail, interview with the author, Bellingham, Washington, September 14, 1998. The St. Aubins also manned Hidden Lake Lookout in 1953, the summer that Snyder was on Sourdough.

P. 3. *By the time he was ten:* Gary Snyder, "Ancient Forests of the Far West," *The Practice of the Wild,* p. 118. "My father put me on one end of a two-man saw when I was ten and gave me the classic instruction of 'don't ride the saw'—don't push, only pull, and I loved the clean swish and ring of the blade, the rhythm, the comradeship, the white curl of the wood that came out with the rakers . . . "

P. 3. *thirteen to fifteen:* Gary Snyder, interview with the author, Kitkitdizze, October 26, 1997. "At thirteen

I started going to a YMCA camp up at Mount Saint Helens where I went into a sort of special category of half camper, half worker — that was a special category for kids that didn't have so much money but were good at taking care of things. So, they started taking me up there even in the off season."

P. 3. *At nineteen he'd taken his first job:* Gary Snyder to Harold Snyder, July 16, 1949, UC Davis. "I got here today & start work Monday on trail and line maintenance work. . . . I do all sorts of work — bucking logs, splicing line, packing food to lookouts, etc."

P. 3. *"highest, most remote . . . lookout":* Snyder interview, October 26, 1997.

P. 3. *"you have no idea . . . ":* ibid.

P. 3. *Gary was sent to Granite Creek Guard Station:* Guard stations were part of the Forest Service's extensive fire suppression network, remote outposts where firefighting tools, food and supplies were cached. In the event of a burn, guard stations also served as a bases for smoke chasers. One or two seasonal "forest guards" or "fire guards" were usually stationed there as well. It was the guards' job to build and maintain area trails, put out small fires in the vicinity, and in general lend support to packers and lookouts.

P. 4. *a "sky hook" crane hoisted him:* Snyder interview, October 26, 1997.

P. 4. *Harold knew the Ruby Creek:* Harold Vail interview, Washington, September 16, 1998.

P. 4. *The other guard — Jim Baxter:* Gary Snyder, telephone interview transcript, November 18, 1998: "I don't know a lot about Jim Baxter. He never said much about himself. He was a seasonal man, and when I think back about it, I remember that Jim was always soft-spoken, mild, mellow and funny. But he never told anything about himself, and I never pursued that."

P. 6. *Shubert Hunter, the lookout:* Shubert Hunter, interview with the author, Marblemount, Washington, August 31, 1998.

P. 6. *Gary and Harold . . . in Slate Creek:* Harold Vail interview, September 16, 1998. "We didn't have a radio or anything, and there was no phone line through there. So we hustled our buns five miles back to the

cabin, to the guard station, to get on the phone to see what the hell was going on, cause we didn't know which way to run and we got back and called and Blackie said 'Well it's all over with, it burned clear to the top of the hill, killed two guys and it's burning out.'"

P. 6. *"The radio told of a great fire":* Philip Whalen to Gary Snyder, July 26, 1952, UC Davis.

P. 6. *"Like living on the bow . . . ":* Gary Snyder, "North Beach," *The Old Ways,* p. 46.

P. 6. *The rent was $35:* Gary Snyder, interview with the author, Kitkitdizze, December 6, 2000.

P. 6. *He had been born in the city:* ibid.

P. 7. *"itching to get . . . Portland":* Painted on the outside of Vesuvio's Bar on Columbus Avenue, across Jack Kerouac Alley from City Lights Bookshop, by San Francisco artist, Shawn Shaughnessy, a Portland native. According to Janet Clyde, one of Vesuvio's current owners, the tagline was inspired by a random quote from a "found" antique postcard.

P. 7. *"West Coast of those days . . . ":* Gary Snyder, "North Beach," *The Old Ways,* p. 45. The poet Lawrence Ferlinghetti, another arrival in San Francisco during those years, draws the North African analogy as well. See Lawrence Ferlinghetti, "The Poetic City That Was," *San Francisco Chronicle,* January 14, 2001. ". . . a small shining white city, looking rather like Tunis seen from seaward, a Mediterranean city with small white houses on hillsides, brilliant in the January sun."

P. 7. *his 200-page senior thesis:* Gary Snyder to Harold Snyder, April 21, 1951, UC Davis. "Thesis is all done but for proofreading, introduction, & bibliography. Title: *Some Dimensions of a Myth:* subject & method: one small Haida Indian myth subjected to an analysis from anthropological, comparative, psychological, metaphysical, linguistic, literary, & functionalist points of view with the dual intention of 1) showing what the range of problems & interpretations are possible in th study of any single version 2) showing that the problems of mythology are extensivet limited to any single discipline, but a synthesis of methods & theories is possible and practical in the study of oral literature."

P. 7. *"most copied Reed thesis"*: David H. French, "Gary Snyder and Reed College," in Jon Halper, ed., *Gary Snyder: Dimensions of a Life,* p. 17. Snyder's thesis, "The Dimensions of a Haida Myth," was published in 1971 as *He Who Hunted Birds in His Father's Village* by Donald Allen's Grey Fox Press.

P. 7. *"on the Montgomery Street drainage"*: Gary Snyder, "Lookout's Journal," *Earth House Hold,* p. 8.

P. 8. *"west to the fresh green breast. . ."*: Gary Snyder, "North Beach Alba," *The Back Country,* p. 75. "tamalpais a fresh green hill in the new sun."

P. 8. *"unearthly . . . summits"*: Gary Snyder, "Ancient Forests of the Far West," *The Practice of the Wild,* p. 117.

P. 10. *John Sutter:* Fred Beckey, *Cascade Alpine Guide: Climbing & High Routes, Vol. 3, Rainy Pass to Fraser River,* p. 191.

P. 10. *"Ruby Creek has gold . . . "*: *Bellingham Bay Mail,* April 19, 1879.

P. 10. *"Nokomokeen"*: Henry Custer, *Report of Reconnaissances,* p. 44. "Nokomokeen" is the name given to the peak in Henry Custer's 1866 report on his 1859 explorations of the Upper Skagit.

P. 10. *gold fever lingered:* Paul C. Pitzer, *Building the Skagit: A Century of Upper Skagit Valley History, 1870–1970,* p. 75.

P. 11. *"Makes trolley buses run"*: Philip Whalen, "Sourdough Mountain Lookout," *Overtime: Selected Poems,* p. 19.

> This year's rock is a spur from the main ridge
> Cuts the valley in two and is broken
> By the river; Ross Dam repairs the break,
> Makes trolley buses run
> Through the streets of dim Seattle far away.

P. 13. *Sometimes Beebe camped:* Although it was called Granite Creek Guard Station, Beebe's cabin was actually on Canyon Creek, which rushed by just ten yards outside the front door. Spanning the creek was a narrow, hand-roped, log footbridge that led to a small barn for pack stock. From the barn, lookouts and their pack strings headed up the Crater Mountain Trail.

P. 13. *At the confluence:* Granite Creek has its source fifteen miles south, high in the cirque lakes of Rainy Pass; Canyon Creek originates deep in the heart of the Pasayten Wilderness, near the Pacific Crest at Holman Pass, twelve miles northeast. The juncture of these streams is a strategic node in the extensive Ruby Creek watershed reaching from the Cascade Crest down to the Skagit.

P. 13. *When Frank Beebe . . . retired:* Jim Baxter to Gary Snyder, December 21, 1958, UC Davis. "The Granite Creek Guard Station is being used for training school kids for Forestry and the Whole District has gone to hell in general."

P. 13. *In the early 1930s Frank Beebe's wife:* Camille Evans, interview with Bee Currie, September 5, 1997, North Cascades National Park archives. Bee Currie was the daughter of Frank Beebe, and lived at his cabin on Canyon Creek. Details of Frank Beebe's life and descriptions of the Granite Creek Guard Station cabin are from her interview.

P. 13. *Just inside the front door:* Harold Vail interview, September 16, 1998. Harold Vail also remembers Gary being an inventive back country chef who could throw together a tasty meal from canned items like spam or corned beef, but also knew enough about wild edibles to steam a pot of fresh nettles or mash up a sweet rhubarb dessert from the juicy shoots growing along the creek bank. Of course, there was always plenty of fish on the menu at Granite Creek, where the cold waters teemed with trout — three pound rainbows and cutthroat twenty inches long, plus Dolly Varden, a delicious char fish so plentiful at that time that most anglers threw them back for junk fish.

P. 13. *reading Damon Runyon:* Gary Snyder, unpublished Crater Mountain journal, July 28, 1952, used by permission of Gary Snyder.

P. 13. *"It is only the sound of running water"*: Gary Snyder, unpublished Crater Mountain journal, July 13, 1952, used by permission of Gary Snyder.

P. 13. *"I am not writing poetry"*: ibid., July 7, 1952. Used by permission of Gary Snyder.

P. 14. *Just before leaving San Francisco:* Gary Snyder, telephone interview transcript, November 12, 1998.

P. 14. *"neat pile on the fragrant trail:* Gary Snyder, "A Berry Feast," *The Back Country,* p. 3.

P. 14. *"Fuck You"*: ibid., p. 5.

P. 14. *"Bearshit-on-the-Trail"*: Comment attributed to Lawrence Ferlinghetti, in Snyder interview, December 6, 2000.

P. 14. *Working from notes:* In our October 1998 interview, Dell Hymes recalled seeing a near-finished draft of the poem at the time of Snyder's departure from Bloomington in January 1952. By the time Gary hitchhiked north to go on lookout in June of 1952, "A Berry Feast" was essentially finished, except for a few changes in punctuation and line breaks.

The earliest extant typescript of "A Berry Feast" among Snyder's papers at UC Davis is dated "1951–1953, Warm Springs — Bloomington — San Francisco." Perhaps the biggest difference between that early version and the poem eventually published in *The Back Country* is the visual look of the poem on the page. In the early typescript, all the lines begin left-justified, with margin notes identifying the animal, vegetable, and human voices of "coyote," "berries," and "people." Snyder kept these dramatic cues as part of the poem through its first publication in the 1957 *Evergreen Review.* For publication in *The Back Country,* he excised them from the margins and simply indicated the alternating choruses by indentation.

P. 14. *"I have been turning out poems":* Gary Snyder to Harold Snyder, November 27, 1950, UC Davis.

P. 14. *It had been very cold then:* Snyder interview, December 6, 2000.

P. 14. *Gary's first folklore:* Gary Snyder to Harold Snyder, December 29, 1949, UC Davis. "I just got back from Warm Springs, collected a fine folk-tale and a fragment of the flood legend from an old Tsimshian who was born in B.C. [British Columbia]. Will spend the rest of the vacation at home, all day every day, reading up on Tsimshian legends and writing a paper around my find."

P. 14. *Tsimshian mythology:* The Tsimshian are a tribe of the North Pacific Coast culture area of British Columbia, part of the "Northern Group," which includes the Haida, Tlingit, and Tsimshian.

P. 15. *The Warm Springs berry feast:* Funk and Wagnalls *Standard Dictionary of Folklore, Mythology, and*

Legend, p. 391. "The concepts underlying first-fruits ceremonies are principally two: 1) The part is representative of the whole; and 2) danger is inherent in new things. Because of this danger, from spirits dwelling in the grain, from the jealous dead, from the gods to whom all things belong, etc., some propitiatory gesture must be made. Therefore, before partaking, the tabu must be removed by giving up a fair share to the gods or spirits, or by indicating to them, by ceremonial approach, that the food is a necessity and that their gift to man will not be wasted."

P. 15. *"Yakima horsemen":* Gary Snyder, "To the Chinese Comrades," *The Back Country,* p. 113.

P. 15. *There was wild gambling:* Gary Snyder to Kenneth Rexroth, "Wednesday 1954," UC Davis. In January 1954, Snyder sent Kenneth Rexroth a finished copy of "A Berry Feast," with an attached letter describing the poem's origins. "Here is a poem of mine that might interest you as an attempt to utilize American Indian material, some Oriental notions, contemporary goings-on in the Northwest, etc. Much of it derives from a stay on the Warm Springs Reservation in the summer of 1950 [1951]. They have, in August, a 'first-fruits' ceremony there called the berry feast — lasts two weeks, & all the Yakima, Wasco, Puyallup, etc. come down for gambling & horse-racing. I sat through all two weeks of it & collected anecdotes about Coyote. Other parts of it derive from logging activities on the Reservation that I was involved in."

P. 15. *"Tools of our time":* Gary Snyder, "History Must Have a Start," *Left Out in the Rain,* pp. 40–41.

P. 15. *Few people then paid any attention:* Robert R. Mierendorf, "An Updated Summary Statement of the Archeology of the North Cascades National Park Service Complex," p. 2. "It was generally thought that Native American people and their ancestors made little if any use of the Cascade Mountain interior, except to cross between interior and coastal regions for purposes of trade. . . . These views were held in spite of the recollections of Native elders, who told of the use of high elevation areas by their ancestors to gather berries, hunt, and practice traditional ceremonies."

P. 16. *The first archeological survey:* For a listing and discussion of early Upper Skagit archeological surveys, see Mierendorf et al., *An Archeological Site Survey and Evaluation,* pp. 23–25. See also, Mierendorf, *People of the North Cascades,* p. 29.

P. 16. *As late as 1986:* Robert R. Mierendorf, E-mail to the author, October 10, 2001.

P. 16. *Not for hundreds, but for thousands:* Robert R. Mierendorf, E-mail to the author, September 1, 1999. "Would it be safe to say that the valley of Ruby Creek was being used by native people for trading purposes at least 5,000 years ago? Probably, but to say so would be by inference using data from the Skagit Valley proper, rather than from sites within Ruby Creek. The sites are there, they just haven't been investigated. So it depends on just how scientifically precise you want to be. I believe Ruby Creek was probably a route for more than 8,000 years, but I have no 'proof' yet."

P. 16. *Long before the miners:* Mierendorf et al., *An Archeological Site Survey and Evaluation,* p. 21.

P. 16. *It was a typically Western situation:* Gary Snyder, "Earth Day and the War Against the Imagination," *A Place in Space,* p. 57. "I hope the time will come when we who live in the foothills will start our story with the Nisenan as our previous teachers and spiritual ancestors, rather than with the brief era of the gold miners. . . ."

P. 16. *"You bastards. . . ":* Gary Snyder, "Dusty Braces," *Turtle Island,* p. 75.

P. 18. *Gary too would have preferred:* Gary Snyder to Harold Snyder, May 8, 1951, UC Davis.

P. 18. *Still, Indiana University:* Dell Hymes, "A Coyote Who Can Sing," in Jon Halper, ed., *Gary Snyder: Dimensions of a Life,* p. 393. "Indeed, Indiana was a reasonable place for someone with Gary's interest in American Indian traditions. The anthropology department had been started and was chaired by a specialist in Indian languages, C. F. Voegelin, who edited there the only journal in the field, *International Journal of American Linguistics;* anthropological interest was strong in the fledgling graduate program in linguistics; there was a folklore program, headed by the dean of American folklore, Stith Thompson, who

had been a dean at Indiana, and whose *Tales of the American Indians* remained a basic source."

P. 18. *Always in the back of his mind:* Gary Snyder to Harold Snyder, November 28, 1949, UC Davis. In the fall of 1949, Gary had begun inquiring about changing his legal residence to his father's address at 1700 Leroy Street, Berkeley, California. "It might save me out-of-state tuition if I go to Berkeley for graduate study." See also, Gary Snyder to Harold Snyder, April 21, 1951, UC Davis. "If it looks like it will take too much effort to pay the fees at Indiana next year, I think I might move down to Berkeley and take a few courses in languages —Chinese, Greek, German; and work part time & read on my own—because I think I can establish residence in California on the basis of you & the fact that I'm a minor."

P. 18. *"the first person I ever talked to":* Snyder interview, December 6, 2000. Also, Robert Richter, telephone interview transcript, August 2, 2001. Richter had met the Zen Master Nyogen Senzaki in Los Angeles in the spring of 1949, while a student in an experimental "independent study" program sponsored by the Cornell-based Telluride Association. "We met this Japanese man who was a Zen Buddhist. He hardly spoke any English, but fortunately, [our instructor] was bilingual and could translate for us. Senzaki gave each of us a book, signed it—a Zen book in Japanese with some drawings and some writing that he had done. He was small, his head was shaved, serious, didn't crack a smile, thin . . . he sat cross-legged on this hotel bed in Japantown—and I was somehow very impressed by him—I think I met him twice—

"So a few months later, we're sitting in this Contemporary European Literature class. And I write this term paper where *Fruits of the Earth* by André Gide is somehow suggestive to me, or I imagined that it was something that I could appropriately compare to Zen Buddhism. Gary was sitting across the aisle from me, and we traded papers. He read mine, and I read his, and that was his first exposure to Zen Buddhism, that's what he later told me."

P. 19. *Suzuki was the first writer:* Gary Snyder, "On the Road with D. T. Suzuki," *A Zen Life: D. T. Suzuki*

Remembered, p. 209. "D. T. Suzuki gave me the push of my life and I can never be too grateful."

P. 19. *Somewhere on the outskirts:* Gary Snyder, E-mail to the author, March 17, 2001. "It was somewhere between Winnemucca and Elko. 40 was just a two lane road, and in those days could be lonely."

P. 19. *Cars were few:* Snyder interview, December 6, 2000. "I had been reading a little about Zen, and I had heard Suzuki's name, but I had never seen any of his actual books. So I bought two or three of the Suzuki books, put them in my pack, and then started heading out in a couple of days, said goodbye to Philip and my father, and I started hitch-hiking for Indiana. And on the road during some very long waits for rides, in Nevada and also in Wyoming, I started reading the Suzuki books . . . and I hadn't gotten very far into them when I said to myself 'I'm not going in the right direction.'"

P. 19. *What impressed him most:* ibid. "It wasn't until I read Suzuki that I ran into those dialogues between students and teachers, and the whole idea of the koans and practice, and when I saw that I said, 'Ah, now this would be fun to do — Practical, practical, not just theoretical.'"

P. 20. *"You cannot give me a blow":* D. T. Suzuki, *Essays in Zen Buddhism, First Series*, p. 253.

P. 20. *"However deep your knowledge":* ibid., p. 247.

P. 20. *And though I didn't know it:* Gary Snyder, "On the Road with D. T. Suzuki," *A Zen Life: D. T. Suzuki Remembered*, p. 207.

P. 20. *"a matter of character":* Suzuki, *Essays in Zen Buddhism, First Series*, p. 246.

P. 20. *Earlier that summer:* Gary Snyder to Thomas Merton, October 10, 1966, Thomas Merton papers, used by permission. "7 Storey — read while hitch-hiking in Oregon 14 years ago — to a logging job — crystallized my determination to go to Japan and study Zen."

P. 20. *In Zen there must be satori:* Suzuki, *Essays in Zen Buddhism, First Series*, p. 262.

P. 20. *In a road-shoulder revelation:* Snyder interview, December 6, 2000. "Well, it was just a practical epiphany, which was that what I really should be doing is going to Japan to study this stuff first hand. And it wasn't like I was discarding my interest in linguistics or Native American anthropology or anything. It was just that this struck me as the next step."

P. 20. *"The Orient":* Gary Snyder to Harold Snyder, September 11, 1951, UC Davis.

P. 21. *one of the greatest Zen masters:* Strictly speaking, Hui-Neng should not be called a "Zen master," since Zen is a Japanese word. The Chinese word for Zen is "Ch'an."

P. 21. *the unschooled woodcutter:* R. H. Blyth, *Zen and Zen Classics*, p. 215.

P. 21. *The story goes that:* The basic outlines of Hui-Neng's story are told in his "Platform Sutra," of which there are numerous translations. "My friend and colleague in Kyoto, Philip Yampolsky, did a translation of it based on a Rinzai interpretation; it is a superb text." Gary Snyder, telephone interview transcript, November 12, 1998.

P. 21. *"Hui-Neng's Platform Sutra is in a way":* Snyder, telephone interview transcript, November 12, 1998.

P. 22. *"People know thereby. . .":* D. T. Suzuki, *Manual of Zen Buddhism*, p. 85.

P. 22. *"Seeing into one's own Nature":* Suzuki, *Essays in Zen Buddhism: First Series*, p. 219. "We can say that Zen has come to its own consciousness by Hui-Neng. According to him, Zen was 'seeing into one's own Nature.' This is the most significant phrase ever coined in the development of Zen Buddhism. . . . Here we have the gist of Zen, and all his later sermons are amplifications of this idea. . . . By 'Nature' he understood 'Buddha Nature,' or more particularly from the intellectual point of view, 'Prajna.'"

P. 22. *"one does not need universities":* Gary Snyder, "Lookout's Journal," *Earth House Hold*, p. 2.

CHAPTER 2: YOUNGSTEIGER

P. 23. *"Aeschylus had . . . scenery as this":* Henry David Thoreau, *The Maine Woods*, p. 640.

P. 23. *who could work a chew:* Gary Snyder, *Earth House Hold*, p. 37. "I knew a packer could chew Copenhagen snoose while eating huckleberries on opposite sides of the mouth and never did mix them up."

P. 23. *"That Andy Wilcox":* Shubert Hunter, interview with the author, Marblemount, Washington, August 31, 1998.

P. 24. *The Chinaman nickname stuck:* Gary Snyder, "To the Chinese Comrades," *The Back Country,* pp. 111–14.

P. 24. *"He wouldn't set in a chair":* Tommy Buller, interview with the author, Marblemount, Washington, September 14, 1998.

P. 24. *Crater Mountain Trail:* Fred Beckey, "McMillan Park-Jackita Ridge Trail," *Cascade Alpine Guide: Climbing & High Routes, Vol. 3,* p. 400.

P. 24. *Crater's cloud-hidden summits:* Crater Mountain has two peaks, a half mile apart and connected by a narrow saddle. East Crater is 7,500 feet; West Crater — the true summit, where Snyder's lookout was located — is 8,129 feet.

P. 25. *lost a fully-loaded mule:* Roger Vail, interview with the author, Burlington, Washington, September 8, 1998.

P. 26. *"When I was up there in the middle of July":* Harold Vail interview with the author, Bellingham, Washington, September 16, 1998.

P. 26. *ice formed:* Gary Snyder to Jack Kerouac, February 22, 1956, Kerouac Estate, used by permission of Gary Snyder.

P. 26. *"fingers are too numb":* Gary Snyder, "Lookout's Journal," *Earth House Hold,* pp. 3–4.

P. 26. *one of the toughest:* Buller interview, September 14, 1998. "Crater was the only lookout in the district where you had to take up your supplies on a winch. I was up there myself, and took my own food and stuff up that cable — crawled up that chimney to the top with that rope as a hand line. Then you winch it up and unload it, then let it back down. And when you're doing it yourself, you make one trip a day." Tommy Buller did a short-season lookout at Crater the year after Snyder.

P. 26. *"It took a full week":* Gary Snyder, interview with the author, Kitkitdizze, October 26, 1997.

P. 28. *"Whoever put that lookout":* George McLeod, interview with the author, Rockport, Washington, August 31, 1998.

P. 28. *wreckage of the old L.O.s:* The lookout on Mount Adams, loftiest in the state, remained intact but had become completely locked in pack ice at the 12,276-foot summit. On Mount St. Helens, the lookout had likewise been left to the snows. And 9,500-foot Anvil Rock Lookout, in Mount Rainier National Park, had been burned down in 1951.

P. 28. *"I was sort of bemused":* Snyder interview, October 26, 1997.

P. 28. *Yet despite the wicked weather:* Snyder, "Lookout's Journal," *Earth House Hold,* p. 4.

P. 28. *"It was perfect":* Snyder interview, October 26, 1997.

P. 28. *Crater Shan:* Snyder, "Lookout's Journal," *Earth House Hold,* p. 4.

P. 28. *By the end of the summer:* Dell Hymes to Gary Snyder, August 25, 1952, UC Davis.

P. 28–29. *On Three Fingers Mountain:* Ira Spring and Byron Fish, *Lookouts: Firewatchers of the Cascades and Olympics,* p. 65.

P. 29. *On the Okanogan:* ibid., pp. 191–210. For elevations and other information concerning fire lookouts, see Appendix I: "Historical Registry of Western Washington Lookouts."

P. 29. *"I really kept myself busy":* Snyder interview, October 26, 1997.

P. 30. *Tibetan Prayer Flags:* ibid. "It was wonderful. It had a Tibetan flavor to be in a place like that. I had been reading *The Hundred Thousand Songs of Milarepa* and *The Life of Milarepa* earlier that year, so I was happy to be in a Tibetan-looking landscape sometimes."

P. 30. *Om Mani Padme Hum:* "Om, jewel in the lotus, hum" is the oldest and most important mantra of Tibetan Buddhism. Briefly, the "jewel in the lotus" is symbolic of the "jewel" of enlightenment that arises in the "lotus" of human consciousness. For Tibetan Buddhists, the six syllables of this mantra are an expression of the basic attitude of compassion, and the recitation of them expresses the longing for liberation.

P. 30. *Gary had tried zazen:* Gary Snyder, *The Real Work,* p. 96. "When I first sat, I recall how very strange, how very un-Western, it felt. I remember at Indiana University I was doing zazen in the apartment that I shared with the anthropologist Dell Hymes. Somebody walked in and caught me sitting there and I felt strange, they felt strange, and then it got all around the university: 'That graduate student from Oregon does weird things.'"

P. 30. *"Crater Mountain was the first"*: Snyder interview, October 26, 1997.

P. 30. *geologically similar*: Rowland Tabor and Ralph Haugerud, *Geology of the North Cascades*, pp. 57–58.

P. 31. *"Blue heaped upon blue"*: Miura Isshu and Ruth Fuller Sasaki, *The Zen Koan: Its History and Use in Rinzai Zen*, p. 105. "Endlessly rise the distant mountains/Blue heaped upon blue."

P. 31. *"her nipple just poking"*: Gary Snyder, journal entry, March 10, 1959, *The Gary Snyder Reader*, p. 342. "Thinking back on Crater Mt. Lookout. . . . A photo of a woman hung on the window; [Lisa Fonssagrives] her nipple just poking Mt. Challenger, Mt. Sourdough by her thigh . . . "

P. 31. *"Natural against natural"*: Gary Snyder, "Lookout's Journal," *Earth House Hold*, p. 7.

P. 31. *"Learn every peak"*: Ray Kresek, *Fire Lookouts of Oregon and Washington*, p. 38.

P. 32. *Mountaineering in the region*: Beckey, Cascade Alpine Guide: Climbing and High Routes, Vol. 3, pp. 272–73.

P. 32. *the ubiquitous Lage Wernstedt*: ibid., p. 268.

P. 34. *"I'd been in the South Cascades"*: Snyder interview, October 26, 1997.

P. 34. *unaware of the blasts*: Gary Snyder, E-mail to the author, November 4, 2001. "The Spirit Lake campers/climbers, or I at any rate, were not aware of the atom bombs being dropped in Japan, and it wasn't until the morning after the climb and reading a big posted newspaper that it sunk in to me."

P. 34. *"an eery, rigorous initiation"*: Gary Snyder, *The Practice of the Wild*, pp. 117–18. "Rising at 3 A.M. at timberline and breaking camp so as to be on glacier ice by six; standing in the rosy sunrise at nine thousand feet on a frozen slope to the crisp tinkle of crampon points on ice — these are some of the esoteric

delights of mountaineering. To be immersed in ice and rock and cold and upper space is to undergo an eery, rigorous initiation and transformation. Being above all the clouds with only a few other high mountains also in the sunshine, the human world still asleep under its gray dawn cloud blanket, is one of the first small steps toward Aldo Leopold's "think like a mountain."

P. 34. *When he came down*: Gary Snyder, E-mail to the author, October 31, 2001.

P. 34. *Gary would always remember*: Gary Snyder, in John P. O'Grady, "Living Landscape: An Interview with Gary Snyder," p. 276. "He was the last person I ever saw who wore the garb of the earlier generation of Pacific Northwest climbers, namely, stagged-off logger's pants, caulked, twelve-inch logger's boots, and a black felt hat. Instead of an ice axe, he carried a long alpenstock, and he covered his face with white zinc ointment to prevent sunburn."

P. 34. *"brotherhood of youthful mountaineers"*: Gary Snyder, "The Youngsteigers."

P. 35. *"We never climbed anything . . . once"*: Snyder interview, October 26, 1997.

P. 35. *"Those guys, I remember"*: Snyder, in O'Grady, "Living Landscape: An Interview with Gary Snyder," pp. 276–77.

P. 35. *"I and the circle"*: Snyder interview, December 6, 2000.

P. 36. *a theme running through*: The Transfer Act of 1905 removed the forest reserves from the administration of the scandal- and patronage-ridden Department of the Interior and placed them under the control of the Department of Agriculture, specifically the U.S. Forest Service, headed by Theodore Roosevelt's friend Gifford Pinchot. With the creation of the National Park Service in 1916, the Department of the Interior began to reclaim it lost public lands.

P. 36. *"To preserve a certain precious"*: Marshall quoted in Roderick Nash, *Wilderness and the American Mind*, p. 204.

P. 36. *North Cascades Primitive Area*: Crater Mountain was within the North Cascades Primitive Area, an 800,000-acre wilderness stretching from Ruby

Creek north to the border with British Columbia and from Ross Lake eastward to the Cascade Crest. This "Primitive Area" was bounded in turn by millions of additional acres under Forest Service jurisdiction — the Okanogan National Forest to the east, the Wenatchee to the south, the Mount Baker Forest to the west. The North Cascades Primitive Area was set aside by the Forest Service under Chief Ferdinand Silcox in 1934.

P. 36. *five Washington volcanos:* Mount Saint Helens, Mount Adams, Mount Rainier, Glacier Peak, and Mount Baker. For a description of the Ice Peaks proposal and its defeat, see David Louter, *Contested Terrain: North Cascades National Park Service Complex, an Administrative History,* pp. 20–25.

P. 37. *"where to put the logging roads":* Harvey Manning, *The Wild Cascades,* p. 114.

P. 37. *seemingly impervious to . . . logging:* The only commercial logging ever attempted on the Upper Skagit was to clear the trees from the flood plain behind Ross Dam when the reservoir was raised — and there was so little profit in that it was years before any company even made a bid for the job. In the late '40s, timber crews had worked in the upstream valley, felling as many trees as possible and leaving them to float up on the rising dam waters. The floating logs were later boomed and hauled uplake by tugs into Canada, then trucked to the Fraser River where they were floated down to Vancouver. In 1952, the boats were still rounding up logs from the surface of Ross Lake and hauling them up towards Hozo-meen, but there was no other logging going on.

P. 37–38. *"seemed like . . . conservative agency":* Snyder, telephone interview transcript, November 12, 1998.

P. 38. *"Forest equals . . . board feet a year":* Gary Snyder, "Lookout's Journal," *Earth House Hold,* p. 12.

P. 38. *"the last righteous years":* Gary Snyder, "Ancient Forests of the Far West," *The Practice of the Wild,* p. 126. "There was a comforting conservationist rhetoric in the world of forestry and lumber from the mid-thirties to the late fifties. The heavy clearcutting that has now devastated the whole Pacific slope from the Kern River to Sitka, Alaska, had not yet begun. In those days

forestry professionals still believed in selective logging and actually practiced sustained yield."

P. 38. *"if that complex radio":* Gary Snyder, "The Lookouts," *Left Out in the Rain,* pp. 38–39.

P. 38. *"Fierce, compact . . . bird":* Snyder, "Lookout's Journal," *Earth House Hold,* p. 4.

P. 38. *"The broken pillar"* Robinson Jeffers, "Hurt Hawks," in Tim Hunt, ed., *The Collected Poetry of Robinson Jefferes: Vol. 1, 1920–1928,* p. 377.

P. 40. *"through the flame-lit surface":* Jeffers, "Oh Lovely Rock," in ibid., Vol. 2, 1928–1938, p. 546.

P. 40. *Jeffers's enormous bitterness:* "Bitter" is one of Jeffers's signature words, appearing in scores of his works — "bitter wonders," "bitter fountain," "bitter earnestness," "bitter dreams," "the bitter war in Korea," "bitter enlightenment." See "Apology for Bad Dreams," "Cassandra," "Boats in a Fog," "Iona: Dreams of the Kings," "De Rerum Virtute," and "Woodrow Wilson," to name a few.

P. 40. *"Boys, be in nothing":* Jeffers, "Shine, Perishing Republic," in Hunt, ed., *The Collected Poetry of Robinson Jefferes: Vol. 1, 1920–1928,* p. 15.

P. 40. *"Fierce consciousness joined":* Jeffers, "Rock and Hawk," ibid., p. 416.

P. 40. *"a shifting of emphasis":* Robinson Jeffers, *The Double Axe & Other Poems,* p. xxi. ". . . called Inhumanism, a shifting of emphasis and significance from man to not-man; the rejection of human solipsism and recognition of the transhuman magnificence." Also Robinson Jeffers, *Selected Letters,* p. 342. "Man is part of nature, but a nearly infinitesimal part; the human race will cease after a while and leave no trace, but the great splendors of nature will go on. Meanwhile, most of our time and energy are necessarily spent on human affairs; that can't be prevented, though I think it should be minimized; but for philosophy, which is an endless research of truth, and for contemplation, which can be a sort of worship, I would suggest that the immense beauty of the earth and the outer universe, the divine 'nature of things,' is a more rewarding object. Certainly it is more ennobling. It is a source of strength; the other of distraction."

P. 40. *"I had more joy"*: Jeffers, "Fawn's Foster Mother," in Hunt, ed., *The Collected Poetry of Robinson Jefferes: Vol. 1, 1920–1928*, p. 387.

P. 40. *"I'd sooner . . . kill a man"*: Jeffers, "Hurt Hawks," ibid., p. 377.

P. 40. *"transhuman . . . glory"*: Jeffers, "De Rerum Virtute," in *ibid., Vol. 3, 1938–1962*, p. 403.

P. 40. *"sick microbe"*: ibid., pp. 402–03.

P. 40. *"transient sickness"*: ibid.

P. 40. *"As for me . . . son of man"*: Jeffers, "Original Sin," in ibid., p. 203–04.

P. 41. *"I was wondering if . . . what Jeffers did"*: Snyder interview, October 26, 1997.

P. 41. *"The poor lonely lookouts"*: Snyder, "Lookout's Journal," *Earth House Hold*, p. 9.

P. 42. *"community of lookouts"*: Gary Snyder to Jack Kerouac, February 22, 1956, Kerouac Estate.

P. 42. *Jack had grown up . . . had to fly twenty more:* Jack Francis, interview with the author, October 6, 1998.

P. 42. *"I kept expecting people"*: Hunter interview, August 31, 1998.

P. 43. *"When I was eleven"*: Snyder interview, October 26, 1997.

P. 43. *"in nothing but a jockstrap"*: Snyder to Kerouac, February 22, 1956, Kerouac Estate. Also, Gary Snyder, journal entry March 14, 1959, *The Gary Snyder Reader*, p. 342. "Thinking back on Crater Mountain . . . shave-headed, bearded, reading, melting last winter's snow to make my tea."

P. 45. *"more than enough time"*: Snyder, "Lookout's Journal," *Earth House Hold*, p. 11.

P. 45. *"a chaotic universe"*: Gary Snyder, *Mountains and Rivers Without End*, p. 153. "Two seasons on lookouts . . . gave me full opportunity to watch the change of mood over vast landscapes, light moving with the day — the countless clouds, the towering cumulus, black thunderstorms moving in with jagged lightning strikes. . . . I became aware of how the energies of mist, white water, rock formations, air swirls — a chaotic universe where everything is in place — are so much part of the East Asian painter's world."

P. 45. *"Aldo Leopold uses the phrase"*: Snyder interview, October 26, 1997.

P. 45. *"eyes tired, teapot empty"*: Snyder, "Lookout's Journal," *Earth House Hold*, p. 10.

P. 45. *Hui-Neng's first enlightenment:* R. H. Blyth, *Zen and Zen Classics*, p. 215. "The Sixth Patriarch, Hui-neng, a man born enlightened, was re-enlightened on hearing the Diamond Sutra . . . "

P. 45. *"It is the scripture . . . the other shore"*: Dwight Goddard, "The Diamond Sutra," *A Buddhist Bible*, p. 107.

P. 46. *"the one of all the sutras"*: D. T. Suzuki, *The Zen Doctrine of No-Mind*, p. 38.

P. 46. *"Ordinary dualistic groove"*: D. T. Suzuki, *Essays in Zen Buddhism, First Series*, p. 275.

P. 46. *a mere raft:* Goddard, "The Diamond Sutra," *A Buddhist Bible*, p. 106. "While the Tathagata, in his teaching, constantly makes use of conceptions and ideas . . . students should keep in mind the unreality of all such conceptions and ideas. They should recall that the Tathagata, in making use of them in explaining the Dharma always uses them in the resemblance of a raft that is of use only to cross a river. As the raft is of no further use after the river is crossed, it should be discarded. So these arbitrary conceptions of things and about things should be wholly given up as one attains enlightenment."

P. 46. *"Those who are not accustomed"*: Suzuki, *Manual of Zen Buddhism*, p. 38.

P. 46. *"Unless one gains . . . Zen"*: Suzuki, *The Zen Doctrine of No-Mind*, p. 108.

P. 46. *"Wherever this sutra is kept"*: Suzuki, "The Kongokyo or Diamond Sutra," *Manual of Zen Buddhism*, p. 44.

P. 46. *"Almost had it"*: Snyder, "Lookout's Journal," *Earth House Hold*, p. 10.

P. 46. *They found him sitting:* Francis, telephone interview transcript, October 6, 1998.

P. 47. *Except for a couple of Boy Scouts:* Jeremy Anderson, "My First Encounter with a Real Poet," in Jon Halper, ed., *Gary Snyder: Dimensions of a Life*, pp. 30–31.

P. 47. *Harold was leaving:* Harold Vail interview, September 14, 1998.

P. 47. *Jack was also going . . . Bremerton:* Jack Francis to Gary Snyder, August 25, 1974, UC Davis. "That was the same day I hiked down from Crater where I was visiting you. Sam Barker gave me a ride up the lake. I hiked up Desolation, closed the lookout, then carried a heavy pack down. That impressed Blackie. I was dead tired, but his attitude made me feel great."

P. 47. *"Dear Hemingway":* Philip Whalen to Gary Snyder, July 26, 1952, Reed.

P. 47. *"Dear Gaygo":* Whalen to Snyder, August 3, 1952, Reed.

P. 47. *"There are worthwhile things":* Dell Hymes to Gary Snyder, July 27, 1952, UC Davis.

P. 47. *Philip wrote to say . . . "mountain of my own":* Whalen to Snyder, July 26, 1952, Reed.

P. 48. *"One does not have":* Snyder, "Lookout's Journal," *Earth House Hold,* p. 11.

P. 48. *mountain was a teaching:* Snyder interview, October 26, 1997. "Crater and then the subsequent summer on Sourdough provided me with a teacher so to speak. It was a teacher, it was a teaching. I was ready to have that space and time given to me. I was able to take advantage of it."

CHAPTER 3: ALL ALONG THE WATCHTOWER

P. 49. *"Ever, ever be on the lookout":* D. T. Suzuki, trans., "Daito Kokushi's Admonition," in *Manual of Zen Buddhism,* p. 147.

P. 49. *sold it for $25:* Roger Vail, interview with the author, Burlington, Washington, August 31, 1998.

P. 50. *In the First World War:* Jack Francis, telephone interview transcript, October 6, 1998.

P. 50. *He was impressive:* Shubert Hunter, interview with the author, Marblemount, Washington, August 31, 1998.

P. 50. *"in that old mold":* Gary Snyder, telephone interview transcript, November 12, 1998. "I've known other people like Blackie over the years—a wonderful style of human being. All of those people that I dedicated *Riprap* to were old style working people. I mean, they had a lot of juice, they had a lot of funny language. They were confident, and not concerned about whether or not they were educated. They also had a

tremendous amount of skill and handiness at what they did—and they were good teachers."

P. 50. *Burns basically ran things:* Harold Vail, interview with the author, Bellingham, Washington, September 16, 1998. "Blackie was a guy that spent his whole life in it. . . . Him and his wife came up and stayed with us two or three days at the guard station [Granite Creek, 1952]. Didn't go up to the lookout, but stayed at the guard station, because the fishing was fantastic. We all took the afternoon off and went fishing and his wife had a big fish feed for us. It was kind of neat. That's the way Blackie was. It was never like, 'Well, I'm here now get the hell out of my way til I get done.'"

P. 50. *"Blackie, the old-timer":* Gary Snyder, unpublished Sourdough Mountain Journal, June 29, 1953, UC Davis.

P. 51. *"big fat bespectacled":* Jack Kerouac, *The Dharma Bums,* pp. 11–12. ". . . the aforementioned booboo big old goodhearted Warren Coughlin [Kerouac's pseudonym for Whalen] a hundred and eighty pounds of poet meat. . . ."

P. 51. *"Philip was not an athletic person":* Gary Snyder, interview with the author, Kitkitdizze, October 26, 1997.

P. 51. *"a pot of money":* Philip Whalen, interview with the author, Hartford Street Zen Center, San Francisco, October 28, 1997.

P. 51. *"It was a very funny feeling":* ibid.

P. 51. *the open road brought nothing:* Gary Snyder, telephone interview transcript, November 12, 1998.

P. 52. *"absorb vitamins":* Philip Whalen, "Interview with Anne Waldman," in Donald Allen, ed., *Off the Wall: Interviews with Philip Whalen,* p. 6.

P. 52. *cheap cuts of horse meat:* Gary Snyder, E-mail to the author, July 5, 1999. "Oregon used to sell horse meat for human consumption legally. It was from the Eastern Oregon wild horse herd, which was huge. Good meat. Cook it like you'd cook venison."

P. 52. *By the time he was twenty-two:* Gary Snyder, "Ancient Forests of the Far West," *The Practice of the Wild,* p. 119. "People love to do hard work together and to feel that the work is real; that is to say primary, productive, needed. Knowing and enjoying the skills of our hands and our well-made tools is fundamental."

P. 52. *Philip was born:* Philip Whalen was born on October 20, 1923, to Glenn and Phyllis Whalen. Glenn Whalen, a traveling salesman for a hardware company, moved the family to Centralia, Washington, soon after Philip's birth. In 1928, the Whalens relocated to The Dalles.

P. 54. *death of his mother:* Phyllis Arminta (Bush) Whalen died in 1939, when Philip was sixteen. See Philip Whalen, "Life and Death and a Letter to My Mother Beyond Them Both," *Overtime,* pp. 79–84.

P. 54. *"witty, articulate, engaging":* Snyder interview, October 26, 1997.

P. 54. *Progressive Party:* In the election of 1948 Henry Wallace, who had been Vice President under Franklin Roosevelt during World War II, ran as a third-party candidate for President on the national ticket of the Progressive Party in the three-way race with President Truman and the Republican candidate, Thomas Dewey. On the local level, many Progressive office seekers were Communist party members.

P. 54. *"wild looking guy":* Whalen interview, October 28, 1997.

P. 54. *Lambert Street house:* Gary Snyder to Harold Snyder, November 20, 1949, UC Davis. "I should tell you about all the people that live here — it is a remarkable collection. In one apartment live three progressives — two from the east coast, one from Jackson Hole Wyo., and all of them mountaineers. One of them — a tall bearded man — spent the summer canoeing from Canada to Portland down the Columbia. They are all philosophy students. Then the chap living with me is from Yonkers and has spent much time driving around the country. Worked for a time in the Anaconda copper mines. Ed Harper — lives with Mahar — studied Zoology for three years at the U of O, then decided to change to Economics and came to Reed. He spent the summer in Spain, France, and Holland. Carol Brown works 40 hours a week at the police station as switchboard operator and carries a full load at school . . . she is a psychology major, has been married twice. There are a couple brothers down

stairs involved in Political Science who have nearly three hundred books in their apartment . . . as you see, it's an interesting group. We don't have much time to be together but at special occasions we manage. If there is ever a war they'll cart us all off to jail, too."

P. 55. *"the original hippies":* Carol Baker, "1414 SE Lambert Street," in Jon Halper, ed., *Gary Snyder: Dimensions of a Life,* p. 28.

P. 55. *"By far the most socially":* J. Michael Mahar, "Scenes from the Sidelines," in Jon Halper, ed., *Gary Snyder: Dimensions of a Life,* p. 10.

P. 55. *the poet Lew Welch:* For a description of Lew Welch's Reed College years, see Louise Steinman, "The Song the Poet Sang," *Reed: A Quarterly Magazine of Personalities, Actions and Ideas,* vol. 78, no. 1, February 1999.

P. 55. *the poet Bill Dickey:* For a description of Bill Dickey's Reed College years, see Nadine Fieldler, "A Voice of Our Time," *Reed,* vol. 78, no. 1, February 1999.

P. 55. *novelist Donald Berry:* For a description of Don Berry's Reed College years, see Jeff Baker, "Reed's Forgotten Beat," *Reed,* vol. 78, no. 1, February 1999.

P. 55. *rooming with Lew Welch:* Gary Snyder to Harold Snyder, June 27, 1949, UC Davis. "I am broke. But I am not starving, I am not pathetic or lonely but on the contrary live in an extremely congenial and comfortable atmosphere with friends in our big old apartment house — which Lew and I manage, and in which we cook, work, study, and have a constructive existence."

P. 55. *"Roy and I teased him":* Whalen interview, October 28, 1997.

P. 55. *"Phil tended to sit back":* J. Michael Mahar, "Scenes from the Sidelines," in Jon Halper, ed., *Gary Snyder: Dimensions of a Life,* p. 11.

P. 55. *"indispensable astringency":* Gary Snyder to Philip Whalen, June 11, 1956, Reed. "I shot the wrong language at you by mistake — you are the only person I know with presence of mind & integrity enough to protest. Which is not by way of compliment, but simply recognition of the indispensable astringency you have always been kind enough to show me."

P. 55. *"he's a lot smarter":* Whalen interview, October 28, 1997.

P. 56. *"a jam session"*: Lew Welch to Dorothy Brownfield, November 4, 1950, Donald Allen, ed., *I Remain: The Letters of Lew Welch and the Correspondence of His Friends,* vol. 1, p. 41. "One hears the language of conversation in a wholly different way after reading him. Words become lively, and poetry unaffected. It was a jam session." See also Williams's recollection of his visit to Reed College in his autobiography.

P. 56. *"to have someone who I thought"*: Philip Whalen, telephone interview transcript, March 11, 1998. Snyder also was greatly encouraged by Williams visit to Reed College. In a November 27, 1950, letter to his father, Snyder wrote: "William Carlos Williams the poet was at Reed for a week and I had many pleasant talks with him. He read some of my poetry, and seemed quite pleased with it — at least said I had attained some confidence and formal certainty. . . . I hope my interest doesn't lag for a while at least."

P. 56. *"We were in the rig"*: Hunter interview, August 31, 1998. "To me it was like one of those history-type things. To me it was normal for anybody to be going through another culture and doing the religion, studying it. It seemed like a natural thing. Gary was really involved in it. It stood out real prominent."

P. 56. *to join the First Zen Institute:* Mary Farkas of First Zen Institute of America to Gary Snyder, October 2, 1952, UC Davis. "Your check received a few days ago has been turned over to the Treasurer of the Institute and you are hereby acknowledged as an Associate Member of the First Zen Institute of America."

P. 56. *written to Nyogen Sensaki:* Gary Snyder, E-mail to the author, June 17, 1999. "I wrote Nyogen several times but never got an answer."

P. 58. *"depend on individual"*: Mary Farkas to Gary Snyder, October 2, 1952, UC Davis.

P. 58. *Sokei-an . . . spiritual adventurer:* For details of the life of Sokei-an, see Rick Fields, *How the Swans Came to the Lake,* pp. 174–94; Mary Farkas, ed., *The Zen Eye,* pp. ix–xxi; and Sokei-an's autobiography, *Footsteps in the Invisible World.*

P. 59. *"A young man with an assured income":* Ruth Fuller Sasaki to Gary Snyder, June 10, 1953, UC Davis. The First Zen Institute taught a koan based practice,

as opposed to the "just sitting" Zen of the Soto school. Koans are nonrational, paradoxical, thought-derailing, answerless questions or dilemmas put to Zen students to foster direct perception rather than habitual thinking. "Listen to the sound of a single hand." and "Does a dog have Buddha-nature?" are two of the most famous Zen koans. Other koans are longer, more in the nature of stories or parables. For a good explanation of koan study, see *The Zen Koan: Its History and Use in Rinzai Zen,* by Isshu Miura and Ruth Fuller Sasaki.

P. 59. *He must be prepared to endure:* Ruth Fuller Sasaki to Gary Snyder, June 10, 1953, UC Davis.

P. 59. *trail crew to Ilabot Creek:* Tommy Buller, interview with the author, Marblemount, Washington, September 14, 1998. "We was up there cleaning out this trail so the timber cruisers could get in there and set up a camp. And we went as far as we could on the road and walked across this unit and got onto the trail and we sat down to eat our lunch, and we're talking and all of a sudden Phil Whalen just climbed up, totally shut up and was looking about like this, and I thought, 'What the heck?' And then he jumped up. We was sitting on a log together, and he just peeled off on his hands and knees and he gets about this far from the ground . . . and he finally looks up and sees I'm about to panic and he says, 'Hey I've studied mosses for years, and this is the first time I've ever seen any of it in spores. This is how it reproduces, and I want to get as close a look as I can. . . . And in my mind, I'm thinking, 'We're picking up a lot of strange people.'"

P. 59. *The two did not see each other:* Gary Snyder, telephone interview transcript, November 12, 1998.

P. 61. *The Skagit Tour:* For a description and history of the Skagit Tour, see Paul Pitzer, *Building the Skagit,* pp. 60–73.

P. 61. *"pleasant white-eyed little horse"*: Snyder, "Lookout's Journal," *Earth House Hold,* pp. 14–15.

P. 62. *Except for an occasional glimpse:* For description of Sourdough Mountain Trail, see Fred Beckey, *Cascade Alpine Guide: Climbing & High Routes,* vol. 3, p. 406.

P. 62. *"Horses look noble"*: Snyder, "Lookout's Journal," *Earth House Hold*, p. 15.

P. 62. *Lucinda Davis:* Paul Pitzer, *Building the Skagit*, pp. 11–14.

P. 63. *"Stetattle"*: Ryan Booth, quoting Carmen Shone, elder of the Upper Skagit tribe and one of the few living speaker-teachers of the Lushootsheed language.

P. 63. *"Mrs. Davis"*: Fred Beckey, *Cascade Alpine Guide, Vol. 3*, p. 196. Sledge Tatum and George Loudon, USGS surveyors, refer to "Mrs. Davis" as one of the peaks visible from Jack Mountain in 1904. Previous to 1904, the mountain was known at Stetattle Peak.

P. 63. *Lucinda Davis and Glee:* "Nomination to the National Historic Lookout Register," Forest Fire Lookout Association, December 15, 1996.

P. 63. *"perfection of chaos"*: Gary Snyder, "Lookout's Journal," *Earth House Hold*, p. 16. "— shifting of light & cloud, perfection of chaos, magnificent *jiji muge*/ interlacing interaction." Gary Snyder, E-mail to the author, June 17, 1999. "In Avatamsaka / Hua-yen / Kegon thought there is an enlightened condition of the universe that is 'all phenomena interacting multidimensionally without obstacle.' In Japanese this is *jiji muge*."

P. 63. *"foehn wind"*: Stephen Pyne, *Fire in America*, p. 413. ". . . a family of winds in North America that spill out of the Great Basin . . . pouring over the Rockies to the east (the Chinook) and over the Cascades [the East wind] and the Sierra [the Mono and Santa Ana winds] to the west. All are foehn winds, part of the family of dry, high velocity, usually warm winds that originate in continental interiors."

P. 63. *"Our route lay through a portion"*: Henry Custer, *Report of Reconnaissances*, p. 20.

P. 65. "Tent Lookout": Will D. Jenkins, Last Frontier in the North Cascades: Tales of the Wild Upper Skagit, p. 34

P. 65. *The following year:* Forest Fire Lookout Association, Sourdough Mountain Lookout: Nomination to the National Historic Lookout Register, 1996.

P. 65. *Harry Clouds:* Jenkins, *Last Frontier in the North Cascades*, p. 34.

P. 66. *"Keep looking across"*: Snyder, "Lookout's Journal," *Earth House Hold*, pp. 15–16.

P. 66. *"like the suburbs"*: Snyder interview, October 26, 1997.

P. 66. *"Sourdough Mountain is very sweet"*: ibid.

P. 67. *Dick Brewer:* Gary Snyder, "August on Sourdough, A Visit from Dick Brewer," *The Back Country*, p. 19.

P. 67. *"by mid-July was ensconced"*: Snyder, "Lookout's Journal," *Earth House Hold*, p. 15. "17 July 53 . . . Just managed to get through to Phil Whalen, on the radio, him up on Sauk Lookout now."

P. 67. *"Shakespeare, plus Chaucer"*: Whalen interview, October 28, 1997.

P. 67. *"small but remarkable"*: Beckey, *Cascade Alpine Guide: Climbing and High Routes*, vol. 3, p. 78. "Sauk Mountain offers training for hikers and joggers and can be good winter climbing. . . . There can be ice climbing given the right conditions."

P. 67. *ash from Glacier Peak:* Roland Tabor and Ralph Haugerud, *Geology of the North Cascades: A Mountain Mosaic*, p. 60.

P. 67. *Mount Sutter:* Ray Jordan, *Yarns of the Skagit Country*, p. 394-5.

P. 67. *Mount Gweht:* Beckey, *Cascades Alpine Guide: Climbing & High Routes, Vol. 3, Rainy Pass to Fraser River*, p. 78.

P. 67. *old man sleeping . . . three wives:* June M. Collins, *Valley of the Spirits: The Upper Skagit Indians of Western Washington*, p. 54.

P. 67. *oracular mountain:* Jordan, *Yarns of the Skagit Country*, p. 395.

P. 67. *peak for spirit quests:* North Cascades National Park archeologist Robert R. Mierendorf, E-mail to the author, January 25, 1999. "That Sauk Mountain was a native vision quest site seems to be common anecdotal knowledge among local people. . . . I have seen a large constructed pit on the side of Sauk Mountain that I believe is an indigenous archeological site — a description of this feature was sent to the Upper Skagit tribe but I don't think it went any further. I have little doubt that this feature was a vision quest site, but it was not test excavated, so again, another loosely substantiated inference.

"Artifactual evidence for this kind of thing is prob-

lematical because there is no clear archeological sig-
nature. Most often, rock piles (cairns) on mountain
summits, when they cannot be related to hunting or
some other activities, are inferred to represent vision
quest sites. Sweat lodges are not much better — if a pit
in the ground has no other obvious function such as
cooking or storage, but it is filled with fire-modified
rocks, it is often suggested as a possible sweat lodge."

P. 67. *Philip Whalen's lookout:* Ira Spring and Byron
Fish, *Lookouts: Firewatchers of the North Cascades,*
pp. 40–41.

P. 68. *angular blocks . . . breccia:* Roland Tabor and
Ralph Haugerud, *Geology of the North Cascades: A
Mountain Mosaic,* p. 60. "This breccia was deposited
in a submarine fan at the toe of a volcano in the
ancient Chilliwack volcanic arc, perhaps 250 million
years ago.

P. 68. *"quite a romantic building":* Whalen interview,
October 28, 1997.

P. 68. *"Great White Watcher":* Beckey, *Cascades Alpine
Guide: Climbing & High Routes, Vol. 3, Rainy Pass to
Fraser River,* p. 27. Beckey also gives the meaning as
"broken" or "damaged."

P. 68. *Since 1946:* Whalen interview, October 28, 1997.

P. 68. *"When I first got out of the army":* ibid.

P. 70. *"unnecessarily complicated":* Philip Whalen,
"Life and Death and a Letter to My Mother Beyond
Them Both," *Overtime,* p. 83. "I don't think it matters
what we name it, you make it on the ideas of God,
peace, quiet, organ music and Mrs. Eddy's representa-
tions of the character and philosophy of Jesus . . . I
don't mean any disrespect, but it seems unnecessarily
complicated to me — that system, those names — it
worked for you, or you worked for it — like Yeats and
his bent gyres and cones and pulleys and belts and
geary numbers —"

P. 70. *"Wow, this is great":* Whalen interview, October
28, 1997.

P. 70. *from the Blue Cliff Record:* Snyder, unpublished
Sourdough Mountain journal, summer 1953, UC
Davis. From the Blue Cliff Record, Snyder read Gen-
sha's commentary on the koan of the Three Invalids —
Blind! Deaf! Dumb! — and he also read the admoni-

tions of Dai and Daito Kokushi. From the sayings of
Matsu, he was introduced to the concept of the
Sravaka, or *arhat* who seeks nirvana for his own indi-
vidual enlightenment — "enlightened yet going
astray" was the phrase Snyder transcribed to his
journal.

P. 70. *Gary also packed . . . Broadway musical:* Gary
Snyder, unpublished Sourdough Mountain journal,
summer 1953, UC Davis.

P. 71. *"similarities between Blake & R. Jeffers":* ibid.,
August 9, 1953, UC Davis.

P. 71. *"Discipline of restraint":* Snyder, "Lookout's
Journal," *Earth House Hold,* pp. 18–19.

P. 71. *"If the doors of perception":* William Blake, "The
Marriage of Heaven and Hell," *The Poetry and Prose of
William Blake,* p. 39.

P. 71. *added simply: "Ah":* ibid., p. 19.

P. 71. *Snyder had never read* Walden: Gary Snyder,
E-mail to the author, June 17, 1999. "I was reading
Thoreau for the first time on Sourdough, and much
enjoyed it. It confirmed a lot of what I was already
doing, including anarchist thinking . . ." Snyder also
recommended *Walden* to Philip Whalen. Philip
Whalen to Gary Snyder, Jan 6, 1954, UC Davis. "I read
Walden the other day, upon your recommendations,
& I was not too displeased. In among all the vegetar-
ian, anti-Hibernian *blague* there are a lot of proper
notions; I'm surprised that it is allowed in Amerkun
schools."

P. 71. *had there been lookouts:* For some interesting
speculations concerning Thoreau and lookouting, see
Don Scheese, "Henry David Thoreau, Fire Lookout,"
Thoreau Society Bulletin, Winter 1990.

P. 71. *"favor . . . to be forever silent":* Henry David
Thoreau, *A Week on the Concord and Merrimack
Rivers,* p. 153. For Thoreau's full account of his journey
on Mount Greylock, see *A Week on the Concord and
Merrimack Rivers,* pp. 147–155.

P. 71. *"The most interesting dwellings":* Henry David
Thoreau, *Walden,* p. 360.

P. 72. *slightly wider than Thoreau's:* In the National
Park Service Pacific Northwest Region inventory,
Sourdough Lookout measures exactly 14'3" x 14'3".

Thoreau's cabin, according to the measurements given in *Walden*, were 10' x 15'. Huck Finn's raft was 12' x 16'.

P. 72. *"a man is rich"*: Henry David Thoreau, *Walden*, p. 387.

P. 72. *"beware of all enterprises"*: Henry David Thoreau, *Walden*, p. 341.

P. 72. *"Only that day dawns"*: ibid., p. 587.

P. 72. *"The morning star is not a star"*: Gary Snyder, *Myths and Texts*, p. 54.

P. 72. *"Ever, ever be on the lookout!"*: D. T. Suzuki, trans., "Daito Kokushi's Admonition," *Manual of Zen Buddhism*, pp. 147–48. See also, Suzuki's gloss on the selection, p. 148. "In those monasteries which are connected in some way with the author of this admonition, it is read or rather chanted before a lecture or Teisho begins."

P. 72. *bristled with various writing plans:* Snyder, unpublished Sourdough journal, August 9–20, 1953, UC Davis.

P. 73. *"human history set agin"*: ibid., August 20, 1953.

P. 73. *"you're practically there"*: Snyder, "Lookout's Journal," *Earth House Hold,* p. 9. In 1998, Shubert Hunter still recalled the difficulty of pinpointing the 1952 fire for the smokechasing crew. Hunter interview, August 31, 1998. "It took me longer than it should have to get that smoke. I got the alignment and we had a panoramic of the area too, so I cross referenced that azimuth with what I had on the fire finder. . . . I wish I could remember the name of that smokechaser's name now, him and another guy, they were two college kids. They were in the area and he says, 'I'm taking a back azimuth and I am two degrees west of your azimuth. Can you pinpoint me on your fire finder and tell me which direction to go?' So, I did that, and say to him, 'So how far out are you?' And he says, 'I have no idea, but I'm going to flash my mirror.' Well, they rattled around in there for a while and they did finally run into the smoke. . . ."

P. 73. *"from Hozomeen slowly"*: Snyder, "Lookout's Journal," *Earth House Hold,* pp. 17–18.

P. 75. *"and then two fires"*: ibid., p. 18.

P. 75. *"up Thunder Creek, high on a ridge"*: Snyder, *Myths and Texts*, p. 42. Snyder interview, October 26,

1997. "The last stanzas of *Myths and Texts* are from my own experience . . . a fire that we had the season I was on Sourdough. That was the smokechaser crew reporting to me on the radio, that was actually their description of it. One of the guys was telling me about it."

P. 75. *The black snag glistens:* Snyder, *Myths and Texts,* p. 42.

P. 75. *"The morning star is not a star"*: ibid.

P. 76. *"famed for his eccentric behavior"*: Diane Scott to Gary Snyder, August 15, 1953, UC Davis.

P. 76. *"I sold the house"*: Snyder, "Lookout's Journal," *Earth House Hold*, p. 22.

P. 76. *"I the poet Gary Snyder"*: Gary Snyder, "Poem Left in Sourdough Lookout," *Left Out in the Rain*, p. 42.

P. 78. *"God, there's some trees"*: Snyder interview, October 26, 1997.

P. 78. *"I like that Snyder feller"*: Jack Francis to Gary Snyder, August 25, 1974, UC Davis. Also, Francis telephone interview transcript, October 6, 1998.

CHAPTER FOUR: HIGHWAY 99

P. 79. *"Although mountains belong to the nation"*: Dogen, "Mountains and Waters Sutra," in Kazuaki Tanahashi, ed., *Moon in a Dewdrop: Writings of Zen Master Dogen*, p. 105.

P. 79. *"small for human beings"*: Gary Snyder to Philip Whalen, March 16, 1954, Reed. In the Vimalakirti Sutra, Vimalakirti's hut was only 10' by 10', but since it was the Abode of Emptiness, it was able to hold the 8,000 Bodhisattvas gathered around Manjusri and Vimalakirti.

P. 79. *where he stayed with friends:* Philip Whalen, telephone interview transcript, March 11, 1998. "The Converses—they were friends of Les Thompson's. Fred Converse and his wife Emily had this huge apartment up above a furniture store that was right on the corner of Western Avenue and Melrose Avenue in Hollywood. And they arranged it for Les to stay there when he was busy getting divorced from his wife. And then I fell down in the middle of all that, and stayed there for a while.

P. 80. *"REXROTH is the one"*: Snyder to Whalen, November 20, 1953, Reed. In the same letter, Snyder continued, "The poetry is sometimes sloppy, & the poem is very uneven, but by god, he has ideas, he says them, & I CHEER — with everybody else in this goddam country turning jello with fright & going queer or anglican, Rexroth is unwobbling, direct, & educated. . . . As far as I'm concerned, at this very moment, with Ezra old & hid, Eliot sick (in the brain) Williams about dead, & Jeffers burned out, Rexroth represents the most positive & fruitful direction for modern poetry."

P. 80. *translations he was working on:* Rexroth at the time was working on the translations for *One Hundred Poems from the Japanese.*

P. 81. *Telling of his Cascadian adventures:* Kenneth Rexroth, *An Autobiographical Novel,* pp. 279–89.

P. 81. *"Siberia of lookouts":* Ira Spring and Byron Fish, *Lookouts: Firewatchers of the Cascades and Olympics,* pp. 150–51.

P. 81. *sent Rexroth "A Berry Feast":* Gary Snyder to Kenneth Rexroth, undated, "Wednesday 1954," UC Davis.

P. 81. *"My own generation . . . cowardly":* ibid.

P. 82. *"favorably imprinted":* Snyder to Whalen, December 9, 1953, Reed.

P. 82. *"intense, diminutive Japanese man":* Gary Snyder, "The Making of *Mountains and Rivers Without End," Mountains and Rivers Without End,* p. 153. In the same essay, Snyder also wrote, "Though I lacked talent, my practice with soot-black ink and brush tuned my eye for looking more closely at paintings. In museums and through books I became aware of how the energies of mist, white water, rock formations, air swirls — a chaotic universe where everything is in place — are so much a part of the East Asian painter's world. In one book I came upon a reference to a hand scroll *(shou-chuan)* called *Mountains and Rivers Without End.* The name stuck in my mind."

P. 82. *"no Zen, consequently no taste":* Snyder to Whalen, November 20, 1953, Reed. "The only sumi painting worth serious consideration IS Zen sumi painting; i.e., done either by Zen monks, or under their direct influence. . . . Sumi painting without the Zen people behind it is mere prettiness, business, bunjinga (that mr. fenellosa [Ernest Fenollosa] so dislikes) etc. . . . Take my teacher, Obata, for example. . . . He showed me a screen he just finished: real Japanese screen 6½ foot high, three folding sections wide, backed with raw silk in dark green: the front all gold-leaf with two deer, two rocks, & a pine tree on it. Handsome & big, but gaudy. . . ."

P. 82. *His work . . . .a potent reflection:* For examples of Chiura Obata's paintings, see *Obata's Yosemite: The Art and Life of Chiura Obata* and *Topaz Moon: Chiura Obata's Art of the Internment.*

P. 83. *Obata's real work:* Snyder, "The Making of *Mountains and Rivers Without End," Mountains and Rivers Without End,* p. 157. In recognition of their kinship, and as an *homage* to his former teacher, Gary in 1996 chose one of Obata's paintings of Yosemite Falls for the cover of the first edition of *Mountains and Rivers Without End.*

P. 83. *"engaged in a bitter fight":* Snyder to Whalen, "2 or 3 November 1953," Reed. Snyder soon amended his callow opinion of Ch'en. Many years later, after reworking these early translations and publishing them, Snyder dedicated the finished poems to Ch'en Shih-hsiang, warmly remembering him as "a remarkable scholar, calligrapher, poet and critic who had a profound appreciation for good poetry of any provenance." *The Gary Snyder Reader,* p. 537.

P. 83. *Ch'en began to appreciate:* Snyder to Whalen, November 12–13, 1953, Reed. "Poetry has improved slightly here. I handed a translation to Mr. Ch'en in forbidden form, & he liked it so much he reversed his stand on the matter. I now have complete freedom in the matter of translation, a special dispensation."

P. 83. *"Chinese poetry is indeed":* Gary Snyder to Philip Whalen, November 12–13, 1953, Reed.

P. 83. *the Tu Fu poem that begins:* Tu Fu, "Spring View," translated by Gary Snyder, *Sixteen T'ang Poems,* from *The Gary Snyder Reader,* p. 542. For a selection of the translations Gary began with Ch'en Shih-hsiang in 1953–54, see his *Sixteen T'ang Poems* and *Bai Juyi's* [Po Chü-i] *Long Bitter Song* in *The Gary*

Snyder Reader. In Ch'en's class in 1954, Gary also blocked out a translation of Po Chü-i's "Song of the Lute," not yet published at this writing.

P. 83. *wrote Phil Whalen . . . to urge him:* Gary Snyder to Philip Whalen, February 2, 1954, Reed.

P. 85. *"I am old and very fat":* Philip Whalen to Gary Snyder, February 7, 1954, UC Davis. "I am old and very fat" foreshadows the opening lines of Whalen's later poem "Sourdough Mountain Lookout"—"I always say I won't go back to the mountains / I am too old and fat there are bugs mean mules / And pancakes every morning of the world."

P. 85. *On February 11 Snyder wrote:* Snyder to Whalen, February 2, 1954, Reed. "I asked Wreaksrath [Kenneth Rexroth] about Sierra lookouting; he says that the only places they put 'em are in the mountain-fringes, not high-country, & being in the Hudsonian zone, rather than alpine zone, are not terribly pleasant places to be. Outside the Sierras, i.e. Coast Range & Trinity alps of north California, one is faced with dread water-shortages & no particular scenery to amuse."

P. 85. *"telling them what I won't take":* Snyder to Whalen, February 11, 1954, Reed.

P. 85. *he too had applied:* Whalen to Snyder, February 14, 1954, UC Davis.

P. 85. *"Because of instructions":* U.S. Department of Agriculture to Gary Snyder, February 10, 1954, UC Davis.

P. 85. *"high summer of the great fear":* David Caute, *The Great Fear: The Anti-Communist Purge Under Truman and Eisenhower,* p. 11.

P. 86. *"I'm disloyal & they figgered it out":* Gary Snyder to Dell Hymes, April 2, 1954, American Philosophical Library.

P. 86. *"A SHAFTLESS ARROW":* Snyder to Whalen, February 16, 1954, Reed.

P. 86. *he tried to brush off his blacklisting:* ibid.

P. 87. *"likely got me blackballed":* ibid.

P. 87. *"Yes, we have been instructed":* U.S. Department of Agriculture to Gary Snyder, March 8, 1954, UC Davis.

P. 87. *his firing . . . Wobbly sympathies:* "(the District Ranger up at Packwood / thought the Wobblies had been dead for forty years / but the FBI smelled treason . . .), "Night Highway 99," *Mountains and Rivers Without End,* p. 16.

P. 87. *passenger-freighter to the Caribbean:* See Gary Snyder, "Cartagena," *Riprap & Cold Mountain Poems,* p. 29.

P. 87. *dishwasher in the passengers' mess:* Gary Snyder, interview with the author, Kitkitdizze, December 6, 2000. "It wasn't exactly a cruise liner, but it had a fairly upscale First Class portion. People didn't fly to the Caribbean in those days, they took ships. So it was serious passengers, plus freight. It was a big ship, and I was in the stewards' department on that trip, actually working on the dish washing line, coming back from the passengers' mess."

P. 87. *two weeks to hitch:* Snyder interview, December 6, 2000. "That was before the Interstate system was in. We took a lot of secondary roads and it took us two weeks. We had a good time . . . with camping gear, so that we slept out in our sleeping bags, scrounged for food, and cooked it."

P. 87. *"You should shit":* Carl Proujan, telephone interview, January 3, 2002.

P. 87. *Carl's parents:* ibid. "Carl lived in New York City and his mother was secretary for the National Maritime Union . . . I stayed in the Proujans' apartment with them for a while. Our plan had been that I would get there and that with a little help from Mrs. Proujan, I would get a ship—that it would be easier for me than normal, without connections. But there was a shipping strike—a union strike had hit just as we got there and the NMU hiring hall was shut down and nobody was going out. So I was sort of marking my time there, waiting for the strike to be over and I know that I wore out my welcome after two or three weeks. So then Mrs. Proujan got the idea that maybe the people over at the Marine Cooks and Stewards Union could help me out. So I went down to the MC&S hiring hall, and sure enough, they had me on a ship in about three days, shipping out to Venezuela, and Cartagena, Columbia."

P. 88. *gays at every level:* Scarlett C. Davis, "The

Marine Cooks and Stewards Union Knew Differences are Small, Solidarity is Big," *The Dispatcher* [magazine of the International Longshoremen & Warehousemen Union], February 1997. "It was widely known that there were gay men at every level of the MCS, even though the union leadership didn't officially discuss it."

P. 88. *MC&S fundraisers:* ibid. ". . . these 'queens' would entertain their fellow merchant seamen and other crewmembers by putting on drag for union benefits and variety shows. The queens, considered to be the most outrageous and campy of the gay men, were also remembered as some of the toughest members of the MCS."

P. 88. *he stayed for a while:* Snyder interview, December 6, 2000. "That was my first experience living in a whole apartment full of gays. They were really nice, took good care of me. I helped them cook, and learned some fancy dishes that I'd never heard of before."

P. 88. *"No Race-Baiting!":* Gary Snyder, E-mail to the author, November 12, 2001." The MC&S was a truly progressive union, as we called them. They were way in advance of the society as a whole. The Communist Party was a strong influence, and was responsible for those enlightened policies. Whatever can be said in criticism of the Communists in the US, and there's plenty, they had their stand on race quite clear . . ."

P. 88. *Nick Bordoise:* Davis, "The Marine Cooks and Stewards Union Knew Differences are Small, Solidarity is Big."

P. 88. *Hugh Bryson:* Norman Leonard Collection, *Records of the National Union of Marine Cooks and Stewards, 1934–1957*, p. 3.

P. 88. *Coast Guard . . . screening:* ibid., p. 2–3. "During the Korean War, Congress passed the Magnuson Act, which authorized the Coast Guard to screen alleged security risks from waterfront industries—longshoremen, seaman, and others. Many MC&S members were barred from their jobs due to this waterfront screening program." The Magnuson Act was signed into law by Harry Truman on August 9, 1950, six weeks after the North Korean invasion of South

Korea. Introduced by Washington's democratic senator Warren Magnuson, its official name was the Port Security Act of 1950, PL 81-679.

P. 88. *The FBI also zeroed in:* Davis, "The Marine Cooks and Stewards Union Knew Differences are Small, Solidarity is Big," *The Dispatcher*. See also, Caute, *The Great Fear*, pp. 392–400.

P. 90. *bitter waterfront purge:* "New Drive Against Waterfront Reds," San Francisco Examiner, April 2, 1952.

P. 90. *"poor security risk":* United States Coast Guard to Gary Snyder, June 24, 1955, UC Davis. "Reference is made to a letter to you dated 10 June 1952 from the Commandant of the Coast Guard wherein you were advised that your application for documents as a merchant seaman had been rejected." This June 24, 1955 letter removed Snyder's former classification as "poor security risk."

P. 90. *he was given clearance:* Snyder interview, December 6, 2000.

P. 90. *father . . . interrogated:* Gary Snyder, E-mail to the author, November 15, 2001. "When the war broke out he was hired by the Veterans Administration (he was a Marine in WWI, though never saw combat) and he stayed with them until he retired. He had been pretty well investigated earlier himself for his left and labor connections in the thirties."

P. 90. *"The Board is informed":* Veterans Administration board of inquiry letter quoted in Gary Snyder to The Secretary of State, March 18, 1955, UC Davis.

P. 90. *"its remarkable accuracy":* J. Michael Mahar, "Scenes from the Sidelines," in Jon Halper, ed., *Gary Snyder: Dimensions of a Life*, p. 9. "The agent cited a report on the people and places that Gary visited, and its remarkable accuracy caused us to ponder the identity of an informer in our midst."

P. 91. *"any behavior, activities or associations":* For a description of the anti-Communist purge of the Civil Service, see Caute, *The Great Fear*, pp. 267–293.

P. 91. *"general unsuitability":* US Department of Agriculture to Gary Snyder, March 23, 1955, UC Davis. "This determination was made on general suitability grounds rather than security grounds."

P. 91. *tentatively offered . . . Lost Lake:* US Department of Agriculture to Gary Snyder, April 16, 1954, UC Davis.

P. 91. *"We certainly would be glad":* Whalen to Snyder, March 2, 1954, UC Davis.

P. 91. *notified to report:* U.S. Department of Agriculture to Gary Snyder, May 19, 1954, UC Davis.

P. 91. *Lost Lake . . . literary tradition:* Ira Spring and Byron Fish, *Lookouts: Firewatchers of the Cascades and Olympics,* pp. 118–20. Martha Hardy had been lookout on Tatoosh in 1943. She wrote her memoir of that summer the following year while at Lost Lake Lookout.

P. 92. *"the Red College":* Barbara Schrecker, *No Ivory Tower,* p. 237. "Many of the folks in Portland, Oregon, hostile to 'the Red College,' erroneously believed that the school had been named for the city's most notorious native son, John Reed; tour bus guides would comment on passing the College 'that it is inclined to be Communist.'"

P. 92. *Two witnesses . . . testified:* "Reed Graduate Acts to Expose Campus Group," *Oregonian,* Portland, Oregon, June 19, 1954.

P. 92. *Smith Act:* The Smith Act, properly The Alien Registration Act of 1940, made it a federal crime to advocate the overthrow of the government or to be a member of organizations that did. Following World War II, the act was used as the basis for many legal cases against Communist Party members.

P. 92. *Owen and Hartle named forty-two:* "Reed Graduate Acts to Expose Campus Group," *Oregonian,* June 19, 1954.

P. 92. *"ratted and ratted":* Gary Snyder, unpublished journal entry, June 22, 1954, used by permission of Gary Snyder.

P. 92. *Owen . . . named Lew Welch:* "Reed Graduate Acts to Expose Campus Group," *Oregonian,* Portland, Oregon, June 19, 1954. The John Reed Clubs, founded in New York in 1929, were originally educational and propaganda cells of the Communist Party. At their height during the Depression, there were more than thirty clubs nationwide, with a combined membership of about 1,200. JRC members made posters for

demonstrations, painted murals, built stage sets for proletarian plays, wrote songs and poems celebrating the class struggle. Only a few chapters, including those in Portland and Seattle, continued after World War II. By then the clubs had become little more than radical salons or discussion groups.

The clubs were named after John Reed, author of *Ten Days That Shook the World,* his eyewitness account the Bolshevik Revolution, and *Insurgent Mexico,* about the Mexican Revolution. Reed was a founder of the Communist Labor Party. Reed died of typhus in Russia in 1920 at age thirty-three and was buried in the Kremlin. Although he was born in Portland, Reed's prosperous family had no connection to Reed College, nor did he attend the college. John Reed himself was a Harvard graduate.

P. 92. *suspended . . . from teaching:* "College to Conduct Inquiry on Three Called from Staff," *Oregonian,* Portland, Oregon, June 23, 1954.

P. 92. *Stanley Moore:* Schrecker, *No Ivory Tower,* p. 236.

P. 93. *Moore was on sabbatical:* "Moore Seeks Open Hearing," *Oregonian,* Portland, Oregon, June 23, 1954. Stanley Moore was fired from Reed in August 1954 for his refusal to testify. Not until 1981 did the Board of Trustees of Reed College admit their error in firing him. For a fuller treatment of the cases of both Lloyd Reynolds and Stanley Moore, see Ellen Schrecker's *No Ivory Tower,* pp. 236–41.

P. 93. *old-timers sent their regards:* Philip Whalen to Gary Snyder, July 18, 1954, UC Davis.

P. 94. *"I have spent . . . hours hassling":* Snyder to Whalen, July 8, 1954, Reed.

P. 94. *"Got fired that day":* Gary Snyder, "Night Highway 99," *Mountains and Rivers Without End,* p. 16.

P. 94. *lynched Wesley Everest:* John Dos Passos, "Paul Bunyan," *U.S.A.,* Book II: *Nineteen-nineteen,* pp. 399–402.

P. 95. *allegiance to the IWW:* Gary Snyder, E-mail to the author, July 5, 1999: "My grandfather, Henry Snyder, read Marx, called himself a Socialist, had soapboxed—they said—in Yesler Square for the I.W.W. at one time. I dropped into the hall in Seattle in the early fifties, once with Allen Ginsberg. In the Sixties I got a Wobbly card via a revived Bay Area movement."

P. 95. *Wobblies in the Pacific Northwest:* Though Marxist, the Wobblies had never been communist, and in 1946, the leadership of the IWW specifically condemned the American Communist Party as "a major menace to the working class." The following year, however, IWW officers refused on principle to provide affidavits of non-membership in the CP as required by the Taft-Hartley Act. As a result, they were put on the Attorney General's list of subversive organizations in 1949. For a comprehensive self-told history of the Industrial Workers of the World, see Fred W. Thompson and Patrick Murfin, *The IWW: Its First Seventy Years, 1905–1975.*

P. 95. *"Chainsaws in a pool of cold oil":* Gary Snyder, "Late Snow & Lumber Strike of the Summer of Fifty-four," *Riprap & Cold Mountain Poems,* p. 2.

P. 95. *"a drifting gull":* Snyder to Whalen, July 8, 1954, Reed.

P. 95. *"burning in sun glare":* Snyder, "Late Snow & Lumber Strike of the Summer of Fifty-four," *Riprap & Cold Mountain Poems,* p. 2.

P. 96. *"alone in a gully":* ibid.

P. 96. *"All in Marblemount":* Whalen to Snyder, July 18, 1954, UC Davis.

P. 96. *"A floating dock":* Gary Snyder, "Lookout's Journal," *Earth House Hold,* pp. 22–23.

P. 96. *"I've been living on the Ross float":* Whalen to Snyder, July 18, 1954, UC Davis.

P. 98. *Philip complained:* Whalen to Snyder, August 7, 1954, UC Davis.

P. 98. *"season is nearly over":* ibid.

P. 98. *"Across the lake":* Philip Whalen, unpublished Skagit story, January 31, 1956, Columbia.

P. 98. *"the great tribe of Tarheels":* ibid., January 29, 1956.

P. 99. *"Junior said, Boy":* ibid., January 31, 1956. Whalen's character "Ryder" takes his name from the real-life Don Rider, who was the fire lookout on Desolation Peak in 1954 and shared the Ross Lake float with Philip Whalen in July of that summer. Most likely, Whalen's "Ryder" is the source of the last name of the

hero of *The Dharma Bums,* "Japhy Ryder," Kerouac's pseudonym for Gary Snyder. Kerouac probably appropriated the name for his own use, either consciously or unconsciously. See Jack Kerouac to Philip Whalen, March 6, 1956 in Kerouac, *Selected Letters, 1940–1956,* p. 564. "Be looking forward to seeing that story of yours about the mountains." Kerouac likely read Whalen's story during April–May, 1956.

P. 99. *"The river flows here":* Henry Custer, "Report of Reconnaissances," pp. 48–49.

P. 99. *first Euro-American:* In July 1858, George Gibb had traveled upstream on the Skagit to a point near present-day Newhalem. George Gibb, "The Northwest Boundary," pp. 332–33. "I ascended it in a canoe, at the end of July 1858, as far as its exit from the cañon, about seventy-five miles from its mouth. . . . At the time of my visit, reports of the existence of gold on the Skagit, and the hope of finding a route to the Frazer River mines, had led quite a number of persons to ascend it."

P. 100. *"Nothing . . . more pleasant":* Henry Custer, *Report of Reconnaissances,* p. 48.

P. 100. *At the foot of Jack Mountain:* ibid., p. 46. "Although I had no positive orders to extend this reconnaissance so far southward, still I thought the opportunity to add this further topographical information to the one already acquired too favorable to miss it. . . . The Indians delighted to steer through the swiftest of rapids—doing so, nothing can secure your safety but the most vigorous plying of the paddle. This the Indians did with a will, shouting and singing at the same time. . . . Nothing equals the pleasant excitement of thus rapidly dashing through the waves of a swift stream with a good canoe and skillful men."

P. 100. *"the East fork":* ibid., p. 49.

P. 100. *"Chinsoloc, A Samona Chief":* ibid., p. 4: "One of the Indians in my employ (Chinsoloc) a Samona Chief, had the most extended geographical Knowledge of any Indian I ever had to deal with. By request he made me a map of the extent of the country he was well acquainted with. It was bounded by the Fraser River to the north, by the Skagit River on the East, by some tributary of this river to the South, and by the

Nookhsahk & Chiloweyuck Rivers to the West. Within these limits his knowledge of the country was most minute & reliable. The map he made of it, although in the most primitive stile, was remarkable for its correctness & completeness. In this way we gained most of our first Knowledge of the country, as also many of the names of its mountains, smaller streams, & lakes."

P. 101. *"apparent absence of native people":* R. Mierendorf et al., *An Archeological Site Survey and Evaluation in the Upper Skagit River Valley,* p. 20. "An interesting phenomenon regarding Native use of the project area [Upper Skagit River from Ross Dam to boundary with British Columbia] is the apparent disappearance of Indian people from the upper Skagit Valley in the last century. Few Native people were encountered in the North Cascades, and none in the project area, at the time of the first explorations by non-natives. At the time of his 1859 travels through the valley to survey the international boundary, Henry Custer observed limited evidence of Native people's presence, noting that 'We found an Indian trail leading through the Klesilkwa valley, faint though as all these trails are, & observed subsequently its continuance through the entire length of the Skagit valley explored by us.' Custer's observations here agree with those of George Gibbs, who noted that many Native American trails throughout the northern Cascades appeared to have 'fallen into disuse.' Gibbs attributed this to 'the diminuation of the tribes and the diversion of trade to the posts.' It is likely that introduced diseases, such as smallpox in ca. 1770, played a major role in reducing Upper Skagit populations, as happened in widespread areas of the Northwest Coast. Whatever the reasons, the accumulating archeological evidence suggests that Native populations, at times in the prehistoric past, made much more use of the valley than the historic record suggests."

P. 101. *Scatters of stone tools:* ibid. See inventory of untested archeological sites nos. 34, 183, 7, 184. Also, Robert R. Mierendorf, E-mail to the author, June 24, 1999. "The evidence indicates that the Skagit gorge was used as a travel route up and down the Skagit River Valley. All the sites near to and in the gorge are

very small and without very many artifacts: they simply consist of small scatters of flaked Hozomeen chert and occasionally other materials, indicating that as they traveled through the gorge, they utilized whatever chert they found along the way and that they sharpened the already-made artifacts that they carried with them, made of stone materials whose sources occur outside of today's park. Another way to look at it: such sites reflect lack of intensive use of the gorge, that the people kept moving through the gorge and didn't spend much time in one spot."

P. 101. *Phil and Volley Reed, backpacking:* Whalen to Snyder, July 18, 1954, UC Davis. ". . . Volley & I forge our way up the Pierce Mtn. Trail into Sourdough, a tedious walking trip. Grub, etc. to be packed in later via jackass — the way it looks at the moment. The 'etcetera' part (personal gear) must be toted personally. Pfui."

P. 102. *"the lakes in two lights":* Philip Whalen, "Sourdough Mountain Lookout," *Overtime: Selected Poems,* p. 15. The strikingly differing colors of Ross and Diablo lakes are attributable to their varying amounts of glacial "rock flour" suspended in their waters. Sunlight scatters through the floating particles of rock flour, with the green wavelengths of light reflecting while other colors are absorbed. Because Diablo Lake is fed by so many nearby glaciers it has a higher concentration of rock flour, and appears a soapy green, especially early in summer. Ross Lake is also fed by glaciers, but because of its greater volume, the rock flour is more widely dispersed, and hence does not exhibit the same green color.

P. 102. *blacktail and mule deer:* Mierendorf et al., *An Archeological Site Survey and Evaluation in the Upper Skagit River Valley,* pp. 21–22.

P. 102. *"I was going around the building":* Whalen interview, October 28, 1997.

P. 102. *"So here's this bear":* ibid.

P. 104. *"Unlike the thick-growing Douglas Fir":* Gary Snyder, "Ancient Forests of the Far West," *The Practice of the Wild,* p. 120.

P. 104. *"Am unmashed only":* Snyder to Whalen, September 17, 1954, UC Davis. For more on setting chokers, see Snyder's evocative description of the work in his essay "Ancient Forests of the Far West."

P. 105. *"My imagination . . . great shape":* Whalen to Snyder, September 7, 1954, UC Davis.

P. 105. *"writing extravagantly":* Whalen to Snyder, October 6, 1954, UC Davis. "I am writing extravagantly, too. We shall flood the market."

P. 105. *drinking just as extravagantly:* Whalen to Snyder, September 20, 1954, UC Davis. "I heard you were *drinking.*"

P. 105. *"D. H. Lawrence & Fu Manchu":* Snyder to Hymes, November 20, 1954, American Philosophical Library.

P. 105. *"yamabushi tendencies":* Gary Snyder, "Anyone with Yamabushi Tendencies," *Zen Notes,* November 1954. See Gary Snyder, "Walking the Great Ridge Omine on the Womb-Diamond Trail," *The Gary Snyder Reader,* p. 372. "The Yamabushi ('those who stay in the mountains') are back country Shaman-Buddhists with strong Shinto connections, who make walking and climbing in deep mountain ranges a large part of their practice."

P. 105. *On a crate beside his bunk:* Gary Snyder, "Ancient Forests of the Far West," *The Practice of the Wild,* pp. 125–26. "I saved a few of the tan free-form scales from the bark of that log and placed them on a tiny altar I kept on a box by my bunk at the logging camp. It and other offerings (a flicker feather, a bit of broken bird's-egg, some obsidian, and a postcard picture of the Boddhisattva of Transcendent Intelligence, Manjusri) were not 'my' offerings to the forest, but the forest's offerings to all of us."

CHAPTER 5: COLD BRILLIANT SUN

P. 107. *"My life has been spent":* Philip Whalen, "Since You Ask Me," *Overtime: Selected Poems,* p. 50.

P. 107. *becoming a seasonal ritual:* The Komo Kulshan station was, and still is, on Baker Lake Road, which connects State Route 20 to Baker Lake. It is home base for the "Baker Lake Hotshots," a crew of U.S. Forest Service wildland firefighters connected to the Mt. Baker District of the Mt. Baker–Snoqualmie National Forest.

P. 107. *sent up the Skagit:* Whalen to Snyder, July 11, 1955, UC Davis. "July 5, after a soaking wet guard school, we all went to Ross Float. Fiddled around Wednesday moving the Lightning Float up the lake [There was also a floating guard station at that time on the Ross Lake shore at the mouth of Lightning Creek. The Lightning Creek Guard Station was for Desolation Lookout.] Thursday blasted & shoveled the Ruby Creek road & began the hay hauling. More hay Friday & returned here. There'll be a lift over Ross Tuesday & Blackie is raving wildly about getting both Desolation & me up on top PDQ, although in this weather I don't see the necessity."

P. 107. *lookout work had turned out:* Gary Snyder, "A Sinecure for P. Whalen," *Left Out in the Rain,* p. 12.

P. 108. *"You could talk":* Tommy Buller, interview with the author, Marblemount, Washington, September 14, 1998.

P. 108. *In early July, Philip sent Gary:* Whalen to Snyder, July 11, 1955, UC Davis.

P. 108. *Buller had nailed . . . fire door:* Buller interview, September 14, 1998.

P. 109. *"I packed fifty pounds":* Whalen to Snyder, July 11, 1955, UC Davis. Reminded of this incident in 1999, Gary Snyder in notes to the author dated June 19, 1999, said, "Let's be real. My whole family doesn't eat 50 pounds in a winter. I probably had about 15 pounds."

P. 109. *"acted on my spirit and mind":* Philip Whalen, "Interview with Anne Waldman," in Donald Allen, ed., *Off the Wall: Interviews with Philip Whalen,* p. 22.

P. 109. *"Great fun reaching":* Whalen to Snyder, June 13, 1955, UC Davis.

P. 109. *positively "Byronic":* Philip Whalen, "Sourdough Mountain Lookout," *Overtime: Selected Poems,* p. 16.

P. 109. *"I was kneeling over the edge":* Whalen, "Interview with Aram Saroyan," in Allen, ed., *Off the Wall: Interviews with Philip Whalen,* p. 45. Also, Philip Whalen, interview with the author, Hartford Street Zen Center, San Francisco, October 28, 1997.

P. 111. *"I the poet Gary Snyder":* In a note to the poem, published in *Left Out in the Rain* in 1986, Snyder wrote that "A later lookout told me this poem was still pinned up in the cabin in 1968."

P. 111. *All through . . . June:* Snyder to Whalen, June 16 and June 21, 1955, Reed.

P. 111. *in February 1955 Snyder:* US Department of Agriculture to Gary Snyder, March 23, 1955, UC Davis. "Your letter of February 1, 1955 . . . has been referred to this office for attention."

P. 111. *"Instructions were issued":* U.S. Department of Agriculture to Gary Snyder, March 23, 1955, UC Davis.

P. 111. *"I am physically sick for wanting":* Snyder to Whalen, June 9, 1955, Reed.

P. 112. *"Everything feels all wrong":* Snyder to Whalen, June 16, 1955, Reed.

P. 112. *"I am suddenly wafted off":* Gary Snyder to Dell Hymes, July 7, 1955, American Philosophical Society.

P. 112. *At the party . . . first taken it:* Whalen to Snyder, April 24, 1955, UC Davis. At that time, peyote was still legal—it would not be criminalized until 1959. Herb dealers like the Tropical Fruit Company in Laredo, Texas, shipped peyote—$12 for a crate of a hundred dried buttons—or $5 for a box of live plants.

P. 112. *After nearly two hours:* Whalen to Snyder, April 24, 1955, UC Davis.

P. 112. *"I was the giant Vishnu":* Whalen to Snyder, April 24, 1955, UC Davis.

P. 113. *Then I was born:* ibid.

P. 113. *"There's no doubt":* Snyder to Whalen, June 16, 1955, Reed.

P. 113. *"An astonishing experience":* Snyder to Whalen, January 2, 1955, Reed. "New Years Eve Claude [Dalenberg], Hatch [Jim Hatch] & I (along with some SF cats) went to Peyote-Land."

P. 113. *"Don't need . . . hallucinations":* Whalen to Snyder, January 25, 1955, UC Davis.

P. 113. *The word "psychedelic":* Dr. Humphrey Osmond invented the word, to describe the action of the peyote-derived drug mescaline. "To fathom hell or soar angelic," Osmond had written to Aldous Huxley, "just take a pinch of psychedelic." Osmond quoted in Martin A. Lee and Bruce Shlain, *Acid Dreams*, p. 55.

P. 114. *"doors of perception":* Interest in peyote jumped considerably in the spring of 1954 with the publication of Aldous Huxley's *The Doors of Perception,* a description of his May 1953 experience with the drug mescaline, the synthesized version of peyote. Huxley's book was extraordinarily influential, and marked the beginning of a psychedelic underground on college campuses.

P. 114. *"If you're really interested":* Snyder to Hymes, January 10, 1955, American Philosophical Society.

P. 114. *"Peyote flows in":* Snyder to Hymes, April 27, 1955, American Philosophical Society.

P. 114. *"widespread shamanic use":* For peyote use in pre-Columbian Mexico, see Richard Evans Schultes and Albert Hoffman, *Plants of the Gods: Their Sacred, Healing and Hallucinogenic Powers.* Rochester, Vermont: Inner Traditions International, Ltd., 2001.

P. 114. *"glorious fields of jewels":* Havelock Ellis, "Mescal: A New Artificial Paradise," *The Contemporary Review.*

P. 114. *Antonin Artaud . . . spiritually renewed:* Antonin Artaud, *The Peyote Dance,* p. 45. ". . . the cataclysm which was my body . . . this dislocated assemblage, this piece of damaged geology."

P. 114. *"Once one has experienced":* ibid., p. 38.

P. 114. *Philip Lamantia, then twenty-three:* Philip Lamantia, interview with the author, San Francisco, December 11, 2000.

P. 114. *"little Berkeley peyotl cult":* Lamantia interview, December 11, 2000.

P. 116. *Lamantia gave Jack Kerouac:* ibid. "It was in that very house that Jack and Neal came up, and I have some peyote—we turn him on, and we turn on—And he [Kerouac] fell asleep on it."

P. 116. *"Everyone . . . marveled that I":* Whalen to Snyder, April 24, 1955, UC Davis.

P. 116. *"a sober ritual":* Lamantia interview, December 11, 2000.

P. 116. *"I'm going . . . peyote party":* Snyder to Whalen, April 2, 1955, Reed.

P. 116. *"low grade samadhi":* Whalen to Snyder, January 25, 1955, UC Davis. "The literary life = low-grade samadhi = peyote & mary jane. Triple phooey."

P. 116. *"I had been apprehensive":* Whalen to Snyder, April 24, 1955, UC Davis.

P. 116. *"Maybe I'm being simple-minded"*: Whalen to Snyder, June 14, 1955, UC Davis.

P. 117. *"Improved from an older"*: Whalen to Snyder, June 14, 1955, UC Davis.

P. 117. *"The Martyrdom of Two Pagans"*: Whalen mailed "The Martyrdom of Two Pagans" to Snyder on March 24, 1955.

P. 117. *"It has . . . crackle"*: Snyder to Whalen, April 2, 1955, Reed.

P. 117. *"I'll probably hammer"*: Whalen to Snyder, March 24, 1955, UC Davis.

P. 117. *"Now and then they ask me"*: Philip Whalen, "Avalanche Lilies" (unpublished), April 3, 1955, Columbia.

P. 117. *"For K.W., Senex"*: Philip Whalen, "For K.W., Senex," April 4, 1955, unpublished manuscript, Columbia.

P. 117. *"Poultry of some kind"*: Whalen to Snyder, April 6, 1955, UC Davis. "Anyway, the season is Spring & the environs academic & the combination of all this has dissociated me completely, hence poultry of some kind keeps happening."

P. 118. *"A new poetickal effusion"*: Whalen to Snyder, May 18, 1955, UC Davis.

P. 118. *Roethke introduced Williams:* Whalen to Snyder, June 14, 1955, UC Davis. "He [Williams] was introduced here by Roethke with a rather florid gesture —"one who teaches us that a poet must be a man"— and that here was a MAN — not a long speech but rather fancy — yet delivered with great passion &c. rather embarrassing. One expected W. in a codpiece."

P. 118. *"Much enfeebled"*: Whalen to Snyder, May 18, 1955, UC Davis.

P. 118. *"It was painful"*: Philip Whalen, "Plums, Metaphysics, an Investigation, a Visit, and a Short Funeral Ode," *Overtime: Selected Poems,* pp. 85–88. The poet Robert Lowell, who caught Williams at the tail of the same tour a few months later back East, used the same verb — deliver — in recalling that Williams "somehow delivered to us what was impossible, something that was both poetry and beyond poetry." Quoted in Ian Hamilton, *Robert Lowell: A Biography,* p. 232.

P. 118. *"Seeing him"*: Whalen to Snyder, May 18, 1955, UC Davis.

P. 118. *"If You're So Smart"*: In a November 12–13, 1953 letter to Philip, Gary Snyder wrote, "Some individuals are absolutely impervious to education, regardless of what formal motions they go through, it would appear. Can it be true that we are really so superior to these creatures as it appears? Theory would deny it, but commonsense every day offers evidence that it is true." Whalen answered, "Superior how? You know that this is one of the things I've puzzled over for fifteen years. . . . 'Commonsense everyday evidence' simply asks me 'If you're so smart, why ain't you rich — or at least able to figure out a reasonably easy way of getting along, which you ain't done?' Which considerably dims the nimbus around my fat head for a day or so." Whalen to Snyder, November 15, 1953, UC Davis. Whalen's 1955 poem may have been inspired partially by William Carlos Williams's visit; it was also written following a visit to the welfare office.

P. 118. *"Whalen was using"*: Michael McClure, *Scratching the Beat Surface,* p. 21.

P. 120. *"an elegant thing"*: Snyder to Whalen, April 9, 1955, Reed.

P. 120. *"Your poetry has a consistent"*: Snyder to Whalen, March 1, 1954, Reed.

P. 120. *"A real hojoki"*: Snyder to Whalen, November 19, 1954, Reed.

P. 120. *"a cunning little one-room thing"*: Jimmy Hubbell, telephone interview transcript, December 31, 1996. "Gary's place was a cunning little one room thing with a charcoal brazier . . . he was the most interesting young man. I remember reading his logging poems back then. I thought, and still think, they were the most beautiful things I've ever read." Jinny Hubbell, formerly Lehrman, was the model for the fictional "Princess" of Kerouac's *The Dharma Bums.* Her maiden name was Baker.

P. 120. *more accurately, his "hojo"*: Gary Snyder, E-mail to the author, September 1, 2001. "In the *Vimalikirti Sutra* the layman adept Vimalikirti is unwell, and many friends, monks, priests, and also various Bodhisattvas, spirits, gods and such all come to pay him a get-well visit. His dwelling is tiny, only ten feet by ten feet, and it would seem that it would be too small to accommodate his guests, but somehow his tiny house holds everyone who comes, even in the millions.

"This tiny room, was given the name, in later tradition, of 'Hojo,' which in Japanese means 'ten feet square.' Buddhist hermits would then call their little places 'hojo' — In medieval Japan, a priest named Kamo no Chomei wrote an account of his life in his tiny place, and it was published as the 'Hojo-ki' which means, 'The Record of my Ten Foot Square Hut.' Ki simply means 'record.' With some confusion, people began calling hermit huts 'hojoki' when they should have said 'hojo.' It also, finally, became the name for the room in which Zen Masters held interviews with their students."

p. 121. *"whose breasts bleed":* Gary Snyder, "A Berry Feast," *The Back Country,* p. 3.

p. 121. *Bear Ceremonialism:* Snyder to Whalen, December 9, 1955, Reed. This woman who "gave birth to slick dark children with sharp teeth" is a presence running through Gary's writing from his earliest work up through the haunting prose of "The Woman Who Married a Bear" and "The Bear Mother," from *Mountains and Rivers Without End.* For further examples, see "The Woman Who Married a Bear," *The Practice of the Wild,* pp. 155–74 and "The Bear Mother," *Mountains and Rivers Without End,* p. 113.

p. 121. *this poem is for bear:* Gary Snyder, *Myths and Texts,* p. 24.

p. 121. *"this poem is for deer":* Snyder to Whalen, January 2, 1955, Reed. Poem included in text of letter to Whalen. For published version of the poem, see *Myths and Texts,* p. 26.

p. 121. *treks in the Olympics:* Whalen to Snyder, February 11, 1955, UC Davis. "Olympics 1947 — odd feeling of Jeffers about some of it."

p. 121. *"I suggest you read up":* Snyder to Hymes, April 27, 1955, American Philosophical Society.

p. 121. *"Song to Be Sung Later":* Included in letter to Dell Hymes, April 2, 1955, American Philosophical Society.

p. 121. *"For a Stone Girl at Sanchi":* Gary Snyder,

"Poem for a Stone Girl at Sanchi," typescript dated June 9, 1955, UC Davis.

p. 121. *"inspired by Greta Garbo":* Snyder to Whalen, June 16, 1955, UC Davis. "I found you again, gone stone/in Zimmer's book of Indian Art . . ." See *Riprap & Cold Mountain Poems,* p. 11.

p. 121. *meeting at the Fairmont:* Snyder to Whalen, April 2, 1955, Reed.

p. 121. *"straight, clear, firm":* Gary Snyder, E-mail to the author, March 17, 2001. "Miura Roshi was indeed the first Zen Master I met, and he was a classical model. Straight, clear, firm, somewhat aloof, no nonsense. There are Zen Masters in the tradition who can be warmer, sillier, and more talkative, as I found out later, but Miura was really like one of the old time guys. Compared to the Japanese teachers, one doesn't even want to mention those Americans who get called Roshi these days. None of them completely fulfill the old model."

p. 122. *"reasonably well expect":* Ruth Fuller Sasaki to Gary Snyder, June 10, 1953, UC Davis.

p. 122. *Alan Watts's Academy:* Alan Watts was son-in-law of Ruth Fuller Sasaki; however, it was not he who introduced Gary Snyder to Mrs. Sasaki. Snyder was already a member of the First Zen Institute when he met Watts. His introduction to Ruth Sasaki was arranged by Donald Shively, one of his professors at Berkeley.

p. 122. *Berkeley's Buddhist Church of America:* Ryo Imamura, "Four Decades with Gary Snyder," in Jon Halper, ed., *Gary Snyder: Dimensions of a Life,* pp. 299–301.

p. 122. *A monk asked Chao-Chou:* Also known as the Koan Mu. According to *The Encyclopedia of Eastern Philosophy and Religion,* p. 231, "it is often the first koan received by a Zen student from his master. When the student has mastered it, it is said that he has become acquainted with 'the world of mu.' In the course of Zen training this mu is to be experienced and demonstrated on ever deeper levels."

p. 122. *"Twenty minutes zazen":* Snyder to Hymes, April 2, 1955, American Philosophical Society. "My mind has been liberated from the intoxication of mythology . . . From the time I read Zimmer's *Myths & Symbols in Indian Art and Civilization* and Robert Graves' *White Goddess* up until about a year ago, I lived in an intense Western Paradise of Gods, Goddesses, & fancy Rites. The thing that freed me was a protracted meditation of the first koan in the *Mumonkwan*."

P. 124. *"It has been suggested":* Ruth Fuller Sasaki to Gary Snyder, letter dated "April 2, 1955" (date incorrect; probably April 12, 1955), UC Davis.

P. 124. *"In your case . . . Communist":* Department of State to Gary Snyder, February 21, 1955, UC Davis.

P. 124. *Ruth B. Shipley:* "Passport Decision Stuns Petticoat Empire Here," *Washington Star,* June 26, 1955, Davis.

P. 124. *"I am not now . . . Communist Party":* Gary Snyder to the Secretary of State, March 18, 1955, UC Davis.

P. 125. *she rescinded . . . but offered:* Sasaki to Snyder, June 3, 1955, UC Davis.

P. 125. *She also consulted:* ibid.

P. 125. *Knight rejected Gary's appeal:* U.S. Department of State to Gary Snyder, June 24, 1955, UC Davis. "Passport facilities cannot be granted to you as it is believed that it is not in the best interests of the United States for you to travel abroad at this time." Also, U.S. Department of State to Senator Richard Neuberger, June 24, 1955, UC Davis. "The Department has carefully reviewed the record of his case, including his affidavit, and has concluded that it is not in the best interests of the United States to issue Mr. Snyder a passport."

P. 125. *"keep up the Japanese":* Sasaki to Snyder, July 5, 1955, UC Davis.

P. 125. *"She must be quite a one":* Whalen to Snyder, June 14, 1955, UC Davis.

P. 125. *Court of Appeals had dealt a blow:* "Passport Decision Stuns Petticoat Empire Here," *Washington Star,* June 26, 1955.

P. 125. *"with the general loosening up":* Sasaki to Snyder, July 5, 1955, UC Davis.

P. 125. *"I am off to Kyoto":* Snyder to Hymes, July 7, 1955, American Philosophical Society.

P. 126. *"I'm surrounded by mountains":* Philip Whalen, "Sourdough Mountain Lookout," *Overtime: Selected Poems,* p. 19.

P. 126. *"Sometimes I was Sakyamuni":* Whalen to Snyder, April 24, 1955, UC Davis.

P. 126. *"another finger pointing":* Whalen to Snyder, May 2, 1955, UC Davis.

P. 128. *"old original rice-bag":* ibid. "The old original rice-bag" is a typical Zen-type reference to the Buddha Sakyamuni. Zen often employs denigrating and irreverent epithets for the Buddha, to stress his non-divinity and the absolute equality and indivisibility of all things. "Meditate. Smarten up," is Whalen's paraphrase of Sakyamuni's reported last words: "Stay awake. Work out your salvation with diligence."

P. 128. *Zen spirit . . . aroused:* Whalen interview, October 28, 1997. "Certainly the peyote had unsealed 'the doors of perception' to the point that this experience of the horse and the lake and the moonlight on the surrounding peaks was really something else."

P. 128. *"The horse was very important":* ibid. "I got a phrase out of the Matthew's Chinese-English dictionary, and it's supposed to mean "Swimming Horse," or "Floating Horse." The characters are probably wrong, but I used them anyway. It's *Ma* [Chinese: "horse"] something, or something *Ma*; anyway, it has 'horse' in it. The horse is there and some other word which means 'swimming' or 'floating' or 'water'. . . . It means childish inability to hold onto things."

P. 128. *"The experience meant a great deal":* ibid.

P. 129. *He wrote Gary that:* Whalen to Snyder, August 14, 1955, UC Davis.

P. 129. *"scattered fragments":* Whalen interview, October 28, 1997.

P. 129. *"I had a lot of bits and pieces":* ibid. In the spring of 1956, Whalen lived at Allen Ginsberg's apartment in Berkeley. Ginsberg was at that time preparing his poem "Howl" for publication by City Lights Books, and Whalen was in an ideal position to observe Ginsberg's editing process.

P. 129. *snow that had persisted:* Photographs taken by the Danielsens during their August 14 visit to Sourdough show snow still covering the area around the lookout. Also, in his July 11, 1955, letter to Gary Snyder, Whalen mentions "the glacier that has taken to inhabiting the top of Sourdough since you left [in 1953]."

P. 130. *lying naked on the slabs of rock:* Whalen, "Sourdough Mountain Lookout," *Overtime*, p. 16. "Outside the lookout I lay nude on the granite/Mountain hot September sun but inside my head/Calm dark night with all the other stars."

P. 130. *Aurora Borealis "shimmying":* ibid., p. 20. "Magnetic storms across the solar plains/Make Aurora Borealis shimmy bright . . . "

P. 130. *"Ireland's fear of unknown":* ibid., p. 16.

P. 130. *"always traveling":* Whalen, "Visiting," unpublished prose manuscript, Columbia.

P. 132. *Philip saw his bootprints:* Whalen, "Sourdough Mountain Lookout," *Overtime: Selected Poems*, p. 15. "I see my bootprints mingle with deer-foot/Bear-paw, mule-shoe in the dusty path to the privy."

P. 132. *"half inch of ice":* ibid., p. 20.

P. 132. *"some of the quartz":* ibid.

P. 133. *"Gary's tiny doghouse":* Philip Whalen, quoted in "Interview with Aram Saroyan," Allen, ed., *Off the Wall: Interviews with Philip Whalen*, p. 49.

P. 133. *"Now if this is true":* Snyder to Whalen, dated only "September 1955," *Gary Snyder Reader*, p. 151. "I got you in on the deal on the basis of three poems, 'Martyrdom,' 'K.W. Senex,' & 'If You're So Smart,' which have achieved a certain subterranean celebration via Rexroth & others. Rexroth got me in."

P. 133. *clearing out his few belongings:* Whalen to Snyder, September 17, 1955, UC Davis.

P. 133. *From the hotel he wrote:* Whalen to Snyder, September 19, 1955, UC Davis.

P. 133. *with keen interest and amazement:* Whalen interview, October 28, 1997. "Gary wrote to me and said he had met this fellow Ginsberg and they were going to do this number and they wanted me to be in it. So I was very interested and amazed."

P. 133. *"There will also be poets":* Snyder to Whalen. "September 1955," *Gary Snyder Reader*, p. 151.

P. 133. *"Unroll the velvet carpets":* Whalen to Snyder, September 19, 1955, UC Davis.

CHAPTER 6: A REMARKABLE COLLECTION OF ANGELS

P. 135. *"Who came to the reading?":* Philip Whalen, "Interview with Anne Waldman," in Donald Allen, ed., *Off the Wall: Interviews with Philip Whalen*, p. 26

P. 135. *"immense triangular arc":* Jack Kerouac, *The Dharma Bums*, p. 5.

P. 137. *"divine and divinely strange":* Jack Kerouac to Allen Ginsberg, September 1–6, 1955. Kerouac, *Selected Letters, 1940–1956*, p. 513.

P. 137. *"the great and final wild . . . ":* Jack Kerouac, *On the Road*, p. 302.

P. 137. *"Mexico is not simple":* William Burroughs to Jack Kerouac, May 1951. *The Letters of William Burroughs*, p. 91.

P. 138. *"hard Durangos and impossible Chihuahuas":* Jack Kerouac, *Some of the Dharma*, p. 339. See also, *The Dharma Bums*, p. 4. ". . . the long cheap bus trip across Zacatecas and Durango and Chihuahua two thousand long miles to the border at El Paso."

P. 138. *"I have just knocked off":* Kerouac to Ginsberg, August 19, 1955. Kerouac, *Selected Letters, 1940–1956*, p. 507.

P. 138. *"Mexico City Blues . . . will do for poetry":* Kerouac to Sterling Lord, August 19, 1955. Kerouac, *Selected Letters, 1940–1956*, p. 510.

P. 138. *"I'm not doing a pitch":* Kerouac to Malcolm Cowley, September 11, 1955. Kerouac, *Selected Letters, 1940–1956*, p. 515.

P. 138. *"all poets like to kick":* Jack Kerouac, *Atop an Underwood*, p. 94. "Like all other poets, I am kicking. I want to kick, you might say. You say, all poets like to kick. And this one here, Jack Kerouac, wants to kick in an original manner, but damned if he can find something original. He wants to be an original kicker, so that people will look at him and say: That fellow is a poet with an original bone to pick."

P. 139. *"Say what you mean":* Jack Kerouac, *Book of Blues*, p. 82.

P. 139. *"blowing a long blues":* Jack Kerouac, Preface, *Mexico City Blues*.

P. 139. *"My ideas vary":* ibid.

P. 139. *In the notebooks:* The original spiral note-books in which Kerouac composed *Mexico City Blues* are in the Berg Collection of the New York Public Library.

P. 139. *Benzedrine, codeine, and Seconal:* Kerouac to Ginsberg, August 19, 1955. Kerouac, *Selected Letters, 1940–1956,* p. 509.

P. 139. *"for excitement, for sleep":* Jack Kerouac, *Desolation Angels,* p. 254.

P. 139. *smoked pot nonstop:* Jack Kerouac, *The Paris Review* Interview with Ted Berrigan and Aram Saroyan, included in *On the Road: Text and Criticism,* pp. 555–56. "I had no other place to write it but on a closed toilet seat in a little tile toilet in Mexico City so as to get away from the guests inside the apartment. There incidentally is a style truly hallucinated as I wrote it all on pot. No pun intended. Ho Ho."

P. 139. *"a charge like a high Benny drive":* Kerouac to John Clellon Holmes, June 5, 1952, Kerouac, *Selected Letters, 1940–1956,* p. 371.

P. 141. *"other maids of honor":* Kerouac to Ginsberg, August 19, 1955. Kerouac, Selected Letters, 1940–1956, p. 508.

P. 141. *"Came to Mexico":* Kerouac to Ginsberg, September 1–6, 1955. Kerouac, Ibid., p. 512. Kerouac's "long short story" was the first half of his novella *Tristessa.*

P. 141. *"high on. . . M":* Jack Kerouac, *The Paris Review* Interview, *On the Road: Text and Criticism,* pp. 564–65. "Poem 230 from *Mexico City Blues* is a poem written purely on morphine. Every line in this poem is written within an hour of one another, high on a big dose of M . . . "

P. 141. *Bill Garver, an elderly addict:* For a description of Bill Garver and Kerouac's time with him on Orizaba Street, see Kerouac, *Desolation Angels,* pp. 245–84. Bill Garver is called "Old Bull Gaines" in *Desolation Angels* and *Tristessa.* He also appears under the name "Gaines" in William Burroughs's novel *Junky.*

P. 141. *Jack did this . . . compassion:* Kerouac, *Desolation Angels,* p. 251.

P. 142. *"Nothin a junkey likes better":* Kerouac, *Mexico City Blues,* p. 59.

P. 142. *"mad sick eyes":* Kerouac, *Some of the Dharma,* p. 337.

P. 142. *"driving myself crazy":* Kerouac to Ginsberg, September 1–6, 1955. Kerouac, *Selected Letters, 1940–1956,* p. 512.

P. 142. *"greatest unpublished writer":* Allen Ginsberg, quoted in Gifford and Lee, *Jack's Book: An Oral Biography of Jack Kerouac,* p. 197. "Rexroth had read his work, knew of his reputation, admired him a great deal, had said he was the greatest unpublished writer in America. Or maybe he told that to Cowley, maybe that's where Cowley got it."

P. 144. *From L.A. he caught:* Kerouac, *The Dharma Bums,* pp. 3–9.

P. 144. *road rat's dream ride:* For an expanded version of this hitchhiking incident, see Kerouac's *Good Blonde & Others,* pp. 3–18.

P. 144. *first night . . . Skid Row hotel:* Kerouac to John Clellon Holmes, October 12, 1955. Kerouac, *Selected Letters, 1940–1956,* p. 523.

P. 144. *"Someday I'll buy":* Kerouac, *Some of the Dharma,* p. 344.

P. 144. *blasting Bach's St. Matthew:* Kerouac to Holmes, October 12, 1955. Kerouac, *Selected Letters, 1940–1956,* p. 524.

P. 144. *"curiously exalted":* Jack Kerouac, *The Town and the City,* p. 365. "Leon Levinsky was about nineteen years old. He was one of the strangest, most curiously exalted youngsters Peter had ever known. . . . Levinsky was an eager, intense, sharply intelligent boy of Russian-Jewish parentage who rushed around New York in a perpetual sweat of emotional activity. . . ."

P. 144. *"sorrowful, poetic con-man":* Kerouac, *On the Road,* p. 7. ". . . the sorrowful poetic con-man with the dark mind that is Carlo Marx."

P. 144. *homoerotic . . . relationship:* For Allen Ginsberg's side of this very complex relationship, see Allen Ginsberg, "Gay Sunshine Interview," in *Spontaneous Mind: Selected Interviews, 1958–1996,* pp. 303–42.

P. 145. *Ginsberg had sent Rexroth:* Allen Ginsberg to Neal Cassady, July 3, 1952, Barry Gifford, ed., *As Ever: The Collected Correspondence of Allen Ginsberg & Neal Cassady,* pp. 129–30. "I am writing Kenneth Rexroth today. He lives in Frisco, believes in Williams, has a lot to do with New Directions poetry selections. . . . Lamantia (Philip) gave me his address. . . . He's an old guy [Rexroth was 47], not really great as writer, too hung up on booklearning, but he does dig all the young subterranean cats like Lamantia."

P. 145. *first part of "Howl":* Allen Ginsberg, *Howl: Original Draft Facsimile, Transcript & Variant Versions, Fully Annotated by Author,* pp. xii–xiii.

P. 145. *"great wild poetry":* Kerouac to Ginsberg, September 1–6, 1955. Kerouac, *Selected Letters, 1940–1956,* p. 513.

P. 145. *On September 2:* Allen Ginsberg, *Journals Mid-Fifties 1954–1958,* p. 178.

P. 145. *On the 8th:* Allen Ginsberg, journal entry, September 9, 1955, in Ann Charters, ed., *Scenes Along the Road,* p. 30.

P. 145. *Gary also suggested:* Snyder interview, December 6, 2000. ". . . and I asked Kenneth to be the Master of Ceremonies. Kenneth was dubious at first—'Buncha drunken fuck-ups!'"

P. 145. *"A bearded interesting Berkeley cat":* Ginsberg, journal entry, September 9, 1955, in Charters, ed., *Scenes Along the Road,* p. 30.

P. 146. *got together on September 23rd:* Gary Snyder, unpublished journal, October 2, 1955, used by permission of Gary Snyder. Mentions meeting "Jack Kerawuack a week ago Friday," i.e., September 23. It was the first chance that the two new arrivals in town—Whalen and Kerouac—had to meet Kenneth Rexroth.

P. 146. *"Jack and Allen . . . from Berkeley":* Philip Whalen, interview with the author, Hartford Street Zen Center, San Francisco, October 28, 1997.

P. 146. *beers at The Place:* Kerouac to Whalen, April 12, 1960. Kerouac, *Selected Letters, 1957–1969,* p. 252.

P. 146. *epicentric watering hole:* Kerouac, *Desolation Angels,* pp. 135–36.

P. 146. *Kerouac's "affable clarity":* Gary Snyder, E-mail to the author, October 13, 1999.

P. 146. *"a great room":* Philip Whalen, telephone interview transcript, March 11, 1998.

P. 147. *Allen had been showing:* Allen Ginsberg, in Gifford and Lee, *Jack's Book: An Oral Biography of Jack Kerouac,* p. 197.

P. 147. *energy and evocation:* Gary Snyder, quoted in ibid., p. 201. "What I liked was the writing, of course, and the energy that was in it, and the evocation of people. Of course, it didn't say 'Jack Kerouac,' it said 'Jean-Louis.'"

P. 147. *"Jazz of the Beat Generation"* appeared in *New World Writing,* no. 7 (spring 1955).

P. 147. *"I flashed that he was Jean-Louis":* Gary Snyder, in Gifford and Lee, *Jack's Book: An Oral Biography of Jack Kerouac,* p. 201.

P. 147. *"And then I knew":* Gary Snyder, E-mail to the author, October 13, 1999.

P. 147. *fashioned from the workbays:* Philip Whalen, "Interview with Anne Waldman," in Donald Allen, ed., *Off the Wall,* pp. 25–26. ". . . called the Six Gallery because it was six artists who paid the rent and showed paintings there. . . . It was actually an old garage that had been a regular repair place for automobiles and then somehow they had built this platform and put a floor in, I think there had only been a dirt floor originally and it was this big sort of gloomy building with all the wall space that they could show pictures on. . . ."

P. 147. *"rundown second-rate":* Ginsberg, *Howl: Original Draft Facsimile,* p. 165.

P. 147. *"someone had knocked together":* Michael McClure, *Scratching the Beat Surface,* p. 13.

P. 147. *"built for a midget . . . to recite The Iliad":* Philip Whalen, "Interview with Anne Waldman," in Donald Allen, ed., *Off the Wall,* p. 21.

P. 148. *"purely amateur":* Ginsberg, *Howl: Original Draft Facsimile,* p. 13.

P. 148. *In Lawrence Ferlinghetti's memory:* Lawrence Ferlinghetti, in Gifford and Lee, *Jack's Book: An Oral Biography of Jack Kerouac,* p. 194.

P. 148. *"a huge room":* McClure, *Scratching the Beat Surface,* p. 13.

P. 148. *upwards of 250:* Philip Whalen, "Interview with Anne Waldman," in Donald Allen, ed., *Off the Wall,* p. 26. "He [Ginsberg] and I sat and addressed seven million dittoed postcards announcing the reading and mailed them out . . . and the Six Gallery was full. The place wasn't big, it couldn't have held more than 250 or maybe 200."

P. 148. *"A surprisingly large number":* Snyder interview, December 6, 2000.

P. 148. *"The Six Gallery reading was open":* McClure, *Scratching the Beat Surface,* pp. 23–24.

P. 148. *"remarkable collection of angels":* The invitation read as follows: "6 POETS AT 6 GALLERY: Philip Lamantia, reading mss. of late John Hoffman—Mike McClure, Allen Ginsberg, Gary Snyder & Phil Whalen—all sharp new straightforward writing—remarkable collection of angels on one stage reading their poetry. No charge, small collection for wine and postcards. Charming event. Kenneth Rexroth M.C." See Gary Snyder's November 20, 1949, letter to his father in which he describes his Lambert Street housemates as "a remarkable collection."

P. 148. *"I doubt much good poetry":* Gary Snyder to Kenneth Rexroth, "Wednesday, 1954," UC Davis. "Now that Williams is very old, I doubt that much good poetry will come from East the Rockies."

P. 148. *Kerouac and Ginsberg . . . felt pretty much the same:* Kerouac, *The Dharma Bums,* p. 98.

P. 148. *"Philip Lamantia . . . bi-coastal":* Philip Lamantia, interview with the author, San Francisco, December 11, 2000. "I can tie together both coasts, since I was on the East Coast—I traveled—I wasn't one of the characters in Kerouac's book, he didn't put me in that book, but I was on the road, man!"

P. 149. *"voice that rises once":* Breton quoted in Nancy J. Peters, "Philip Lamantia," *Dictionary of Literary Biography,* vol. 16, p. 330.

P. 149. *"among the finest":* Kenneth Rexroth, "The Influence of French Poetry on American," *World Outside the Window,* p. 167.

P. 149. *"that Renaissance":* In *The Dharma Bums,* Kerouac describes the Six Gallery reading as "the night of the birth of the San Francisco Poetry Renaissance" (p. 13); however, that Renaissance had really begun several years before. For an account of the earliest beginnings of the Berkeley and San Francisco

Renaissance of the late 1940s, see Ekbert Faas, *Young Robert Duncan,* pp. 192–201.

P. 149. *Ginsberg had taken note:* Allen Ginsberg to Neal Cassady and Jack Kerouac, February 15, 1952, in Barry Gifford, ed., *As Ever: Collected Correspondence of Allen Ginsberg and Neal Cassady,* p. 118. "I used to haunt the Art Library at Columbia . . . and read Surrealist Magazines. Well, I was astounded one day, when in *VVV* a N.Y. Transplantation of the style, a Magazine like *View,* I ran into the poems of 13 year old Lamantia (1944–5)—and I even remember envying and admiring him. . . . I followed his career vaguely, & ran into him in N.Y. also 2 years ago with great joy at the widening circle."

P. 149. *Ginsberg would include Lamantia:* Ginsberg, *Howl: Original Facsimile,* p. 124.

P. 149. *McClure . . . Artaud:* McClure, *Scratching the Beat Surface,* p. 24. "One of my first exchanges with Philip Lamantia on meeting him in 1954 was to ask where I could find more works by Artaud."

P. 149. *considered Rexroth a mentor:* Author's note: When I first met Philip Lamantia, in December 2000, he stood on Columbus Avenue in North Beach, outside the City Lights Bookstore, encouraging me to "not forget Rexie" in *Poets on the Peaks.* "Rexroth was himself a peak," said Lamantia, "—a peak-man, a man-peak!"

P. 150. *"I used to have endless":* Lamantia interview, December 11, 2000.

P. 150. *"a great mentor":* Snyder interview, December 6, 2000.

P. 150. *Washo tribe:* Philip Lamantia, *Becoming Visible,* Notes. "Washo—a tribe whose original territory lay in the verdant area of Lake Tahoe, on both sides of the California and Nevada border. Their peyote rite 'The Tipi Way' in which I participated in the early 1950s has been a constant source of poetic inspiration."

P. 150. *Cora Indians of Mexico:* ibid. "In the spring of 1955 during an extended stay in their village of Jesus-Maria, I joined the Coras in a night-ritual celebrating yana (the Cora name for tobacco).

P. 150. *Hoffmann . . . died in Mexico:* The circumstances of John Hoffmann's death were unclear. Kerouac, in *The Dharma Bums*, p. 15, perpetuated the story that Hoffmann, whom he gives the pseudonym "Altman" had died of peyote poisoning. ". . . Altman who'd eaten too much peyote in Chihuahua (or died of polio. . .)."

P. 150. *Burroughs had mentioned him:* William Burroughs, *Junky*, p. 147. "One of these junkies came down to Mexico and started taking peyote with the Indians. He was using it all the time in large quantities: up to twelve buttons in one dose. He died of a condition that was diagnosed as polio. I understand, however, that the symptoms of peyote poisoning and polio are identical."

P. 150. *"got busted":* Ginsberg, *Howl: Original Draft Facsimile*, p. 124.

P. 150. *"disappeared into the volcanoes":* ibid., p. 129.

P. 150. *"reputed to be":* Allen Ginsberg to Neal Cassady, February 15, 1952, Gifford, ed., *As Ever*, p. 118.

P. 150. *Hoffmann was highly regarded:* Ginsberg, *Howl: Original Draft Facsimile*, p. 129.

P. 151. *Journey to the End:* In November 2000, Kolourmein Press of "Oaktown," California, produced a limited edition of two dozen copies of *Journey to the End* from the Hoffmann poems in Lamantia's possession.

P. 151. *"oracular style":* What Kerouac later satirized as "a delicate Englishy voice that had me crying with inside laughter" (Kerouac, *The Dharma Bums*, p. 15), McClure heard as "an oracular English style, with lovely intonation" (McClure, "Nights in North Beach," *The Sixties*, p. 28).

P. 151. *Lamantia had nearly died:* Lamantia interview, December 11, 2000. "When I got bitten by the scorpion it was like taking a powerful drug. The venom really lays you out. I was paralyzed for about twelve hours at least, and couldn't move and I vomited constantly. I passed out about five times. The first time I passed out—that is why I returned to the Church above all—As I passed out, the first thing I say—I feel I'm gonna die—I'm only twenty-four years old, I mean I haven't had any experience like this before, so out of my—What?—Out of what?—I say, 'Ah, Madonna! Madonna, save me!' *Madonna?* I hated the Church! I

was an atheist by the time I was fourteen. I left it with hatred, became a Surrealist. . ."

P. 151. *"a crisis of conversion":* ibid. See also Kenneth Rexroth, "San Francisco Letter," *World Outside the Window*, p. 61. "Lamantia's poetry is illuminated, ecstatic, with the mystic's intense autonomy. Unfortunately, since his surrealist days, although he has written a great deal, he has published practically nothing. Poems he has read locally have been deeply moving, but each in turn he has put by and gone on, dissatisfied, to something else. As it is so often the case with the mystic temperament, art seems to have become a means rather than even a temporary end. I hope that soon he will find what he is seeking, at least in a measure, and then, of course, his previous work will fall into place and be seen as satisfactory enough to publish—I hope."

P. 151. *McClure first read a letter:* Michael McClure, in Gifford and Lee, eds., *Jack's Book: An Oral Biography of Jack Kerouac*, p. 196.

P. 152. *"more to Duncan than any other":* Kenneth Rexroth, *Assays*, p. 192.

P. 152. *McClure considered Duncan:* Michael McClure, *Lighting the Corners*, pp. 91–92. "As brilliant and 'major' as Rexroth was it was Duncan who seemed to be even more international. It did not matter that Duncan was unknown or that he said he'd be happy to have just five hundred readers—the scope of intention and smoldering liveliness in his poems made Duncan seem to be the most international among us. We could imagine Robert speaking with Picasso and Cocteau and Stein and D. H. Lawrence."

P. 152. *Duncan . . . had helped to establish:* It was Duncan, with his life partner, the painter Jess Collins, who had established the Six Gallery's predecessor—the Ubu Gallery—at the same Fillmore Street address. And Duncan had already performed at the Six Gallery —earlier in 1955 he had staged a reading of his play *Faust Foutu* ("Faust Fucked"), a wild music drama for which he'd composed the score and acted out the role of each character. At the end of his piece, Duncan had ripped off his clothes and stood naked before the audience, a shocking gesture at the time, which helped foster the gallery's reputation as a place where anything might happen. See McClure, *Scratching the Beat Surface*, p. 12.

P. 152. *made an impression on Gary Snyder:* Snyder interview, December 6, 2000. "Certainly Duncan was a presence there. . . . What's really interesting isn't the 'Beat Generation,' it was the period leading up to it. That's where all the action was. Allen's and Jack's and our thing was all built on that, we all took off from that launching pad, which was laid earlier by Spicer and Duncan and Rexroth. Duncan was such an elegant poet. We crossed paths and met several times, that first year I was in San Francisco, and I had tremendous admiration for both his poetics and his politics, which were Anarchist."

P. 152. *"addressed to Artaud":* Michael McClure, telephone interview transcript, April 25, 2001.

P. 152. *Whalen now came shyly:* Will Petersen, "September Ridge," in Jon Halper, ed., *Gary Snyder: Dimensions of a Life*, p. 76.

P. 152. *"Funny and dry":* Gary Snyder, E-mail to the author, October 13, 1999.

P. 152. *McClure, who had never seen:* McClure interview, December 9, 2000.

P. 152. *"As I watched him read":* McClure, *Scratching the Beat Surface*, pp. 21–23.

P. 153. *"When Philip started reading":* McClure interview, December 9, 2000.

P. 153. *Kerouac and his drinking buddy Bob Donlin:* Kerouac, *The Dharma Bums*, pp. 13–14. "And I was the one who got things jumping by going around collecting dimes and quarters from the rather stiff audience standing around in the gallery and coming back with three huge jugs of California Burgundy and getting them all piffed. . . ."

P. 153. *surprisingly clear-headed:* Ginsberg, *Howl: Original Draft Facsimile*, p. 165. "The reading was delivered by the poet, rather surprised at his own power, drunk on the platform, becoming increasingly sober as he read. . . ."

P. 153. *"strange ecstatic intensity":* ibid.

P. 154. *McClure was totally unprepared:* McClure interview, December 9, 2000.

P. 154. *"from quiet, brilliant burning":* McClure, *Scratching the Beat Surface*, p. 15.

P. 154. *"and stand before you":* Ginsberg, "Howl," *Collected Poems, 1947–1980*, pp. 130–31.

P. 154. *"tears which restored":* Ginsberg, *Howl: Original Draft Facsimile*, p. 165.

P. 154. *"secret hero":* Ginsberg, "Howl," *Collected Poems, 1947–1980*, p. 128.

P. 154. *"Allen m'boy, I'm proud":* Ginsberg, *Howl: Original Draft Facsimile*, p. 167. "—the nicest thing I heard that night. It was completely, unabashedly, friendly, happy approval."

P. 154. *". . . and when Irwin had finished":* Jack Kerouac, *Desolation Angels*, p. 205.

P. 155. *"Ginsberg left us standing":* McClure, *Scratching the Beat Surface*, p. 15.

P. 155. *which he had just titled:* A September 19, 1955 journal entry refers to "Myths & Texts"; also, October 2, 1955, journal entry, used by permission of Gary Snyder. "Spent the last two days arranging *Texts and Myths* on the floor."

P. 155. *arranging them in three groups:* Gary Snyder, E-mail to the author, October 13, 1999. "I had spread out al the poems that I sensed belonged together, and read them as a whole, to find their relationships. In the following days I wrote a few further poems to fill in the vacant niches, and then established their right sequence. The first person I showed the finished sequence to was Kenneth Rexroth, who seemed to like it a lot."

P. 155. *"with heroic firmness":* McClure, "North Beach Nights," *The Sixties*, p. 28.

P. 156. *"the sawmill temples":* Gary Snyder, *Myths and Texts*, p. 15.

P. 156. *"Dead city in dry summer":* Gary Snyder, "A Berry Feast," *The Back Country*, p. 7.

P. 156. *"Save the invitation":* Will Petersen, "September Ridge," in Jon Halper, ed., in *Gary Snyder: Dimensions of a Life*, p. 77. "'Save the invitation,' Gary confided: 'Some day it will be worth something.' He was somehow certain of immortality, back then. In an impoverished Taoist unpublished poet sort of way."

CHAPTER 7: WHEN MEN AND MOUNTAINS MEET

P. 157. *"Great things are done":* William Blake, "Satiric Verses & Epigrams," *The Poetry & Prose of William Blake*, p. 511.

P. 157. *"From that night on":* Gary Snyder, *A Place in Space*, p. 8. "We had a sudden feeling that we had finally broken through to a new form of expression, had shattered the stranglehold of universities on poets, and gone beyond the tedious and pointless arguments of Bolshevik versus capitalist. . . ."

P. 157. *offer to publish "Howl":* Howl and Other Poems became Number Four in the new paperback series, behind Ferlinghetti's own *Pictures of a Gone World*, Rexroth's *Thirty Spanish Poems of Love and Exile*, and Kenneth Patchen's *Poems of Humor and Protest*.

P. 158. *while Kerouac leaned:* Barry Miles, *Ginsberg: A Biography*, p. 200.

P. 158. *In the Yosemite:* Jim Snyder, "Riprap and the Old Ways: Gary Snyder in the Yosemite, 1955," in Jon Halper, ed., *Gary Snyder: Dimensions of a Life*, pp. 35–42.

P. 158. *"If they ask you":* Philip Whalen, "Memorial to the Throne," September 29, 1955, Columbia.

P. 158. *Poetry is Shit:* Kerouac to Whalen, October 17, 1961. Kerouac, *Selected Letters, 1957–1969*, pp. 304–5.

P. 159. *"I don't want to hear about it":* Whalen, "Memorial to the Throne," September 29, 1955, Columbia.

P. 159. *"Allen Ginsberg has arranged":* Kerouac to Malcolm Cowley, September 20, 1955. Kerouac, *Selected Letters, 1940–1956*, p. 519.

P. 159. *"earnest and strong":* Jack Kerouac, *The Dharma Bums*, p. 14.

P. 159. *"the only one who didn't":* ibid., p. 11.

P. 159. *"The other poets":* ibid., p. 15.

P. 159. *"aridly unemotional":* Kerouac to Whalen, June 19, 1962, Reed.

P. 161. *"Damn you, I told you":* Kerouac to Whalen, January 5, 1956. Kerouac, *Selected Letters, 1940–1956*, p. 537.

P. 161. *"one for solitude":* Henry David Thoreau, *Walden*, p. 434.

P. 161. *"one sentimental rocking chair":* Kerouac, *The Dharma Bums*, p. 18.

P. 161. *covered with a cougar hide:* Walter Lehrman, telephone interview with the author, April 15, 2000.

P. 161. *"In the corner was his famous rucksack":* Kerouac, *The Dharma Bums*, p. 18.

P. 162. *"Long, Bitter Song":* Snyder to Whalen, March 1, 1954, Reed. The letter includes eighteen lines of Po Chü-i's "Long Bitter Song."

P. 162. *"Song of the Lute":* Snyder interview, December 6, 2000.

P. 162. *Ch'en, who had once written:* Chiang Yee, *The Silent Traveler in San Francisco*, pp. 328–31.

P. 162. *"Who can leap":* Snyder, *Riprap & Cold Mountain Poems*, p. 44.

P. 162. *"My heart's not the same":* ibid., p. 42.

P. 162. *Kuo Ching monastery:* Bill Porter [Red Pine], *The Collected Songs of Cold Mountain*, pp. 4–5. "He [Han Shan] often availed himself of the hospitality of Kuoching Temple at the foot of Mount Tientai, a long day's hike to the Northeast . . . the monk Chih-yi founded the influential Tientai school of Buddhism there in the sixth century. In his will, Chih-yi asked his followers to build a temple on the site of his former hut. It was completed in 598, the year after his death, and named Tientai Temple. In 605, this was changed to Kuoching."

P. 162. *Sometimes sage and governor:* Bill Porter, *The Road to Heaven: Encounters with Chinese Hermits*, pp. 24–34.

P. 162. *Han Shan . . . called them thieves:* This incident, recorded in a T'ang era preface to Han Shan's poems by one Lu Ch'iu-Yin, was taken up by both Kerouac and Snyder in their depictions of Han Shan. Kerouac uses the episode at the end of *The Dharma Bums*, in the words of his character Ray Smith, who says (p. 243), "And suddenly it seemed I saw that unimaginable little Chinese . . . and he stood there saying nothing. 'Go away, thieves of the mind!' he cried down the hollows of the unbelievable Cascades . . . "

In the twelfth poem of the "Burning" section of *Myths and Texts*, Snyder alludes to the event as well, in describing the Cascadian landscape.

Han Shan could have lived here,
& no scissorbill stooge of the
Emperor would have come trying to steal
his last poor shred of sense.

P. 163. *The cave where Han Shan:* Bill Porter, who visited Han Shan's hermitage in 1989, writes: "It's actually more of a huge overhang than a cave. Roughly sixty meters across, thirty meters deep, and ten meters high, it faces south toward the course of the sun and the moon." For directions to Hanyen and photographs of Han Shan's cave—as well as the only English translation of all 300 Han Shan poems—see Bill Porter, *The Collected Songs of Cold Mountain,* p. 4.

P. 163. *Han Shan's writings:* For a discussion of the issues concerning the dating and identity of Han Shan, see Bill Porter's preface to *The Collected Songs of Cold Mountain,* pp. 3–18.

P. 163. *"You sometimes run into them":* Snyder, *Riprap & Cold Mountain Poems,* p. 33. "[Han Shan] and his sidekick Shih-te (Jittoku in Japanese) became great favorites with Zen painters of later days—the scroll, the broom, the wild hair and laughter. They became Immortals and you sometimes run into them today in the skidrows, orchards, hobo jungles, and logging camps of America."

P. 163. *when Arthur Waley published:* Arthur Waley, "Twenty-seven Poems by Han Shan," *Encounter,* vol. 3, no. 3, 1954.

P. 163. *Wang-Wei and Meng Hao-jan:* Gary Snyder, "Sixteen T'ang Poems," *The Gary Snyder Reader,* pp. 538–39.

P. 163. *poetic "communion":* Kenneth Rexroth, "The Poet as Translator," *World Outside the Window,* p. 189. "Communion is as important to the poet-translator as communication."

P. 164. *came across Han Shan:* Kerouac, *Some of the Dharma,* p. 311.

P. 164. *"I believed that I was an oldtime bhikku":* Kerouac, *The Dharma Bums,* p. 5.

P. 164. *"I don't want to live":* Jack Kerouac, *The Subterraneans,* p. 198. Also, Jack Kerouac, "The Last Word," *Good Blonde & Others,* p. 165. "So I was wiser when I was younger after a bad love affair and sat in my lonely November room thinking, 'It's all a big crrrock, I wanta die' . . . yet these thoughts didn't stand up to the Four Noble Truths as propounded by Buddha and which I memorized under a streetlamp in the cold wind of night."

P. 164. *At Columbia:* Kerouac, *A Jack Kerouac Romnibus*/Archive/Writers &Writing/Notebook entry, 1940.

P. 164. *not until late 1953:* Jack Kerouac, *Some of the Dharma,* p. 103.

P. 166. *"If a disciple will simply practice kindness":* Kerouac here is referring to his discovery of the Diamond Sutra. See Dwight Goddard, ed., "The Diamond Sutra," *A Buddhist Bible,* p. 91. "If any disciple will simply practice kindness, he will soon attain Anuttara-samyak-sambhodi [Highest Perfect Wisdom]."

P. 166. *"the sad eyes of Sebastian":* Jack Kerouac to Stella Sampas, October 12, 1955. Kerouac, *Selected Letters, 1940–1956,* pp. 525–26.

P. 166. *"A Buddhist Bible, like Suzuki's Manual":* Robert Aitken, Foreword to Dwight Goddard's *A Buddhist Bible,* p. ix. "It is tempting to compare *A Buddhist Bible* with D. T. Suzuki's *Manual of Zen Buddhism,* published in the same decade. Indeed, the two books overlap to some extent, for both contain the Heart Sutra, and selections from the Diamond, Surangama, Lankavatara, and Platform sutras. Suzuki and Goddard selected different sections from the original texts, however, and their translations vary. *The Manual of Zen Buddhism* is quite sectarian, whereas *A Buddhist Bible* includes a broad selection of Mahayana texts as well as selections from the Pali and Tibetan canon."

P. 166. *"the diamond that cuts through":* Jack Kerouac, *Book of Blues,* p. 147.

P. 166. *brilliant imitations:* For examples of Kerouac's early poems, see Jack Kerouac, *Atop an Underwood: Early Stories and Other Writings.*

P. 167. *began thinking of them as blues:* Jack Kerouac, *Book of Blues,* p. 2. "In my system, the form of blues choruses is limited by the small page of the breast-pocket notebook in which they are written, like the form of a set number of bars in a jazz blues chorus, and so sometimes the word-meaning can carry from one chorus into another, or not, just like the phrase-meaning can carry harmonically for one chorus to the other, or not, in jazz. . . ."

P. 167. *"It's taken me all my life":* Jack Kerouac to Malcolm Cowley, September 11, 1955. Kerouac, *Selected Letters, 1940–1956,* p. 516.

P. 167. *"Charley Parker Looked like Buddha":* Jack Kerouac, *Mexico City Blues,* pp. 241–43.

P. 168. *"I think that both Gary and I":* Philip Whalen, in David Meltzer, ed., *San Francisco Beat: Talking with the Poets,* p. 337.

P. 169. *the idea of living alone:* Kerouac, *Atop an Underwood: Early Stories and Other Writings,* p. 80. "A little shack on the slope of a mountain . . . with a bedroom overlooking the great projecting earth's grandest summits, snow-capped, sadly lost in clouds . . . "

P. 169. *where he had rowed:* Mary Di Benedetto, interview with the author, Lowell, Massachusetts, December 7, 1992. Mary Di Benedetto (formerly Carney) was Kerouac's girlfriend in high school, and the model for his Duluoz legend character Maggie Cassidy. In 1992 she was still living in the Carney family home on Billerica Street in South Lowell, where Kerouac had wooed her more than fifty years before. I interviewed her three times in the fall of 1992, when she recounted her times with Jack and showed me the Concord River bridges under which they had rowed together in her father's boat.

P. 169. *"I'll buy a saddlehorse":* Jack Kerouac to Allen Ginsberg, June 10, 1949. Kerouac, *Selected Letters, 1940–1956,* p. 193.

P. 169. *"Someday I'm going to be a hermit":* Jack Kerouac to John Clellon Holmes, June 5, 1952. Kerouac, *Selected Letters, 1940–1956,* p. 371.

P. 169. *"Go somewhere":* Kerouac, *Some of the Dharma,* p. 11.

P. 169. *"one should have his abode":* Dwight Goddard, ed., "The Lankavatara Scripture," *A Buddhist Bible,* p. 318.

P. 169. *"I don't want to be":* ibid., p. 63.

P. 171. *"an Indian thing":* Jack Kerouac, "Mexico Fellaheen," *Lonesome Traveler,* p. 22.

P. 171. *"I'll go down to Mexico":* Jack Kerouac, *Some of the Dharma,* p. 32.

P. 171. *"My own little vihara":* ibid., p. 312.

P. 171. *"Get to Thy Hermitage!":* ibid., p. 167.

P. 171. *"The woods are easier":* ibid., p. 143.

P. 171. *"Dear Lord above":* ibid., 167.

P. 171. *his sister Caroline:* Kerouac's sister Caroline, or "Nin," as she was known in the family, was three years Jack's senior, born in 1918. In 1945, Caroline married Paul Blake, an electrical engineer. During the 1950s, Jack often stayed with the Blakes in their homes in North Carolina and Florida.

P. 171. *"Twin Tree Grove":* For a description of Kerouac's meditation grove, as well as his meditation practices there, see *Some of the Dharma,* pp. 253–331.

P. 172. *"got sick first day":* Kerouac to Ginsberg, August 7, 1955. Kerouac, *Selected Letters, 1940–1956,* p. 505.

P. 172. *Listening to Gary and Phil:* Snyder interview, December 6, 2000.

P. 172. *"Who can leap the world's ties":* Gary Snyder, *Riprap & Cold Mountain Poems,* p. 44.

P. 173. *He had ridden:* Jack Kerouac, in "On the Road Again," *The New Yorker,* June 22–29, 1998. "February 6, 1949. Portland to Butte."

P. 173. *"commemorated in . . . The Dharma Bums:* Kerouac, *The Dharma Bums,* pp. 35–94. Also see Gary Snyder's poems, "Late October Camping in the Sawtooths" in *Left Out in the Rain,* and "On Climbing the Sierra Matterhorn Again After Thirty-one Years" in *The Gary Snyder Reader.*

P. 173. *"our rock dhyana":* Jack Kerouac to Gary Snyder, February 23, 1959. Kerouac, *Selected Letters, 1957–1969,* p. 186. "Dhyana" is a Sanskrit word for meditation, roughly equivalent to the Chinese "Ch'an" and Japanese "Zen."

P. 173. *"Jean-Louis Kerouac, a great Hero":* Gary Snyder, unpublished journal, October 22, 1955, used by permission of Gary Snyder. "—with Jean-Louis Kerouac; camped under a huge out-leaning boulder; a great pitch-log burning. John Montgomery camped alone, somewhere below."

P. 173. *October Chill:* Snyder to Kerouac, November 1,

1960, Kerouac Estate. "I always think of our trip to the Matterhorn on Cold Frosty October nights."

P. 173. *"We were at a girl's house"*: Kerouac, *Some of the Dharma*, p. 346.

P. 174. *"Good old silence at last"*: ibid., p. 346.

P. 174. *"an earlier Buddhist religious argument"*: Carolyn Cassady, *Off the Road: My Life with Cassady, Kerouac, and Ginsberg*, pp. 234–35.

P. 174. *"people went to Skid Row"*: Kerouac, *Some of the Dharma*, p. 346.

P. 174. *"San Francisco Blues"*: Kerouac, *Book of Blues*, p. 81.

P. 174. *"my first intimation"*: Kerouac, *Some of the Dharma*, p. 38. "Tonight March 25 1954 in San Francisco I attained suddenly the Diamond Samadhi which is the buzz of my intrinsic hearing, the pure liquid accommodating vibrating sea-hush stuff that receives imprints of transitory sounds and g-l-u-r-s them till finally I began to hear as on cocaine the roar of many things—I thought up till now that there would never be an actual breakthrough to the other world to support my belief."

Such aural phenomena—as well as episodes involving the other senses—are common to the practice of zazen and are known as *mayko*. In Philip Kapleau's *Three Pillars of Zen*, pp. 43–44, the roshi Hakuun Yasutani explains *makyo* experiences, saying, "They are temporary mental states which arise during zazen when our ability to concentrate has developed to a certain point and our practice is beginning to ripen. Such visions are certainly a sign that you are at a crucial point in your sitting, and that if you exert yourself to the utmost, you can surely experience kensho. . . . Whenever *makyo* appear, simply ignore them and continue sitting wholeheartedly."

P. 175. *"The beauty of the Cameo"*: Kerouac, *Some of the Dharma*, p. 346.

P. 175. *suicide of Natalie Jackson*: For an explanation of the circumstances leading up to the death of Natalie Jackson, see Carolyn Cassady, *Off the Road: My Years with Cassady, Kerouac, and Ginsberg*, pp. 258–76. Kerouac fictionalized Natalie as "Rosie Buchanan" in *The Dharma Bums*.

P. 175. *"I tried to tell her"*: Kerouac, *Some of the Dharma*, p. 346.

P. 175. *"Had a horrible dream"*: ibid., p. 352.

P. 175. *"You come to me"*: Philip Whalen, "Unfinished," *On Bear's Head*, p. 45.

P. 176. *"Granite sierras"*: Gary Snyder, "The Rainy Season," *Left Out in the Rain*, pp. 50–51.

CHAPTER 8: BHIKKU HOSTEL

P. 177. *"Jack Kerouac in smoky flame"*: Gary Snyder, "Ballad of Rolling Heads," *Left Out in the Rain*, p. 192.

P. 177. *In mid-December 1955*: For a description of this cross-country trip, see Jack Kerouac, *Some of the Dharma*, pp. 363–66. For his fictive treatment of it, see Jack Kerouac, *The Dharma Bums*, pp. 116–33.

P. 177. *"book of sorrows"*: Jack Kerouac to Philip Whalen, January 16, 1956, Kerouac, *Selected Letters, 1957–1969*, p. 540.

P. 177. *guilt and grief*: Jack Kerouac to Neal Cassady, January 3, 1951. Kerouac, *Selected Letters, 1940–1956*, p. 273.

P. 177. *"The whole reason why"*: Jack Kerouac, *Visions of Gerard*, p. 112.

P. 177. *Kerouac's first creative treatment*: Kerouac to Cassady, December 28, 1950. Kerouac, *Selected Letters, 1940–1956*, p. 255.

P. 178. *"his pure and tranquil face"*: Kerouac, *Visions of Gerard*, p. 1.

P. 178. *"fast blowing sessions"*: Jack Kerouac, *Some of the Dharma*, p. 358.

P. 178. *popped some Benzedrine*: Kerouac, *Some of the Dharma*, p. 365. On December 15, 1955, Kerouac crossed the border to Mexicali to restock his drug supply for the winter in Rocky Mount. ". . . went to drugstore around to left and bought 60 codeinettas and 50 benzedrines ($3.50 in all) and put in flap and headed for Gate where I was stopped by unpleasant American guards (3 of them) and whole bag was searched but they overlooked Flap and barely touched my earlier-this-year-in-Mexico-bought goofballs . . ."

P. 178. *"continual lifework"*: ibid., p. 358.

P. 178. *first . . . Dharmic prose work*: *Tristessa*, begun in the summer of 1955 at Orizaba Street, was Kerouac's first attempt at a Buddhist prose work, but it was not completed until late 1956.

P. 178. *Gerard's story was to be:* Kerouac, *Some of the Dharma*, p. 367. "Today I begin the opening novel (chronologically) of DULUOZ LEGEND—VISIONS OF GERARD, the story of the first four years of my life, of my brother who is my true self as Bodhisattva Hero—the mournful idealistic little boy in the gloomy rain—If I can't handle this I'm lost—Took Benny for kickoff—Unpackt all my notebooks and manuscripts and ranged them on the Workdesk."

P. 178. *"Brotherhood Ideal":* Kerouac, *Visions of Gerard*, p. 7.

P. 178. *sometimes writing . . . 3,000 words per hour:* Kerouac, *Some of the Dharma*, p. 374.

P. 178. *prodigious correspondence:* See Kerouac, *Selected Letters, 1940–1956*, pp. 535–80, for letters written during this period.

P. 179. *To Jack, at such peaks:* See Kerouac, *Some of the Dharma*, pp. 367–80 for an indication of Kerouac's frame of mind during this period.

P. 179. *applying to the Forest Service:* Kerouac to Whalen, January 5, 1956. Kerouac, *Selected Letters, 1940–1956*, p. 535. "Just wrote off my four letters to the district rangers up in Wash. applying for the fire-spotting jobs."

P. 179. *"Glad and surprised":* Kerouac to Whalen, February 7, 1956, ibid., p. 547.

P. 179. *"O boy, O boy":* Kerouac quoted in Carolyn Cassady, *Off the Road: My Life with Cassady, Kerouac, and Ginsberg*, p. 279.

P. 179. *"If I don't get a vision":* Kerouac to Lucien Carr, February 24, 1956. Kerouac, *Selected Letters, 1940–1956*, p. 564.

P. 179. *"emptiness aspect of things":* Kerouac, *Some of the Dharma*, p. 394.

P. 179. *with his Buddhist Bible propped:* See *Some of the Dharma*, pp. 391–420, for Kerouac's journal entries during this period.

P. 179. *"Prajna-paramita Wringer":* Kerouac, *Some of the Dharma*, p. 394. An example of the use of the "Wringer" is on page 392. Other examples from this period abound in Kerouac's letters to his friends. See

Kerouac to Philip Whalen on February 7, *Selected Letters, 1940–1956*, p. 548; Kerouac to Lucien Carr on February 24, *Selected Letters, 1940–1956*, p. 564; and Kerouac to Gary Snyder on March 8, *Selected Letters, 1940–1956*, pp. 569–70.

P. 181. *"Money is emptiness":* Kerouac, *Some of the Dharma*, p. 400.

P. 181. *"I know it works":* Kerouac to Snyder, March 8, 1956. Kerouac, *Selected Letters, 1940–1956*, p. 570.

P. 181. *Snyder and Ginsberg had embarked:* Allen Ginsberg, *Journals: Mid-Fifties, 1954–1958*, pp. 217–26.

P. 181. *"No reasonable doubt exists":* U.S. Department of State to Senator Richard L. Neuberger, November 10, 1955, UC Davis. "A further investigation which has been made in this case has developed that no reasonable doubt exists as to Mr. Snyder's loyalty. I shall be glad to have a passport issued to Mr. Snyder if he will forward to the Passport Office the passport fee of $9.00. . . ."

P. 181. *to learn more about Gary's:* Michael McClure, interview with the author, Oakland, California, December 9, 2000. "Allen had respect for Gary in a way that he didn't for some other people. He wanted to learn from Gary. . . . Nature, hitchhiking, the things he did in fact learn."

P. 181. *riding across the rez:* Gary Snyder to Philip Whalen, January 27, 1956, *The Gary Snyder Reader*, p. 152. ". . . a long snowy ride up 97 & through Warm Springs . . ."

P. 181. *gambling with the Wasco:* Gary Snyder, "To the Chinese Comrades," *The Back Country*, p. 113.

P. 182. *Joyce Matson, baby on hip:* Gary Snyder, telephone interview transcript, November 12, 1998.

P. 182. *"Her breasts, black-nippled":* Gary Snyder, "A Berry Feast," *The Back Country*, p. 4.

P. 182. *"[Ginsberg] is reconsidering":* Snyder to Whalen, January 27, 1956, *The Gary Snyder Reader*, p. 152.

P. 182. *"Five old ladies ran out":* Allen Ginsberg to Neal Cassady, February 7, 1956, in Gifford, ed., *As Ever*, p. 183. See also Will Baker, "Poets on the Bum," in Halper, ed., *Gary Snyder: Dimensions of a Life*, pp. 43–49, for an eyewitness account of the Parrington Hall reading.

P. 182. *Everett Massacre:* The "Everett Massacre" refers to a violent event in November 1916 on the docks of Everett, Washington, twenty-five miles north of Seattle on Puget Sound. Two hundred Wobblies from Seattle had sailed on the ferry *Verona* to march in solidarity with striking shingle weavers in Everett. The *Verona* was met at the Everett dock by two hundred vigilantes organized by local lumber companies. A gunfight ensued in which scores of men were shot. Five lumberman and perhaps a dozen Wobblies were killed. Some bodies were never recovered from the water. The *Verona* returned to Seattle, where the Wobblies were arrested en masse and charged with murder as they disembarked. Five months later all were acquitted; none of the Everett deputies were charged.

P. 182. *Those old trees:* Gary Snyder, *Myths and Texts,* p. 4. "San Francisco 2x4s were the woods around Seattle."

P. 183. *Rexroth claimed:* Kenneth Rexroth, *An Autobiographical Novel,* p. 279.

P. 183. *Swedes and Finns:* Snyder, *Myths and Texts,* p. 44.

P. 183. *"Tell the boys":* John Dos Passos, *USA: Nineteen-nineteen,* p. 401.

P. 183. *"Forming the New Society":* ibid., p. 44.

P. 183. *"Problem is":* Ginsberg, *Journals Mid-Fifties, 1954–58,* p. 220. ". . . the Wobblie Hall, the mandala of Labor, one Big Union, 'We eat for you.' Old men bleareyed & cardplaying behind counter and round table with surreal posters. Pamphlets. Soldiers of discontent—talk about the young fellers cant see ahead and we have nothing to offer."

P. 183. *"Where I cut one off":* Snyder, *Myths and Texts,* p. 7.

P. 183. *"O Karl":* ibid., p. 7.

P. 183. *dreary Communist Party hall:* Gary Snyder, interview with the author, Kitkitdizze, December 6, 2000. "Allen was trying to find a way out of continuing the involvement in his mother's Communist Party membership, and the red-diaper baby complex. He knew he wanted to be free from that. And Kenneth [Rexroth], with his political stance, his outright anti-

Stalinism, and then the nonviolent, communitarian anarchism of both Rexroth and Duncan, and then myself, coming from the Northwest with a kind of IWW anarchist position, also anti-Stalinist, provided Allen with a way to be leftist without being Stalinist. And so that was a big help to him."

P. 184. *"their bleak lone cries":* Allen Ginsberg, "Afternoon Seattle," *Reality Sandwiches,* pp. 60–61.

P. 184. *out to the Lummi Reservation:* Gary Snyder, "Lookout's Journal," *Earth House Hold,* p. 13.

P. 184. *Baxter was dressed:* Gary Snyder, "Night Highway 99," *Mountains and Rivers Without End,* p. 11.

P. 184. *Roy sat in a stuffed chair:* Details suggested from the poem "Night Highway 99."

P. 184. *"He'll never be any good":* Jim Baxter to Gary Snyder, November 13, 1955, UC Davis. "I see Roy Raymond every week. He's around but he'll never be any good again."

P. 184. *"Today in Bellingham":* Ginsberg, *Journals Mid-Fifties, 1954–58,* pp. 223–24.

P. 184. *"Impassive giant":* ibid., p. 221.

P. 185. *"All America south and east":* Snyder, "Nooksack Valley," *Riprap & Cold Mountain Poems,* p. 15.

P. 185. *"better means of Revolution":* Locke McCorkle, in Gifford and Lee, eds., *Jack's Book: An Oral Biography of Jack Kerouac,* p. 209.

P. 186. *"the Rucksack Revolution":* The "Rucksack Revolution" refers to the Snyder-based character Japhy Ryder's vision in *The Dharma Bums* of ". . . a great rucksack revolution thousands or even millions of young Americans wandering around with rucksacks, going up to mountains to pray. . . ." Part of the overall vision entailed the creation of a network of "monasteries for fellows to monastrate and meditate in . . . groups of shacks up in the Sierras or the High Cascades. . . ." In early 1956, Gary Snyder saw McCorkle's Montford Road shack as one of the first nodes in the envisioned network. For the full fictive vision of the "Rucksack Revolution," see Kerouac, *The Dharma Bums,* pp. 97–99.

P. 186. *The rent for the entire:* Locke McCorkle, telephone interview, April 15, 2001.

P. 186. *Gary felled and corded:* Details from Gary

Snyder letter to Jack Kerouac, February 22, 1956, Kerouac Estate.

P. 186. *"The cabin on my friend's place"*: Snyder to Kerouac, February 22, 1956, Kerouac Estate.

P. 186. *"any tips"*: Kerouac to Snyder, February 14, 1956. Kerouac, *Selected Letters, 1940–1956*, p. 560.

P. 186. *"Just play it straight"*: Snyder to Kerouac, February 22, 1956, Kerouac Estate.

P. 186. *Gary dug into his own journals:* ibid.

P. 186. *"Your human history"*: Kerouac to Snyder, March 8, 1956. Kerouac, *Selected Letters, 1940–1956*, p. 568.

P. 186. Compare "Greenest Kid You Ever Saw" passages in Snyder's *Earth House Hold*, p. 15, with Kerouac's *The Dharma Bums*, p. 227.

P. 188. *"Marin-An"*: Gary Snyder, E-mail to the author, September 1, 2001. "This is entirely Japanese pronunciation, no Chinese mixed in, although Ma — 'horse' — is pronounced the same in both languages. 'An' means a small Buddhist temple, actually. Not as small as a 'hojo.'"

P. 188. *"The Marin Poems"*: Gary Snyder, "Migration of Birds," typescript, UC Davis. Page includes handwritten heading, *The Marin Poems,* with "Migration of Birds" as number 1 in the projected sequence.

P. 188. *"I still remember the day"*: Snyder, *Mountains and Rivers Without End*, p. 155.

P. 188. *"I asked him"*: Snyder interview, December 6, 2000.

P. 188. *Mountains and Rivers Without End:* Snyder, *Mountains and Rivers Without End*, p. 155.

P. 189. *Visions of Gary:* Kerouac, *Some of the Dharma*, p. 360.

P. 189. *character-driven mode:* Kerouac, *Some of the Dharma*, p. 342.

P. 189. *chanting the Triple Refuge:* Kerouac, *The Dharma Bums*, p. 171.

P. 189. *"singing like a millionaire"*: ibid., p. 213.

P. 189. *and death:* Kerouac to Snyder, May 24, 1957. Kerouac, *Selected Letters, 1957–1969*, p. 38. "... those sad nights discussing death ..."

P. 191. *"Jack Kerouac outside"*: Snyder, "Migration of Birds," *Riprap & Cold Mountain Poems*, p. 17.

P. 191. *"Read, as I'm doing"*: Kerouac to Ginsberg, July 14, 1955. Kerouac, *Selected Letters, 1940–1956*, p. 498.

P. 191. *even by Philip Whalen:* Philip Whalen, in Gifford and Lee, eds., *Jack's Book: An Oral Biography of Jack Kerouac*, p. 217. "As far as I can see, honestly, his interest in Buddhism was pretty much literary. ..." Also, Whalen in David Meltzer, ed., *San Francisco Beat: Talking with the Poets*, p. 337. "I never supposed that he became a Buddhist, but he was certainly interested in the teaching. ... He had quite a lot of insight into Buddhist writings, actually."

P. 191. *"poisonous word"*: Sokei-an Sasaki, "The Harmful View of Emptiness," quoted in Mary Farkas, ed., *The Zen Eye: A Collection of Talks by Sokei-an*, p. 77. "The Buddha said that anyone who falls into this harmful view can never be saved. So the Buddhist teaches the true view of Emptiness very carefully."

P. 192. *"Hui-Neng's concept"*: D. T. Suzuki, *The Zen Doctrine of No-Mind*, p. 24.

P. 192. *hugest seaman's duffel:* Philip Lamantia, interview with the author, San Francisco, December 11, 2000. "I was at Gary's party just before his departure with this *huge* seaman's bag, about eight feet high and about this thick around [gesturing with both arms] cause he had been a seaman, and he was taking all this stuff to Japan, his books and all. ..."

P. 192. *"hooftrompling" his sleep:* Jack Kerouac, *Old Angel Midnight*, p. 17.

P. 192. *"Dostoevsky's death mask"*: Kerouac, *The Dharma Bums*, p. 208.

P. 192. *"O what a vision"*: Kerouac to Snyder, undated "May 1956." Kerouac, *Selected Letters, 1940–1956*, p. 584.

P. 193. *"his eyes real"*: Gary Snyder, "Spring Sesshin at Shokoku-ji," *Earth House Hold*, p. 47.

P. 193. *"I went around"*: Snyder to Whalen, May 23, 1956, Reed.

P. 193. *hiked Mount Atago:* Gary Snyder, "Walking the Great Ridge Omine on the Womb-Diamond Trail," *The Gary Snyder Reader*, p. 371.

P. 193. *"like a peyote dream"*: Gary Snyder, "Japan First Time Around," *Earth House Hold*, p. 34.

P. 193. *"the only superstitions":* ibid., p. 34.

P. 193. *"The center of this world":* Snyder, "Japan First Time Around," *Earth House Hold,* p. 33.

P. 194. *"There's no need":* Snyder to Whalen, May 23, 1956, Reed.

P. 194. *"You sound dangerously":* Whalen to Snyder, June 7, 1956, UC Davis.

P. 194. *"although I confess":* Snyder to Whalen, June 11, 1956, Reed.

P. 194. *Ginsberg on a sea voyage:* On June 9, 1956, Allen's mother Naomi died. A week later he shipped aboard the USNS *Pendleton* on an Arctic voyage to Northern Alaska. He returned to San Francisco briefly in September before traveling to Mexico and returning to the East Coast.

P. 194. *America's last and greatest wilderness:* David Louter, *Contested Terrain: North Cascades National Park Service Complex, An Administrative History,* p. 26. "At midcentury, despite its lack of formal wilderness classification, the North Cascades were still one of the most unknown and virtually undeveloped sections of a nation undergoing rapid population and economic growth after World War II. This growth seemed destined to consume the last expanses of American wilderness for material gain. Thus when wilderness preservationists gathered forces in the postwar era, they perceived in Washington's northern Cascades one of the country's 'most untouched primeval regions,' a sanctuary from the complicated life of modern society, 'one of the country's last and perhaps its greatest.'"

CHAPTER 9: DESOLATION ADVENTURE

P. 197. *"How the gravity of Nature":* Johann Wolfgang von Goethe, quoted in Aldous Huxley, *The Doors of Perception and Heaven and Hell,* p. 74.

P. 197. *its "heaving bulk":* Jack Kerouac, "Alone on a Mountaintop," *Lonesome Traveler,* p. 120.

P. 198. *"the moving mountain":* Jack Kerouac, *Desolation Angels,* p. 97.

P. 198. *"Now we must all get out":* Jack Kerouac, *On the Road,* p. 140.

P. 198. An early version of *On the Road* is in the Kerouac Archives in a leather bound journal entitled "Rain and Rivers."

P. 198. *Jack wrote many haiku:* Kerouac to Snyder, December 18, 1956, UC Davis.

P. 198. *fun, but "small":* Kerouac to Whalen, January 16, 1956. Kerouac, *Selected Letters, 1940–1956,* p. 542.

P. 198. *who just enjoy the passage:* Kerouac to John Clellon Holmes, May 27, 1956. Kerouac, *Selected Letters, 1940–1956,* p. 578.

P. 198. *book of a thousand haikus:* Allen Ginsberg, "The Dharma Bums Review," *Deliberate Prose: Selected Essays 1952–1995,* p. 347.

P. 198. *There are instances:* Jack Kerouac, *The Dharma Bums,* pp. 225–26. Beginning with the phrase "As I looked up the clouds assumed," on page 225, there are eight consecutive sentences that were originally written as haiku on the banks of the Skagit River outside Marblemount. Included in an unpublished December 18, 1956, letter from Jack Kerouac to Gary Snyder, UC Davis.

P. 200. *aerogram letter from Gary:* Kerouac to Snyder, December 18, 1956, UC Davis (included in letter from Allen Ginsberg). "Notebook say: 'Found letter from Gary on cookhouse table.' . . . "

P. 200. *"Keep your socks darned":* Snyder to Kerouac, June 21, 1956, Kerouac Estate.

P. 200. *mouse droppings:* Gary Snyder, "Japan First Time Around," *Earth House Hold,* p. 36. "Poking about in the abandoned monks' rooms — smell of an old unused mining cabin or logging shanty — a cupboard of bindles the boys left behind, a drawer full of letters, notebooks, seals; like magazines and coffee cups full of dust and mouseshit."

P. 200. *The monk's drum:* ibid., p. 35. "I heard the subtle steady single-beat of oldest American-Asian shamanism. The basic song." Also, Snyder to Whalen, July 22, 1956, Reed. ". . . got up at 4 every day & did zazen while the monk chanted sutras for an hour accompanying himself on a wooden drum & two bells. . . . The drum beat is just like old Warm Springs dance & gambling, & the whole sutra-chanting business has an incredible ancient prehistoric shamanism sound to it."

P. 201. *the face of a man:* ibid., p. 36.

P. 201. *horse barge behind:* Kerouac to Snyder, December 18, 1956, UC Davis.

P. 201. *the mare Mabel:* Kerouac, *The Dharma Bums,* p. 229. "... then myself on the mare Mabel ..." In his Sourdough Mountain journal for 1953, Snyder mentions Mabel as one of the four horses in his packstring. Whalen, in our 1997 interview, also recalled Mabel by name as well, in his recounting of the incident at Ross Dam, making Mabel the most chronicled horse in the Beat Generation.

P. 201. *The Desolation Trail:* Fred Beckey, *Cascade Alpine Guide: Climbing & High Routes,* vol. 3, p. 393. "The trail gains 4,400 feet in 4.8 miles from the lake to the summit lookout."

P. 201. *great sixteenth century fires:* James Agee et al., *The Fire History of Desolation Peak,* p. 47. "The southwest aspect [of Desolation] probably has the greatest representation of all possible age classes due to its history of more frequent and lower severity disturbance. ... All of these aspects have patches of 300 to 334 year old trees, protected by certain topographic features, and surrounded by post-1926 cohort."

P. 202. *new novel ... Ozone Park in the mid-1940s:* Jack Kerouac, "Golden West" Desolation Journal, July 5–10. Kerouac Estate. Also John Suiter, "Beat a Path to Kerouac Country," *The Independent/Sunday Review,* p. 77; and "Desolation Revisited: Jack Kerouac's Peak Experience," *Shambhala Sun,* p. 62.

P. 202. *"hundreds of miles":* Kerouac, *The Dharma Bums,* p. 234.

P. 204. *"names Japhy had sung":* ibid., p. 235.

P. 204. *Gary had made his brush painting:* Snyder to Kerouac, February 22, 1956. Kerouac Estate.

P. 204. *Hozomeen ... "unforgettable":* Beckey, *Cascade Alpine Guide: Climbing and High Routes,* vol. 3, p. 201. "The remarkable double peak of Hozomeen, closely E of upper Ross Lake and S of the International Boundary, is one of the classic landmarks of the North Cascades. Though not of regionally outstanding height, the solitary location, vast local relief, and steeply pitched walls of the massive and spectacular summits make the mountain unforgettable."

P. 204. *"Hozomeen, Hozomeen":* See Kerouac, *Desolation Angels,* p. 4; *The Dharma Bums,* p. 234; *Book of Blues,* p. 117; *Pomes All Sizes,* p. 163.

P. 205. *"inaccessible horn":* Beckey, *Cascade Alpine Guide: Climbing and High Routes,* vol. 3, p. 201. "Reginald A. Daly commented on 'the nearly or quite inaccessible horn' of the South Peak.'"

P. 205. *"mess of double-pointed rock":* Jack Kerouac, *Book of Blues,* p. 117.

P. 205. *"a little too much":* Kerouac, "Alone on a Mountaintop," *Lonesome Traveler,* p. 125.

P. 207. *"You realize the ghosts":* Kerouac, *Desolation Angels,* p. 79.

P. 207. *same rock as Hozomeen:* Beckey, *Cascade Alpine Guide: Climbing and High Routes,* vol. 3, p. 196. "The mountain and its surroundings consist largely of a thick sequence of highly sheared and fractured Paleozoic greenstones (the same volcanic rocks of Hozomeen Mountain)."

P. 207. *Hozomeen Terrane:* Rowland Tabor and Ralph Haugerud, *Geology of the North Cascades,* p. 28.

P. 207. *Jack is one of the highest:* Beckey, *Cascade Alpine Guide,* p. 197. "Reaburn told pioneer Glee Davis that Jack Mountain was the hardest of his Cascade Range ascents."

P. 207. *Kerouac's writing table:* Kerouac, *Desolation Angels,* p. 8.

P. 207. *"thousand football fields of snow":* ibid., p. 8.

P. 208. *his new life as a Zen trainee:* Snyder to Whalen, July 22, 1956, Reed. "One day I had to formally ask to be his [Miura's] disciple, which called forth a long speech from him about how Zen training is only hard if you think it is, & another day he cooked up a little ceremony to make me formally into a Buddhist — I had to recite the three refuges before him & the butsuden in the main temple of Rinko-in 3 times, After he and another man chanted Mahaprajnaparamita together, & then we went to visit his Master's grave (old Nanshinken) at Nanzenji."

P. 208. *"I take refuge in the Buddha":* D. T. Suzuki, trans., *Manual of Zen Buddhism,* p. 14.

P. 208. *Four Great Buddhist Vows:* Miura Isshu and

Ruth Fuller Sasaki, *The Zen Koan: Its History and Use in Rinzai Zen*, p. 36.

P. 208. *Nanshinken:* ibid., p. 40. "Nanshinken . . . in his day had the reputation of being the most severe of all the sodo roshis in Japan. Whenever he found any of us negligent in our practice, he would wield his nyoi ruthlessly, and, every O Sesshin, many of us would bear the resultant bumps on our heads. I am still deeply grateful for Nanshinken's nyoi."

P. 210. *"if enlightenment's a real thing":* Snyder to Whalen, July 22, 1956, Reed.

P. 210. *"Something will happen":* Kerouac to Snyder, March 8, 1956. Kerouac, *Selected Letters, 1940–1956,* p. 567.

P. 210. *"just devote yourselves":* D. T. Suzuki, trans., *Manual of Zen Buddhism,* p. 84. ". . . just devote yourselves to the one volume of the Vajracchedika-prajna-paramita Sutra, and you will, seeing into the nature of your being, enter upon the Prajna-samadhi. It should be known that the merit of such a person is immeasurable, as is distinctly praised in the sutras, of which I need not speak in detail."

P. 211. *mountains were their mind:* Gary Snyder, *Myths and Texts,* p. 53. "The cloud mutters/The mountains are your mind."

P. 211. *"Yes, for I'd thought":* Kerouac, *Desolation Angels,* p. 4.

P. 211. *He worked on long letters:* Jack Kerouac, "Golden West" Desolation Journal, July 22, 1956. Kerouac Estate.

P. 211. *To entertain himself:* ibid.

P. 212. *solitaire baseball game:* Kerouac, *Desolation Angels,* pp. 14–17. See also, "Kerouac's Baseball Card Game," and "Playing 'Baseball' with Kerouac," in *A Jack Kerouac Romnibus*/Archive/Sports.

P. 212. *15,000 words of the Ozone Park novel:* Jack Kerouac, "Golden West" Desolation Journal, July 15, 1956. Kerouac Estate. See also Suiter, "Beat a Path to Kerouac Country," p. 77; and "Desolation Revisited: Jack Kerouac's Peak Experience," p. 62.

P. 212. *added to "The Martin Family":* Jack Kerouac, "Golden West" Desolation Journal, undated early August 1956, Kerouac Estate. See also Suiter, "Beat a Path to Kerouac Country," p. 77; and "Desolation Revisited: Jack Kerouac's Peak Experience," p. 65.

P. 212. *"Desolation Adventure":* Kerouac, "Golden West" Desolation Journal, August 10, 1956. See also Suiter, "Beat a Path to Kerouac Country,, p. 77; and "Desolation Revisited: Jack Kerouac's Peak Experience," p. 65.

P. 212. *"written up there in boredom":* Kerouac to Whalen, January 10, 1965. *Kerouac, Selected Letters, 1957–1969,* p. 391.

P. 212. *"little Samhadi":* Jack Kerouac, *Some of the Dharma,* p. 342.

P. 214. *"transliteration":* Kerouac to Snyder, March 8, 1956. Kerouac, *Selected Letters, 1940–1956,* p. 567. "I'm busy translating the Diamond Sutra from the English-of-the-Translators to an English to be understood by ordinary people. . . . For instance, I think 'imaginary judgment' will be a good translation of 'arbitrary conception,' which is such a tough phrase, even I couldn't understand it with all my philological considerings. . . . Dharma would be 'truth law,' Nirvana, 'Blown-out-ness'. . . Tathata, 'That-Which-Every-thing-Is' and Tathagata 'Attainer-to-That-Which Everything-Is'. . . Bodhisattva-Mahasattvas, 'Beings of Great Wisdom'. . . ."

P. 214. *sometimes ponderous translations:* The English translation of the Diamond Sutra in *A Buddhist Bible* was done by Dwight Goddard and the Chinese scholar Bhikshu Wai-tao in 1935. It was based on the Sanskrit-to-Chinese translation by Kumarajiva in 412 A.D. D. T. Suzuki's English translation of the sutra in *Manual of Zen Buddhism* was also based on Kumarajiva's version.

P. 214. *promise of future merit:* Dwight Goddard, ed., "The Diamond Sutra," *A Buddhist Bible,* p. 89. "If any good and pious disciple, man or woman, for the sake of charity has been sacrificing his or her life for generation after generation as many as the grains of sand in the three thousand great universes, and another disciple has been simply studying and observing even one stanza of this Scripture and explaining it to others, his blessing and merit will be far greater."

P. 214. *"The Diamond Vow of God's Wisdom":* "The

Diamond Vow of God's Wisdom" is from *A Jack Kerouac Romnibus*/Archive; "The Diamond Cutter of the Wise Vow" is from *Desolation Angels*, p. 94; "The Diamondcutter of Ideal Wisdom" is from Kerouac to Snyder, March 8, 1956, *Selected Letters, 1957–1969*, p. 567.

P. 214. *He planned . . . hand-lettered version:* Kerouac to Snyder, March 8, 1956. Kerouac, *Selected Letters, 1940–1956*, p. 567. "I bought a little 5&10 black bindbook and on the tiny pages have typed out the Diamond Sutra using above 'translations' and divided the reading-chore into seven days, that is, Monday Sila Kindness, Sunday Dana Charity, etc. to Saturday Samadhi Ecstasy (adding that 7th invisible paramita). . . . The Diamondcutter of Ideal Wisdom . . . a splendid little Book of Prayers to fit right in the flap of my rucksack instead of that vast arbitrary Goddard Bible. . . . "

P. 214. *his Desolation transliteration:* Jack Kerouac, "Golden West" Desolation Journal, August 25, 1956. *A Jack Kerouac Romnibus*/Archive/Buddhism/ "Notebook #11." "THE DIAMONDCUTTER OF PERFECT KNOWING: A TRANSLITERATION FROM THE ENGLISH AND SANSKRIT Divided for Daily Reading by John Kerouac."

P. 214. *"poems about hearts":* Kerouac, *Desolation Angels*, p. 68.

P. 214. *"too bored here to write":* Jack Kerouac, "Golden West" Desolation journal, August 20, 1956.

P. 215. *"One thing's sure":* ibid., undated August, 1956. See also Suiter, "Beat a Path to Kerouac Country," p. 77; and "Desolation Revisited: Jack Kerouac's Peak Experience," p. 62.

P. 215. *"Glacier Creek":* Henry Custer, *Report of Reconnaissances*, p. 36.

P. 215. *the Challenger Glacier:* ibid., p. 35. "We found a good camp near the banks of a creek in an open forest. Opposite us is the magnificent glaciers. Below it, we see numerous cascades hundreds of feet high, sending their dust-like waters over the rocky precipitous cliffs of the adjacent Mts, all intent to increase the volume of the creek near us."

P. 215. *"Wila-Kin-ghasist":* ibid., p. 33. "Nothing ever seen before could compare to the matchless grandeur of this feature in nature. All the glaciers in the surrounding mountains to the East of us — and there are many of them — vanish before it into insignificance in comparison with this colossus of glaciers. Imagine the Niagara Fall tens of times magnified in height and size, and this vast sheet of falling water instantly crystallized and rendered permanently solid, and you have a somewhat adequate idea of the immensity of this natural phenomena."

P. 215. *noted the "desolate" character:* ibid., p. 44. "The Country has a dry desolate look . . . "

P. 215. *The fire of 1926:* James Agee et al., *The Fire History of Desolation Peak*, p. 45. "The 1926 fire is described as starting in the area of Big Beaver Creek and moving north and east towards Desolation Peak, where it stopped. The fire burned from July 4 until late in October, with several periods of rapid spread. In the area of Desolation Peak, it was reported to have moved five miles in 15 minutes, which would be a spread rate of 20 mph. This spread rate is too high to be believable; the fire did chase crews from the vicinity, however, and probably was spotting up Desolation as it burned upslope."

P. 217. *big burns that had shaped:* ibid., p. 1. "Desolation Peak may have received its name in this century for its burned-over landscape, but that landscape has dynamically evolved with fire for eons."

P. 217. *On average, a fire:* ibid., p. 72. "Natural fires have been common in the past and fairly frequent if fire presence within this study area is a criterion. Roughly every 14 years a fire has occurred on Desolation Peak for the last four hundred years."

P. 217. *"strand of electricity":* Kerouac, *Desolation Angels*, p. 43.

P. 218. *Jack, uninvolved:* ibid., pp. 53–54. In *Desolation Angels*, Kerouac describes himself as disinterestedly listening to the suppression efforts unfolding over his radio, but like Gary before him he also scribbled copious notes of what he was hearing over the radio for later literary uses. His descriptions of the fire fighting, as heard over his squawking Packmaster radio, still bristle with urgency fifty years after the event.

P. 218. *"being forestry careerists":* ibid., p. 54.

P. 218. *"Forestry Bodhisattvas"*: Jack Kerouac, "Golden West" Desolation notebook.

P. 218. *"What American loses"*: Kerouac, *Desolation Angels*, pp. 48–49.

P. 218. *"front for the lumber interests"*: ibid., p. 48.

P. 218. *"sharp, like a sharp knife"*: G. P. V. and Helen B. Akrigg, *British Columbia Place Names*, p. 135. "Miss Annie York of Spuzzum, who speaks the Lower Thompson Indian language, gives the meaning of Hozomeen as 'sharp, like a sharp knife.'" The place name is anglicized from the Interior Salish language.

P. 218. *name may have originally derived*: Robert R. Mierendorf, E-mail to the author, May 18, 2001. "Regarding your comment that the etymology of the word goes back to the knives and blades, etc., that is what I tried to convey in my 1993 chert procurement report, where I acknowledge that the meaning of the word also embodies the entire long tradition of the use of this material for tools that we can trace archeologically for at least 8,000 years."

P. 218. *ancient people had been quarrying*: Mierendorf et al., *An Archeological Site Survey*, p. 361. Bits of tools and weapons made of chert quarried on the Upper Skagit have been found in archeological sites along Puget Sound, from the lower Fraser River south to Seattle, and at the northern end of Lake Chelan, indicating an extensive regional trade in Hozomeen chert. "Exotic" materials, that is, projectile points, etc. from outside the area, have been found along the shores of present day Ross Lake — obsidian and other "glassy volcanics" from as far away as Sugar Mountain in Northern California and the Upper Similkameen River in British Columbia are proof of an extensive regional trade network of which the Upper Skagit was a major node . . . going back eight thousand years.

P. 220. *one of the largest. . . old chert quarries*: ibid., p. 35. "The site is a large chert quarry that appears to have been used more or less continuously for the last 7,600 years, with the most intensive use occurring between 3,500 and 5,000 years ago." Ages are based on thirteen radiocarbon estimates. The 7,600-year date given is the raw radiocarbon dating, which translates to 8,400 calendar years.

P. 220. *first chert quarries were not discovered*: ibid., p. 24. The Desolation Chert Quarry was test excavated between 1987 and 1989.

P. 220. *"I don't think the Skagit Indians ever penetrated"*: Snyder to Kerouac, February 22, 1956.

P. 220. *"Desolation was aptly named"*: Jack Francis, telephone interview transcript, October 6, 1998.

P. 220. *"with the mountains steeped"*: Jack Kerouac, "If I Were Wealthy," *Atop an Underwood*, p. 81.

P. 220. *"How sad my . . . face"*: Kerouac, *Desolation Angels*, p. 70.

P. 220. *"I think that no experience I have"*: Henry David Thoreau, Journal II, pp. 306–7.

P. 221. *"My hair was long"*: Kerouac, *The Dharma Bums*, p. 242.

P. 221. *If Dostoevsky could write*: Dostoevsky turned forty in 1861. His greatest novels were written after the age of forty-four: *Notes from Underground* (1864); *Crime and Punishment* (1865–66); *The Gambler* (1866); *The Idiot* (1869); *The Possessed* (1871). *The Brothers Karamazov* was written when Dostoevsky was nearly sixty and published the year before he died.

P. 221. *"Where the top of this arch"*: Dante Alighieri, *The Convivo*: IV, xxiii, p. 216.

P. 221. *"Now I'll go on, into truly mighty work"*: Jack Kerouac, "Golden West" Desolation Journal, September 1, 1956. See also Suiter, "Desolation Revisited: Jack Kerouac's Peak Experience," p. 62; and "Beat a Path to Kerouac Country," p. 77.

P. 223. *"ecstasy of mind"*: Kerouac to Snyder, June 24, 1957, Reed. Kerouac, *Selected Letters, 1957–1969*, p. 46.

P. 223. *"I'd rather have drugs"*: Jack Kerouac, "Golden West" Desolation Journal, late August 1956.

P. 223. *"the warm arms of Esperanza"*: ibid., July 23, 1956. *A Jack Kerouac Romnibus*/Archive/Travel/ "Dharma Desolation notebook, 1956." "Going to Mexico City to the warm arms of Esperanza — wrote thousands of words well." See also, Jack Kerouac, *Tristessa*, p. 63. ". . . went north to Desolation Peak and spent a summer surling in the Wilderness, eating and sleeping alone — said, 'Soon I go back, to the warm arms of Tristessa' —"

P. 223. *"Enough of rocks"*: Kerouac, *Desolation Angels,* p. 69.

P. 223. *"Yippiee I yelled"*: Kerouac, "Golden West" Desolation Journal, August 25, 1956. See also Suiter, "Beat a Path to Kerouac Country," p. 77 and "Desolation Revisited: Jack Kerouac's Peak Experience," p. 62.

P. 223. *huckleberries were ripening:* In his "Golden West" Desolation notebook, Kerouac records picking blueberries on August 27. The report of Henry Custer, who was in the vicinity of Desolation Peak during the same time of month ninety-seven years before, also mentions the profusion of ripe berries. See Custer, *Report of Reconnaissances,* p.52. "August 25 [1859] . . . the mountainsides were covered with extensive patches of Hookle berries, the largest and finest of peculiar brownish blue color that could be seen. They are of excellent flavor. To withstand the temptation of a large tract literally covered with these delicious berries goes beyond the moral strength of a white man, much less that of an Indian. To halt and eat and to eat and halt is all you can do under these circumstances; and if, during an hour or two, you can manage to bring yourself and particularly your Indians through one of these belts where these berries grow exclusively, you may say you have done well . . . "Washington country may be properly called the country of berries, because nowhere I saw such endless number of different species of berries, each species again with many different varieties. . . ."

P. 223. *"a mile-long patch"*: Kerouac, *The Dharma Bums,* p. 243.

P. 223. *birds fluttering over it:* Kerouac, "Golden West" Desolation Journal, September 5, 1956. *A Jack Kerouac Romnibus*/Archive/Buddhism/"Notebook, Desolation Peak, 1956." "Birds fly over the shack rejoicing . . . "

P. 224. *"Avalokitesvra the Bear"*: Kerouac, *Desolation Angels,* p. 62. Also *The Dharma Bums,* p. 242, and "Alone on a Mountaintop," *Lonesome Traveler,* pp. 130–31.

P. 224. *Thoreau said that:* Henry David Thoreau, *Walden,* p. 427. "I have never felt lonesome, or in the least oppressed by a sense of solitude, but once, and that was a few weeks after I came to the woods, when, for an hour, I doubted if the near neighborhood of man was not essential to a serene and healthy life. To be alone was something unpleasant. But I was at the same time conscious of a slight insanity in my mood, and seemed to foresee my recovery."

P. 224. *mind was "in rags"*: Kerouac, *Desolation Angels,* p. 68.

P. 224. *"ruined Kerouac as a writer"*: Andrew O'Hagan, "The Road to Desolation," BBC documentary film, September *1997.*

P. 224. *"whistled at the moon"*: Miura Isshu and Ruth Fuller Sasaki, *The Zen Koan: Its History and Use in Rinzai Zen,* p. 119. "On top of the solitary peak / he whistles at the moon and sleeps in the clouds."

P. 225. *"Desolation Adventure has power"*: Kerouac, "Golden West" Desolation Journal, September 5, 1956. *A Jack Kerouac Romnibus*/Archive/Buddhism/"Notebook, Desolation Peak, 1956."

P. 225. *Virya:* Virya is also sometimes translated as "energy," "will power," "exertion." It is identical with the sixth of the "eightfold paths"—Perfect Effort.

P. 225. *"wherever this Scripture"*: Dwight Goddard, ed., "The Diamond Sutra," *A Buddhist Bible,* p. 97.

P. 225. *"Such places," the Diamondcutter prophesied:* ibid., p. 97.

P. 225. *"Such places (where the scripture is observed)"*: Kerouac, "Golden West" Desolation Journal, September 5, 1956. *A Jack Kerouac Romnibus*/Archive/Buddhism/"Notebook, Desolation Peak, 1956." See also Suiter, "Beat a Path to Kerouac Country," p. 77 and "Desolation Revisited: Jack Kerouac's Peak Experience," p. 65.

P. 226. *"Tomorrow morning at 11 AM"*: Kerouac, "Golden West" Desolation Journal, September 5, 1956. *A Jack Kerouac Romnibus*/Archive/Buddhism/"Notebook, Desolation Peak, 1956."

CHAPTER 10: A DECENT MAD NARRATIVE

P. 227. *Gilbert Millstein's New York Times review:* Gilbert Millstein, "Books of the Times," *New York Times,* September 5, 1957. "*On the Road* is the most beautifully executed, the clearest and the most important utterance yet made by the generation Kerouac himself named years ago as 'beat,' and whose principal avatar he is. Just as, more than any other novel of the Twenties, *The Sun Also Rises* came to be regarded as the testament of the 'Lost Generation,' so it seems certain that *On the Road* will come to be known as that of the 'Beat Generation.'"

P. 227. *"It was all very thrilling"*: Joyce Johnson, *Minor Characters*, p. 185.

P. 228. *"a new bathtub and refrigerator"*: Jack Kerouac, "Golden West" Desolation Journal, August 8, 1956, Kerouac Estate. See also Suiter, "Beat a Path to Kerouac Country," p. 77 and "Desolation Revisited: Jack Kerouac's Peak Experience," p. 65.

P. 228. *half dozen manuscripts*: In late 1957 Kerouac had completed manuscripts with his agent Sterling Lord for the following works: *Doctor Sax, Visions of Gerard, Maggie Cassidy, Tristessa, Mexico City Blues*. *The Subterraneans* had been sold to Grove Press and was scheduled for March 1958 publication.

P. 228. *"After ROAD comes out"*: Kerouac to Malcolm Cowley, March 8, 1957. Kerouac, *Selected Letters, 1957–1969*, p. 12.

P. 228. *He had been itching*: Jack Kerouac, *Some of the Dharma*, p. 360. Kerouac first mentions plans for a VISIONS OF GARY in his journal for December 14, 1955.

P. 228. *"lying in bed contemplating"*: Kerouac to Snyder, April 3, 1957. Kerouac, *Selected Letters, 1957–1969*, p. 24.

P. 228. *sometimes as "Dharma Bums"*: By the summer of 1957, Kerouac had envisioned how the San Francisco scenes in *The Dharma Bums* would commence. See Kerouac to Philip Whalen, undated, summer 1957, Reed.

P. 228. *"Avalokitesvara"*: Kerouac to Sterling Lord, May 31, 1957. Kerouac, *Selected Letters, 1957–1969*, p. 38. "Meanwhile, I've just started and am working furiously on a new narrative adventure (I don't write 'novels' as you know), the title: AVALOKITESVARA, which is a picaresque account of how I discovered Buddha and what happened in my experiences, often

hilarious, as an American Dharma Bum (or bhikku, wandering religious teacher). . . . It has all kinds of hitchhiking scenes, girls, new characters I've never written about (such as Gary Snyder who wanders in the mountains alone for months and comes down to, among other things, organize Tibetan yabyum orgies with the girls), railroads, wine, dialog, the story of the San Francisco poetry movement which began one drunken night, my meditations in the North Carolina woods, all written in a wild undisciplined way which is consistent with the spirit of the freedom of Tao (the Chinese Way). . . . "

P. 228. *"bogged down in metaphysical"*: Kerouac to Allen Ginsberg, June 7, 1957. Kerouac, *Selected Letters, 1957–1969*, pp. 41–42.

P. 229. *"he [Gary] is really the only character"*: Kerouac to Philip Whalen, undated, Summer 1957, Reed.

P. 229. *rather slapstick effort*: Jack Kerouac, *Desolation Angels*, pp. 389–409.

P. 229. *Jack and Memere lived in the rear apartment*: Bob Kealing, "The Road to Kerouac."

P. 229. *"with a good firm fast touch"*: Kerouac to Joyce Johnson, November 1, 1957. *Door Wide Open*, p. 90. "I think I will buy it cause it's a bitch, with a good firm fast touch, nice small keys, nice quiet sound . . . on this machine I can swing and swing and swing. I think I can go 95 words a minute on this one. . . ."

P. 229. *when writing On the Road*: Kerouac promoted the myth that *On the Road* was written on a continuous scroll during a spontaneous three-week burst in April of 1951, but subsequent research in his archives by several authors has shown that the book was begun in 1948, and that many preliminary outlines and chapter drafts contributed to his inspired April 1951 "scroll" session.

P. 229. *On November 26*: Jack Kerouac, *A Jack Kerouac Romnibus*/Archive/Writing & Writers/ "Notebook entry, November 26, 1957."

P. 229. *Kerouac spread out his spiral notebooks*: For an insight into Kerouac's compositional method in *The Dharma Bums*, compare books Nine and Ten of *Some of the Dharma*—Kerouac's dharma journal—with chapters 19–21 of *The Dharma Bums*.

P. 229. *Jack used their actual names:* ibid., Archive/Writing & Writers/"Jack's notebook #9, December 7–8, 1957." Kerouac substituted pseudonyms for his main characters immediately after finishing his first draft scroll of *The Dharma Bums* on December 8, 1957. His journal for that date gives a character key for the five main characters in the book under "Names for DHARMA BUMS." In the published edition of *The Dharma Bums,* an apparent copyediting error left the name "Gary" in the text in a single instance, at the end of Chapter 23, p. 161.

P. 231. *"Started Dharma Bums":* Kerouac, *A Jack Kerouac Romnibus*/Archive/Writing & Writers/"Notebook entry, November 26, 1957."

P. 231. *"splendid chapter about Rocky Mount":* ibid., "Notebook entry, December 2, 1957."

P. 231. *read Don Quixote:* ibid. Kerouac, who saw his task as the writing of an American picaresque, read *Don Quixote* concurrently with the composition of *The Dharma Bums,* and there are several tangential references to Cervantes and Quixote throughout the text. See also *A Jack Kerouac Romnibus*/Archive/Writing & Writers/"Notebook entry, November 26, 1957." "Everything that ever lived is Don Quixote, since existence itself is an illusion. . . . Think of all the snide critics who laugh at Quixote and Quixotism!"

P. 231. *Jackie Wilson:* Kerouac, *A Jack Kerouac Romnibus*/Archive/Writing & Writers/"Notebook entry, December 2, 1957." "Jackie Wilson great new blues singer."

P. 231. *"Wrote a little Lucien Midnight":* ibid., "Notebook entries, December 4–5, 1957."

P. 233. *"Long day shooting baskets":* ibid.

P. 233. *"Duluoz seems to be moving":* Kerouac, *Selected Letters, 1957–1969,* pp. 10–11.

P. 233. *writer had to believe:* Jack Kerouac, "Belief & Technique for Modern Prose," in Ann Charters, ed., *The Portable Beat Reader,* p. 59.

P. 233. *Snyder described the Skagit:* Snyder to Kerouac, February 22, 1956, Kerouac Estate.

P. 233. *Jack drew on the dream:* Kerouac to Snyder, undated, "May 1956." Kerouac, *Selected Letters, 1940–1956,* p. 584.

P. 233. *"And suddenly it seemed I saw":* Kerouac, *The Dharma Bums,* pp. 243–44.

P. 233. *"finally completing. . . December 7":* Kerouac, *A Jack Kerouac Romnibus*/Archive/Writing & Writers/ "Jack's notebook #9, December 7–8, 1957." "Finished DHARMA BUMS at midnight."

P. 234. *"'Japhy,' I said":* Kerouac, *The Dharma Bums,* p. 244.

P. 234. *"I'm glad to just have it all":* Kerouac, *A Jack Kerouac Romnibus*/Archive/Writing & Writers/"Jack's notebook #9, December 7–8, 1957." The "scroll" was actually sixty feet long, composed of six ten-foot sections taped together, according to description of the typescript in Christie's auction catalog in December 2001.

P. 234. *just-launched Soviet Sputnik:* Kerouac, *A Jack Kerouac Romnibus*/Archive/Writing & Writers/ "Notebook entry, Orlando 1957." ". . . saw Sputnik II's rockets, a brown star racing northward, at 10:45 PM, called Ma — nice cold starry night no crickets Avalokitesvara night. . . ."

P. 234. *"explosive significance":* Kerouac, *A Jack Kerouac Romnibus*/Archive/Writing & Writers/"Jack's notebook #9, December 7–8, 1957." "I think DHARMA BUMS is not as dramatic as *On the Road* but it's a better book (more important) — Technically almost just as good in any case — if Viking doesn't want to publish it they'll be mistaken, + sorry later on — it packs explosive significance, + is worth its weight in gold."

P. 234. *"better than* On the Road*":* ibid.

P. 234. *"Proem, Narrative":* Allen Ginsberg, *Kaddish and Other Poems, 1958–1960.* Subtitle of poem on Contents page.

P. 234. *"sea where the heroes sail":* Gary Snyder to Will Petersen, December 22, 1957, *The Gary Snyder Reader,* p. 162.

P. 235. *"laughing covered with grease":* ibid.

P. 235. *"just floating around":* ibid.

P. 235. *"the dharma bums, my new novel":* Kerouac to Snyder, January 15, 1958. Kerouac, *Selected Letters, 1957–1969,* p. 106.

P. 235. *"Maybe this is the year":* Snyder to Kerouac, February 25, 1958, Kerouac Estate.

p. 235. *"1958 will be a great year"*: Kerouac to Whalen, January 7, 1958. Kerouac, *Selected Letters, 1957–1969*, p. 97.

p. 236. *train north to Oakland*: Gary Snyder to Will Petersen, April 22, 1958, in Jon Halper, ed., *Gary Snyder: Dimensions of a Life*, p. 88. "Ah Pete, we came through. Made it back to white clean sea-air San Francisco unrolled or unrobbed."

p. 236. *"crazy new America"*: Gary Snyder, journal entry, May 13, 1958, UC Davis.

p. 237. *"I did see indeed the scene"*: Snyder to Kerouac, April 21, 1958, Kerouac Estate.

p. 237. *The Subterraneans*: The real-life events upon which Kerouac based *The Subterraneans* took place in New York during the summer and fall of 1953, but in order to avoid possible libel suits, the setting was transposed to San Francisco.

p. 237. *"My, your name is being throwed about"*: Snyder to Kerouac, April 21, 1958, Kerouac Estate.

p. 237. *"was drunk 2 weeks ago"*: Kerouac to Whalen, undated, probably late April 1958. Kerouac, *Selected Letters, 1957–1969*, p. 123. A year later, Kerouac suspected that his San Remo attack had effected him more than he had realized at the time. See also, Kerouac to Allen Ginsberg, March 24, 1959. *Selected Letters, 1957–1969*, p. 193. "As to my recent belligerent drunkenness I just noticed today it all began last April right after that bum pounded my brain head with his big fingered fist ring . . . maybe I got brain damage, maybe once I was kind drunk, but now am brain-clogged drunk with the kindness valve clogged by injury."

p. 237. *Neal Cassady . . . arrested*: Carolyn Cassady, *Off the Road: My Life with Cassady, Kerouac, and Ginsberg*, pp. 296–320.

p. 237. *"afraid to come to Frisco"*: Kerouac to Whalen, undated, early June 1958. Kerouac, *Selected Letters, 1957–1969*, p. 129.

p. 237. *"I told Whalen"*: Kerouac to Snyder, June 19, 1958. Kerouac, *Selected Letters, 1957–1969*, p. 136.

p. 238. *"Marin-an shack was so ugly"*: Gary Snyder, journal entry May 13, 1958, UC Davis.

p. 238. *"Now tis clean & pure"*: ibid.

p. 238. *Gary put down fresh mats*: Snyder to Whalen, July 1958. *The Gary Snyder Reader*, p. 154. "I am living in the hermitage of Ma-rin now, with brand new Coleman lamp for reading light & spiffy coleman stove for quick cooking & wood stove for heat & cheer, & big cupboard full of Crystal Palace goodies like polenta, wheat flour, bulghur, rice, dates, etc. Mats on the floor & a fine black pot Shandel gave, & lots of books rescued from other people, & long crosscut saw & broadaxe, galvanized washtub & washboard, a samurai sword my sis' longshoreman boyfriend gave me, cougar hide, sleeping bag, iron teapot japonaise, meditation hall in other room with big zendo bell & clackers, a goodwill leather jacket & denim railroad man's jacket & new pair levis, new pair tennis shoes, All in order. Also this typewriter I bought for $15.00."

p. 238. *In the cabin he'd even found*: Gary Snyder, journal entry May 13, 1958, UC Davis. "[Found] letter to Jack from Gabrielle & Jack's old blue T shirts & blue-jeans, I wear one T shirt now. . . . Now reading On the Road & beautiful rolling book it is."

p. 238. *"You know, it's just fine"*: Snyder to Kerouac, dated "in the fifth month," 1958, Kerouac Estate.

p. 239. *"O there's no end"*: ibid.

p. 239. *"Don't ever get mad at me"*: Kerouac to Snyder, June 19, 1958. Kerouac, *Selected Letters, 1957–1969*, p. 135.

p. 239. *"Why not dedicate"*: Snyder to Kerouac, June 30, 1958, Kerouac Estate.

p. 239. *inserting Han Shan*: Kerouac to Snyder, July 14, 1958, UC Davis.

p. 239. *"I don't know if this"*: Whalen to Snyder, October 1, 1958, UC Davis.

p. 240. *"a beautiful book"*: Snyder to Kerouac, October 12, 1958, Kerouac Estate.

p. 240. *"I do wish Jack"*: Snyder to Whalen, October 9, 1958. *The Gary Snyder Reader*, p. 155.

p. 240. *"quite a chronicle"*: ibid.

p. 240. *"I expect by the time"*: Whalen to Snyder, undated, October 1958, UC Davis.

p. 240. *noncommittal about* The Dharma Bums: Philip Whalen, "Interview with Anne Waldman," in Donald Allen, ed., *Off the Wall: Interviews with Philip Whalen*, p. 24. "It was very interesting later to read *[The]*

Dharma Bums which was made up of a lot of scenes that I actually saw and to see his account of them and his selection and his rendering of them into language was really superb because it's not recording, it's not factual photographic reproduction of what happened but a very careful selection of certain incidents and certain persons that he could handle and make into things . . . when I first read that book I was annoyed because it seemed like what he said wasn't true, because if I had been writing about that scene it would've taken a very large volume and it would've involved very many people and very many scenes and many places and with a whole lot of different explanations of what was happening, whereas Jack was able to get it into a much neater package which was quite remarkable."

P. 240. *"Jack . . . now I've read"*: Whalen to Kerouac and Snyder, October 24, 1958, UC Davis. "Only trouble is, people will HAVE to read it in college American literature course & it will be a Classic and scare everybody & nobody will really read it *[The Subterraneans]* any more except PhD's in HUDSON REVIEW. But I mean it will survive even all that kind of baloney & will still be around, 100 years from now. . . ."

P. 240. *"We can take off"*: Kerouac, *A Jack Kerouac Romnibus*/Archive/Correspondence/"Gary Snyder, May 5, 1958."

P. 241. *"I'll see you probably"*: Kerouac to Snyder, July 14, 1958. Kerouac, *Selected Letters, 1957–1969*, p. 139.

P. 241. *"NW trip was great"*: Snyder to Kerouac, October 12, 1958, Kerouac Estate.

P. 241. *"dreadful ragged confusing"*: Gary Snyder, unpublished journal entry, October 15, 1958, UC Davis.

P. 241. *with Claude Dalenberg*: Snyder to Kerouac, October 12, 1958, Kerouac Estate.

P. 241. *"tiny zendo for a small group"*: Snyder to Whalen, October 9, 1958. *The Gary Snyder Reader*, p. 155. "I started my Zendo going last week, from 8 to 10 every Tuesday, Wednesday & Thursday evenings & people are coming in droves, & sitting very nicely & being very willing and apt pupils re the formalities of bows, entrances, exits, etc. I am really astounded at the response."

P. 241. *"Week nights people come"*: Snyder to Kerouac, October 12, 1958, Kerouac Estate.

P. 241. *Locke, Claude Dalenberg. . . :* Rick Fields, *How the Swans Came to the Lake: A Narrative History of Buddhism in America*, p. 220. ". . . a small informal *zazenkai,* a zazen group, took shape. Gary sat regularly in the evenings and he was joined by a few friends — Claude Dalenberg, who had been the janitor at the Academy of Asian Studies, the poet Lew Welch, a roommate of Snyder's and Whalen's at Reed, and Albert Saijo, who had come up from Los Angeles where he had studied with Senzaki."

P. 241. *the poet Joanne Kyger*: Gary Snyder, journal entry, June 8, 1958. "Evening went to Poetry Center reading. Various hands . . . then Coffee Gallery & Place; interesting bit with Joanne Kyger/Kryger who read at the reading — girl with a broke ankle — blonde & loony, 23-year-old; 'I want to be the best girl beat generation poet on North Beach.'"

P. 241. *Rohatsu sesshin*: Gary Snyder to Joanne Kyger, December 1, 1958, UC Davis. "Today is the beginning of Asceticism week (every December from first to the eighth is Asceticism week for Historical reasons) also known as *Rohatsu Great Sesshin* because you meditate mostly all week. Anyway, Claude, Albert Saijo, Nick the Greek, & such like local Bodhisattvas will be striving for the benefit of all beings all week long up in this poor mountain hermitage & if you would like to put your shoulder to the wheel for an evening give the East-West House a call & maybe they can arrange your transportation some night, eight until ten P.M. zazen."

P. 242. *"calm and steadily"*: Yasutani-roshi quoted in Philip Kapleau, *The Three Pillars of Zen*, p. 37.

P. 242. *"Gary would have us crashing"*: Joanne Kyger, interview with the author, Bolinas, December 4, 2000.

P. 242. *"I haven't written"*: Kerouac to Snyder, December 1, 1958. Kerouac, *Selected Letters, 1957–1969*, p. 167.

P. 242. *"a shade too self-conscious"*: Alan Watts, "Beat Zen, Square Zen, and Zen," *This Is It and Other Essays on Zen and Spiritual Experience*, p. 92.

P. 242. *"Even Susuki"*: Kerouac to Snyder, February 23, 1959. Kerouac, *Selected Letters, 1957–1969*, p. 186. For a description of Kerouac's meeting with Suzuki, see Kerouac to Philip Whalen, "early November," 1958. Kerouac, *Selected Letters, 1957–1969*, pp. 164–65.

P. 243. *"I'd be ashamed"*: Kerouac to Whalen, January 10, 1959, ibid., p. 177.

P. 243. *"nodding my head"*: Kerouac to Whalen, March 15, 1959, ibid., p. 190.

P. 243. *"Why doesn't Gary just get"*: Kerouac to Whalen, January 10, 1959, ibid., p. 177.

P. 243. *"Since Dharma Bums came out"*: Kerouac to Snyder, February 23, 1959. Kerouac, *Selected Letters, 1957–1969*, p. 186.

P. 243. *"when you look . . . in future years"*: Snyder interview, December 6, 2000. "I was annoyed by what I thought was the sloppy writing. It's too cartoonish. It crams ideas, thoughts, vocabulary together much too densely. It makes the Japhy Ryder character and a lot of the other people into cartoons — laughing, yelling, jumping around. It totally lacks subtlety, which is a sign of the haste with which he wrote it. Although there are some very sweet things about it, a genuine kind of compassionate Buddhist spirit, and a certain amount of expert intention . . . it still comes off as a really second-rate book, and it could have been better if he'd have given it more time and attention and thought . . . with what our ideas were, I mean, it could have been a good story. As it happens, people still did read it and still do read it . . . it does have energy, and it's readable, and we read it even though we know it's kind of silly."

P. 243. *"I don't understand"*: Kerouac to Snyder, February 23, 1959. Kerouac, *Selected Letters, 1957–1969*, p. 186.

P. 245. *February 21, 1959*: Gary Snyder, "Japan, 'Of All the Wild Sakura,'" *The Gary Snyder Reader*, p. 342. "Pier 9 Saturday/afternoon at 5 o'clock, the twenty-first/of February 19 hundred fifty-nine."

P. 245. *Hiyeharu-maru*: Gary Snyder to Joanne Kyger, March 8, 1959, UC Davis. "The name of this ship 'Hiyeharu-maru' means 'Spring on Mt. Hiei' I found out. (Hiei + haru, spring) HA HA. Hiei is the Tamalpais of Kyoto, with a number of ancient Buddhist temples on it; & I am probably the only person on this

ship — perhaps in all of Shinnibon Steamship Lines — who has actually been hiking on Hiei in the spring. It *is* lovely; wild azaleas all blooming."

P. 245. *"I told you I liked it"*: Snyder to Kerouac, March 10, 1959, Kerouac Estate.

P. 245. *"I've become soft"*: Kerouac to Snyder, February 23, 1959. Kerouac, *Selected Letters, 1957–1969*, p. 186.

P. 245. *"If you come here"*: Snyder to Kerouac, March 10, 1959, Kerouac Estate

P. 245. *"I guess he's done with me"*: Kerouac to Whalen, March 15, 1959. Kerouac, *Selected Letters, 1957–1969*, pp. 188–89.

P. 245. *"Hermitage in the Dust"*: Gary Snyder, "Japan, 'Of All the Wild Sakura,'" *The Gary Snyder Reader*, p. 346.

P. 245. *"This house is five miles"*: Snyder to Kerouac, June 10, 1959, Kerouac Estate.

P. 245. *"There are no Hui Neng's"*: Kerouac to Snyder, February 23, 1959. Kerouac, *Selected Letters, 1957–1969*, p. 186.

P. 245. *"snobbish aristocratic & insular"*: Snyder quoted in Will Petersen, "September Ridge," in Jon Halper, ed., *Gary Snyder: Dimensions of a Life*, p. 79.

P. 246. *temple most open*: Gary Snyder, "On Rinzai Masters and Western Students in Japan," *Wind Bell*, Fall 1969, p. 27. ". . . when Oda Roshi, the Dharma heir of Goto Roshi, became Kancho and also Roshi of the monastery of Daitoku-ji, Goto Roshi said to him, 'You should be open to foreigners,' and so Daitoku-ji became the orthodox Rinzai temple that was open to foreigners as none of the others ever were really and aren't today. Foreigners could come and sit in the monastery and then if they were still around after a year and had learned Japanese, they might be accepted as disciples of Oda Roshi."

P. 246. *"an extremely subtle man"*: Gary Snyder, "The East-West Interview," *The Gary Snyder Reader*, pp. 95–96. ". . . the way the transmission works is that you don't see *how* it works for a long time. It begins to come clear later. Oda Roshi delivered *teisho* lectures in so soft a voice nobody could hear him. Year after year, we would sit at lectures — lectures that only roshis can give, spontaneous commentaries on classical texts — and not hear what he was saying. Several years after Oda Roshi had died one of the head monks, with whom I became very close, said to me, 'You know those lectures that Oda Roshi gave that we couldn't hear? I'm beginning to hear them now.'"

P. 246. *"throwing young kids"*: Kerouac, *The Dharma Bums*, p. 13.

P. 246. *"especially gentle and quiet"*: Gary Snyder, "The East-West Interview," *The Gary Snyder Reader*, p. 95.

P. 246. *"Listen to the sound"*: Gary Snyder, journal entry April 30, 1959, *The Gary Snyder Reader*, p. 346. "And start regular sanzen interviews with Oda Sesso Roshi [Monastic roshi and Kancho of Daitokuji]. Rain at 3 A.M. teisho at 9. Koan received: hear the sound of a single hand. 'Sekishu no onjo wo kitte koyo.' —Hakuin."

This koan is sometimes referred to simply as "Sekishu." According to *The Encyclopedia of Eastern Philosophy and Religion* (p. 310), "This is the best known koan stemming from a Japanese Zen Master, Hakuin Zenji. Hakuin saw it, with the koan Mu as one of the most effective hosshin koans, i.e., as a koan particularly suitable for aid a practitioner working with it to come to a first enlightenment experience."

P. 246. *"So I get up at 3 A.M."*: Snyder to Kerouac, June 1, 1959, Kerouac Estate. See also Gary Snyder, "Three Worlds, Three Realms, Six Roads," *Mountains and Rivers Without End*, p. 29. "Getting up at four in the morning to go meet with the Old Man." See also Janwillem van de Wetering, *The Empty Mirror*, p. 57. Van de Wetering was a fellow student of Gary's at Daitokuji in 1959, and describes Gary thus: "His self-discipline was beyond reproach: even if he was running a temperature he would arrive in the morning, or at night, park his motorcycle near the gate and visit the master, trembling with physical misery."

P. 246. *"eye-openers"*: Isshu Miura and Ruth Fuller Sasaki, *The Zen Koan*, p. 44.

P. 247. *"gunning the cycle"*: Gary Snyder, journal entry May 8, 1959, *The Gary Snyder Reader*, p. 346.

P. 247. *"Dumb as a newborn"*: Snyder to Kerouac, June 1, 1959, Kerouac Estate.

P. 247. *"I sit here below Mt. Hiei"*: Gary Snyder, journal entry May 28, 1959, *The Gary Snyder Reader*, p. 348.

CHAPTER 11: FIRE ON THE MOUNTAIN

P. 249. *"You many think that in mountains"*: Dogen, "Mountains and Waters Sutra," in Kazuaki Tanahashi, ed., *Moon in a Dewdrop: Writings of Zen Master Dogen*, p. 105.

P. 249. *North Cascades National Park:* Public Law 90–544, 90th Congress, S. 1321, October 2, 1968, also known as the North Cascades Act.

P. 249. *huge, contiguous, permanently-protected:* David Louter, *Contested Terrain: North Cascades National Park Service Complex, An Administrative History,* p. 59. "The North Cascades Act created a park complex of the two-unit North Cascades National Park, which embraced nearly 505,000 acres, Ross Lake National Recreation Area of some 105,000 acres, and Lake Chelan National Recreation Area of 62,000 acres. The North Cascades Act also created the 520,000-acre Pasayten Wilderness and provided for a 10,000-acre addition to the Glacier Peak Wilderness. Altogether, the act set aside some 1.2 million acres of wild alpine country."

P. 250. *married Masa Uehara:* Hisao Kanaseki, "An Easy Rider at Yase," in Jon Halper, ed., *Gary Snyder: Dimensions of a Life,* p. 75. "Masa Uehara . . . the brightest and most vivacious girl in all the English Department."

P. 250. *"push of his life"*: Gary Snyder, "On the Road with D. T. Suzuki," in Masao Abe, ed., *A Zen Life: D. T. Suzuki Remembered,* p. 209.

P. 250. *"I got to bow my head"*: ibid.

P. 250. *"Dharma name—Chofu"*: Gary Snyder, E-mail to the author, March 17, 2001. "I received my Dharma name from my second teacher, Oda Sesso Roshi, after I had worked with him for three years. The name is *Chofu,* "Listen to the Wind."

P. 250. *"In Zen they tell you"*: Gary Snyder, E-mail to the author, November 12, 2001.

P. 250. *Sakaki's tribe:* Katsunori Yamazato, "Snyder, Sakaki, and the Tribe," in Jon Halper, ed., *Gary Snyder: Dimensions of a Life,* pp. 93–106.

p. 250. *joined the Suwanose communards:* Gary Snyder, "Suwa-No-Se Island and the Banyan Ashram," *Earth House Hold,* pp. 137–38.

p. 251. *Gary and Masa were married:* ibid., pp. 141–42.

p. 251. *"women he'd known . . . married, lost":* Masa Uehara was Snyder's third wife. His first marriage, to Alison Gass in 1950, had lasted only seven months before they separated. They were divorced in 1953. Gary's second marriage was to Joanne Kyger, from 1960 to 1965. Gary and Masa were married for twenty-two years; they divorced in 1989. In 1991, Gary married Carole Koda.

p. 251. *Miyazawa Kenji:* Hisao Kanaseki, "An Easy Rider at Yase," in Halper, ed., *Gary Snyder: Dimensions of a Life,* p. 74. "I think literary historians in both countries should pay more attention to these translations because they were the results of the beautiful meeting of different poets from different cultures, reminding one of what happened between Poe and Baudelaire, and Li Po and Ezra Pound."

p. 251. *"the new/old name":* Gary Snyder, "Introductory Note," *Turtle Island,* p. 1. "Turtle Island — the old/new name for the continent, based on many creation myths of the people who have been living here for millennia, and reapplied by some of them to 'North America' in recent years."

p. 251. *beginning again with the plants:* Gary Snyder, *The Real Work,* p. 69. "We haven't discovered North America yet. People live on it without knowing what it is or where they are. They live on it literally like invaders. You know whether or not a person knows where he is by whether or not he knows the plants. By whether or not he knows what the soils and waters do. Now that is so fundamental and basic, and so true that it's easy to overlook."

p. 251. *Swami Kryananda:* Yogic name of J. Donald Walters, founder of the Ananda Community, an ashram adjacent to Snyder's Kitkitdizze homestead on San Juan Ridge. Gary Snyder, E-mail to the author, November 24, 2001. "Partners in Bald Mountain Association were Dick Baker, Allen Ginsberg, and J. Donald Walters."

p. 251. *eventually establish a homestead:* Gary Snyder,

"Kitkitdizze: A Node in the Net," *A Place in Space,* p. 253. "Once, while I was on a visit to California, some friends suggested that I join them in buying mountain land. I put down the money for a twenty-five acre share of the hundred acres and returned to Japan. In 1969, back for good in California, we drove out to the land and made a family decision to put our life there."

p. 252. *settled in Muir Woods:* Gary Snyder, E-mail to the author, March 17, 2001. "I was doing a lot of readings to save up money to build our place, a fair amount of environmental activist meetings and talks in the Bay Area, leading some zazen sessions, and taking care of my family."

p. 253. *"I'm still writing":* Philip Whalen, "Author's Note," *On Bear's Head,* p. vii. See also Whalen to Snyder, May 17, 1969, UC Davis. "ON BEAR'S HEAD has arrived, & it looks very strange to me — totally silly & vacuous babbling."

p. 253. *"homesick" for Kyoto:* Philip Whalen, in David Meltzer, ed., *San Francisco Beat: Talking with the Poets,* p. 329. "I came back here to work on the publication of *On Bear's Head* because I didn't want to do it by overseas mail. That was a mistake, because it wasn't very long before I was homesick for Kyoto."

p. 253. *"No matter how late":* ibid., p. 329. "Doing it every morning at my place, no matter what. As Issan used to say, 'No matter how late, no matter how drunk, get up and do it.'"

p. 253. *Noh song along the Kamo:* Philip Whalen, "White River Ode," *Overtime,* p. 147. "I hear one singing a No song as he walks beside the river . . . "

p. 254. *had also lived in Kyoto:* Philip Whalen, "White River Ode," *Overtime,* p. 147. "Basho and Murasaki, Seami and Buson/All used to live in this town . . . "

p. 254. *"It's wonderful to be there":* Whalen, in Meltzer, ed., *San Francisco Beat: Talking with the Poets,* p. 328.

p. 254. *great deal of goody:* Philip Whalen, "Interview with Aram Saroyan," in Allen, ed., *Off the Wall: Interviews with Philip Whalen,* p. 49.

p. 254. *did a lot of writing:* Whalen, in Meltzer, ed., *San Francisco Beat: Talking with the Poets,* p. 329.

p. 254. *"When Philip Whalen, in his red whiskers":*

Kenneth Rexroth, "The Authentic Joy of Philip Whalen," *With Eye and Ear*, pp. 210–12.

P. 254. *"I'm fat, dejected"*: Kerouac to Snyder, undated, probably early February, 1960. Kerouac, *Selected Letters, 1957–1969*, p. 235. Editor Ann Charters supposes that this letter was written in "early December 1959," but Kerouac is clearly responding in it to items in Snyder's January 20, 1960 letter.

P. 254. *"I must get a cabin"*: ibid.

P. 254. *"cabin in the hills is what you need"*: Snyder to Kerouac, April 27, 1960, Kerouac Estate.

P. 255. *"This coast crying out"*: Robinson Jeffers, "Apology for Bad Dreams," in Tim Hunt, ed., *The Collected Poetry of Robinson Jeffers: Vol. 1, 1920–28*, p. 209.

P. 255. *"Peace mechanisms"*: Jack Kerouac, *Big Sur*, p. 18.

P. 255. *nervous breakdown or . . . satori*: Kerouac to Whalen, mid-September, 1960. Kerouac, *Selected Letters, 1957–1969*, p. 265.

P. 255. *never knew satori*: Kerouac to Snyder, September 20, 1960, UC Davis.

P. 255. *"Jack's Zen"*: Kerouac to Whalen, February 7, 1963. Kerouac, *A Jack Kerouac Romnibus*/Archive/Correspondence/Philip Whalen.

P. 255. *the Highlands*: Paul Marion, editor of Kerouac's *Atop an Underwood: Early Stories and Other Writings*, and a lifelong Lowell resident, writes: "Back in 1967 that would have been a toney area to move to, and Stella would have been mindful of that, given that she was a person who had lived on the border of Highlands (Lower Highlands), the Acre, and Pawtucketville."

P. 257. *Thoreau as literary "neighbor"*: Jack Kerouac, *Vanity of Duluoz*, p. 35. "Henry David Thoreau, a neighbor of mine at Walden Pond near Concord, trees of which I can see on clear days from this present upstairs bedroom where I'm writing this *Vanity of Duluoz*."

P. 257. *"Who's going to come out"*: Kerouac, *Vanity of Duluoz*, p. 263.

P. 257. *"dead of a gastric hemorrhage"*: John Suiter, "End of the Road for Kerouac," *Berkeley Barb*, October 23, 1969.

P. 257. *"I wonder which one"*: Jack Kerouac, *The Dharma Bums*, p. 213.

P. 257. *"It was very sad"*: Gary Snyder, interview with the author, Kitkitdizze, December 6, 2000.

P. 257. *"When I think of Jack"*: Snyder interview, December 6, 2000.

P. 258. *Photographs at the cemetery*: Ann Charters, *Beats and Company: Portrait of a Literary Generation*, pp. 121–24.

P. 259. *October to me*: Kerouac, *A Jack Kerouac Romnibus*/Archive/Personal/Letter to Myself, September 5, 1945." "My art, my god. This is King in my soul. Then there are the princes or demigods of my private religion. October is top prince of them all. October to me is more than a month, it's an ecstasy. I can reach a fuller understanding with this immense prince than with people . . ."

P. 259. *"In a previous life"*: Kerouac to Whalen, January 16, 1969. Kerouac, *Selected Letters, 1957–1969*, p. 466.

P. 259. *"Well, I can't say"*: Philip Whalen, telephone interview transcript, March 11, 1998.

P. 260. *Park Service Lookout*: With the establishment of the National Park, Desolation and Sourdough lookouts came within the administration of the Park Service. Crater Mountain and Sauk Mountain remained within Forest Service jurisdiction, Crater on the Okanogan, Sauk on the Mount Baker National Forest. The Park assumed control of the Marblemount Ranger Station.

P. 260. *"Kerouac worshipers"*: Gerry Cook, interview with the author, Marblemount, Washington, September 14, 1998.

P. 260. *"In 1970 the job they offered"*: ibid.

P. 260. *"that makes it so special"*: Maxine Franklin, interview with the author, Marblemount, Washington, September 8, 1998.

P. 261. *"Ever since I've been here"*: Cook interview, September 14, 1998.

P. 261. *"When I first read Kerouac"*: Franklin interview, September 8, 1998.

P. 263. *Glacier Peak Wilderness*: The Glacier Peak Wilderness Area had been included in the preservation system established by the Wilderness Act of 1964.

P. 263. *decree of the Secretary*: Harvey Manning, *The*

Wild Cascades, p. 115. "In his order of September 6, 1960, setting aside a 458,505 acre Glacier Peak Wilderness Area, the Secretary of Agriculture rejected Forest Service recommendations by completely closing to logging the disputed corridors of the upper Suiattle, Agnes, and Philps. Also in opposition to Forest Service desires, he ordered that the country northward from Cascade Pass, though omitted from the wilderness, should be managed primarily for recreation and scenic preservation, with logging allowed only when compatible with these aims."

P. 263. *"So many mountains":* Gary Snyder, "Glacier Peak Wilderness Area," *Earth House Hold,* p. 101.

P. 263. *"You mean there's a Senator":* Allen Ginsberg, quoted in Snyder, "Glacier Peak Wilderness Area," *Earth House Hold,* p. 101.

P. 263. *key environmental essay:* "The Wilderness" was originally given as an address at the Center for Democratic Institutions, in Santa Barbara, California, in 1970. It was later included in *Turtle Island.*

P. 263. *"climax of preservationist environmentalism":* Wallace Stegner, "A Capsule History of Conservation," *Where the Bluebird Sings,* p. 131.

P. 264. *to the death, some said:* Edward Zahniser, telephone interview with the author, November 21, 2001. "Without the nine-year stress of that work he may have held on a few years longer, but I think it's probably an overstatement to say it killed him any more than the Hetch-Hetchy fight killed John Muir." Howard Zahniser died at the age of fifty-eight on May 5, 1964, three months before the bill was signed into law. His son, Ed Zahniser, in our interview, pointed out that his father had had a major heart attack in 1946, and had struggled with various other health problems as well.

P. 264. *"an area where the earth":* Wilderness Act of 1964, PL 88-577, *Statutes at Large,* Vol. 78, stat. 890.

P. 264. *"member of the natural community":* "Wilderness Bill," s.4013, p. 3, 14-15.

P. 264. *"I would like to think of a new definition":* Gary Snyder, "The Wilderness," *Turtle Island,* p. 106. ". . . one of the clearest days I had ever seen. When we reached the summit of Glacier Peak we could see

almost to the Selkirks in Canada. We could see south far beyond the Columbia River to Mount Hood and Mount Jefferson. And, of course, we could see Mount Adams and Mount Rainier. We could see across Puget Sound to the ranges of the Olympic Mountains. My companion, who is a poet, said: 'You mean there's a senator for all this?'"

P. 264. *last time Gary saw him:* Gary Snyder, "Night Highway 99," *Mountains and Rivers Without End,* p. 11.

P. 264. *body was found floating:* Jim Baxter to Gary Snyder, undated — Spring 1960, UC Davis. "Did you know that Roy Raymond disappeared? A couple of years ago — maybe I've already told you. They found a body floating in the Skagit River resembling his but no one ever proved it anyway He left his Hotel room one day with His pack and no one has seen him since."

P. 264. *"Don't let those old Buddhist priests":* Baxter to Snyder, December 16, 1960, UC Davis.

P. 265. *Baxter died in his bunk:* Jack Francis to Gary Snyder, October 5, 1970, UC Davis. "A few years ago while working as a caretaker at a boy scout camp on Silver Lake, a lake not far from Glacier, he had to go out on the water during a northeast storm to round up some rowboats which had drifted away. Somehow he got wet, went back to his cabin, failed to get a fire going and died of exposure."

P. 265. *"Blackie says he regrets":* Francis to Snyder, October 5, 1970, UC Davis.

P. 265. *"After I got aboard":* Francis to Snyder, August 25, 1974, UC Davis.

P. 266. *"A box of junk":* Francis to Snyder, December 5, 1974, UC Davis.

P. 266. *5,000 fire watch cabins:* Ira Spring and Byron Fish, *Lookouts: Firewatchers of the Cascades and Olympics,* p. 22.

P. 268. *last two operational:* Hidden Lake Lookout, the "Hilton" manned by the Vail brothers in the early 1950s, still stands, but is maintained as a hikers' shelter by a group of fire lookout enthusiasts, no longer a working L.O. Copper Mountain Lookout functions as a back country ranger station for the North Cascades National Park.

P. 268. *both lookouts were added:* Tim Manns, Chief of

Interpretation, North Cascades National Park,
E-mail to the author, January 19, 1996. "Desolation
Lookout was nominated along with virtually all other
historic structures in the Park in a 'multiple resource'
nomination. The Keeper of the National Register in
Washington, D.C. accepted and added everything to
the Register on February 10, 1989." See also National
Park Service, Cultural Resources Division, *Pacific
Northwest Regional Office Inventory.* "The U.S. Forest
Service erected fire lookouts as part of their fire pro-
tection system for the forests. Most of the lookouts
were built between 1929 and 1935. WWII brought a
perceived threat from across the Pacific and this led to
the manning of some lookouts as part of the military's
Aircraft Warning System. After the war, aerial surveil-
lance and other technological advances rendered the
old lookouts obsolete. Many were torn down in the
1960s. Desolation Peak Lookout was constructed by
USFS employee Oscar Banner in 1932. One of Desola-
tion's past lookouts was writer Jack Kerouac whose
book *Desolation Angels* describes the summer he spent
there in 1956. A new roof was installed in 1980 by the
NPS. This lookout is similar in appearance to Sour-
dough Mountain Lookout."

Bibliography

Books by Gary Snyder

POETRY

Axe Handles. San Francisco: North Point Press, 1983.

The Back Country. New York: New Directions, 1968.

The Gary Snyder Reader: Prose, Poetry, and Translations, 1952–1998. Washington, D.C.: Counterpoint, 1999.

Left Out in the Rain: New Poems, 1947–1985. New York: North Point Press, 1986.

Mountains and Rivers Without End. Washington, D.C.: Counterpoint, 1996.

Myths and Texts. New York: New Directions, 1978.

Regarding Wave. New York: New Directions, 1970.

Riprap & Cold Mountain Poems. San Francisco: Grey Fox Press, 1982.

Turtle Island. New York: New Directions, 1974.

PROSE

Earth House Hold: Technical Notes & Queries to Fellow Dharma Revolutionaries. New York: New Directions, 1969.

He Who Hunted Birds in His Father's Village: The Dimensions of a Haida Myth. San Francisco: Grey Fox Press, 1979.

The Old Ways: Six Essays. San Francisco: City Lights Books, 1977.

Passage Through India. San Francisco: Grey Fox Press, 1992.

A Place in Space: Ethics, Aesthetics and Watersheds. Washington, D.C.: Counterpoint, 1995.

The Practice of the Wild. New York: North Point Press, 1990.

The Real Work: Interviews & Talks 1964–1979. New York: New Directions, 1980.

ARTICLES AND ESSAYS

"Anyone with Yama-Bushi Tendencies," *Zen Notes,* November 1954, New York, The First Zen Institute of America.

"On Rinzai Masters and Western Students in Japan." *Wind Bell*, vol. VIII, nos. 1–2. San Francisco: Zen Center, Fall 1969.

"On the Road with D. T. Suzuki," from Maseo Abe, ed., *A Zen Life: D. T. Suzuki Remembered*. New York: Weatherhill, 1987.

"The Youngsteigers," *Mazama*, vol. 29, no. 13 (December 1947).

Books by Philip Whalen

Canoeing Up Cabarga Creek: Buddhist Poems, 1955–1986. Berkeley: Parallax Press, 1996.

On Bear's Head. New York: Harcourt, Brace and World, 1969.

Overtime: Selected Poems. New York: Penguin Books, 1999.

Two Novels: You Didn't Even Try & Imaginary Speeches for a Brazen Head. Somerville, Mass.: Zephyr Press, 1985.

Books by Jack Kerouac

PROSE

Atop an Underwood: Early Stories and Other Writings. New York: Viking Press, 1999.

Big Sur. New York: Penguin, 1992.

Desolation Angels. New York: Riverhead Books, 1995.

The Dharma Bums. New York: Penguin, 1976.

Doctor Sax. New York: Grove Press, 1959.

Good Blonde & Others. San Francisco: Grey Fox Press, 1993.

Lonesome Traveler. New York: Grove Press, 1989.

Old Angel Midnight. San Francisco: Grey Fox Press, 1993.

On the Road. New York: Penguin Books, 1991.

On the Road: Text and Criticism. Scott Donaldson, ed. New York: Viking Critical Library, 1979.

Satori in Paris and Pic. New York: Grove Press, 1988.

Selected Letters of Jack Kerouac: 1940–1956. Ann Charters, ed. New York: Viking Penguin, 1995.

Selected Letters of Jack Kerouac: 1957–1969. Ann Charters, ed. New York: Viking Penguin, 1999.

Some of the Dharma. New York: Viking Press, 1997.

The Subterraneans. New York: Grove Press, 1989.

The Town and the City. New York: Harcourt, Brace, Jovanovich, 1978.

Tristessa. New York: Penguin, 1992.

Vanity of Duluoz. New York: Penguin, 1994.

Visions of Cody. New York: Penguin, 1993.

Visions of Gerard. New York: Penguin Books, 1991.

POETRY

Book of Blues. New York: Penguin Books, 1995.

Heaven & Other Poems. San Francisco: Grey Fox Press, 1977.

Mexico City Blues. New York: Grove Press, 1990.

Pomes All Sizes. San Francisco: City Lights Books, 1992.

Scattered Poems. San Francisco: City Lights Books, 1971.

ARTICLES

"On the Road Again." Douglas Brinkley, ed. *The New Yorker,* June 22 and 29, 1998.

MULTIMEDIA

A Jack Kerouac Romnibus. New York: Penguin Electronic, 1996.

General Bibliography

Abbey, Edward. *The Journey Home: Some Words in Defense of the American West.* New York: E. P. Dutton, 1977.

Agee, James K. et al. *The Fire History of Desolation Peak.* Seattle: National Park Service Cooperative Unit, College of Forest Resources, University of Washington, 1986.

Akrigg, G. P. V. and Akrigg, Helen B. *British Columbia Place Names.* Victoria, B.C.: Sono Nis Press, 1986.

Alighieri, Dante. *The Convivio.* Richard Lansing, trans. Garland, New York: Garland Library of Medieval Literature, 1990.

Allen, Donald, ed. *I Remain: The Letters of Lew Welch and the Correspondence of His Friends.* Two volumes. Bolinas, Cal.: Grey Fox, 1980.

_____. *Off the Wall: Interviews with Philip Whalen.* Bolinas, Cal.: Four Seasons Foundation, 1978.

Antoninus, Brother (William Everson). *Robinson Jeffers: Fragments of an Older Fury.* Berkeley, Cal.: Oyez, 1968.

Artaud, Antonin. *The Peyote Dance.* New York: Farrar, Straus and Giroux, 1976.

Beckey, Fred. *Cascade Alpine Guide: Climbing and High Routes, Volume 3: Rainy Pass to Fraser River,* 2d ed. Seattle: The Mountaineers, 1995.

_____. *Challenge of the North Cascades.* Seattle: The Mountaineers, 1969.

Blake, William. *The Poetry and Prose of William Blake.* David V. Erdman, ed. New York: Doubleday, 1988.

Blyth, R. H. *Haiku, Volume One: Eastern Culture.* South San Francisco: Heian International, 1981.

_____. *Zen and Zen Classics.* Union City, Cal.: Heian International, 1991.

Brower, David R. "Crisis in the Northern Cascades: 'The Missing Million.'" *Sierra Club Bulletin,* vol. 44, no. 2 (February 1959), p. 104.

_____, ed. *Not Man Apart: Lines from Robinson Jeffers.* San Francisco, Sierra Club, 1965.

Buckley, William F. *The Committee and Its Critics: A Calm Review of the House Committee on Un-American Activities.* New York: G. P. Putnam, 1962.

Burnet, John. *Early Greek Philosophy.* London: A. and C. Black, Ltd., 1958.

Burroughs, William S. *Junky.* New York: Penguin, 1977.

_____. *Queer.* New York: Penguin Books, 1987.

_____. *Letters 1945–1959,* Oliver Harris, ed., New York: Penguin, 1993.

Bynner, Witter, trans. *The Jade Mountain: A Chinese Anthology.* New York: Vintage, 1972.

Cassady, Carolyn. *Off the Road: My Years with Cassady, Kerouac, and Ginsberg.* New York: William Morrow, 1990.

Caute, David. *The Great Fear: The Anti-Communist Purge Under Truman and Eisenhower.* New York: Simon and Schuster, 1978.

Charters, Ann. *Beats & Company: Portrait of a Literary Generation.* Garden City, N.Y.: Doubleday, 1986.

_____. "The Beats: Literary Bohemians in Postwar America." In vol. 16, parts 1 and 2 of *Dictionary of Literary Biography.* Detroit: Gale Research Co., 1983.

_____. *Kerouac: A Biography.* New York: Warner Paperback Library, 1974.

_____, ed. *Scenes Along the Road: Photographs of the Desolation Angels, 1944–1960.* San Francisco: City Lights, 1984.

_____, ed. *Viking Portable Beat Reader.* New York: Viking Penguin, 1992.

Christie's Auction Catalog: "Jack Kerouac: including the Typescript for *The Dharma Bums.*" London: Christie's International Media Division, 2001.

Cleary, Thomas, trans. *The Sutra of Hui-Neng: Grand Master of Zen.* Boston: Shambhala, 1998.

Collins, June M. *Valley of the Spirits: The Upper Skagit Indians of Western Washington.* Seattle: University of Washington Press, 1974.

Custer, Henry. "Report of Henry Custer, Assistant of Reconnaissances, Made in 1859 over the routes in the Cascades Mountains in the vicinity of the 49th parallel." Typed manuscript. Seattle: National Park Service, Pacific Northwest Region, 1866.

Dardis, Tom. *The Thirsty Muse: Alcohol and the American Writer.* New York: Ticknor and Fields, 1989.

Davis, Scarlett C. "The Marine Cooks and Stewards Union Knew Differences are Small, Solidarity is Big." *The Dispatcher* [Magazine of the International Longshoremen & Warehousemen Union], February 1997.

Dos Passos, John. *U.S.A.* Boston: Houghton Mifflin, 1946.

Douglas, George W. and Taylor, Ronald J. *Mountain Plants of the Pacific Northwest: A Field Guide to Washington, Western British Columbia, and Southeastern Alaska.* Missoula, Mont.: Mountain Press Publishing Company, 1995.

Dower, John W. *Embracing Defeat: Japan in the Wake of World War II.* New York: W. W. Norton, 1999.

Durbin, Katie. *Tree Huggers: Victory, Defeat & Renewal in the Northwest Ancient Forest Campaign.* Seattle: The Mountaineers, 1996.

Einarsen, John, ed. *The Sacred Mountains of Asia.* Boston: Shamabhala, 1995.

Ellis, Havelock. "Mescal: A New Artificial Paradise." *The Contemporary Review,* January 1898.

Evans, Camille. "Interview with Bee Currie concerning Frank Beebe and Life on Granite Creek." Unpublished paper. Marblemount, Wash.: North Cascades National Park Service, 1997.

Ferlinghetti, Lawrence and Peters, Nancy J. *Literary San Francisco: A Pictorial History from Its Beginnings to the Present Day.* San Francisco: Harper and Row, 1980.

Fields, Rick. *How the Swans Came to the Lake: A Narrative History of Buddhism in America,* third edition. Boston: Shambhala Publications, 1992.

Frome, Michael. *The Forest Service.* New York: Praeger Publishers, 1971.

Fuller, Margaret. *Forest Fires: An Introduction to Wildland Fire Behavior, Management, Firefighting, and Prevention.* New York: John Wiley and Sons, 1991.

Gifford, Barry, ed. *As Ever: The Collected Correspondence of Allen Ginsberg and Neal Cassady.* Berkeley, Cal.: Creative Arts Book Company, 1977.

_____ and Lee, Lawrence. *Jack's Book: An Oral Biography of Jack Kerouac.* New York: St. Martin's Press, 1978.

Ginsberg, Allen. *Collected Poems: 1947–1980.* New York: Harper-Perennial, 1988.

_____. *Deliberate Prose: Selected Essays 1952–1995,* ed. Bill Morgan. New York: HarperCollins, 2000.

_____. *Howl: Original Draft Facsimile, Transcript & Variant Versions, Fully Annotated by Author.* New York: HarperCollins, 1995.

_____. *Journals Mid-Fifties: 1954–1958.* New York: HarperCollins, 1995.

_____. *Spontaneous Mind: Selected Interviews, 1958–1996.* David Carter, ed. New York: HarperCollins, 2001.

Goddard, Dwight, ed. *A Buddhist Bible.* Boston: Beacon Press, 1994.

Halberstam, David. *The Fifties.* New York: Ballantine Books, 1994.

Halper, Jon, ed. *Gary Snyder: Dimensions of a Life.* San Francisco: Sierra Club Books, 1991.

Hamalian, Linda. *A Life of Kenneth Rexroth.* New York: W. W. Norton, 1991.

Hamilton, Ian. *Robert Lowell: A Biography.* New York: Random House, 1982.

Hardy, Martha. *Tatoosh.* New York: Macmillan, 1947; Seattle: The Mountaineers, 1980.

Hill, Kimi Kodani. *Topaz Moon: Chiura Obata's Art of the Internment.* Berkeley, Cal.: Heyday Books, 2000.

Hoffmann, John. *Journey to the End.* "Oaktown" [Oakland], Cal.: Kolourmein Press, 2000.

Huber, J. Parker, ed. *Elevating Ourselves: Thoreau on Mountains.* Boston: Houghton Mifflin, 1999.

Huxley, Aldous. *The Doors of Perception & Heaven and Hell.* New York: Harper and Row, 1990.

Jamison, Kay Redfield. *Touched with Fire: Manic-Depressive Illness and the Artistic Temperament.* New York: Simon and Schuster, 1993.

Jeffers, Robinson, *The Collected Poetry of Robinson Jeffers: Volume 1, 1920–1928,* Tim Hunt, ed., Stanford, California: Stanford University Press, 1988.

_____. *The Collected Poetry of Robinson Jeffers: Volume 2, 1928–1938,* Tim Hunt, ed., Stanford, California: Stanford University Press, 1989.

_____. *The Collected Poetry of Robinson Jeffers: Volume 3, 1938–1962,* Tim Hunt, ed., Stanford, California: Stanford University Press, 1991.

_____. *The Double Axe & Other Poems,* New York: Liveright, 1977.

_____. *The Selected Letters of Robinson Jeffers.* Ann N. Ridgeway, ed. Baltimore: Johns Hopkins University Press, 1968.

Jenkins, Will, D. *Last Frontier in the North Cascades: Tales of the Wild Upper Skagit.* La Conner, Washington: Skagit County Historical Society, 1985.

Johnson, Joyce. *Minor Characters.* Boston: Houghton-Mifflin, 1983.

_____ and Kerouac, Jack. *Door Wide Open: A Beat Love Affair in Letters, 1957–1958.* New York: Viking, 2000.

Jordan, Ray. *Yarns of the Skagit Country.* Everett, Washington: The Printers, 1974.

Kapleau, Philip. *The Three Pillars of Zen.* New York: Doubleday, 1989.

Kealing, Bob. "The Road to Kerouac." *Florida Magazine,* March 9, 1997.

Knight, Arthur and Kit, eds. *Kerouac and the Beats: A Primary Sourcebook.* New York: Paragon House, 1988.

Kornbluh, Joyce L., ed. *Rebel Voices: An I.W.W. Anthology.* Ann Arbor: University of Michigan Press, 1964.

Kresek, Ray. *Fire Lookouts of Oregon and Washington.* Fairfield, Wash.: Ye Galleon Press, 1985.

_____. *Fire Lookouts of the Northwest,* Fairfield, WA: Ye Galleon Press, 1985.

Kropotkin, Peter. *Mutual Aid: A Factor of Evolution.* New York: New York University Press, 1972.

Kyger, Joanne. *Strange Big Moon: The Japan and India Journals, 1960–64.* Berkeley, Cal.: North Atlantic Books, 2000.

Lamantia, Philip. *Becoming Visible.* San Francisco: City Lights Books, 1981.

_____. *Bed of Sphinxes: New & Selected Poems 1943–1993.* San Francisco: City Lights Books, 1997.

Leach, Maria, ed. *Funk and Wagnalls Standard Dictionary of Folklore, Mythology, and Legend.* New York: Harper and Row, 1984.

Lee, Martin A. and Shlain, Bruce. *Acid Dreams: The CIA, LSD and the Sixties Rebellion.* New York: Grove Press, 1985.

Lincoln, Frederick C. *Migration of Birds.* Garden City, N.Y.: Doubleday, 1952.

Louter, David. *Contested Terrain: North Cascades National Park Service Complex, An Administrative History.* Seattle: National Park Service, 1998.

Luxenberg, Gretchen A. "Boundary Commission: Henry Custer's Explorations (1857)." *Historic Resource Study.* North Cascades National Park Service Complex, 1986.

Manning, Harvey. *The Wild Cascades: Forgotten Parkland.* San Francisco: Sierra Club Books, 1965.

Marshall, Robert. "The Northern Cascades Wilderness." *Living Wilderness,* vol. 1, no. 10 (September 1935).

Matthews, Daniel. *Cascade-Olympic Natural History: A Trailside Reference.* Portland, Ore.: Raven Editions, 1990.

McClure, Michael. *Lighting the Corners: On Art, Nature, and the Visionary.* Albuquerque: University of New Mexico Press, 1993.

_____. "Nights in North Beach," from Obst, Lynda, ed., *The Sixties.* San Francisco: Rolling Stone Press, 1977, p. 26.

_____. *Scratching the Beat Surface.* San Francisco: North Point Press, 1982.

_____. *Selected Poems.* New York: New Directions, 1986.

McCord, Howard. *Some Notes to Gary Snyder's Myths & Texts.* Berkeley, Cal.: Sand Dollar Press, 1971.

Meltzer, David, ed. *San Francisco Beat: Talking with the Poets.* San Francisco: City Lights Books, 2001.

Merton, Thomas. *The Seven Storey Mountain.* New York: Harcourt, Brace and Company, 1948.

Mierendorf, Robert R. et al., eds. *An Archeological Site Survey and Evaluation in the Upper Skagit River Valley, Whatcom County, Washington.* Sedro-Woolley, Wash.: North Cascades National Park Service Complex, 1998.

_____. *People of the North Cascades.* Seattle: North Cascades National Park Service Complex, 1986.

_____. "An Updated Summary Statement of the Archeology of the North Cascades National Park Service Complex, Sedro-Woolley." Sedro-Woolley, Wash.: North Cascades National Park Service Complex, 1998.

Miura, Isshü and Sasaki, Ruth Fuller. *The Zen Koan: Its History and Use in Rinzai Zen.* New York: Harcourt, Brace and World, 1965.

Nash, Roderick. *Wilderness and the American Mind,* third ed. New Haven and London: Yale University Press, 1982.

Nicosia, Gerald. *Memory Babe: A Critical Biography of Jack Kerouac.* New York: Grove Press, 1983.

O'Grady, John P. "Living Landscape: An Interview with Gary Snyder." *Western American Literature* (Fall 1998), pp. 275–91.

Okakura, Kakuzo. *The Book of Tea.* New York: Dover Publications, 1964.

O'Neill, Maureen and Suiter, John (photos). "Desolation Summer: Keeping Company with Kerouac." *Seattle Times/Pacific Magazine,* June 9, 1996.

Perry, Charles. *The Haight-Ashbury: A History.* New York: Vintage, 1985.

Pinchot, Gifford. *Breaking New Ground.* New York: Harcourt, Brace and Co., 1947.

Pitzer, Paul C. *Building the Skagit: A Century of Upper Skagit Valley History, 1870-1970.* Portland, Ore.: Galley Press, 1978.

Porter, Bill. *The Collected Songs of Cold Mountain, translated by Red Pine.* Port Townsend, Wash.: Copper Canyon Press, 2000.

_____. *Road to Heaven: Encounters with Chinese Hermits.* San Francisco: Mercury House, 1993.

Price, A. F. and Wong, Mou-lam, trans. *The Diamond Sutra & the Sutra of Hui-neng.* Boston: Shambhala Publications, 1990.

Pyne, Stephen J. *Fire in America: A Cultural History of Wildland and Rural Fire.* Seattle: University of Washington Press, 1997.

Rexroth, Kenneth. *An Autobiographical Novel.* Garden City, N.Y.: Doubleday, 1966.

_____. *With Eye and Ear.* New York: Herder & Herder, 1970.

_____. *World Outside the Window: Selected Essays.* New York: New Directions, 1987.

Ross, Nancy Wilson. *Buddhism: A Way of Life and Thought.* New York: Alfred A. Knopf, 1980.

Scheese, Don. "Henry David Thoreau, Fire Lookout." *Thoreau Society Bulletin,* no. 190 (Winter 1990).

Schrecker, Ellen. *Many Are the Crimes: McCarthyism in America.* New York: Little, Brown, 1998.

_____. *No Ivory Tower: McCarthyism and the Universities.* New York: Oxford University Press, 1986.

Schumacher, Michael. *Dharma Lion: A Biography of Allen Ginsberg.* New York: St. Martin's Press, 1992.

Simons, David. *Brief: The Need for Scenic Resource Conservation in the Northern Cascades of Washington.* San Francisco: Sierra Club, 1959.

Spring, Ira and Fish, Byron. *Lookouts: Firewatchers of the Cascades and Olympics,* 2nd ed. Seattle: The Mountaineers, 1996.

Spring, Ira and Manning, Harvey. *100 Hikes in Washington's North Cascades National Park Region.* 2nd ed. Seattle: The Mountaineers, 1997.

Stegner, Wallace. *Where the Bluebird Sings to the Lemonade Springs: Living and Writing in the West.* New York: Random House, 1992.

Steuding, Bob. *Gary Snyder.* Boston: G. K. Hall, 1976.

Stier, Maggie and McAdow, Ron. *Into the Mountains: Stories of New England's Most Celebrated Peaks.* Boston: Appalachian Mountain Club, 1995.

Suiter, John. "Beat a Path to Kerouac Country." *The Independent* (London), October 20, 1996.

_____. "Desolation Revisited: Jack Kerouac's Peak Experience." *Shambhala Sun* (Halifax, N.S.), vol. 5, no. 4 (March 1997).

_____. "Rolling Toward the Moon: Jack Kerouac's Last Great Adventure." *Sierra,* March–April 1998.

Suzuki, D. T. *Essays in Zen Buddhism: First Series.* New York: Grove Press, 1961.

_____. *Manual of Zen Buddhism.* New York: Grove Press, 1960.

_____. *Zen and Japanese Culture.* Princeton: Princeton University Press, 1959.

_____. *The Zen Doctrine of No-Mind: The Significance of the Sutra of Hui-Neng.* York Beach, Maine: Samuel Weiser, 1972.

Tabor, Roland and Haugerud, Ralph. *Geology of the North Cascades: A Mountain Mosaic.* Seattle: The Mountaineers, 1999.

Tanahashi, Kazuaki, ed. *Moon in a Dewdrop: The Writings of Zen Master Dogen.* New York: North Point Press, 1985.

Thompson, Fred W. and Murfin, Patrick. *The I.W.W.: Its First Seventy Years, 1905–1975.* Chicago: Industrial Workers of the World, 1976.

Thoreau, Henry David. *Cape Cod; The Maine Woods; Walden; A Week on the Concord and Merrimack Rivers.* New York: Literary Classics of the United States, 1985.

Tonkinson, Carole, ed. *Big Sky Mind: Buddhism and the Beat Generation.* New York: Riverhead Books, 1995.

Ulrichs, Hermann F. "The Cascade Range in Northern Washington." *Sierra Club Bulletin,* vol. 22, no. 1 (February 1937), p. 69.

van de Wetering, Janwillem. *The Empty Mirror: Experiences in a Japanese Zen Monastery.* New York: St. Martin's, 1999.

Waley, Arthur. *The No Plays of Japan.* New York: Grove Press, 1957.

Watson, Steven. *The Birth of the Beat Generation: Visionaries, Rebels, and Hipsters, 1944–1960.* New York: Pantheon, 1995.

Watts, Alan. *This is It and Other Essays on Zen and Spiritual Experience.* New York: Vintage Books (Random House), 1973.

Yee, Chiang. *The Silent Traveler in San Francisco.* New York: W. W. Norton, 1964.

Yip, Wai-lim, ed. and trans. *Chinese Poetry: An Anthology of Major Modes and Genres.* Durham, N.C.: Duke University Press, 1997.

Zahniser, Howard. "Wilderness in the Cascades." *Living Wilderness,* vol. 58 (Fall-Winter 1956–57), editorial page.

Acknowledgments

Gary Snyder has been this book's great benefactor and challenger. Working with, and learning from him has turned out to be one of the pleasures of my professional life. I especially thank Gary and his wife, the writer Carole Koda, for their hospitality in inviting me to their home at Kitkitdizze. Meeting Philip Whalen was another high point of the project. I will always appreciate his uncomplaining participation in our interviews, often under great physical discomfort, but never without wit and precision.

I never knew Kerouac; he was long dead when this book was conceived. However, through my collaboration with John Sampas, Kerouac's brother-in-law and literary executor, with whom I worked on several projects during the 1990s, I was privileged to "meet" Jack as only a few scholars and biographers have, through his then-unpublished letters and journals. In 1994, I worked closely with John Sampas on *A Jack Kerouac Romnibus,* an important CD-Rom production which first introduced the public to the literary riches of the Kerouac archives. Also, after my visit to Desolation Peak in July 1995, John graciously shared Jack's own Desolation journal with me for the photo-essays I was working on at the time. Those articles evolved into this book.

At North Cascades I had expert assistance from many knowledgeable people. Tim Manns, Chief of Interpretation at North Cascades, was of the greatest help throughout, but many other Park Service people are also here in these pages: Superintendent Bill Paleck, Andriz Vezis and Janet Kailen of the Marblemount fire office, Jennifer Weldon, who packed me up to Desolation in '95, and Brent Hooper who packed me down; Steve Schindler who went to Crater Mountain with me in '98; Paula Ogden and Val Normand who hiked with me to Sourdough Lookout, also in '98. A special note of thanks to Bob Mierendorf, the Park's chief archeologist, for helping me see the big picture. Thanks also to Jesse Kennedy, Camille Evans, Marshall & Dawn Plumer, Margaret Goodro, Alison Deerlove, Jim Harris, Cindy Bjorklund, Merlene Buller, Joyce Brown, Ryan Booth, Craig Holmquist, Jon Riedel, and Paul Jensen. And gratitude to Felix DeMello of Seattle City Light, for his assistance in arranging a base of operations for me at the foot of Sourdough Mountain in 1997 and 1998.

In the Skagit I was also fortunate to meet some of the former Forest Service men who worked with Gary, Philip and Jack during the 1950s: Shubert Hunter, Harold and Roger Vail, Tommy Buller, and Jack Francis. Their recollections, language and spirit have contributed greatly to this project, and I salute them. Thanks likewise to former lookouts Maxine Franklin and Gerry Cook for sharing their memories of Sourdough and Desolation during the 1970s.

The poets Michael McClure, Philip Lamantia, and Joanne Kyger strengthened the book greatly; they too are peaks. I also thank Michael Rothenberg, Locke McCorkle, Walter Lehrman, Bob Richter, Dell Hymes, Carl Proujan, Mary Carney (di Benedetto) — Kerouac's high school sweetheart; Jinny Baker (Hubbell) — the life model for his character "Princess" in *The Dharma Bums.*

This book is for Hozomeen, but it wouldn't have happened without a mountain of support from many "rocks." Gratitude and love to my mother, for her enduring faith in me, from the beginning. To my old high school friends, Tim Kelley of Vancouver, and Barbara Bloodwell of Berkeley, who put me up on my West Coast trips. Also, to our teacher from those days — and these — Harry LeFever. To Alice Wu, who saw me off at the start (with prayer flags); and Sungrim Kim who was there in the home stretch. Also, to Susana Enríquez in Mexico City — "Viva la Vida."

In Lowell, Massachusetts, thanks to Dan Walsh and Mark Bograd of the National Park Service, to Paul Marion, poet and editor of *Atop an Underwood,* for fourteen years of friendship around things Kerouackian; to old buddy Dave Green for thirty; to Lee Lockwood of the National Writers' Union for his solidarity and always solid advice; to Thoreau scholar, Tom Blanding; to Ray Kresek of Spokane's Fire Lookout Association; writer Bill Wilson in New York; Ed Zahniser, Bruce Kinch, Sue Anne Hodges, Roger Brunelle, and Errol Selkirk, from whom I first heard the word "Zen."

I am proud to be associated with Counterpoint Press. Many thanks to publisher Jack Shoemaker, for his belief, generosity, and resoluteness; to the indefatigable Trish Hoard, Managing Editor and midwife of this book; also to Norman MacAfee, David Bullen, Heather McLeod, Keltie Hawkins, and John McLeod.

Finally, many able research librarians and archivists fed the book its daily bread of documents and facts — too many to name here. But I would be remiss not to thank John Skarstad, head of the Special Collections Department of Shields Library at the University of California, Davis, where the Gary Snyder Papers are housed. John's interested, knowledgeable, and rapid responses to my many queries were indispensable to my research efforts.

Photo Credits
and Permissions

generous permission of Philip Whalen.

Quotes from *Off the Wall: Interviews with Philip Whalen* used by permission of Donald Allen.

Quotes by Philip Whalen in *San Francisco Beat: Talking with the Poets*, ed. David Meltzer © 2001 by David Meltzer, used by permission of City Lights Publishers.

Quotes from *The Dharma Bums* by Jack Kerouac © 1958 by Jack Kerouac, renewed 1986 by Stella Kerouac and Jan Kerouac; quotations from *On the Road* by Jack Kerouac © 1955 & 1957 by Jack Kerouac, renewed 1986 by Stella and Jan Kerouac. Used by permission of Viking Penguin, a division of Penguin Putnam Inc.

Quotes from Jack Kerouac's writings in *A Jack Kerouac Romnibus* © 1995 Black Mountain Multimedia Inc. and Penguin Books USA Inc. Used by permission of Viking Penguin, a division of Penguin Putnam Inc.

Quotes from the following books by Jack Kerouac are all used by permission of Sterling Lord Literistic, Inc.: *Desolation Angels* © 1965 by Jack Kerouac; *Lonesome Traveler* © 1960 by Jack Kerouac; *Mexico City Blues* © 1959 by Jack Kerouac; *Book of Blues* © 1995 by Estate of Stella Kerouac; *Selected Letters, 1940–1956* © 1995 by Estate of Stella Kerouac; *Selected Letters, 1957–1969* © 1999 by Estate of Stella Kerouac, *Some of the Dharma* © 1997 by Estate of Stella Kerouac, John Sampas, Literary Representative;

Excerpt from Jack Kerouac's letter to Philip Whalen is from the Philip Whalen Papers, Special Collections, Reed College Library, copyrighted by the Estate of Stella Kerouac, John Sampas, Literary Representative, and used by permission of Sterling Lord

Literistic, Inc. Excerpts from Jack Kerouac's Desolation notebook are copyrighted by the Estate of Stella Kerouac, John Sampas, Literary Representative, and used by permission of Sterling Lord Literistic, Inc.

Excerpts from *Collected Poems: 1947–1980*, by Allen Ginsberg © 1984 by Allen Ginsberg; *Howl: Original Draft Facsimile, Transcript & Variant Versions, Fully Annotated* © 1986 by Allen Ginsberg; and *Journals Mid-Fifties: 1954–1956* © 1995 by Allen Ginsberg are used by permission of HarperCollins Publishers.

Allen Ginsberg's journal entry and excerpts from Allen Ginsberg's letters to Neal Cassady are copyrighted and used by the generous permission of the Allen Ginsberg Trust.

Excerpts from *Scratching the Beat Surface*, by Michael McClure © 1982 by Michael McClure used by permission of North Point Press, a division of Farrar, Straus, and Giroux.

Excerpts from *A Buddhist Bible*, edited by Dwight Goddard © 1938, 1966 by E.P. Dutton & Co., Inc. are used by permission of Penguin Putnam Inc.

Excerpts from *Manual of Zen Buddhism*, edited by D. T. Suzuki are used by permission of Grove Press.

Excerpts from *Cascade Alpine Guide: Climbing & High Routes Volume 3: Rainy Pass to Fraser River* by Fred Beckey © 1995 Fred Beckey, used with permission of the publisher, The Mountaineers, Seattle WA.